THE CHICAGO BEARS

NSON GEPFORD MAC WHERTER LANUM KOEHLER VEACH STERNAMAN DRESSEN

YOUNG SHANK MAY HIGH ADKINS CLARK FEITCHINGER PEARCE LOTSHAW Trainer

TRAFTON JONES INGWERSEN HALAS BLACKLOCK PETTY MINTUN

1920 STALEY TEAM

THE CHICAGO BEARS

From George Halas
to Super Bowl XX

An Illustrated History

REVISED AND UPDATED

by Richard Whittingham
Introduction by Mike Ditka

A FIRESIDE BOOK
Published by Simon & Schuster, Inc.
NEW YORK

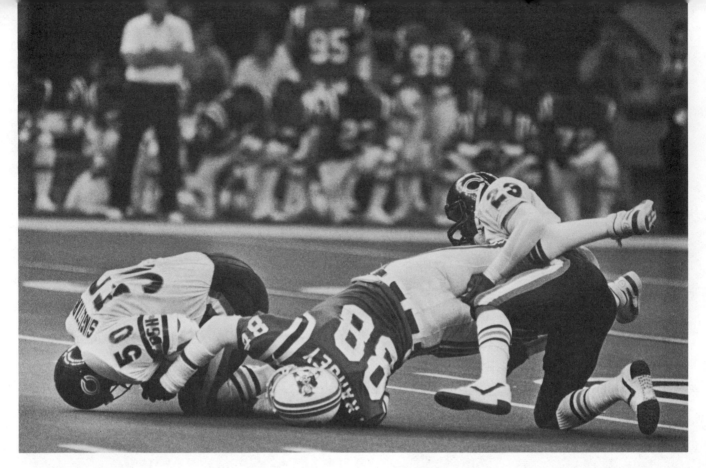

ACKNOWLEDGMENTS: The author and publisher wish to extend their thanks to all the people and organizations whose cooperation and help were instrumental in the creation of this book, most notably:

The family of the late Edward C. ("Dutch") Sternaman, especially Peg Holmes, Dutch's daughter, whose aid was immeasurable and whose time and efforts were given so generously; John Sternaman, Dutch's son; and in-law Myrtle Brunkow Baumann, who diligently and accurately researched and recorded so many of the facts and events from the Bears' early history.

The Pro Football Hall of Fame in Canton, Ohio, for the use of their vast resources, and especially Joe Horrigan, curator and chief researcher, for his expert guidance.

Richard Youhn, Bear fan and authority, whose consultation on all aspects of the Bear story from 1950 to the present was invaluable.

Steve Sutton, whose untimely death in May, 1979, prevented him from seeing this book in its final form, but whose contributions in terms of editorial counsel, motivation, and standards of quality are indelibly imprinted on it.

Mary Chiaro, for her editorial expertise and dedication to the book, and the staff she guided in the enormous task of substantiating all the facts and statistics that appear in it.

The author would additionally like to thank the many persons whose remembrances helped him in telling the story of the Chicago Bears and who graciously gave of their time in interviews.

Acknowledgment is also made and appreciation extended to photographers Keith A. Smith of Manitowoc, Wisconsin, and Ron Shankle of Canton, Ohio, who photographed the many items of memorabilia in this book.

The author and publisher also extend their gratitude for permission to reprint the following passages from copyrighted works:

Excerpt from the book *Magic* by William Goldman. Copyright © 1976 by William Goldman. Reprinted (on pages 123-125) by permission of Delacorte Press.

Quotation (reprinted on page 101) from the book *My Life with the Redskins* by Corinne Griffith. Published by A. S. Barnes & Company, Inc., 1947.

A Fireside Book,
Published by Simon & Schuster, Inc.
Simon & Schuster Building
Rockefeller Center
1230 Avenue of the Americas
New York, New York 10020

This is a revised edition of a book published in 1979 and 1982 by Rand McNally & Company

FIRESIDE and colophon are registered trademarks of Simon & Schuster, Inc.

Designed by Mario Pagliai

Manufactured in the United States of America

10 9 8 7 6 5 4 3 2 1 Pbk.

Library of Congress Cataloging-in-Publication Data

Whittingham, Richard, date.
  The Chicago Bears.

  "A Fireside book."
  Includes index.
  1. Chicago Bears (Football team)—History. I. Title.
GV956.C5W47   1986   796.332'64'0977311   86-14816
ISBN 0-671-62885-2 Pbk.

CONTENTS

*For Chuck and
Jean Whittingham*

FOREWORD

THE BEARS were the only team I would have played with. I had been a fan of theirs way back, when I was in high school and they were the Decatur Staleys. Besides, George Halas, who had played baseball and football at Illinois, and Dutch Sternaman, who was also from Illinois, not only coached the Bears but were on the team.

The colleges in the 1920s were viciously against professional football. My coach at Illinois, Bob Zuppke, actually didn't speak to me for about three years after I turned pro. All the college coaches were against it. However, in 1925—my senior year—I met a fellow in Champaign, Charley Pyle, who owned two movie theaters there, and he sold me on the idea of playing pro ball. I knew Halas was interested in my joining the Bears, and I was impressed with him and how the team was run. So was Pyle, later called "Cash and Carry" by the newspaper writers.

I always thought of the Bears as my alma mater and so did many of the other players, like Paddy Driscoll. And George Halas built the Bears into what they are today. When I joined them, George used to sell a half-dozen tickets and run across the road and buy tape and tape the players' ankles before they would run on the field. He ran everything at the ball park. Nobody ever worked as hard as George. And I think if it hadn't been for the Bears and the Green Bay Packers I don't believe there would have been a National Football

League. A little later the New York Giants came in under Tim Mara, but Halas and Curly Lambeau really made the NFL. They got it going, then TV came along in the 1950s and gave it a big boost.

I think it's a better game today. When I first joined the Bears, they had only 18 players (the league limit) and you played both offense and defense. Today you have 45 players on the squad and two separate teams. But I think at least two rule changes made football what it is today—being able to pass anywhere behind the line of scrimmage and free substitutions. In my day you had to be 5 yards back or more before you could throw the ball and you couldn't return to the game until the next quarter. And come to think of it, I haven't seen a new football play since high school—there are really only so many ways you can move the ball—though the ball itself has been changed three times since then, to make it longer and narrower so you could throw it better. The biggest change, in general, has been in the defense, not the offense. The offenses haven't changed all that much, in my opinion, but the defenses have changed tremendously.

Another rule change that has helped today's game was moving the hashmarks in for the start of the next play after the ball goes out-of-bounds. When I was playing, the ball was brought in just one yard. Actually the rule came about because of that championship game we had to play indoors in the Chicago Stadium in

1932 against Portsmouth. The walls were right up against the sidelines, so they decided that when the ball went out-of-bounds it would be brought in 10 yards from the wall. Well the next year Halas talked to the rules committee about that, and it was adopted by the National Football League. The hashmarks are in a lot more today, of course.

George Halas was a different kind of coach. I remember an incident in 1934 with Johnny Sisk. Sisk didn't like to practice and would complain about injuries, but he was always ready to go on game days. He came out one Tuesday and told Halas he couldn't practice because he had hurt his knee on Sunday. He was limping around, and Halas let him go sit in the stands. After the practice session, everyone went into the dressing room and Sisk went out to get into his new car. Halas was at the window watching him limp along. Well somebody put a smoke bomb in Sisk's car, and when he started it the bomb went off and he jumped out and came flying back to the clubhouse—he was a sprinter, you know. George just looked at him and said, "OK, John, six laps."

There was never any question that George was tough. At times there were factions on the team—most teams have them off and on. Generally, nobody paid much attention to it, but I guess it bothered George. One time in 1934, before going out to practice, he said he wanted to talk to us. Instead he started to call certain players by name and told them to line up in two different groups. Then George said, "Here are the guys who are breaking up the team into factions, and I'll fight you all, one by one, or all together." And that was the end of the faction. He minced no words. He often said, "There are only two things I'm interested in: my family and the Bears."

There were a lot of colorful personalities in pro ball when it was just getting started. Here are a couple of my favorite stories about those early days:

They had a referee in the 1920s, Jim Durfee, who was a character. He and George were pretty good friends. But Durfee loved to penalize the Bears right in front of the bench. When Halas was riding him pretty hard in a game one day, Jim began marching off a 5-yard penalty. Halas got really hot. "What's that for?" he hollered.

"Coaching from the sidelines," Jim yelled back. (You couldn't do that in those days.)

"Well," said George, "that just proves how dumb you are. That's 15 yards not 5 yards!"

"Yeah," said Jim, "but the penalty for your kind of coaching is only 5 yards."

Another day Jim was penalizing the Bears 15 yards, and Halas cupped his hands and yelled, "You stink!" Jim just marched off another 15 yards, then turned and shouted, "How do I smell from here?"

After the game, however, they'd probably have a drink together.

And there was the time we went to the White House. This was in December, 1925, a couple of weeks after I joined the Bears. We were playing an exhibition game with a team called the Washington All-Stars, and it was the first time the Bears played in Washington, D.C. Senator McKinley, of Illinois, called George and me and asked if we wanted to meet President Coolidge. The senator sent his car to pick us up, and when we arrived he introduced me to the President as "Red Grange, who plays with the Bears." Coolidge shook hands and said, "Young man, I always liked animal acts."

It was good to be part of it all, and to see football grow to what it is today. I'm from the Chicago area, the Bears are Chicago, and I'm glad to be a part of their history.

Red Grange

INTRODUCTION

WHEN DICK WHITTINGHAM first wrote this book, he ended it by saying that the game has changed, the league has changed, and the people who watch the game have changed, too. But he went on to say that professional football really is the same sport it's always been, the same for the Bears of the 1980s as it was for the Bears of the 1920s.

I think that's right, and I hope it never changes.

The book is revised now to include the story of the 1985 Chicago Bears and their victory in Super Bowl XX.

From our standpoint, that's great . . . it's a thrill for me to reflect on the fact that I was a part of what happened in a very special season.

But, you want to know something? Winning the Super Bowl doesn't tell the story of the Chicago Bears. The Super Bowl trophy is sort of like an ornament on a Christmas tree . . . it's beautiful, but what's holding it up is the tree, and the tree is the Chicago Bears.

I'm not sure what to call it . . . tradition, whatever. It's an unbroken line of men who, for more than sixty years, have worn the uniform. It's a lot of other people, too, coaches and staff.

And Coach Halas. It started with him, and he's still a part of it. It all happened because of him.

It's pride, really—pride in being a Bear.

When I came back to Chicago in 1982 to coach, I talked to the players about the pride I had known in pulling on a Bear jersey. It was something I wanted them to feel.

Vernon Biever

9

I think that pride was there in 1985 . . . our players took pride in meeting the challenges. They won some games when we absolutely had to have them and they won some games when we didn't have to . . . when the only thing at stake was our pride.

It's funny, I look at our 1985 season and it's a good feeling . . . it's very satisfying. But I can look back at the history of this club, at the people and their achievements and the pride they brought to the Bears, and that's a thrill for me.

There aren't any secrets in this business . . . there never have been.

Grange and Nagurski, McAfee and Trafton, Connor and Driscoll, Bulldog Turner and Sid Luckman, Bill George and Doug Atkins . . . that's just a few names from the Bear past. Butkus and Sayers—they're more recent. Payton and Singletary—they're today's Bears.

All of those guys won, and I don't care what the scores of their games were. They won because of the fierce pride they took in their profession. They recognized the gifts the Good Lord gave to them, and they made the most out of them. Those are the people who are the winners, regardless of what they happen to do for a living.

What happened this past season was important; what our team was able to do on the field brought enjoyment to a lot of people. It was important, too, because it permitted all of us to see what can be done, when you put "we" ahead of "me."

For sure, I know one thing about this present Bears team: every one of us owes thanks to all those Bears past, because they're the people who made our success possible.

I just hope we can measure up to them in the years ahead.

—*Mike Ditka*

WHERE IT ALL BEGAN

FOR MOST of the 2.7 million people who lived in Chicago in 1921, the 16th of October was just another ordinary Sunday. In the early morning hours, with the temperature already in the mid-50s and the sun climbing into a clear eastern sky over Lake Michigan, a few people could be found strolling under the brilliant autumn colors of the trees that lined almost all the city streets in those days. From time to time, cars that carried spare tires on their trunks or running boards and had canvas tops and isinglass side curtains would motor by. The noise from the automobiles, along with the occasional screech of a streetcar's steel wheels and the familiar clang of its bell, was about all that interrupted the quiet of the morning. For the most part, a Sunday in the city in 1921 was a restful, family-oriented day, a respite after the 5½-day or the 6-day workweek that most people were saddled with back then.

But it wasn't a day of leisure for everyone; for some it would not be an ordinary day at all. Sixteen young men would labor that afternoon on the field at Cubs Park, up on the North Side, and introduce to the city the Chicago Bears professional football team, although at that time they were still called the Staleys.

Two of these young men—George S. Halas and Edward C. ("Dutch") Sternaman, both 26—were also up at an early hour that Sunday morning. But they harbored no thoughts of strolls through the cavernous halls of the recently completed Field Museum of Natural History, or fancy brunches at the Edgewater Beach Hotel, or family rides on one of the city's double-decker buses. As co-owners and co-coaches of the Staleys, as well as an end and a halfback respectively, Halas and Sternaman were thinking only about football. They had just moved their team up from Decatur—a small town about 125 miles southwest of Chicago—where they had played the year before under the benevolence of A. E. Staley, owner of the Staley Manufacturing Company, a maker of corn products. But now the team was on its own, the sole property of two young men whose overriding interest was the game of football and whose dream was that professional football, and their team in particular, would achieve respect and support from the public and grow to be a success.

On that morning in October, 1921, Halas and Sternaman had no way of knowing whether or not their dream would come true. All they could do was hope that enough people would show up that day at Cubs Park and pay the $1 for a ticket to watch them perform. After all, there were 16 salaries to be paid and a variety of other expenses to be met. The two men had taken out a couple of small ads in the newspapers, personally handed out leaflets around town, and done everything else they could think of to make people aware that they were in business. Even so, they

11

couldn't help but wonder just how many spectators they could legitimately expect on a day when the city's other professional football team, the Cardinals, who had been established in Chicago for more than a year now, would be playing at the same hour directly across town. And besides that, there would be at least 20 semi-pro games going on at various other fields around the city.

Halas and Sternaman, as well as most of the players on the Chicago Staleys, were now living in the Blackwood Hotel. It was an inexpensive, apartment-type hotel that accommodated both transient and permanent residents and had the distinct advantage of being within walking distance of Cubs Park. Its versatility was a virtue too, since Halas and Sternaman did not know at the time whether they would be permanent or transient guests. Actually, neither of them expected to turn a profit at the start of their venture, and both had other jobs on the side—Halas as a car salesman and Sternaman in a gas station.

The newspapers they read that morning also gave them some cause to worry. The lead stories were all about the union brotherhoods who were threatening a nationwide railroad strike, one that could put 2 million people out of work and bring the nation's railroads to a complete halt. President Warren G. Harding had announced he was doing everything possible to prevent the walkout. But if he wasn't successful, how, Halas and Sternaman wondered, would such teams as the Dayton Triangles and the Buffalo All-Americans and the Canton Bulldogs get their players to Chicago to face the Staleys in the games scheduled for the coming weeks?

The news on the sports pages wasn't discouraging, however. True, Halas and Sternaman's alma mater, the University of Illinois, had been beaten decisively by Iowa 14–2 on Saturday, the same day that Cornell had, with a notable lack of mercy, clobbered Western Reserve 110–0. But the college box scores that dominated the Sunday sports news were filled with names which Halas and Sternaman looked forward to adding one day to the Bears' roster—and many they would: Jim McMillen and Laurie Walquist of Illinois and Heartley ("Hunk") Anderson and Johnny Mohardt of Notre Dame, were a few of them. Lesser space was devoted to the news that Jack Dempsey was in Chicago as part of a vaudeville tour he was involved with, apparently to supplement his earnings from the ring, and that Babe Ruth was planning to defy baseball commissioner Judge Kenesaw Mountain Landis by playing in an exhibition baseball game. And there on an inside page of one paper was a six-inch, single-column story about the game that afternoon between

Co-owners, co-coaches, fellow players, and fellow alumni of the University of Illinois, George Halas (left) and Dutch Sternaman were the two men who brought the Staleys from Decatur and turned them into the Chicago Bears. –Sternaman Collection

the Chicago Staleys and the Rochester (N.Y.) Jeffersons. There was even a small picture of Joe DuMoe, one of the Rochester ends.

As the morning moved along, many of the Chicago players began drifting into a little restaurant near the ball park where they could get a breakfast of bacon, eggs, toast, milk, and coffee for about 35¢ or a lunch of meat, potatoes, vegetables, salad, soup, dessert, and beverage for 75¢. But by noon most of the players, feeling the first pangs of nervousness deep in their stomachs that all athletes, professional or amateur, experience before a contest, were walking over to Cubs Park to get their ankles taped, warm up a little, and listen to a Halas/Sternaman pep talk before the game that was scheduled for 2:30.

While all this was going on, people from different areas of the city began to think about football too. And many of them anted up a dime apiece to ride the Northwestern elevated train to the Addison Street stop, which was only about a block east of Cubs Park, while others opted to invest 7¢ for a ride on the streetcar that would deposit them right at the entrance to the ball park. A few people drove their Model T Fords and Maxwells, even a Pierce-Arrow or two, and parked them in the large vacant prairie just west of the playing field. Parking at the stadium in 1921 was free and totally uncomplicated.

By game time, approximately 8,000 spectators, exclusively male, were sitting in the bleachers of Cubs Park. It turned out to be a larger crowd than Halas and Sternaman had expected, even though there were still quite a few empty spaces in the 14,000-seat Cubs Park of 1921.

The team Chicagoans were introduced to that day was actually one of the finest and most well-rounded in all of pro football. Four of the Staley starters—Charles ("Chick") Harley and Pete Stinchcomb from Ohio State, Guy Chamberlin from Nebraska, and Ralph Scott from Wisconsin—had been named to Walter Camp's national All-American teams, which for many years was the highest accolade a college football player could attain. But the men who played professional football at that time were not as big, on the average, as those on today's squads. In fact, in the 1920s they were about the same size as the youngsters who play major *high school* football in the 1970s. The vital statistics of the Staleys' starting line-up on that October afternoon illustrate this:

LE	Guy Chamberlin	6'	190 lbs.
LT	Ralph Scott	6'2"	234 lbs.
LG	John Taylor	5'11"	170 lbs.
C	George Trafton	6'1"	230 lbs.
RG	Russ Smith	5'10"	220 lbs.
RT	Hugh Blacklock	6'	220 lbs.
RE	George Halas	6'	175 lbs.
QB	Pete Stinchcomb	5'8"	152 lbs.
LH	Dutch Sternaman	5'7"	170 lbs.
RH	Chick Harley	5'8"	165 lbs.
FB	Ken Huffine	6'	208 lbs.

But regardless of their size, most of the pros in the early years played the game for 60 solid minutes, offense and defense, coming out only if they were hurt or too exhausted to function effectively.

When the Staleys took the field that afternoon in the colors of midnight blue and orange which the Bears would keep over all the ensuing years, they gave Chicago football fans the first of what would prove to be a long history of exciting moments to cheer about. The Rochester Jeffersons got out to a 3-point lead in the first quarter, but Dutch Sternaman tied it up in the next period with a 30-yard field goal (Halas, a true partner, held for the placekick). Then another field goal by the Jeffersons put them back out in front. The Staleys fell further behind in the third quarter when

Rochester halfback Howard Berry intercepted a Staley pass, ran it back 85 yards for a touchdown, and kicked the extra point. The Staleys were losing 13–3. But later in the quarter, the Jeffersons, with their backs to their own goal line, had to give up the ball. George ("Tiny") Trafton crashed through to block the punt, and Ralph Scott fell on the ball in the end zone for a Staley touchdown. Then in the final quarter, Ken Huffine plunged over for a touchdown and Sternaman kicked the extra point to give the Staleys a 16–13 victory in their new hometown.

The newspapers in 1921 were not impressed enough with the fledgling sport of professional football to send their own writers to cover the game, so George Halas paid a press agent $10 to do it. After the game, both Halas and Sternaman took the story down to the various Chicago newspapers of the day—the *Tribune*, the *Herald-Examiner*, the *American*, and the *Journal*—in the hope that they might garner some publicity the next day to help their cause. The last line of the press agent's story was reassuring, even comforting: "The game was hard fought and cleanly played." In one paper, the account of the game appeared in an interior column somewhat subordinate to one that had this to say:

"Autumn winds presaging snow are sweeping down from the north. The days grow shorter, the nights are crisp, frosty and from above come the notes of migrating birds. Forests flame with color. . . . Corn is in the shock, prairie chickens and quail are gleaning the stubble for grain. . . . Mallards, canvasbacks, widgeon and other favorites are considering their southward flight to more hospitable climes." But that's the way it was in 1921.

Pro football, of course, did not begin with that first game in Cubs Park, nor did the Chicago Bears as a team for that matter. The game, played for money, is traced all the way back to November 12, 1892, when William ("Pudge") Heffelfinger, a teammate of Amos Alonzo Stagg on the Yale squad, was paid $500 to play for the Allegheny Athletic Association in a game against the Pittsburgh Athletic Club. This was the first recorded instance of an athlete receiving money for playing football. The most publicized of the other early football games in which a player was paid took place August 31, 1895, between a YMCA team from Latrobe, Pennsylvania, and a squad from nearby Jeannette. Latrobe's quarterback, who was paid "$10 and cakes" (expenses), for decades was erroneously credited with being the first "pro."

Local teams then began to emerge that would actually represent cities in those early days of the sport,

Pudge Heffelfinger, who was paid $500 to play in a game for the Allegheny Athletic Association back in 1892, is recognized now as the first professional football player in America. This was three years before the Latrobe-Jeannette game in Pennsylvania that has often, but erroneously, been called the first pro game.
–Pro Football Hall of Fame

especially in rugged coal-mining towns like Pottsville, Pennsylvania, and in the steel towns of Ohio—Canton, Massillon, and Akron, for example. The players worked in plants, mills, and mines during the week and came out to play a little football on weekends for a few extra dollars. The rivalry was intense among these teams, the fans wildly partisan, and the local newspapers carried lengthy, play-by-play accounts of the games. The wide-open gambling and rowdyism associated with the pro sport gave it an unsavory reputation that would take years to erase. Nevertheless, many a collegian—using a different name—played on these early teams.

Today, of course, pro football squads are not just bands of local talent but instead are the results of a program of recruiting the top players available from various places and bringing them together as one team. And the choicest recruiting ground has always been the

arena of college football. This approach to organizing a pro team began, according to a story often told by Dutch Sternaman, with a game in 1919 that ironically was never played.

The game was to involve the Decatur Staleys and a team called the Independents from the nearby town of Arcola. The Staleys, whose members were regular employees of the Staley Manufacturing Company, had beaten another team from Arcola earlier in the year 41–0. A group of football-loving Arcola businessmen and farmers, who loved the sport of wagering even more and who had been humiliated by the trouncing, decided to avenge the honor of their town and make a few dollars on the side. The way to do that was with a rematch, but this time they would field a team with the best players they could lay their hands on. And those young men were on the college football fields. But they could be recruited to play for money *after* the college season. So one of the townsmen, a conductor on the Illinois Central Railroad who traveled through most of northern Indiana and Illinois, was lined up as the contact man. He became perhaps pro football's first recruiter when he visited Dutch Sternaman, the University of Illinois's top running back, and enlisted him in the cause. Between them, they contacted other football stars of the day, not only from Illinois but from such

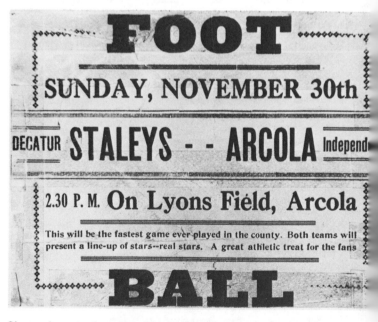

Shown here is the poster for the 1919 game between the Decatur Staleys and the Arcola Independents that was never played. Dutch Sternaman, with an Arcola team loaded with collegiate stars, showed up for the game, but the Staleys wisely did not. The Arcola maneuver, however, prompted A. E. Staley to begin his own recruiting program, which brought Sternaman and George Halas to Decatur the next year. –Sternaman Collection

universities as Indiana, Purdue, and Notre Dame (including the fabled George Gipp, who wanted to play but, as it turned out, couldn't because he became ill).

Arcola collected its roster of college stars, arranged the game with the Staleys, and printed posters. The townspeople laid down bets on the team and then brought their new players to Arcola several days before the game so they could practice together. Vengeance was going to be sweet *and* lucrative. The game was scheduled for 2:30 on Sunday, November 30, but when that time rolled around the only players on Lyons Field in Arcola were the Independents. They waited until 3:00, then until 3:30. Finally someone telephoned A. E. Staley, who, it seems, had gotten word of the "new" Arcola team and had decided to spare his players the fate the Arcolans had cooked up for them. But the act was not wasted on Staley. He saw very clearly how a topflight football team could be put together, and that planted the seed in *his* mind.

So Mr. Staley contacted Dutch Sternaman for his own purposes. He asked the young college senior to see him in Decatur during the Christmas vacation of 1919. Staley told Sternaman when they met that he wanted a player and organizer like him on the company payroll. Sternaman, however, was still working toward a degree in mechanical engineering, and at the moment was more interested in a job when he finished school in the spring than in playing pro football. In fact, he was looking for a job in boiler and combustion engineering, he told the man. Staley took him over to the office window and pointed out to a large plant with towering smokestacks. "We're building a big business here," he said, "with just the kind of training ground you're looking for. There's a power plant, a filtration plant, manufacturing facilities out there. You can learn your trade right in the boiler rooms here, and you can play football and help organize the best team around at the same time." Sternaman admitted he was interested and said he would think about it; then he went back to get his engineering degree at Illinois.

Not one for waiting around, Staley got hold of George Halas in March, 1920. Halas, Staley had heard, was a player of professional caliber not only in football but also in baseball, and Staley had an equal and abiding love for both sports. Halas had played end at the University of Illinois. After graduating he became a member of the Great Lakes Naval Training Station football squad during the last year of World War I. Two other young men on that team were John L. ("Paddy") Driscoll, fresh from Northwestern University, and Jimmy Conzelman, from Washington University in St. Louis. Each of them would later play both with and against the Bears and eventually join

Halas in the pro football Hall of Fame. The Great Lakes squad was good enough to play in the Rose Bowl game on January 1, 1919. With Halas contributing to the score, Great Lakes Navy shut out the favored Mare Island Marines—who had won the bowl game the year before—17–0.

A. E. Staley, owner of the Decatur, Illinois, corn products company that bore his name, sponsor of the Decatur Staleys, and the Chicago Bears' premiere fan and first financial backer.
–Sternaman Collection

As a New York Yankee under manager Miller Huggins, George Halas injured his hip during spring training, in 1919, which effectively ended his major league baseball career. –Pro Football Hall of Fame

After he was discharged from the Navy, Halas tried his fortunes on the baseball diamond, earning a try-out with the New York Yankees. Miller Huggins, the Yankee manager, signed him to a contract, and in 1919 Halas reported for spring training at Jacksonville, Florida. In an exhibition game there against the Brooklyn Dodgers, he hit a double off Rube Marquard, but trying to stretch it into a triple he slid into third and injured his hip. He was hurt badly enough to keep him out of major league baseball, although he was in the Yankee line-up early in the regular season. He wound up his baseball career playing with the St. Paul, Minnesota, minor league club. Halas returned to Chicago, took a job with the Chicago, Burlington & Quincy Railroad, and joined his friend Paddy Driscoll on weekends to play with the Hammond Pros, a local and loosely organized pro football team.

When he got the call from A. E. Staley, Halas went down to Decatur to see what the man had to offer. Staley told Halas that he wanted him to play for his baseball team, which was managed by former major league pitcher Joe ("Iron Man") McGinnity, one of the game's early greats who would later be inducted into baseball's Hall of Fame. He also wanted Halas to

The Staley baseball team of 1920. Standing at the far left is company owner and team sponsor A. E. Staley. Next to him is team captain George Halas. Standing third from the right is future Chicago Bear and Chicago Cub trainer Andy Lotshaw; in the center of the middle row is manager Iron Man Joe McGinnity. –Sternaman Collection

organize a Staley football team like the one Arcola had put together for the game that never took place. "Bring in the best players around," Staley said. "I'll give them jobs—they'll earn a living here, and they'll play football for us." Halas himself would receive a good salary to work in the Staley plant.

George Halas, whose great loves were playing baseball and football, thought the idea of having a job with a regular paycheck along with the opportunity to play both sports on an organized, big-time level was a wonderful one. He accepted Staley's offer.

When the school year was over in June, Dutch Sternaman also took a job with the Staley company. There he joined Halas in contacting prospective players to get them to come to Decatur to play football and work for Staley. The two young men also agreed to share the coaching duties of the team they had reorganized.

By midsummer the Staleys had the nucleus of a team. Playing one end was the jewel of their acquisition efforts, Guy Chamberlin. Among the greatest of the players in that era, he would go on to coach and play his way into the Hall of Fame. Halas held down the other end position. Hugh Blacklock from Michigan State and Burt Ingwersen from Illinois were the tackles, Jerry Jones from Notre Dame and Ross Petty from Illinois the guards. Another Notre Dame alumnus, George Trafton, who would become one of the all-time Bear greats and a Hall-of-Famer, was signed on at center. Quarterbacking chores were to be shared between Walter ("Pard") Pearce from the University of Pennsylvania and Charlie Dressen, who would later make much more of a name for himself as a major league baseball manager. Dutch Sternaman was at left halfback and Jimmy Conzelman, one of the game's more famous names, at right halfback. Bob Koehler from Northwestern, who signed on to play fullback, would move over to the Chicago Cardinals after that season and come back to harass the Bears with his superb running abilities. Another Staley employee, Andy Lotshaw, a millwright who had played on the company's baseball team, was signed on as trainer and manager. In that capacity, Lotshaw would become a legend in Chicago, tending to the ailments and pains of both the Bears and the Cubs for decades to come.

Now that Halas and Sternaman had their team, they confronted the next problem—lining up some competition. There were a number of professional and semi-pro teams around in 1920, and a few of these had brief periods of success and stability. But most of them could not even be counted on to show up for a scheduled game. The Canton Bulldogs were one of the more substantial teams, and when Halas approached

George Trafton, long-time Bear center during the early years of the team's existence, had a well-earned reputation for ferocity around the league, similar to those earned by players like Ed Sprinkle and Dick Butkus in later years. During one particular game with the Independents at Rock Island in 1920, a number of their players had to leave the game with assorted injuries after encounters with Trafton. The crowd, already angry, became enraged when Rock Island tailback Fred Chicken joined the casualty list as he tried to race around end and out of Trafton's reach.

"I tackled him right on the sideline," Trafton said. "There was a fence close to the field, and after I hit Chicken he spun up against a fence post and broke his leg. After that the fans were really on me." An understatement, to say the least. At the end of the game, they chased him out of the stadium and down the street under a shower of rocks, empty bottles, and other lethal objects at hand that were throwable. Dutch Sternaman tried to pick him up in a cab, but the pursuers were too close. Trafton finally managed to escape with the help of a passing motorist.

The next time that the Bears appeared in Rock Island, the game was again an especially physical one and the crowd grew almost as ornery as it had the time before. When this game ended and George Halas was handed $7,000 in cash—the Bears' share of the gate receipts—he gave the money over to Trafton for safekeeping. "I knew that if trouble came," Halas said, "I'd be running only for the $7,000. Trafton would be running for his life."

Decatur Staley and Chicago Bear halfback Dutch Sternaman.
–Sternaman Collection

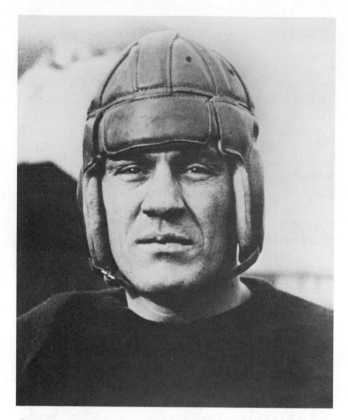

Jimmy Conzelman played with the Staleys of 1920, then came back to haunt them as one of the finest halfbacks of his day, playing against them on various teams during the next decade. And as coach of the Chicago Cardinals in 1940-42 and 1946-48, he was a key contributor to the great intra-city rivalry between the two Chicago franchises. –Pro Football Hall of Fame

them about playing with the Staleys, he learned from their owner, Ralph Hay, that plans were under way to organize a league. Sternaman and Halas both felt that there should be some structure to the season, and the formation of a league made up of the best pro teams seemed the only way to go about it. A few interested team owners got together in Akron in August and decided to hold a meeting for the express purpose of organizing a league. Hay offered to host the meeting and to contact all the better pro teams he normally played against and get them to attend too.

The meeting took place September 17, 1920, at Hay's Hupmobile Agency in Canton. George Halas went to Ohio to represent the Decatur Staleys. "That meeting in Hay's showroom must have been the most informal on record," Halas said later. "There were no chairs. We lounged around on fenders and running boards and talked things over." Besides the Staleys and the Bulldogs, nine pro teams were represented that day. One of these was a team from Chicago's South Side, the Racine Cardinals, who began playing

pro ball just before World War I but date back to 1899. They took the first part of their name from the street next to where they played in 1901 and the last part from the color of their "new" jerseys, which were actually faded maroon hand-me-downs discarded by the University of Chicago. The other teams who sent representatives to the meeting were the Akron Pros, Cleveland Indians, Dayton Triangles, Hammond Pros, Massillon (Ohio) Tigers, Muncie (Ind.) Flyers, Rochester Jeffersons, and Rock Island Independents.

The league formed at the Canton meeting was called the American Professional Football Association. It was, in fact, the beginning of the National Football League, although it would not go by that name for the first two years of its existence. For promotional value, Jim Thorpe, the game's most famous figure, was chosen president of the APFA. This would be an office in name and honor only, for at this time the future Hall-of-Famer was still the running and kicking star, as well as coach, of the Canton Bulldogs, but he had ended his major league baseball career the year before. George Halas also remembered this about the historic meeting: "To give the new organization an appearance of financial stability, we announced that the membership fee for individual clubs had been set at $100. However, I can testify that no money changed hands. Why I doubt if there was a hundred bucks in the whole room."

Two things were agreed on at that meeting. First the league would attempt to win the goodwill of college football (which would be about as easy to accomplish as chopping up Mount Everest and fashioning the pieces into cobblestone bricks) by not signing up collegians before their playing careers were over; second, no team would tamper with players on another team, a rule the Staleys would manage to violate before this first league season was over.

The official minutes of the meeting also show that "Mr. Marshall of the Brunswick-Balke Collender Company, Tire Division, presented a silver loving cup to be given the team awarded the championship by the association. Any team winning the cup three times should be adjudged the owner." There is no record, however, of any team ever having been awarded Mr. Marshall's trophy.

And so in the year 1920, when America was about to begin what F. Scott Fitzgerald would describe as "the greatest gaudiest spree in history," the type of professional football we know today and the Chicago Bears were both launched right along with it. It was the Jazz Age, a time when men with patent-leather hair wore knickers and raccoon coats, when women bobbed their hair and wore flapper dresses and rolled-

THE NATIONAL FOOTBALL LEAGUE

JOS. F. CARR, Columbus, Ohio..................President
JOHN DUNN, Minneapolis, Minn................Vice-President
CARL L. STORCK, Dayton, Ohio..............Secretary-Treasurer

CODE OF ETHICS

Members of this League are expected to conduct themselves as gentlemen and sportsmen. Any flagrant violation of this principle may subject the offending member to suspension or expulsion.

No member shall knowingly make false representations through advertising as to the personnel of his or a competitive team in an effort to deceive the public for his own financia betterment. The confidence of the public is to be desired above all else.

No member shall have a player on his team under an assumed name.

Tampering with players on College teams shall not be tolerated by this League. The same creates much unfavorable public sentiment against professional football and is deplored and discouraged by this League. An adequate supply of football players who have completed their academic status exist and by confining ourselves to these men much favorable public sentiment shall be ours.

down hose; when the freer spirits of both took to smoking cigarettes and drinking bootleg hooch, as they called it in the jargon of the day. It had come time for names like Harold ("Red") Grange, Earl ("Curly") Lambeau, and Ernie Nevers to take their places on the pages of newspapers next to those of Babe Ruth, Jack Dempsey, Gene Tunney, Bill Tilden, and the other sports celebrities of the age. It was perhaps the perfect climate in which to launch a frantic sport like professional football.

The American Professional Football Association of 1920 was not really a league, like the NFL turned out to be. The APFA was more like a loosely knit association, formed to help teams cooperate with each other and to provide at least some semblance of organization. It did not set schedules, keep records, make official pronouncements or decisions, or even publish rules or regulations. League members played nonleague teams, and there were no provisions for determining the season's champion. But all that would change shortly.

By the time the APFA teams got their season under way in October, the Massillon Tigers, for years the legendary rivals of the Canton Bulldogs, had already folded. Four others, however, eagerly joined the new league—the Buffalo All-Americans, Detroit Heralds, Chicago Tigers, and Columbus Panhandles—giving the APFA a total of 14 teams. But one of these, the hapless Muncie Flyers, which fielded a squad deemed "out of its league," was soon forced out.

In 1920 the teams in the APFA would play only those in nearby cities. None of them had the money to transport maybe 15 to 18 players and a manager to towns more than a short distance away. Of the eight league games the Decatur Staleys played that year, for example, two were against the Cardinals in Chicago, two against the Tigers in that same city, two against the Independents in Rock Island, Illinois, and one against the Pros from Hammond, Indiana, who came to Decatur. All the towns were within 125 miles of each other. (The Cardinals and the Tigers apparently were a little *too* close to each other for both to survive financially, so they decided to play a game for the "rights" to Chicago; the loser would drop out of the league. The Cardinals won, 6–3, on a touchdown scored by Paddy Driscoll, who had been signed up earlier that year, and as agreed, the Tigers disbanded.)

The first game the Staleys played in 1920 was not against a league team. Halas and Sternaman brought their new team out onto Staley Field before the excited eyes of A. E. Staley and a thousand or so eager fans on October 3, 1920, to face the Moline Tractors, an independent pro team from that small Illinois town over on the Mississippi River. The Staleys' debut was a success, as they easily defeated the Tractors 20–0.

1920 STALEY TEAM

SEASON 1920

Professional Football

Staleys vs. Moline Tractors

Staley Field—Decatur, Illinois

Sunday, October 3

3:00 P. M.

PERSONNEL OF TWO TEAMS

STALEYS—		MOLINE—	
1	LANUM (Illinois)	1	KOLLS
2	STERNAMAN (Illinois)	2	ROHWER
3	KOEHLER (Northwestern)	3	WIEDERQUIST
4	PEARCE (Pennsylvania)	4	MULLINIX
5	DRESSEN (Independent)	5	SIES
6	GEPFORD (Millikin)	6	HUFFORD
7	HALAS (Illinois)	7	SODERSTROM
8	JOHNSON (Millikin)	8	WOODYATT
10	INGWERSEN (Illinois)	9	MEERSMAN
11	FEICHTINGER (Multnomah A. C.)	10	SWANSON
12	JONES (Notre Dame)	11	ALLEN
13	TRAFTON (Notre Dame)	12	NORTON
14	McWHERTER (Millikin)	13	VERSLUS
15	VEACH (Independent)	14	CRAWFORD
16	YOUNG (Millikin)	15	VALENTINE
17	PETTY (Illinois)	16	DONOVAN
18	SHANK (Maryland State)	17	HAYDEN
19	MAY (Independent)	18	BURNS
20	MINTUN (Independent)		
21	BLACKLOCK (Michigan Aggies)		
22	ADKINS (Millikin)		
23	CLARK (Independent)		
24	HIGH (Eastern Normal)		

SCORE BY QUARTERS

	1	2	3	4	TOTAL
STALEYS					
MOLINE					

OFFICIALS

Referee—WALTER ECKERSAL .... (Chicago)

Umpire—HOWARD MILLARD .... (Illinois Wesleyan)

Head Linesman—FRED YOUNG .... (Illinois Wesleyan)

Program and roster from the first game played by the Decatur Staleys under George Halas and Dutch Sternaman. –Sternaman Collection

The Staleys lost only one game that year, to the Cardinals, who hosted them at Normal Park out at 61st and Racine on Chicago's South Side. This win by the Cardinals must rank among the most questionable in NFL history. With the Cardinals losing 6–0 late in the game, one of their receivers caught a pass along the sidelines, but as he was about to be tackled he scrambled to safety behind a group of partisan spectators, who had drifted onto the gridiron. Using them as blockers he went in for a touchdown. Afraid of the fans' frenzied reaction if he called the play back, the referee allowed the score, and the Cardinals won 7–6.

As the last game of the season approached, the Staleys had an APFA league record of five wins, one loss, and one tie. The team they were to play, however, the Akron Pros, were undefeated. Led by tailback Fritz Pollard, the Pros boasted a 6–0–1 record. The game was being heralded as the first "pro football championship game." To help their cause, Halas and Sternaman lured Paddy Driscoll down from Chicago. Driscoll had already proved himself one of the best backs and kickers in the game, and his team, the Cardinals, had ended their season the week before. The Decatur coaches put him in a Staley uniform, choosing to ignore the unwritten agreement about not tampering with another team's players, but in the end it did them no good. The Decatur-Akron game ended in a scoreless tie, and with it the first organized pro football season came to a close. No official standings were kept, so there was no official APFA champion for 1920. If a title were to be bestowed, however, it probably would have gone to the Akron Pros, who did not lose a game all year.

The Staleys actually ended their season with a record of 10–1–2 because they had played five independent teams during that autumn (besides Moline, teams from three other Illinois towns—Kewanee, Rockford, and Champaign—and the Minneapolis Marines). The high scorer for the year was Dutch Sternaman, who accounted for 98 of the Staleys' 166 points in their 13 games. The season was a very real success for the Staleys, and when the profits from the gate receipts were toted up, each member of the Decatur team received a check for $1,900, which was a very hefty bonus to be added to anyone's regular earnings in 1920.

But prosperity for the Staley starchworkers was to be short-lived, for 1921 would prove to be a different kind of year entirely. The nation's economy took a sudden downhill turn. Many people lost their jobs, and those who weren't laid off were forced to accept large pay cuts. It was a minor depression, and it reached out to Decatur, forcing an unhappy A. E. Staley to call George Halas from his job in the company's glucose department and give him the grim news. Because of the financial situation, he was going to have to severely curtail the Staley athletic program.

"I know you're more interested in football than the starch business," he said to Halas, "but we simply can't underwrite the team's expenses any longer. Why don't you move the boys up to Chicago? I think pro football can go over in a big way there—and I'll give you $5,000 to help you get started. All I ask is that you continue to call the team the Staleys for one season."

Halas, and Sternaman, who agreed to come in as a full 50/50 partner, decided to give it a try. First though, they needed a place to play. So Halas and Sternaman paid a call on William L. Veeck, then one of the owners and president of the Chicago Cubs (father of Bill Veeck, Jr., who would later run the Cleveland Indians, St. Louis Browns, and Chicago White Sox baseball franchises) to see what the possibilities would be of playing pro football in Cubs Park. Veeck had long been a football fan. He was not so sure, however, about the survival prospects of professional football in Chicago. On the other hand, he knew that many people truly liked the sport of football (no one could fail to notice the 50,000 to 70,000 fans who would turn out for a major college game, even in those days). Besides, the ball park sat idle on Sundays in the autumn and early winter and any income would be a nice extra. Veeck was interested.

"How much would it cost to rent the park?" Halas asked.

Veeck was not going to make it difficult for the young owners. "Fifteen percent of the gross gate

1920 SEASON   .909
Won 10   Lost 1   Tied 2

George Halas,
Dutch Sternaman—Coaches

	Bears*	Opponents
Moline	20	0
Kewanee	27	0
Rock Island	7	0
Chicago Tigers	10	0
Rockford	29	0
Champaign	20	0
Hammond	28	7
Rock Island	0	0
Minneapolis	3	0
Chicago Tigers	6	0
Racine (Chicago) Cardinals	6	7
Racine (Chicago) Cardinals	10	0
Akron	0	0
Totals	166	14

*Decatur Staleys; schedule includes non-league games

ERWIN L. WENZEL
PRESIDENT

H. J. McCOMB
ASST. TO PRESIDENT

HOTEL PLANTERS

PHONE RANDOLPH 4800

CLARK NEAR MADISON ST.

CHICAGO,   19

ABSOLUTELY FIRE PROOF-ALL MODERN
300 ROOMS - 200 ROOMS WITH BATH
RATES $2.00 UP
W. G. RIDDLE, MGR.

When George Halas and Dutch Sternaman signed up some recent college graduates in the lobby of this downtown Chicago hotel, they got more publicity than they bargained for—most of it distinctly unfavorable. –Sternaman Collection

receipts. And we keep the profits from the concessions.'' The rental would increase to 20% when the gross receipts reached $10,000.

It was the ideal arrangement for Halas and Sternaman and the tenuous existence of their enterprise. They would not be burdened with a fixed rental they might not be able to meet should the crowds they hoped for fail to materialize on certain Sundays. They would simply have to share a small portion of the revenue they took in. Then Halas, in the midst of his first real business deal, showed the hard-bargaining

Dutch Sternaman kicking, George Halas holding was only one of the ways the two partners teamed up in the early 1920s. This picture was taken in the Bears' new home at Cubs Park, later renamed Wrigley Field. –Sternaman Collection

business sense that would become his trademark over the years. "But we keep the profits from the program sales," he added.

Veeck agreed, and the Staleys had a home. The negotiations, according to Halas, "took all of seventy-five seconds," but these arrangements would endure unchanged for 50 years, until the Bears moved their operation to Soldier Field in 1971.

Many of the 1920 Staleys moved north with the team. The salary deal varied from player to player, but the range was $75 to $100 a game. All Halas and Sternaman agreed to take for their playing, coaching, administering, promoting, errand-running, ankle-taping, and worrying was a wage of $100 per game. Among the players they recruited for the coming season were Chick Harley and Pete Stinchcomb. Signing them, which Halas and Sternaman did in the lobby of the Hotel Planters in downtown Chicago, where they did much of their business that year because they couldn't afford to rent office space, got more publicity than anyone expected. Favorable reports of the signing included such statements as, "and with Dutch Sternaman [Harley and Stinchcomb] will give the Decatur [Chicago] eleven the greatest professional backfield in the country." Most of the printed words, however, were in the form of scathing attacks on the immorality of collegians playing this wholesome game for, of all things, money. Amos Alonzo Stagg, famous coach of the University of Chicago, especially was vehement in his criticism of the pro game. A *Chicago Daily News* story on November 2, 1921, was headlined, "Stagg Condemns Pro Football Contests," then went on: "Says Sunday-playing Teams Debauch College Sport and Athletes." After denouncing gambling as an insidious force out to destroy college football, Stagg added, "And now along comes another serious menace, possibly greater than all others, viz., Sunday professional football." He would lead the parade for years to come against what he called "the scourge of pro football." The APFA's hopes of winning over the college football establishment were not faring so well.

In order to sign Chick Harley, the hottest name in college football the year before, Halas and Sternaman had to agree to bring both him and his brother Bill (his manager) into the organization as partners. An initial agreement was signed and their names were added to the Staleys' letterhead. But when the final contract was drawn up, the Harleys, holding out for certain benefits that had not been included, tore it up, an action they would regret dearly the following year. So the Staleys got Chick Harley for 1921, and Halas and Sternaman kept full ownership of the team. The Staleys also signed on a tough little guard from Ohio State, John

("Tarzan") Taylor, and their biggest lineman, tackle Ralph Scott, who weighed in at 234 pounds.

There were some changes in the APFA itself too. The league was reorganized, and Joseph F. Carr, long-time manager of the Columbus Panhandles, replaced Jim Thorpe as president. A sportswriter, Carr had also been involved with professional baseball and basketball. Firmly, but fairly, he would guide the National Football League through all the problems of its formative years, providing eminent leadership for the next 18 years, until his death in 1939.

Jim Thorpe also left the Canton Bulldogs, taking along with him his fellow backs, Pete Calac and Hall-of-Famer Joe Guyon, to organize a new franchise, the Cleveland Indians. The APFA, in fact, swelled to 18 teams in 1921, although five would drop out before the end of the season.

Before the November, 1921, game between the Bears and the Cleveland Indians, the three most famous Indians in pro football—Pete Calac, Jim Thorpe, and Joe Guyon (left to right)—pose for the camera. The Bears won that game 22–7. –Sternaman Collection

The letter of agreement dividing ownership of the Staleys equally among Halas, Sternaman, Chick Harley, and Chick's brother William. It never became a valid contract, however, and the Harleys' association with the team lasted for only one season (1921). –Sternaman Collection

At the very start, the Chicago Staleys, now headquartered at the Blackwood Hotel, were optimistic enough about their survival to print up their new stationery. Note the Harleys' names on the letterhead. –Sternaman Collection

EDWARD C. STERNAMAN   GEO. S. HALAS

CUBS PARK HOME OF THE STALEYS

STALEY FOOTBALL CLUB

Blackwood Hotel
4518 Clarendon Avenue
CHICAGO, ILL.
Phone Edgewater 8600

WILLIAM G. HARLEY   CHAS. W. HARLEY

One of the new franchises that would not drop out—but came close—was awarded to a team up in Green Bay, Wisconsin, sponsored by the Acme Packing Company and to be led by coach and tailback Curly Lambeau.

The Packers had been organized two years earlier, when Lambeau, an employee of the firm's predecessor, the Indian Packing Company, persuaded his boss to back a football team. But after the 1921 season, Joe Carr ordered the franchise returned to the league because Green Bay had been fielding college players using assumed names. Promising he would obey the rules, Lambeau paid the $50 fee to get the franchise back. To keep the team from folding when bad weather turned the 1922 season into a financial disaster, the town fathers formed a nonprofit corporation to operate the team, retaining tailback and future Hall-of-Famer Lambeau as manager/coach.

The Chicago Staleys opened the 1921 season with an exhibition game at Staley Field in Decatur against a semi-pro team called the Waukegan American Legion and demolished them 35–0. They also played their first league game in Decatur. More than 4,000 fans came out to Staley Field, the largest crowd ever to attend a game there, to watch the Staleys in their farewell appearance beat the Rock Island Independents 14–10.

The Staleys then went to Chicago to play nine straight home games at Cubs Park. By the end of November, the new Chicago franchise had a league record of six wins and no losses, certainly enough to impress and delight its benefactor, A. E. Staley, who traveled up to see the team almost every Sunday. Also undefeated, however, were the Buffalo All-Americans, who came to visit the Staleys in Cubs Park on November 24th. This game was being billed by Buffalo as the battle for the "world championship." But it didn't turn out that way, because even though Buffalo defeated the Staleys 7–6 they didn't win the "world championship"—or the APFA championship for that matter.

Three days later, Green Bay invaded Chicago for the first game in what George Halas would later describe as "the most fierce rivalry in pro football." Along with the team came 300 loyal fans as well as a brass band whose musicians were garbed in woodsmen's costumes. The whole contingent—team, fans, and band—traveled on a special train. But none of this hoopla helped the Packers. The Staleys, with touchdowns by Pard Pearce, Pete Stinchcomb, and George Halas and two extra points kicked by Dutch Sternaman, shut out the Pack 20–0.

Buffalo returned to Cubs Park a week later, but this time the Staleys were ready. With Guy Chamberlin scoring a touchdown and turning in a fine defensive performance, the Staleys won 10–7 and clinched the first pro football league championship. Their final record was 10–1–1 (if you included that non-league

Curly Lambeau, the Green Bay Packers' great tailback and coach, was an integral part of the Packer-Bear rivalry for 30 years, until he retired from the Packers in 1949. As a coach, only George Halas has won more pro football games than Curly Lambeau. –Pro Football Hall of Fame

The 1921 Staleys. This team picture was taken in front of the Staley plant in Decatur, even though the Bears played only their first game of the season there before moving to Chicago. From the left: George E. Chamberlain (Staley plant manager), Ralph Scott, George Trafton, Guy Chamberlin, Ken Huffine, Russ Smith, Hugh Blacklock, Harry Englund, Jake Lanum, George Bolan, George Halas, Jack Mintun, Burt Ingwersen, Tarzan Taylor, Chick Harley, Pete Stinchcomb, Pard Pearce, Dutch Sternaman, Andy Lotshaw (trainer). –Pro Football Hall of Fame

game with Waukegan, which the Staleys did), a short step ahead of the Buffalo All-Americans, who ended their season with a 9–1–2 record. Buffalo protested, claiming at least a share of the league title, but Joe Carr ruled in favor of the Staleys. They had the championship—the first officially recognized by the NFL—but would have to be satisfied with just the glory of winning it, because the team ended up losing money. Fortunately the total loss was only $71.63.

1921 SEASON .909*
Won 10 Lost 1 Tied 1

George Halas,

Dutch Sternaman—Coaches	Bears†	Opponents
Waukegan (non-league team)	35	0
Rock Island Independents	14	10
Rochester (N.Y.) Jeffersons	16	13
Dayton Triangles	7	0
Detroit Heralds	20	9
Rock Island Independents	3	0
Cleveland Indians	22	7
Buffalo All-Americans	6	7
Green Bay Packers	20	0
Buffalo All-Americans	10	7
Canton Bulldogs	10	0
Racine (Chicago) Cardinals	0	0
Totals	163	53

*APFA champions
†Chicago Staleys

Joe Carr headed the NFL from 1921 until his death in 1939. He was instrumental in sustaining the league during the turbulent years of its early existence. As a result, he was often at loggerheads with team owners—with George Halas and Dutch Sternaman, it was over the Paddy Driscoll, Red Grange, and Joe Savoldi incidents, among others. –Pro Football Hall of Fame

A NEW IDENTITY

IN 1922 the American Professional Football Association changed its name, at the suggestion of George Halas, to the National Football League. And earlier in the year, the Chicago Staleys became the Chicago Bears. Halas and Sternaman chose the name Bears because they wanted some link to the Chicago Cubs baseball team they were sharing facilities with and perhaps because they hoped that some of the success the Cubs had already achieved would rub off on their team.

Late in January, pro football was accorded full-fledged press coverage for the first time, but it was hardly the kind of publicity the league would have chosen. The banner headline in the *Chicago Herald-Examiner* read: "Stagg Says [Big Ten] Conference Will Break Professional Football Menace." This time the brouhaha was the result of a game that had taken place in November but because it was played between small-town teams in southern Illinois—Carlinville and Taylorville—the story didn't surface for two months. It was a grudge match, and betting was heavy. That was bad enough, but what really riled Stagg was the revelation that collegians, from Illinois and Notre Dame universities, had participated in the game. Two of the Illinois players were future Bears, one of them a long-time standout with the team. The Taylorville quarterback in the second half (he replaced former Staley Charlie Dressen) was 5-feet-6 and weighed only

150 pounds. His face was painted and patterned over with strips of adhesive tape, but Joey Sternaman's size and skill—he kicked three field goals that day—gave him away. Another Illinois player who later joined the Bear roster was Laurie Walquist. Sternaman and the other 16 collegians involved, were made scapegoats for doing what everyone knew had been going on for decades and were declared ineligible. The furor over this incident culminated in the absurdity of the Big Ten Conference ordering all football pros who had played in college to return their varsity letters.

On May 2, 1922, Halas and Dutch Sternaman filed for incorporation in the state of Illinois as the Chicago Bears Football Club, Inc. They paid the $20 fee and a franchise tax of $13.34 and listed only one other person on their board of directors—ironically enough, Paddy Driscoll of their crosstown rivals, the Cardinals. It was all part of a deal to get Driscoll into a Chicago Bear uniform. He was just about the best player in the league, and he was a consistent plague on Halas and Sternaman's team. The ploy, however, did not work. Joe Carr, NFL president, ruled that Driscoll was the property of the Cardinals and the Bears had no right to him unless the Cardinals agreed to it. They didn't, of course. So Driscoll's part ownership of the Bears, along with his membership on their board of directors, was cancelled on September 15, 1922, and he went back to the Cardinals. His team, meanwhile, had changed its name to the Chicago Cardinals, when an NFL franchise was awarded to the Racine (Wis.) Legion. The Cardinals also began playing their home games in Comiskey Park that year.

The initial issuance of stock in the Bears' new corporation was 150 shares, each having a par value of $100. (Driscoll was to have had 25 of these shares.) As far as administration of the corporation was concerned, Halas and Sternaman agreed to serve as president and secretary respectively, and then switch those roles every year.

The Bears may have gained a new name in 1922, but they lost one of their prize properties. Guy Cham-

berlin left to coach and play for the Canton Bulldogs. It was a loss that would hurt the Bears sorely by the time the season ended. Tarzan Taylor also moved to Canton. Another player who departed was Chick Harley. He had hardly lived up to what Halas and Sternaman had expected of an All-American who had been so highly touted. They did not choose to invite him back and removed him from the Bears' payroll. With that, the Chicago Bears were presented with their first lawsuit. Bill Harley, still his brother's manager, brought an action against the Bears organization, and against Halas and Sternaman personally, in the Superior Court of Illinois. As reported in the *Chicago Herald-*

The Chicago Bears became a corporation on May 2, 1922. One of the three principals named on the incorporation papers (shown here) is Paddy Driscoll, who at the time was a member of the Chicago Cardinals. Ownership, stock, and a directorship were enticements offered by Halas and Sternaman to bring him over to the Bears. NFL President Joe Carr, however, called it "tampering," and Driscoll had to relinquish his part ownership of the Bears. —Sternaman Collection

---

POLICY OF THE CHICAGO BEARS FOOTBALL CLUB, INC.

——o——

Member of the National Football League.

The policy of the Chicago Bears Football Club, Inc., is to promote clean, healthful sport; to maintain for the City of Chicago a football team that will be a leader in this great American out-door sport. This team is composed of American College stars and will have the leading football teams of the country as opponents. Our City will gain added publicity in supporting games that will attract nation-wide attention and be recognized as a promoter of clean sports and recreation.

Examiner, the Bears management "permitted a situation to arise on the Bear team . . . which broke Chick Harley's heart." The *Chicago Tribune* reported the specifics:

"The suit contends that Chick Harley was the unremitting object of attempts to belittle his playing ability, that the Staleys' line gave way in games of 1921 in order to let opposing players spill him, and that he was driven into a state of mental collapse by the 'freeze out' treatment which culminated in the team's refusal to accept his insertion into the second half of the game with Buffalo late in the 1921 season, with 10,000 people looking on. For months following this episode, Chick Harley was in sanitaria."

The case did go to court. When he appeared before the judge, Dutch Sternaman was asked what the net worth of the Bears was at that particular time. Sternaman shrugged and said, "Eleven jocks in the locker room." The case eventually drifted into oblivion, as had the Harleys' share in the partnership when they failed to sign the formal contract with Halas and Sternaman the year before.

In 1922 Dutch Sternaman coaxed his younger brother into joining the Bears. "Little Joey," as many people referred to him in those days was indeed small by today's pro football standards, but he was fast, tough, durable, and afraid of no one, no matter what his size. One Chicago writer described him as having the "unique characteristics of a combined bantam rooster and pit bulldog." He was good enough to take the starting quarterback position away from Pete Stinchcomb and Pard Pearce, who had been sharing it, and he became the Bears' primary field-goal and extra-point kicker. He would prove to be one of the pro game's best drop-kickers over the next nine years.

The Bears also added guard Hunk Anderson, an All-American, and Laurie Walquist, a fine running

Joey Sternaman was the Bears' chief extra-point and field-goal kicker for most of the eight years he spent with the team. A drop-kicker, he was consistently among the NFL's top kicking specialists during the 1920s. The rounded shape of the ball in those days was obviously much more suited to drop-kicking than the type of ball used now. –Sternaman Collection

Ed Healey was "the most versatile tackle of all time," in the words of George Halas, and was also one of the game's greatest linemen. He came to the Bears in 1922 from the Rock Island Independents in the first player deal in Bear history (his contract was purchased for $100) and remained with them for the rest of his career. –Pro Football Hall of Fame

back. Midway through the season, the Bears made their first player deal by buying up the contract of tackle Ed Healey from the Rock Island Independents for $100. Both Halas and Sternaman have stories as to how it came about. Halas remembers it as a result of a most unpleasant confrontation with Healey the first time they played against each other. Halas, realizing he couldn't effectively block this big, fast lineman, took to holding him when the referee wasn't looking. Healey didn't cotton to the idea too well and took a vicious swipe at Halas, burying his fist up to the wrist in the ground. "I decided then and there I'd much rather have Healey playing on our side than against us," Halas said later. Sternaman remembers the same game: "Healey kept stopping me on every off-tackle smash I tried. Finally, I told Blacklock (who had been trying to block Healey) just to get out of the way and let

me hit Healey head on. I did, and Ed just picked me up. That night I met Flanagan [the owner of the Rock Island team] in the Sherman Hotel. He needed some money, about $75 I think it was, and I told him I wouldn't give him a loan but I'd buy Ed Healey's contract for $100."

How it happened is apparently a matter of opinion, but the acquisition of Healey was an inspired move. Healey went on to play for the Bears for six years, during which time he proved to be one of the finest tackles who ever played the game. (He was elected to the pro football Hall of Fame in 1964.)

The Bears, defending their league championship, opened the season on October 1, 1922, at Cubs Park against the Racine Legion, whose biggest threat was Charlie Dressen. The Bears beat Racine, then Rock Island, Rochester, and Buffalo, before they came up against the revitalized Canton Bulldogs. Halas and Sternaman knew only too well how good Guy Chamberlin was; they also respected the reputations of Canton's linemen Roy ("Link") Lyman and Wilbur Henry, better known as Pete or "Fats." The Bulldogs were far from the mediocre fifth-place team they had been the year before, the Bears found out to their dismay when they hosted the team at Cubs Park at the end of October. The Bulldogs beat them 7–6.

Two weeks later, the Bears took on the Oorang Indians from Marion, Ohio, a new, all-Indian team organized and coached by halfback Jim Thorpe. Now 34 years old, Thorpe was still a powerful player, as George Halas could testify: "To have Thorpe tackle you from behind was an experience you couldn't forget. He wouldn't actually tackle you. With his great speed he'd run you down and then throw his huge body crosswise into your back. It was like having a redwood tree fall on you." The Oorang Indians, who took the first part of their name from a dog kennel that originally sponsored the team, played road games only. Besides Thorpe, Joe Guyon, and Pete Calac the roster included Deer Slayer, Joe Little Twig, Laughing Gas, Baptiste Thunder, Red Fang, and Chief Xavier Downwind. The Bears beat Thorpe's Indians, as the team was also known, 33–6.

The Bears appeared to have a decent chance at catching the Canton Bulldogs, who were still undefeated as the season came down to its last three games. But then the Bears' hardhearted rivals from the South Side of town, the Cardinals, led by the young man they coveted, Paddy Driscoll, defeated them 6–0 on Thanksgiving Day and again 10 days later 9–0. The Bears ended the season with a record of 9–3–0, in second place behind the new NFL titleholders, the Canton Bulldogs.

This photo of the 1922 Chicago Bears was taken at the Bears' practice field that year, a vacant lot at the corner of Webster and Sheffield Streets on Chicago's North Side. That is part of DePaul University in the background. Front row, from the left: Carl Hanke, Fred Larson, Russ Smith, Hunk Anderson, Hugh Blacklock, Jake Lanum, Harry Englund, Joe LaFleur. Back row: George Halas, Laurie Walquist, George Bolan, Andy Lotshaw, Hec Garvey, Dutch Sternaman, Pete Stinchcomb, Joey Sternaman. –Sternaman Collection

In 1922 the Sternaman brothers accounted for 73 of the Bears' total of 123 points—Dutch, with 41, was third highest in the NFL and Joey, with 32, ranked eighth. And the team ended up in the black; George Halas and Dutch Sternaman had a profit of $1,476.92 to split when the books were closed for the season.

As the 1923 season opened, the NFL numbered 20 team franchises. But again some of them would play only a few games and then quietly drift away. One of the new teams, the Duluth Kelleys, lured Joey Sternaman away from the Bears, offering him more money to both coach and play. The Bears added Oscar Knop, an alumnus of Illinois, they obtained from the Hammond Pros. Knop would be the Bears' starting fullback for the next five years. They also signed up a first-rate end in Frank ("Duke") Hanny from Indiana, who

would also start over the next five seasons. And Johnny Bryan, a quarterback and running back from the University of Chicago, was picked up to replace Joey Sternaman, who, however, would return to the Bears late in the season.

The Bears began the 1923 season with a loss to a team that had never defeated them before. The Rock Island Independents, who would win only two games that year, astonished their hometown fans by shutting out the mighty Bears 3–0. Two weeks later, the Bears, who had not played the Packers in 1922, invaded Green Bay for the first time. With this game in 1923, which the Bears won 3–0, the two teams embarked on what was to become the longest uninterrupted rivalry—never missing a season—in NFL history. The Bears' home opener was against the Canton Bulldogs,

–Sternaman Collection

RALPH E. HAY, PRESIDENT & GEN. MGR.   LESTER HIGGINS, SECRETARY & TREAS.   GEO. GOETZL, TRAINER

Canton-Bulldogs
FOOTBALL TEAM
ORGANIZED 1905
Canton, Ohio

COACH AND CAPTAIN
GUY B. CHAMBERLIN

RALPH E. HAY

The Chicago Bears were the first professional football team to have their own fight song. This song was composed for the Bears in 1922, and for many years it was sung at the games played in Cubs Park. The lyrics:

> *From the East and from the West,*
> *They send their very best*
> *To play against the pride of old Chicago.*
> *There is none of them compare with our*
> * Chicago Bears.*
> *Through the line they go,*
> *Hold them down Chicago, Hold them down,*
> *Is the cry of everybody in our town.*
> *Just watch the way they meet and tumble their*
> * foe,*
> *Out to win Chicago Bears, they will always go.*
> *Cross that line Chicago, cross that line,*
> *That's the way to play, you're doing fine,*
> *And when the season's o'er and you have to*
> * play no more,*
> *Chicago Bears will stand out fore.*

who came to Chicago with a 3–0 record. Once again behind the great defensive play of Guy Chamberlin, which this time was complemented by the fine kicking of tackle Pete Henry (two field goals that day), the Bulldogs beat the Bears 6–0. That, however, was the Bears' last loss of the season. They went on to win six of their next seven games tied only by the Milwaukee Badgers in the second-last game of the season. But for the second year in a row, Canton went undefeated and the Bears ended up in second place.

1922 SEASON .750

Won 9 Lost 3 Tied 0

George Halas,
Dutch Sternaman—Coaches

	Bears	Opponents
Racine (Wis.) Legion	6	0
Rock Island Independents	10	6
Rochester (N.Y.) Jeffersons	7	0
Buffalo All-Americans	7	0
Canton Bulldogs	6	7
Dayton Triangles	9	0
Oorang (Marion, Ohio) Indians	33	6
Rock Island Independents	3	0
Akron Pros/Indians	20	10
Chicago Cardinals	0	6
Toledo Maroons	22	0
Chicago Cardinals	0	9
Totals	123	44

During the 1923 season, there was one truly memorable play. It occurred on a sloppy, muddy Cubs Park field on November 4 against Jim Thorpe and his Oorang Indians. The Indians, threatening on their only scoring drive of the game, had the ball on the Bears' 5-yard line. Behind the blocking of Joe Little Twig, Buffalo, Gray Horse, and Long Time Sleep, Jim Thorpe himself crashed over the left side of the line, but the slippery ball went scooting out of his hands and into the waiting arms of George Halas at the 2-yard line. Halas took off, his eyes set on the goal all the way at the other end of the field. But he heard the sloshing of Jim Thorpe pounding behind him. Halas, ever aware of the "redwood tree" that could fall on him at any moment, zigzagged his way down the field, preventing Thorpe from unleashing one of his famous flying blocks. At the 5-yard line, Thorpe made a desperate lunge but it only helped to propel Halas into the end zone. That 98-yard runback of a fumble remained an NFL record for 50 years, until Jack Tatum of the Oakland Raiders ran one back 104 yards against Green Bay in 1972. Halas later contended that he must have actually run "about 198 yards" trying to keep away from Thorpe.

Dutch Sternaman ended up as the Bears' leading scorer and third highest in the league, with 51 points, which included four touchdowns rushing and another receiving, five field goals, and six points after touchdowns. Johnny Bryan contributed 30 points, second among the Bears.

The difference between the Bears and the Canton Bulldogs in the 1922 and 1923 seasons was that Canton was the better team. But there was another difference and it was quite important. Whereas the Bears made money, a little anyway, the Bulldogs did not. Their stadium was too small, their payroll was too high—they lost money each year even though they were winning league championships. Glory can carry a pro team only so far; so in 1924 Ralph Hay decided he

1923 SEASON   .818
Won 9   Lost 2   Tied 1

George Halas,

Dutch Sternaman—Coaches	Bears	Opponents
Rock Island Independents	0	3
Racine (Wis.) Legion	3	0
Green Bay Packers	3	0
Buffalo All-Americans.	18	3
Canton Bulldogs	0	6
Oorang (Marion, Ohio) Indians	26	0
Akron Pros/Indians	20	6
Rock Island Independents	7	3
Hammond Pros	14	7
Chicago Cardinals	3	0
Milwaukee Badgers	0	0
Rock Island Independents	29	7
Totals.	123	35

Fats Henry was one of the finest kickers and linemen around in the early days of the NFL, and the Bears wanted him. In the telegram to Sam Deutsch, owner of the Cleveland Bulldogs, Dutch Sternaman suggests trading Ed Healey or Hunk Anderson for Henry, a deal that never got beyond the talking stage.
–Top, Pro Football Hall of Fame; bottom, Sternaman Collection.

Guy Chamberlin, here in his Canton uniform and posing with a fan, made his pro football debut with the Staleys (1920-21) but immortalized his name as player/coach with the Canton Bulldogs, Cleveland Bulldogs, and Frankford Yellow Jackets. The Bears let him get away in 1922 and then watched him lead Canton (1922 and 1923), Cleveland (1924), and Frankford (1926) to NFL championships. –Pro Football Hall of Fame

WESTERN UNION TELEGRAM

NEWCOMB CARLTON, PRESIDENT   GEORGE W. E. ATKINS, FIRST VICE-PRESIDENT

Send the following message, subject to the terms on back hereof, which are hereby agreed to

Oct 14 19 24

To   Samuel H. Deutsch
Street and No. (or Telephone Number)   1269 Euclid ave
Place   Cleveland, Ohio

How about trade Healey for Henry or Anderson for Henry, must know immeadiately

Edw C Sternaman

5726 Calumet
chgo   normal 4592

OFFICIAL PROGRAM

Season 1923

CHICAGO BEARS

FOOTBALL CLUB INC.

CHICAGO
vs
Thorpe's Indians
Sunday, Nov. 4, 1923
2:15 P. M.

CUBS PARK
PRICE 10¢

A program spread from the November 4, 1923, meeting between the Bears and Jim Thorpe's team. Thorpe's Indians, as they were sometimes called, listed each member's tribe as well as his college affiliation. They were also known as the Oorang Indians (for a local dog kennel that once sponsored the team). The Bears won that particular game 26–0. –Sternaman Collection

CHICAGO

No.	Name	Position	College	Wgt.
19	HANNY	L. E.	INDIANA	195
16	HEALY	L. T.	DARTMOUTH	196
18	ANDERSON	L. G.	NOTRE DAME	192
13	TRAFTON	C.	NOTRE DAME	235
6	GARVEY	R. G.	NOTRE DAME	253
12	USHER	R. T.	SYRACUSE	242
7	HALAS	R. E.	ILLINOIS	178
8	BRYAN	Q. B.	CHICAGO	165
3	STERNAMAN	L. H.	ILLINOIS	182
11	KNOP	F. B.	ILLINOIS	195
9	LANUM	R. H.	ILLINOIS	190
2	LA FLEUR	BACK	MARQUETTE	232
15	FLAHERTY	END	WASHINGTON	198
10	FETZ	BACK	INDEPENDENT	158
17	SCOTT	T.	WISCONSIN	234
5	BOLAN	F. B.	PURDUE	194

SUNDAY, NOVEMBER 11
CHICAGO VS. AKRON
CUBS PARK—2:15 P. M. SHARP
REFEREE—P. S. MOORE
UMPIRE—THOMAS, ILLINOIS.

LINESMAN—

THORPE'S INDIANS

No.	Name	Position	College	Tribe
5	LITTLE TWIG	L. E.	CARLISLE	Mohawk
18	PUFFALO	L. T.	HASKELL	Chippewa
30	GRAY HORSE	L. G.	CARLISLE	Chippewa
7	LONG TIME SLEEP	C.	CARLISLE	Flat Head
22	LONE WOLF	R. G.	CARLISLE	Chippewa
26	BIG BEAR	R. T.	CARLISLE	Chippewa
16	RUNNING DEER	R. E.	HASKELL	Chippewa
11	RED FOX	Q. B.	HASKELL	Cheerokee
1	JIM THORPE	L. H.	CARLISLE	Sac and Fox
12	TOMAHAWK	R. H.	MIAMI	Wyandotte
6	PETE CALAC	F. B.	CARLISLE	California
--	WOODCHUCK	END	MIAMI	Chippewa
28	JACK THORPE	BACK	CARLISLE	Sac and Fox
11	RED FOX	BACK	HASKELL	Cheerokee
32	EAGLE FEATHER	BACK	CARLISLE	Mohican
8	LU BOUTWELL	GUARD	CARLISLE	Chippewa

	1st	2nd	3rd	4th	CHICAGO VS.
CHICAGO					AKRON
INDIANS					SUNDAY, NOV. 11, AT 2:15 P. M.

would have to move his franchise to a larger city. The Bulldogs went to Cleveland. Most of the players and star/coach Guy Chamberlin went along. But their fine kicker, tackle, and future Hall-of-Famer Pete Henry did not. The Bears were quite interested in obtaining him and tried a number of times to entice him, but for some unexplained reason, Henry opted to drop out of the NFL completely and sign with an independent pro team in Pennsylvania, the Pottsville Maroons. The Bears did add Jim McMillen, a fine guard from the University of Illinois.

For the NFL, 1924 was a strange year all around. A franchise was awarded to the Frankford Yellow Jackets, who played out of Philadelphia, and since Pennsylvania's blue laws prohibited any sporting event to be held in the state on a Sunday, Frankford scheduled an away game on that day and a home game on the Saturday before. Several teams played more games than they were supposed to that year. And in Kansas City, Fred ("Duke") Slater, star tackle of the Rock Island Independents, was forced to sit out a game on the bench because the Kansas City Cowboys—another new franchise that year—refused to allow a black man to play in their town. (The Cowboys, incidentally, had a rookie on their roster who was destined to enter the Hall of Fame—tackle Steve Owen.) Pro football was still frowned upon by the major colleges, and the nation's large-city newspapers still paid only occasional attention to it.

Halas and Sternaman continued to handle all the coaching chores, and pep talks were still an important ritual before each game. Dutch Sternaman used to write notes to himself as to how he would inspire the team. One sheet of these words of wisdom, saved over the years since 1924, includes such standard urgings as "Everybody tackle" and "Don't take time out if we're going good." And there was also this item, which has stood the test of time: "When in doubt, punt!"

Joey Sternaman takes off around end in a game at Cubs Park in 1924, back in the days when a quarterback was better known for his running abilities than his passing talents. He scored four touchdowns rushing during the regular season that year, and led the NFL in total points, with 75. –Sternaman Collection

The Bears started the 1924 season with their first loss to the Green Bay Packers, 5–0. The following week, the Rock Island Independents, improved somewhat from the year before and now with the itinerant Jim Thorpe as one of their running backs (the Oorang Indians had folded at the end of the 1923 season), held the Bears to a scoreless tie. The unheralded Racine Legion showed up at Cubs Park for the Bears' home opener, bringing with them a fleet of former Bears that included Johnny Mohardt, Don Murry, and Milt Romney. The Bears underestimated them, and could only eke out a 10–10 tie.

One week after the Bears' first win—over the Cardinals, 6–0—the Frankford Yellow Jackets came to Chicago. Even though they were a new team, they were one of the toughest and soundest in the NFL. For the Bears, it was a very important game. They already had one loss, and the perennially powerful Bulldogs were repeating their undefeated ways in Cleveland. The Yellow Jackets had only one loss in five games, and they had their eyes set just as intently on the NFL title as did the Bears.

A crowd of about 6,000 showed up at Cubs Park. The Yellow Jackets posted the first score with a field goal. But then the Bears managed to put their act together. Consecutive touchdowns by Joey Sternaman, Dutch Sternaman, Laurie Walquist, and Johnny Bryan; a safety; and a Joey Sternaman field goal and four extra points from his toe added up to a 33–3 victory. And the Bears, for the first time that season, had something to cheer about.

The Bears did not lose another game during the regular 1924 season, ending up with a record of 6–1–4. But the NFL schedules were elastic in those early days. Many of them were adapted or changed to fit the needs or whims of any team, and there was no set number of games played. Because of the Yellow Jackets' back-to-back weekend scheduling, for example, they played a significantly larger number of games than most teams. (League teams also played nonleague teams, not counting in the standings but adding to the difficulties faced by the record keepers of that period.)

At the end of the 1924 season, three teams—the Cleveland Bulldogs, the Frankford Yellow Jackets, and the Bears—were claiming the championship. Seeing an opportunity to extend the season and bring in some much-needed revenue, they decided that they might as well play a few more games to determine the title for that year.

The Bears and the Bulldogs scheduled a game for December 7, to be played at Cubs Park and billed as the NFL championship game. The Yellow Jackets were not going to sit still for that, and they scheduled a game with the winner to be dubbed the "true" game for the NFL championship of 1924.

As it turned out, the Bears trounced the Cleveland Bulldogs 23–0, with touchdowns contributed by the Sternaman brothers and by Jim Kendrick, a newcomer that year, and a field goal and two extra points by Joey Sternaman. A week later, the Bears also defeated the Yellow Jackets, 13–10. Then they returned to Chicago and played another game against the Rock Island Independents, who were not in contention for the championship, and, surprisingly, lost 7–6.

When all the games were played—regular league games and those that were tacked on afterward—the records of the teams involved were somewhat of a mishmash, and now four teams were claiming the title for that year. Cleveland, with a 7–2–1 record, Frankford with 11–3–1, the Bears with 8–2–4, and even the Duluth Kelleys with 4–1–0, all laid claim to the NFL championship.

NFL president Joe Carr decided the squabble at the post-season meeting of owners when he ruled that none of the games played in December, that is, after the regular season, would be counted. So the title went to the Cleveland Bulldogs, whose 7–1–1 regular season record was the best winning percentage (.875)—ties were not included in the calculation for determining win percentages. The Bears were once again in second place, their 6–1–4 record showing a win percentage of .857, just a little lower than the Bulldogs'. Joey Sternaman was the league's leading scorer (regular season games only were included), with a total of 75 points. He was also the top field-goal kicker that year, with nine.

With the extra games, the melodrama the Bears were able to build for the various post-season "champi-

One of Joey Sternaman's fonder memories of the early-day Bear games was the time that fullback Oscar Knop intercepted a pass and took off for the goal line . . . only it was the wrong goal he was racing toward. It happened in 1924 against the Columbus Tigers. The ball bounced off the chest of the intended Tiger receiver and into the arms of a surprised Oscar Knop, who somehow got turned around on the play. "The entire Tiger team just stood there and watched as he started running the wrong way," Joey Sternaman recalled. "Most of them were laughing, I think. I took off after him, yelling, but I guess he couldn't hear me. Ed Healey was after him too, and he made a lunging tackle that stopped Knop just before he got to the goal. If it weren't for Healey, Knop would have had the distinction of being the first pro to score some points for the other team." It was not quickly forgotten either. "Before practice the next day, our trainer, Andy Lotshaw, came up to me as we were all getting ready and started wrapping my index finger in a big white bandage," Sternaman said. "I asked him what he was doing, there wasn't anything wrong with my finger. He said loud enough for everyone to hear that he wanted to make it conspicuous in case I had to point out the right goal line to some of the other players."

In this game at Cubs Park in 1924, one of three the Bears played after the season ended, Joey Sternaman drop-kicks an extra point for the Bears in their 23–0 rout of the Cleveland Bulldogs. But NFL President Joe Carr ruled that post-season games would not count in the official records, and the Bulldogs were declared the NFL champs that year. –Sternaman Collection

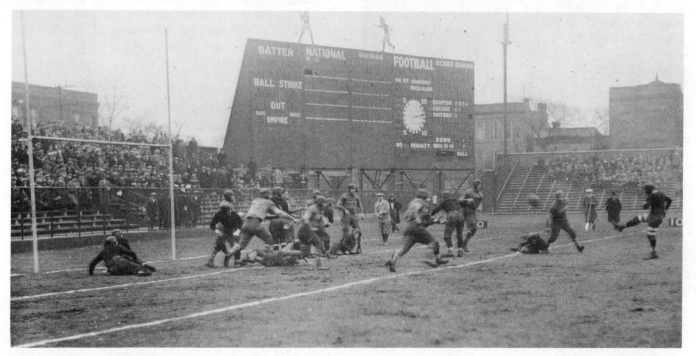

The 1924 Bears, looking as if they were queuing up for a fast Bunny Hop, pose in front of the scoreboard at Cubs Park. From the left: Ralph Scott, Oscar Knop, George Trafton, Ed Healey, Jim McMillen, Verne Mullen, Hugh Blacklock, Duke Hanny, Joe LaFleur, Jake Lanum, Roy White, George Halas, Hunk Anderson, Laurie Walquist, Dutch Sternaman, Joey Sternaman. —Sternaman Collection

Bear quarterback Joey Sternaman is shown here with the team's first mascot before a 1924 game. When the bear grew larger, it was released on waivers to a local zoo. —Joey Sternaman

onships'' that really weren't, and the flush economy of 1924, the Bears had their first truly successful season in terms of finances. When everything was added up, there was a profit of $20,000. For the first time, Halas and Sternaman could breathe a little more easily.

But neither Halas nor Sternaman was happy with playing on or owning a team that always ended up in second place. They had something very definite in mind to change that situation. And 1925, which would prove to be a milestone year in professional football, was to become that because of what Halas and Sternaman were thinking about in the summer months of that year.

1924 SEASON .857

Won 6 Lost 1 Tied 4

George Halas,
Dutch Sternaman—Coaches

	Bears	Opponents
Green Bay Packers	0	5
Rock Island Independents	0	0
Racine (Wis.) Legion	10	10
Chicago Cardinals	6	0
Frankford (Pa.) Yellow Jackets	33	3
Rock Island Independents	3	3
Columbus Tigers	12	6
Racine (Wis.) Legion	3	3
Green Bay Packers	3	0
Chicago Cardinals	21	0
Milwaukee Badgers	31	14
Totals	122	44

THE YEAR OF THE GHOST

ON AN EVENING in early August, 1925, two young men walked into the Virginia Theatre in Champaign, Illinois, a college town about 100 miles south of Chicago. Each flashed one of the free passes that the theater owner, Charles C. Pyle, had handed out to all the players on the University of Illinois football team, and then settled into their seats to watch Harold Lloyd in the silent film comedy *The Freshman.*

They were interrupted, however, when an usher came down the aisle and tapped one of the football players on the shoulder. "Mr. Pyle would like to see you upstairs in his office," he said.

"Probably wants your autograph," said the other player, who was Illinois's starting fullback, Earl Britton.

"Probably wants some free tickets for a game," his friend said as he started to get up. That young man, the one who then followed the usher up the aisle, was Britton's running partner at Illinois, left halfback Harold Grange, better known to millions of sports fans throughout the country as "Red," or the "Galloping Ghost," or the "Wheaton Iceman" (because he had worked summers hauling blocks of ice around that suburb of Chicago), or just "No. 77."

What Pyle wanted from Grange was not an autograph or free football tickets. C. C. Pyle had an idea, a plan that would irrevocably alter the course of professional football, and what he wanted was to talk it over with Red Grange. And because of their discussion, although neither of them was aware of it at that moment, the 1925 football season was destined to become one of the most important in the evolution of professional football.

The sequence of events actually began in the office of the Chicago Bears a month or two before the season started. With the frustrations and disappointments of three consecutive second-place seasons all too fresh in their minds, owners George Halas and Dutch Sternaman knew that they needed something extra— anything—to push the Bears over into a league championship. Besides wanting a winner, they were troubled by the economics of the game. Costs were rising sharply, but attendance was not. In those early days of pro football, only 5,000 or 6,000 fans could ordinarily be coaxed to invest $1 for a bleacher seat or $2 for a box seat to watch a Sunday Bear game. Maybe 10,000 or 11,000 spectators would show up if the weather was perfect and the opponent was their crosstown rivals, the Cardinals, or a team that could display Jim Thorpe, whom people still wanted to see even though by 1925 he was pretty much past his prime. College football, on the other hand, was the nation's autumn pastime; just 10 miles south of Cubs Park, 40,000 or 50,000 fans would turn out to watch a University of Chicago game at Stagg Field, and other Big Ten games might draw close to 75,000 paying spectators. It was disillusioning for Halas and Sternaman to see filled Sunday after

Sunday only about one-fourth of the 30,000 seats of the recently enlarged Cubs Park. It was also becoming economically precarious, they knew. "Something had to be done to bring in customers if we were to continue," George Halas said. "We decided what the Bears needed was a big-name star."

And *the* biggest-name star ever to play the game of football, everyone in 1925 knew, was Red Grange.

Red Grange was a senior at the University of Illinois that year and at 5-feet-11 and 175 pounds the most dazzling running back ever to carry a football on an American gridiron. A breakaway runner with speed and the ability to make the sharpest cuts and the most exciting moves, he was already a legend, at 22 years of age as revered in his sport as Babe Ruth, Jack Dempsey, Bill Tilden, and Bobby Jones were in theirs. No one drew more fans into a stadium than "No. 77." Everywhere he went, newspaper reporters hounded him for quotes. Newsreel cameramen from *Movietone* and *Pathé* wanted to capture him on film, whether he was playing football or simply walking down a street. Radio broadcasters were forever putting microphones before his face for a few words to be carried over the airwaves to the millions of people throughout the country who knew his name and his reputation.

But Red Grange was not just a name. He had earned his fame on the football field. Those who questioned his abilities did not do so for long. Fielding ("Hurry-Up") Yost, coach of Michigan in 1924 when his team was considered the best in the nation, for example, said somewhat snidely of Grange before the Michigan-Illinois game: "All Grange can do is run." He quickly learned how dreadfully right he was on one count and how wrong on another. First, Grange could indeed run—for five touchdowns, four in the first quarter, against Yost's team, compiling a phenomenal game total of 402 yards on 21 carries. Second, Grange could in fact do more than run, which he proved when he threw six completed passes, one for a touchdown, as Illinois crushed top-ranked Michigan 39–14. That was only one of his many spectacular games, however. By the end of his college career, he had been named to the All-America team three years in a row, had rushed for a total of 3,637 yards, and scored 31 touchdowns.

Red Grange was "the big name" that George Halas and Dutch Sternaman wanted for the Chicago Bears. And so they wrote several letters to him in the early summer of 1925 regarding the possibility of his becoming a pro—more precisely, a Chicago Bear—at the end of the coming college season. None of the letters were answered. Pro football was just not one of his considerations then.

"I hadn't thought really about turning professional," Grange explains. "Not at first, anyway. I hadn't talked to anybody about it. Not until that night I was sitting in the movie house in Champaign."

One of Grange's reasons for not giving it much thought was that in 1925 professional football was still generally disdained, considered crassly commercial, if not morally destitute, by most people. Professional baseball was well accepted, while football was looked on as so disreputable that many of the pros took to advertising their game as "Post Graduate Football."

Whatever the reasons for Grange's reluctance to talk with the Bear owners, the heart of the matter was that when the Bears lined up for the first kickoff of the 1925 season, they did it without the "big name" they were looking for. Nor had they found that something extra, that vital property they felt would move them beyond the level of just a runner-up.

The Bears were, in fact, fielding almost the same team they had the year before. The backfield, with the Sternaman brothers, Laurie Walquist, and Oscar Knop,

Red Grange, the greatest college football player of his day, starts out on one of his famous gallops in a game at the University of Illinois, following the blocking of his friend and tandem running back, Earl Britton. Britton was also at the Virginia Theatre in Champaign the night C. C. Pyle approached Grange with the idea of turning pro. A fullback, Britton joined the Bears for the two Red Grange tours, in late 1925 and early 1926. –Pro Football Hall of Fame

One of Red Grange's nicknames was "the Wheaton Iceman," dubbed so because during his college years he worked summers delivering large blocks of the stuff. By the time this promotional picture was taken, however, Red Grange's days as an iceman were well in the past. –Sternaman Collection

was still among the best in the league. Halas and Duke Hanny were back at ends. Ed Healey, at 30, was as outstanding a tackle as ever; George Trafton, now 28, was still the best center in the league; and Jim McMillen held down one of the guard positions again. But Bill Fleckenstein, a 192-pound newcomer to the pros from the University of Iowa, replaced Hunk Anderson at the other starting guard position. And Don Murry, whose contract the Bears had purchased from the now-defunct Racine Legion, took over the other starting tackle position from Ralph Scott. Those were the only two changes in the line-up.

It was 1925, and the league was a mere five years old; it was far from the age when you could trade future draft choices for players that you needed *now*, or even trade for anybody, for that matter. It was a time when you *kept* those players you were lucky enough to sign to a contract because there were not many players good enough to compete who were also willing to associate themselves with this "morally corrupt" and so far poor-paying, sparsely attended sport.

Still, competition had continued to grow tougher each year. The Chicago Cardinals, led by tailback

Paddy Driscoll, were a team to be reckoned with; so were the Green Bay Packers under tailback/coach Curly Lambeau. With Guy Chamberlin now leading them, the Frankford Yellow Jackets were fearsome, coming off an 11–2–1 record from the year before; and there was a very real threat from the Detroit Panthers, a new franchise put together by player/coach/owner Jimmy Conzelman. Two other new teams in the league, the New York Giants (owned by future Hall-of-Famer Tim Mara) and the Pottsville (Pa.) Maroons, were rumored to be as good as any team that had ever taken to the pro football field.

The season began more dismally for the Bears than either Halas or Sternaman had expected. In two of the first three games they managed only 0–0 ties (with the Rock Island Independents and the Detroit Panthers), which at least were better than their 14–10 loss to Green Bay in the other game. The Bears did turn it all around after that, however, and win six of their next seven games. But events even more important for the Bears than these victories were now taking place behind the scenes, all of which began that night in the Virginia Theatre in Champaign.

C. C. Pyle, whose initials sportswriters would later say stood for "Cash and Carry" or "Cold Cash," was not your ordinary theater owner. In the words of Red Grange: "He was a dapper little guy, sort of a peacock strutting in spats and carrying a cane." Pyle, however, was more than a figure of sartorial elegance; he was also an entrepreneur, a promoter, and an ambitious businessman whose aims were far loftier than simply owning a few movie theaters in places like Kokomo, Indiana, and Champaign. He had always had his eyes

One of the promotional stunts the Chicago Bears used to herald the opening of their 1925 season. The flower-bedecked car, with a full-size stuffed bear straddling the hood, motored about the city to spread its message. –Sternaman Collection

POST GRADUATE
FOOTBALL

Detroit Panthers vs. Chicago Bears

**Sunday
November
15th**
AT
**CUBS
Park**
2:15 P. M.

ED HEALY, Dartmouth,
Left Tackle for Chicago Bears

P. J. Carr Day

JAMES CONZELMAN,
Manager, Detroit Panthers

A handbill that also served as a poster in 1925. Because of the deep-seated sentiment against young men playing football for money in those days, the professionals came up with a fine euphemism to describe their game: "Post Graduate Football." This game, against Jimmy Conzelman's Detroit Panthers, was won by the Bears, 14–0. –Sternaman Collection

open for that one opportunity to break out of the small-town syndrome and into the big time. When Grange walked into his office and sat down across the desk from him, Pyle knew that his opportunity had finally arrived.

"Red, how would you like to make a hundred thousand dollars . . . maybe even a million?"

Grange looked at him suspiciously. That was the kind of money a gambler might talk about. "How?" he asked.

"Playing football, my boy, just playing football," Pyle answered, and went on to explain his plan. Grange would finish up his college season, then join a pro team to finish up their longer-lasting season, and *then* they would take that team on a whirlwind tour of the country. Hundreds of thousands of people would turn out to see the famous Red Grange play in cities where they had never had the chance before. The team would travel to places like New York and Boston, of course, but also down to Florida and out to California. He would arrange everything, Pyle said. He would be Grange's manager.

Grange was overwhelmed with the possibilities, and said that he was interested. He also mentioned that the Bears' organization up in Chicago had expressed interest in him. Pyle nodded; he had already suspected that the Bears would be interested in the talents of "No. 77." He, in fact, had thought Chicago would be the ideal place for Grange. The team was good, it needed a Grange to make it great, and he was impressed with the way the team was handled. He would contact the Bears.

Pyle was correct. Halas and Sternaman were definitely still interested in the prospect of Red Grange joining their organization. So Pyle took a train to Chicago and paid a call on Halas and Sternaman. Grange went back to the classrooms and the football field of Illinois, with a warning from Pyle not to discuss with anyone the possibility of his turning pro at the end of the college season.

There was a tenet in the NFL's Code of Ethics, written by President Joe Carr himself, that read:

"Tampering with players on College teams
shall not be tolerated by this League."

But what constituted tampering, other than the outright recruiting of a player before he had finished his college playing eligibility, had never been clearly defined. Pyle did not want to take any chances. It was touchy enough to join the pros in 1925, especially for a famous player like Grange, and Pyle wisely wanted nothing to interfere with or tarnish the move once it took place.

In Chicago, three of the shrewdest, most resolute bargainers to be found anywhere in 1925 sat down and agreed in principle as to the football future of Red Grange. Sternaman and Halas had been surprised at the suggestion of a full-scale national tour, but they liked the idea. Details of the financial arrangements, however, would not be settled until *after* Grange's last game of the college season, nor would any money exchange hands in any form until that time. In that way, there could be no charge of "tampering," they felt. But negotiations would begin immediately after the final gun of Grange's last game, which was scheduled for November 21, when Illinois would play Ohio State at Columbus. Pyle, Halas, and Sternaman agreed to meet in the Morrison Hotel in Chicago that very Saturday and, when the game ended, to work there until every last financial detail was settled.

Despite the secrecy of the behind-the-scenes maneuvering of Pyle and the Bears' owners, rumors began to pop up all over regarding the possibility of Red Grange becoming a pro when his college football days were over. Some people were saying that he had already secretly signed a contract with the Bears, others that the signed contract was in the hands of Tim Mara of the New York Giants. There was also the story that a promoter was putting together a team that included Grange and the Four Horsemen of Notre Dame, who had ended their college careers the season before, to tour the country playing against pro teams. As the season moved along, the rumors grew in number. And so did the criticism. Newswriters, coaches, college officials all spoke out on the subject of Grange possibly playing football for money. "He is a living legend now," one Chicago news reporter wrote. "Why go and sully it."

Even his football coach at Illinois, Bob Zuppke, the same man who had coached Halas and Sternaman and more than a half-dozen other players who in 1925 were on the Chicago Bears' roster, counseled Grange against making any such move. "Football isn't meant to be played for money. Stay away from professionalism," Zuppke urged him.

But Grange could not subscribe to that kind of reasoning. "You get paid for coaching, Zup," he replied. "Why should it be wrong for me to get paid for playing?"

It was a question that Zuppke could not really answer. Still, it did not sway him from his opposition to Grange's becoming a pro. He told Red that if professional football thrived it would turn college football into a mere training ground for the pros. That would destroy college football in the end, he said. "Zuppke was correct," Dutch Sternaman later observed. "College football did become a training ground, but that never adversely affected the game played by collegians. If anything, it strengthened it."

Zuppke also told Red he ought to go back to Wheaton and talk with his father before making any decision about his future. Coach Zuppke felt sure that Lyle Grange would advise his son against joining up to play football for "tainted" money. Red did go to see his father, and Coach Zuppke was right; Lyle Grange voiced the opinion that his son would be better off pursuing some other career. "But when you turned 21, I told you that you would have to make your own decisions," he reminded Red. "And this is one of them. But whatever decision you make, I'll stand behind you." The decision had, in fact, already been made. Now it was simply reaffirmed in Red's mind.

By the time the last game of the college season approached, the rumors had it that Grange was already signed up by a pro team, and they were so widespread that serious questions were raised as to whether or not he could play in the game. If he had signed, he was no longer an amateur athlete and would be ineligible to play for Illinois. Both Coach Zuppke and Illinois's

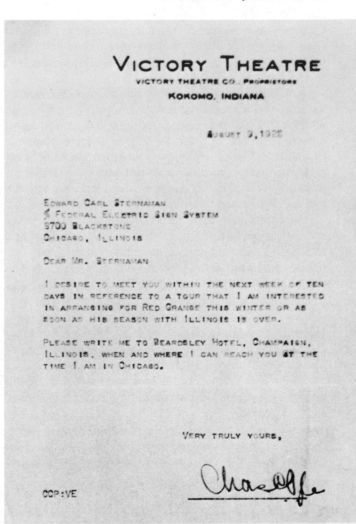

This is the letter from C. C. Pyle to Dutch Sternaman that launched the Red Grange/Chicago Bear affair, which would irrevocably change the course of professional football. –Sternaman Collection

athletic director George Huff were forced to confront Grange to see if there was any truth to the rumors. There was not, Grange told them emphatically. Then, hoping to end all the speculation, he went on record with a statement to the working press: "After the game I'm going to listen to offers. Maybe I'll accept one of them . . . But you can be sure I haven't signed a scrap of paper with anyone, and I haven't told anybody what I'm going to do."

In Columbus, Ohio, on November 21, Red Grange trotted out onto the field to play his last college game, against Ohio State. More than 70,000 people were on hand—"half of them, it seemed, were newspaper writers and photographers," one observer commented. "No. 77" led Illinois to a 14–9 win. When the final gun was sounded, his college career over at last,

Grange was besieged on the field by reporters. He told them simply: ''I intend to sign an agreement to play with the Chicago Bears,'' and then he disappeared into the locker room.

And with that, George Halas and Dutch Sternaman sat down in a room in the Morrison Hotel in Chicago with C. C. Pyle and Frank Zambreno, a theatrical agent whom Pyle had enlisted to help in the negotiations. ''Cash and Carry'' Pyle knew what he wanted for his prize property, and he was not going to settle for anything less. The discussions went on through the night. ''We made a tactical error,'' Halas said later. ''Sternaman and I sat together to lend each other moral support through all this haggling. Pyle and Zambreno were smarter. They'd take turns. While one talked the other would sneak off and snatch a few winks of sleep.'' As it turned out, however, no one was really the smarter because the agreement the four men worked out in that Chicago hotel room on that cold November night would prove to benefit not only Grange, Pyle, and the Chicago Bears, but all of professional football as well.

While Pyle, Halas, and Sternaman were arguing the dollars and cents of the situation, Red Grange was trying to elude the literally hundreds of news media people who wanted to talk with him. He managed to get back to his hotel in Columbus, but the lobby was so awash with reporters, well-wishers, and curiosity-seekers that he was forced to make his exit down an old fire escape into an alley. He did not plan to travel back to Champaign with the team; instead, with hat pulled down over his eyes and coat collar turned up, looking more like a henchman of Al Capone than a young college football player, he boarded a train for Chicago. When word somehow leaked out that Halas, Sternaman, and Pyle were meeting in the Morrison Hotel to hash out Grange's contract, the lobby there was quickly carpeted with newsmen. They had also heard the rumor that Grange himself would be arriving at the Morrison to sign the final document, but that was not true. From the train station in Chicago he took a taxi to the Belmont Hotel, about four miles from the Morrison, registered under a bogus name, and waited there to hear from Pyle.

Finally, in the early morning hours of Sunday, November 22, an agreement was reached. It called for the ''Red Grange/C. C. Pyle Company'' to receive a guarantee of $2,000 per game against a percentage of

The signing of Red Grange brought together for the media Bear co-owners George Halas and Dutch Sternaman, the star, and his agent C. C. Pyle. From this moment on, photographs of Grange taken over the next two years, off the field anyway, invariably included the face of his mentor Pyle. –Pro Football Hall of Fame

DWARD ST AMAN   GEORGE HALAS   HAROLD 'RED' GRANGE   C. C. PYLE

"RED" SIGNS HIS FIRST PRO CONTRACT, NOVEMBER 1925.

When C. C. Pyle negotiated the highly lucrative financial deal with the Chicago Bears for Red Grange, the young halfback immediately went out and bought the most chic item of the day, a raccoon coat, for which he paid the hefty sum of $500.
–Sternaman Collection

the gate both for the remaining league games and for the exhibition games in the "Red Grange/Chicago Bears" tour of the nation. Grange and Pyle would split their earnings 60/40, with the larger share going to Grange and with Pyle paying any business expenses that they would incur. The actual contract would not be signed until Monday because the two tired Bear owners still had a football game to play and coach that afternoon.

The game was against the Green Bay Packers. About 7,000 fans turned out at Cubs Park to watch it. Fueled perhaps by the adrenalin that came with signing up Grange, the Bears went out and mauled the Packers, who had beaten them earlier in the season, 21–0. And on the bench but in ordinary street clothes—including a raccoon coat—was the newest Chicago Bear, Red Grange. It was announced that on the coming Thursday, Thanksgiving Day, Grange would don a Chicago Bear uniform and play his first professional football game. It was *the* sporting news of the year. But the tone of the news was not necessarily positive. This wire service story, not exactly in the tradition of objective journalism, was one of the milder ones.

Chicago, Nov. 22 (AP)—Harold (Red) Grange today plunged into the business of capitalizing on his gridiron fame by signing to play professional football, against the wishes of his father as well as George Huff, director of athletics of the University of Illinois, Coach Robert Zuppke and others who had hoped he would accept other offers held out to him.

The big question now being asked was: would Red Grange be able to bring out for the pros the tens of thousands of fans that he had when he was playing for Illinois?

That question was answered very shortly. Tickets for the Thanksgiving Day game against the Chicago Cardinals went on sale Monday at the Spalding Sporting Goods Store on State Street in downtown Chicago. People were lined up for blocks, and within three hours all 20,000 tickets that had been printed were sold. It was promised, however, that a new printing would make more tickets available the following day and that they would also be sold at the ball park on the day of the game; that is, if there were any left. By game time on Thanksgiving Day, a standing-room-only crowd of 36,000 people filled Cubs Park to watch Red Grange play. And all the tickets that had been printed for the game a few days later against a little-known team, the Columbus Tigers, were already sold out. In the words of George Halas: "There had never been such evidence of public interest since our professional league began in 1920. I knew then and there that pro football was destined to be a big-time sport." And, of course, from that moment on, it was.

After the Thanksgiving Day meeting with the Cardinals and the next Sunday's with the Tigers at Cubs Park, the Bears would go on the road. The entire project loomed so large, so complicated, so financially awesome that C. C. Pyle hired an assistant manager to help him handle Red Grange and the tour. Pyle then revealed the logistics of the tour he had arranged. It would actually be two tours, one of eight games and the other of nine. But it quickly became apparent that he had never been a football player himself. The first tour had the Bears playing *eight* games in *eight* different cities in a *12-day* period, a schedule unheard of before in any form of organized football. It would include the last games of the regular season. After the first tour, the team would have a week and a half to rest before the first game of the second tour, which would be played on Christmas Day. The other eight games in the second tour would be played over a more sensible period of one month, but during that time the team would travel by train from Chicago to the tip of Florida, as far west as the California coast, and as far north as Seattle. Nothing, it could be said, stood in the way of "Cash and Carry" Pyle's scheduling.

Before he suited up for his first pro game, Grange was given a crash three-day course on the Bears' plays by Halas and Sternaman. And someone hastily sewed a "77" on a Bear jersey (up to then no other player on the Bears' team had a number higher than 29). But on Thursday, the 36,000 people who postponed their

Red Grange sets out on one of his first jaunts with the ball as a pro during the Thanksgiving Day game between the Bears and Cardinals at Cubs Park (top). Leading interference for him is guard Bill Fleckenstein. Blocking the Cardinal in the foreground is guard Jim McMillen, and the Bear on the ground at the right is end George Halas. On another of his 16 carries of the day (bottom), Grange tries to go around left end, but with the Cardinals keying on him, he finds the going a little difficult. –Sternaman Collection

turkey dinners to sit in the damp November cold and watch Red Grange perform in the mud of Cubs Park found little to get excited about. Grange carried the ball from scrimmage 16 times, gaining a total of only 36 yards, and threw six passes, completing none. Nor did he have a chance to exercise one of his most devastating specialties—returning punts. Paddy Driscoll, the Cardinals' premier back and punter, figured wisely that it would be in his team's interest not to kick the ball anywhere near Grange. As Driscoll later explained: "It was a question of which of us would look bad— Grange or Driscoll. I decided it wouldn't be Paddy." And Driscoll was a fine enough punter to accomplish just that. But no one played any better than "No. 77" that day, and the game ended in a 0–0 tie. Yet young Red Grange was suddenly a lot wealthier than he had been the week before, when he was rooming in the Zeta Psi fraternity house in Champaign. That afternoon

On the bench for a short rest during the Bear-Cardinal game of 1925, three serious faces. From the left are George Halas, Bill Fleckenstein, and Red Grange . . . and, of course, C. C. Pyle.
–Sternaman Collection

Red Grange is mobbed as he is escorted off the field by a coterie of policemen at Cubs Park following his debut as a professional football player and a Chicago Bear. A more-than-capacity crowd of 36,000, the biggest in the Bears' six-year history, turned out that Thanksgiving Day, 1925, to watch the "Galloping Ghost" and the other Bears play their arch rivals, the Chicago Cardinals, to a scoreless tie. –Sternaman Collection

The Chicago Cardinals' quadruple-threat star—passer, running back, punter, and field-goal kicker Paddy Driscoll. –Pro Football Hall of Fame

After this game, Earl Britton, Grange's running mate from Illinois and seat mate in the Virginia Theatre that fateful night earlier in the year, and a few other players were added to the team for the grueling tour that lay ahead. As it turned out, the Bears would need every able, healthy body they could get in order to field a team, as game after game in such quick succession took a brutal toll on the players.

Tuesday the team left for St. Louis for a Wednesday afternoon game against a team of professional and semi-pro players that had been hastily put together by Francis Donnelly, a St. Louis mortician and sometime promoter. The temperature at game time reached a high for the day of 12 degrees above zero, and only 8,000 spectators were willing to endure the bitter cold on that weekday afternoon to watch a football game. But those who did show up saw Red Grange deliver his finest performance as a pro. He scored four touchdowns, and that, along with touchdowns by Joey

Red Grange and family in front of the lock-up in Wheaton, Illinois, where Grange's father, Lyle (left), served as chief of police. In the center is Red's younger brother Garland, better known as "Gardie," who later signed with the Bears and played end for them from 1929 through 1931. –Sternaman Collection

he earned the handsome sum of $12,000, not bad for a few hours' work in that era of minimal income taxes, when you could buy an Auburn Roadster for less than $1,500 or bed down in a first-class hotel, with three meals thrown in, for $6.50.

Three days later, neither Grange's less-than-spectacular debut nor a heavy snowstorm would keep 28,000 fans from gathering again at Cubs Park to watch the Bears play. It was a truly miserable day and if the Bears had not been showcasing "No. 77" they probably would not have drawn more than one or two thousand die-hard fans to watch them play the Columbus Tigers. But pro football, at least in Chicago, had changed—there was no doubt about it. As one Chicago newspaper headlined in its sports section, "A New Era in Pro Football Has Begun."

The snow and cold did not seem to bother Red Grange, however. That afternoon he gained twice as many yards rushing (72) as he had the game before, caught two passes, and returned a kickoff for 28 yards. With a touchdown by Joey Sternaman, another by Laurie Walquist, and two successful extra points kicked by Joey, the Bears were able to squeeze out a 14–13 victory over the Tigers.

Three days after his debut at Cubs Park, Red Grange was right back on the same field, this time carrying the ball against the Columbus Tigers (top). On that snowy day, he gained 72 yards rushing. In this same game, quarterback Joey Sternaman, streaking around left end (bottom), unveils what was to become one of the most effective plays in the Bear offensive strategy of 1925. With Grange a marked man on every play, Sternaman would fake a handoff to Grange going around one end, hide the ball behind his hip, and bootleg it around the other end. Against Columbus that day, Sternaman ran for one touchdown and drop-kicked two extra points to lead the Bears to a 14–13 win. –Sternaman Collection

CUBS PARK HOME OF THE BEARS

Chicago Bears Football Club

=== (INC) ===

CHICAGO, ILL.

The Bear letterhead of 1925—a bit gothic in style and remindful of the logo of the Chicago Tribune. –Sternaman Collection

Sternaman and Verne Mullen, a second-string end who played behind George Halas, was enough for an impressive 39–6 victory. The only touchdown for the St. Louis team was contributed by Jimmy Conzelman, who had taken a temporary leave of absence from his Detroit Panther team to play in the game. After St. Louis, the Bears luxuriated in a two-day rest, the longest they would have on the first tour; but one day of it was spent traveling by train to Philadelphia.

The tour, with the aid of Pyle's huckstering, was gathering much more publicity than pro football ordinarily would in those days. At one time or another during the tour the nation's most widely read sportswriters—Damon Runyon, Grantland Rice, Westbrook Pegler, even Ford Frick, the future commissioner

of major league baseball—would travel with the Bears.

Philadelphia welcomed the Bears with a driving rainstorm for their Saturday afternoon game against the Frankford Yellow Jackets. Under Guy Chamberlin, the Yellow Jackets had a first-rate roster, including Link Lyman, who had come over from Cleveland with Chamberlin, and a cast of lesser-knowns like the Mutt and Jeff combination of Jug Earpe (6-feet-2, 240 pounds) and Two Bits Homan (5-feet-5, 144 pounds). Lyman, however, would join the Bears in two weeks for their second tour and stay around to play seven seasons with them.

Grange again ran the Bears to a victory (14–7) by scoring both touchdowns; the conversions were contributed by Joey Sternaman. As Westbrook Pegler,

The Chicago Bears, dressed to kill, pose here before boarding the train on the first leg of the 1925-26 Red Grange/Chicago Bear tours. This train would take them to St. Louis for the first road game of the tours. Jimmy Conzelman was featured in the St. Louis backfield, but he made little difference in the Bears' lopsided, 39–6, win that day. Other trains would carry the Bears about 12,000 miles during their two months of touring. –Sternaman Collection

then traveling with the team, put it in his sports column: "Red Grange, the only football player who ever enjoyed the luxury of a manager and a substitute manager, scored two personal touchdowns and a personal victory over the Frankford Yellow Jackets . . . some 35,000 soggy customers melted away in the early dusk, drenched and satisfied."

The Bears were equally drenched by the downpour in Philadelphia, but after the game they weren't able to melt away into the early dusk. They had to rush to the train station, still in their wet, muddy uniforms, and catch the last train to New York because the schedule called for them to face the Giants at the Polo Grounds the next afternoon. As the players were changing out of their uniforms aboard the train, everyone was painfully aware that the soggy jerseys and mud-splotched pants couldn't be cleaned in time for the game and probably wouldn't even be dry by then. C. C. Pyle, who it seemed was never more than a few feet away from the team or the young man he managed, leaned over to George Halas and said: "This tour will make you so wealthy, Halas, that next year you'll be able to afford two sets of uniforms."

It was a tired and bruised Chicago Bear team that finally checked into the Astor Hotel in Times Square that Saturday night. But they were also buoyed up by the prospect of what awaited them the next day. Damon Runyon, one of the newswriters who would cover the game, conveyed the excitement of that afternoon when he described it later:

"I here preach from the old familiar text, 'It pays to advertise.'

"There gathered at the Polo Grounds in Harlem this afternoon the largest crowd that ever witnessed a football game on the island of Manhattan, drawn by the publicity that has been given one individual—Red Harold Grange, late of the University of Illinois.

"Seventy thousand men, women and children were in the stands, blocking the aisles and runways. Twenty thousand more were perched on Coogan's Bluff and the roofs of apartment houses overlooking the baseball home of McGraw's club, content with just an occasional glimpse of the whirling mass of players on the field far below and wondering which was Red Grange."

Actually, when all the fence climbers and gate-crashers were added to those who purchased tickets to the game, the crowd was estimated at more than 73,000 (the official seating capacity of the Polo Grounds in 1925 was 65,000). Never in the short history of professional football had a crowd so large been enticed into a sports stadium.

The Chicago Bears who traveled on the 1925-26 Red Grange tours. Bottom row, from the left: Hugh Blacklock, Russ Smith, Jim McMillen, Dutch Sternaman, George Trafton, Red Grange, George Halas, Johnny Mohardt, Joey Sternaman, Roy White. Middle row: Don Murry, Hunk Anderson, Ed Healey, Laurie Walquist, Johnny Bryan, Milt Romney, Ralph Scott, Oscar Knop, Earl Britton. Top row: Andy Lotshaw (trainer), Mush Crawford, Bill Fleckenstein, Duke Hanny, Verne Mullen. –Sternaman Collection

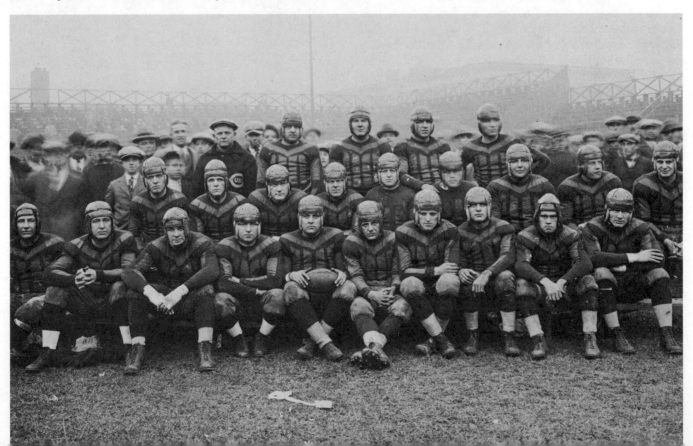

Most famous for his dazzling open-field running, Red Grange was also a fine passer and surprised many a defense when he pulled up on a would-be end run and let go with a pass, like he was about to do here during a game on the first Red Grange/Chicago Bear tour of 1925. Running interference in front of him is quarterback Joey Sternaman. The other Bear in the picture is guard Hunk Anderson. –Pro Football Hall of Fame

What they saw was a powerful Bears team that easily defeated the Giants, 19–7. They also saw Red Grange play for 35 of the game's 60 minutes, during which time he rushed 11 times for a total of 53 yards, ran back two punts for 13 yards, completed two short forward passes, picked off a pass thrown by Bill Rooney, and ran the interception back 35 yards for a touchdown. Actually Joey Sternaman, who played the full 60 minutes of that game just as he had in the game the day before, outrushed Grange, scored the other two touchdowns, and drop-kicked an extra point for the Bears. But the publicity was reserved for the "Ghost," whether he galloped or not. As sportswriter B. G. FitzGibbon put it in the language of the 1920s: "Red Grange did his stuff . . . he convinced the 70,000-and-odd persons assembled in the Polo Grounds that he was, slangily speaking, 'the berries'."

Monday was a day off for the Bears, which afforded them the luxury of having their uniforms cleaned and dried and time to nurse the wounds, bruises, and sore muscles they had picked up by playing three football games in the past five days.

Some of the players were content to spend the day resting up; others took in the sights around the island of Manhattan. Still others sought out their own particular pleasures in the sprawling city of speakeasies and sophistication that only the month before had come under the indulgent rule of Mayor Jimmy Walker, sometimes known as "Beau James."

Red Grange, however, spent the day with his manager going over the other ways that his name and his presence could be merchandised—movies, product endorsements, personal appearances, nothing would be overlooked by Pyle. Entrepreneur Pyle felt sure that he and Grange could earn at least as much money from these ventures as they would from Grange's football playing. As it turned out, he was right. The Red Grange/C. C. Pyle Company, it is estimated, grossed about $125,000 from these outside enterprises, about equal to the amount it reaped from gate receipt guarantees and percentages from the two tours.

A visitor also dropped by C. C. Pyle's suite in the Astor Hotel that day. The Sultan of Swat, Babe Ruth of the New York Yankees, decided to stop in and introduce himself to the young man with whom he was now sharing the sports page headlines. Red Grange remem-

Sternaman Collection

bers that the Babe was full of advice, which over the years has been variously reported to include such bits of wisdom as:

"Kid, don't believe anything they write about you."

"Get the dough while the getting is good, but don't break your heart trying to get it."

"Don't pick up too many checks."

Washington, D.C., was the next stop. And it was the beginning of a portion of the trip that made the previous phase of three games in five days seem like a lark. This segment called for three games in three days: Tuesday in Washington, Wednesday in Boston, and Thursday in Pittsburgh.

The exhaustion and the pain of the tour were beginning to show on all the Bear players. But the road show itself was not without its lighter moments. The Washington stopover, in fact, has always prompted one of Red Grange's favorite stories. Whisked to the White House and introduced to President Calvin Coolidge as "Red Grange, who plays with the Bears," he was quickly humbled, when the austere Coolidge nodded and then said, "Young man, I always liked animal acts."

Later that day, the Bears handily defeated a group of eastern pro and semi-pro players who went under the name of the Washington All-Stars, 19–0. But the glorious string of victories ended that afternoon in the Washington stadium. The following day in Boston, the Providence Steam Roller, who had signed up two of the legendary Four Horsemen of Notre Dame—Jim Crowley and Don Miller—beat the Bears 9–6 in an official league game. A tired Red Grange did not play much that day, and he was credited with gaining only 18½ yards in the game. The 25,000 spectators who jammed Boston Braves Field were not happy with the afternoon's entertainment, and at the end of the game, the Bears had to virtually fight their way through a jeering, rioting crowd to get to their locker room.

The loss to the Providence Steam Roller was the first the Bears had suffered since Grange had joined the team. But it was not the last. The fatigued and injury-ridden Bears were slaughtered the next day by a Pittsburgh team of unknowns that had been specially assembled for the game. The score was 24–0. Grange saw action for only one play. On his first run from scrimmage, he tore a muscle in his left arm and had to leave the game.

The injury was severe enough to keep him from playing in the game against Jimmy Conzelman's Detroit Panthers two days later. When it was announced in that city that Grange would be conspicuously absent from the field of play, 10,000 people demanded (and

In Hartford, Connecticut, Ed Curley was trying to put together a team to play the Bears, which would feature several of Notre Dame's former Four Horsemen. He was not successful, and the game was never written into the tour schedule. Two of the Four Horsemen—Don Miller and Jim Crowley—signed on with the Providence Steam Roller to play against Grange and the Bears in the Boston tour stop and contributed enough to hand them their first defeat of the tour, 9–6. It was the fourth game the Bears had played in four different East Coast cities within five days. –Sternaman Collection

received) refunds on the tickets they had purchased. A meager crowd of just over 4,000 paid to watch the Panthers destroy a battered Bear team 21–0.

How badly were they battered at this stage of their tour? Howard Roberts, a Chicago newsman, chronicled the problems. Besides the injury to Grange, "Laurie Walquist had a broken toe, Milt Romney a twisted ankle, Dutch Sternaman an injured shoulder, Joe Sternaman a lame knee, Ed Healey and George Trafton leg injuries and Halas himself, not to be outdone, developed a boil on his neck." It was so bad

One day, as the first Bear-Grange tour was coming to an end, "Cash and Carry" Pyle cornered Westbrook Pegler, who was never known to treat anyone gently in his writings. "I don't understand it, Pegler," he said. "Through this whole tour, you drink all my booze and then write all these bad things about me in your column."

"Look, Pyle," Pegler said. "You don't have to worry about anything I write about you until I stop referring to your name in the singular."

that trainer Andy Lotshaw, who had enough on his hands just tending to the injured and tired players, was enlisted to play tackle so that the Bears could field an 11-man team, even though he hadn't played in a game for years.

The final game of the tour was back at Cubs Park. Tim Mara, who had been on the verge of going out of business until the Bears and Red Grange lured more than 73,000 people into the Polo Grounds a week earlier, now had plenty of money to transport his New York Giants to Chicago for the last league game of the season. The Bears who took the field that day were a decimated team. But Grange was back in uniform, despite his very sore arm, because no one wanted to see a repeat of what had happened in Detroit the day before, when thousands of people rushed to return their tickets. Even so, only about 18,000 fans showed up for the game, far fewer than the record crowds that had jammed Cubs Park for Grange's first two appearances. And for those who did show up that cold Sunday in December, it was a disheartening experience. The Bears lost 9–0, and Grange was able to do little more than protect his arm from further damage.

It had now been 18 days since Red Grange put on his first pro football uniform, and in that 2½-week period, he had played in nine games and earned approximately $50,000.

The game with the Giants officially ended the 1925 season for the Bears. Their record of 9–5–3 included three losses to league teams in the last week of their

The name Red Grange in 1925 was not associated merely with the game of football. "Cash and Carry" Pyle saw to it that it was attached to a variety of products. Among the items that carried Grange's name or endorsement that year were:

a candy bar	*ginger ale*
a brand of cigarettes	*sweaters*
yeast foam malted milk	*a cap*
a doll	*shoes*
a fountain pen	*socks*

Grange's fame and the effect of his endorsement in the commercial world would pave the way for later stars to peddle a wide assortment of products, ranging from Fords (by Dick Butkus) and rental cars (O. J. Simpson) to pantyhose (Joe Namath).

tour and left them in seventh place in the final NFL standings, the lowest they had ever been in their six seasons of pro ball. The Chicago Cardinals, with an 11–2–1 record, were awarded the championship that year, following another of those contested claims to the title that had to be settled by NFL president Joe Carr.

Red Grange had brought glamour to the latter part of the season and, of course, he had brought the spectators out to the ball parks where he played. But if a football hero on the team were to be singled out, it would have to be Joey Sternaman, who accounted for 62 points, the third highest total in the NFL (after Charlie Berry of the Pottsville Maroons and Paddy Driscoll of the Cardinals). Sternaman rushed for five touchdowns, caught one touchdown pass, threw passes for three more, and kicked three field goals and 17 extra points.

The NFL season had ended, but the Bears' season was far from over. Their second tour was about to commence. For this one, Pyle arranged for the players to have their own Pullman car and a personal porter so they could travel in appropriate style. He also saw to it that each player was outfitted with a sweater with "Bears" emblazoned on the front, matching knickers, and bright-colored knee socks. With that flourish, the team chugged out of the sleet and ice of Chicago to the midwinter warmth of sunny Florida.

The nine teams the Bears would encounter in the next month would comprise players picked up in each city especially for that particular exhibition game. Some of the players were exceptionally good but most of them were locals of dubious quality, and the teams lacked the advantage of having played together except for a few practice sessions.

1925 SEASON   .643
Won 9   Lost 5   Tied 3

George Halas, Dutch Sternaman—Coaches

	Bears	Opponents
Rock Island Independents	0	0
Green Bay Packers	10	14
Detroit Panthers	0	0
Hammond Pros	28	7
Cleveland Bulldogs	7	0
Chicago Cardinals	0	9
Rock Island Independents	6	0
Frankford (Pa.) Yellow Jackets	19	0
Detroit Panthers	14	0
Green Bay Packers	21	0
Chicago Cardinals	0	0
Columbus Tigers	14	13
Frankford (Pa.) Yellow Jackets	14	7
New York Giants	19	7
Providence (Mass.) Steam Roller	6	9
Detroit Panthers	0	21
New York Giants	0	9
Totals	158	96

The first stop was Coral Gables, just outside Miami, where a temporary stadium had been erected for the game. The Bears defeated the Coral Gables Collegians 7–3, with Grange scoring the game's only touchdown. From there, the Bears began working their way back up the Florida peninsula. In Tampa, on New Year's Day, they faced a team calling themselves the Cardinals, who had recruited a 37-year-old and sadly-out-of-shape Jim Thorpe. To no avail—the Bears trounced Tampa 17–3.

Jacksonville, the next stop, was to be something really special. John S. O'Brien, who would have liked to be the successful promoter that C. C. Pyle had become, was putting together the Jacksonville Stars along with a few other Florida backers. He had succeeded in getting himself named the manager of Stanford's great fullback Ernie Nevers, who, after Grange, was the most famous college football player of the day. O'Brien had grandiose plans, but he was no match for Pyle.

In a February, 1926, issue of *Liberty* magazine, Walter Davenport reported on this exchange between the two promoters:

"It should be the battle of the century, Mr. Pyle," said Mr. O'Brien. "I aim to cover the South with announcements that no red-blooded man should miss the titanic struggle between the Galloping Ghost and the Lion of the Sierras—Red and Ernie. It will be a sell-out with lamentable numbers turned away at the gate."

"I'm glad to hear it," said Mr. Pyle, "because you will now read with less pain our contract, which, I regret to say, has embarrassed other managers . . . ."

Ernie Nevers did show up for the game. So did Red Grange, C. C. Pyle, and the other Bears (with an already-banked $20,000 guarantee for the game and a 65% share of all earnings from it). But the spectators didn't. Inflated ticket prices ranged from $8.50 down to $5.50 (more than four times what was charged in Cubs Park), and a depressed Florida economy obviously contributed to a dismal attendance figure of 6,700 fans. The Jacksonville promoters absorbed a loss of about $12,500. And the collision on the football field of the two college goliaths was less than spectacular. Grange gained 29 yards in five carries and threw one touchdown pass. Nevers rushed for a total of 46 yards and scored one touchdown. The Bears won easily, 19–6.

In the opulence of their private railroad car, the Bears then made their way along the Gulf Coast to New Orleans, where they defeated a team called the All-Stars 14–0. As part of the pre-game fanfare and hype, all the Bears were taken out to Fair Grounds Racetrack to watch the newly named feature race, the

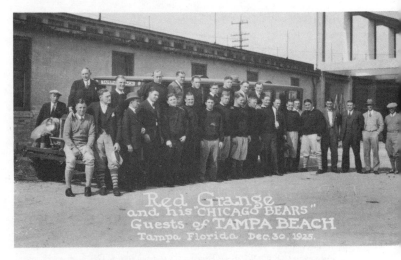

This picture of the Bears was taken two days before they faced a team representing the city of Tampa, Florida, which had enticed an aging Jim Thorpe to play for them. The Bears won easily, 17–3. The title below the picture illustrates the potency of Red Grange's name in 1925. –Sternaman Collection

In California, Red Grange and the Bears met many silent movie stars of the day. Here he poses with comedian Harold Lloyd, whose picture, The Freshman, *he had been watching a few months earlier in Champaign, Illinois, which was interrupted for him by C. C. Pyle's proposition to turn pro. Behind and to the left of Grange is Dutch Sternaman and to the left of him is Joey Sternaman. Directly behind Lloyd is the ever-present Pyle. The others are a random gathering of Bear players and movie actors.* –Sternaman Collection

Red Grange Handicap. A horse called Prickly Heat won the race, and Grange himself went to the winner's circle to present the jockey with an enormous pink floral football.

The second tour was turning into more of a barnstorming sideshow with Pyle leading the theatrics and pyrotechnics like a true P. T. Barnum. But no one seemed to mind.

In Los Angeles, the next stop, Pyle had Grange and the other Bears posing with everyone from Mary Pickford to Charlie Chaplin. He even gathered several members of the team on the roof of the Biltmore Hotel, where they were staying, to throw footballs down into a crowd of 5,000 that had gathered for a Pyle-sponsored gimmick. Any person to catch one—no easy feat considering the speed and angle of a football rocketing down 13 stories—would be awarded $25 and get to keep the football. This publicity stunt cost Pyle a total of $100.

Ticket prices for the tour games varied from city to city—most were higher than regular-season tickets. So was the cost of a program, like this one inflated from the standard 10¢ to 25¢ for the game between the Bears and the Los Angeles Tigers.

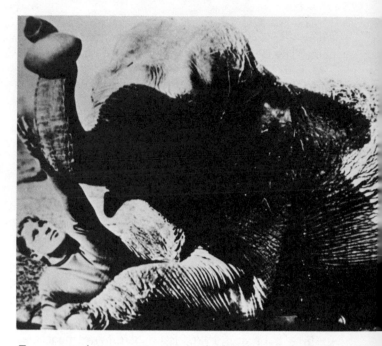

To promote the upcoming game at the Los Angeles Coliseum between the Chicago Bears and his all-star team, the Los Angeles Tigers, Wildcat Wilson posed with a variety of animals.
—Sternaman Collection

The promotion and the pizzazz paid off, at least in Los Angeles. A crowd estimated at more than 75,000 filled the Los Angeles Coliseum to watch the Bears pummel a make-up team called the L. A. Tigers that was headed by George ("Wildcat") Wilson, an All-American from the University of Washington. The score was 17–7. Playing on the line for the Tigers that day was a large, gravel-voiced young man who would go on to make a name for himself in the movies—Andy Devine.

The Bears then traveled down to San Diego to defeat a team called the Collegians 14–0 and up to San Francisco, where they suffered their only loss of the tour (14–9). From there they went on to Portland, Oregon, for a 60–3 devastation of a predominantly semi-pro aggregate of athletes who called themselves the All-Stars and finally to Seattle for an easy 34–0 win on the last day of January, 1926.

The tour was finally over. Grange and Pyle had pocketed roughly $150,000 from the gate receipts alone, bringing their total for the two tours to $250,-000. The Chicago Bears' organization had earned a little more than $100,000 from both tours. In the words of George Halas, it was "the first financial cushion we'd managed to accumulate." For the other Bear players, however, it was not a financial bonanza—they had worked hard to earn the $100 to $200 a game each was paid. But they did have an opportunity to build an

CHiCAGO BEARS
v.s.
LOS ANGELES
T I G E R S
Jan 15, 1926

incredible scrapbook of memories on a pilgrimage that had taken them from Cubs Park to Times Square, the White House, Miami Beach, New Orleans' French Quarter, Hollywood, the Wrigley mansion on Santa Catalina Island, Tijuana, the palatial estate of William Randolph Hearst at San Simeon, Fisherman's Wharf, and a raft of other interesting and out-of-the-ordinary ports of call.

For the Bears as a team, the official NFL season was disappointing. But what had taken place during and after the regular season, when looked at in proper perspective, was much more important. As George

---

Red Grange/Chicago Bear Tours
1925–26

(All games on the road, except Dec. 13)

Tour 1		Bears	Opponents
Dec. 2	St. Louis	39	6
Dec. 5	Frankford Yellow Jackets (at Philadelphia)*	14	7
Dec. 6	New York Giants*	19	7
Dec. 8	Washington, D.C.	19	0
Dec. 9	Providence Steam Roller (at Boston)*	6	9
Dec. 10	Pittsburgh	0	24
Dec. 12	Detroit Panthers*	0	21
Dec. 13	New York Giants*	0	9

Tour 2		Bears	Opponents
Dec. 25	Coral Gables	7	3
Jan. 1	Tampa	17	3
Jan. 2	Jacksonville	19	6
Jan. 10	New Orleans	14	0
Jan. 16	Los Angeles	17	7
Jan. 17	San Diego	14	0
Jan. 24	San Francisco	9	14
Jan. 30	Portland, Ore.	60	3
Jan. 31	Seattle	34	0

*League games; all others exhibition games

This is the handwritten first draft of some sterling advice Red Grange wrote for William Randolph Hearst's son Randolph. Another note was written to the other Hearst son, Elbert, and both were personally delivered to the boys by Grange when the Chicago Bears visited the magnificent Hearst estate at San Simeon in California. –Sternaman Collection

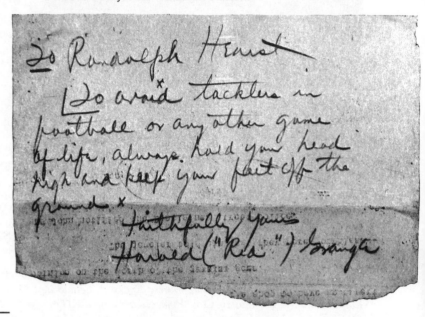

More than 75,000 people—the biggest crowd ever to attend a professional football game, by 1926 anyway—came to the Los Angeles Coliseum to see the Chicago Bears and Red Grange play. They watched the Bears defeat the Los Angeles Tigers, a hastily put-together team of West Coast all-stars, 17–7. –Pro Football Hall of Fame

During the tour, the Bears visited Luther Burbank, world famous botanist, at his ranch in Santa Rosa, California (where this picture was taken). The group: squatting, Harold Erickson; behind him, George Trafton; in tiers from left to right and in ascending order, Luther Burbank, Ed Garvey, C. C. Pyle, Oscar Knop; Red Grange, Bill Fleckenstein, Jim McMillen; Bill McElwain, Ralph Scott, Verne Mullen; Duke Hanny, Link Lyman; Dutch Sternaman, Laurie Walquist, unidentified Bear, Earl Britton; and at the right, Andy Lotshaw. Burbank died less than three months after this photograph was taken. –Sternaman Collection

Halas put it some 30 years later, ''I believe that as a result of our Grange tour, pro football for the first time took on true national stature.'' Indeed it did. Professional football was introduced in cities across the country, to people who up to that time had only heard vague rumblings about its existence and the questions regarding its commercialism and alleged lack of ''solid moral fiber.'' Now one of the nation's great sports idols was part of it, and the people came in droves to see him play the game. It would still take many more years before pro football would become the enormously popular spectator sport it is today, but the season of 1925 was the first real step in that direction.

Red Grange did not make professional football respectable. Joe Carr, George Halas, Dutch Sternaman, Curly Lambeau, Jimmy Conzelman, Jim Thorpe, and the other founding fathers of the NFL had already done that. But the public just hadn't accepted it yet. What Red Grange did was to popularize the game. He brought people out to see for themselves that pro football really was a respectable, entertaining, and exciting sport.

THE LEAGUE STRUGGLES FOR SURVIVAL

AS THE CHICAGO BEARS climbed aboard the train in Seattle for the ride back home after that last game of the 1925-26 tours, George Halas and Dutch Sternaman had every right to look forward to the 1926 NFL season. There was the reality of Red Grange and his ability to draw large crowds, their team was now both powerful and experienced, they would face a sensible league schedule, and there was money in the bank. But the Bears' angel of good fortune, who had traveled with the team over the 12,000 miles of their two-session tour and sat in 17 different stadiums with the 400,000 spectators to watch them play, got off the train somewhere between Seattle and Chicago.

It happened when C. C. Pyle met with Halas and Sternaman in a corner of their Pullman car during that trip to discuss what financial incentives would be needed to put Grange in a Chicago Bear uniform for the coming season. Halas and Sternaman thought the profit split of 1925, although lopsided in favor of Pyle and Grange, would be acceptable. And Pyle agreed to that arrangement, *but* only if it was supplemented by a one-third ownership of the team for the Red Grange/ C. C. Pyle Company. Halas and Sternaman rejected that proposal on the spot.

Over the next few days, on and off the train, the three men who only a few months earlier had huddled in an all-night bargaining session and been able to hammer out a "Red Grange deal" that was acceptable to everyone, found that this was no longer a possibility. On the question of restructuring the partnership of the Bears' organization, neither side was willing to budge or even compromise.

Pyle's only alternative, he said, would be to start his own team, building it around the star attraction of Red Grange. Halas and Sternaman were unmoved. With that, Pyle put his plan into motion. He had to act fast, however, because the official NFL post-season meeting of club owners was only days away. But time limitations were never an obstacle to Pyle. First, he wangled a five-year lease for the use of the recently finished Yankee Stadium in the Bronx, called the "house that Babe Ruth built" because the old ball park couldn't accommodate the tens of thousands of fans who wanted to watch him play. It was also the ideal stadium to display the equally awesome talents of Red Grange, Pyle had determined. Then at the official NFL meeting he went before the gathering of owners and requested a franchise for his team, which he had named the New York Yankees. The owner of the New York Giants, Tim Mara, knew too well what another New York team—especially one with Red Grange—would do to his already shaky franchise, which played its games just across the Harlem River at the Polo Grounds. He vociferously opposed the granting of a new franchise to Pyle, and the other owners supported him. Pyle's New York Yankees would not play in the NFL in 1926.

Red Grange was gone from the Bears in 1926, a year in which he divided his time between New York City, where he played with the football Yankees in the new American Football League, and Hollywood, where he was making movies. In this scene from One Minute to Play, *he tries to explain something about football to his leading lady, Mary McAllister.* –Pro Football Hall of Fame

"Cash and Carry" Pyle was not a man easily daunted. If the NFL wouldn't have him, he would establish his own league. And he did just that. The result was the first of several new leagues that would be created over the next 50 years to challenge the NFL. The American Football League, as Pyle called it, was formed around his own New York Yankee franchise and eight other teams—the Chicago Bulls, Boston Bulldogs, Cleveland Panthers, Philadelphia Quakers, Los Angeles Wildcats (strictly a road team), Brooklyn Horsemen, Newark Bears, and Rock Island Independents (the NFL team, which moved, totally intact, over to the AFL).

The new league proved to be a major threat to the NFL, not only because it had Red Grange but also because it was attracting a number of talented, well-established players from various NFL teams. The AFL was also able to entice some former college superstars, like Harry Stuhldreher of Notre Dame's Four Horsemen; Colgate's Eddie Tryon, one of the college game's all-time great running backs; and Wildcat Wilson, the All-American from Washington who had played against Grange and the Bears on the West Coast leg of their 1925-26 tours.

The city of Chicago encountered more than its share of the problems presented by the newly estab-

lished AFL. First the Bears lost their fine quarterback and leading scorer, Joey Sternaman, who quit to head up the Chicago Bulls. Then the Bulls managed to lease Comiskey Park out from under the Chicago Cardinals, forcing the illustrious NFL defending champions to play in tiny Normal Park, which they were using when they joined the league six years earlier.

The Bears' 1926 season, which had appeared so promising back in early February, began to look like it would be a disappointing one. George Halas and Dutch Sternaman, like most of the other NFL club owners, were very much aware of the problems facing the individual teams and the league in general. Halas was bitterly opposed to the AFL. He said over and over that the game was not yet big enough to support two separate, competing leagues. Sternaman was in complete agreement. Ironically, it was Halas and Sternaman, along with Grange and Pyle, who had created the climate in which this expansion could occur. They had brought pro football into the limelight the year before and revealed its very real potential as a money-making operation. Investors and promoters of every stripe suddenly saw the pro game as one that could attract tens of thousands of *paying* customers. And so it was not altogether unbelievable to see nine new teams rise up to form a new league. But the Bears' owners knew

After Red Grange was lost to the New York Yankees in the American Football League for the 1926 season, the Bears' woes were further compounded when quarterback and leading scorer, Joey Sternaman, left to lead the Chicago Bulls, also in the AFL. This is his letter of resignation. –Sternaman Collection

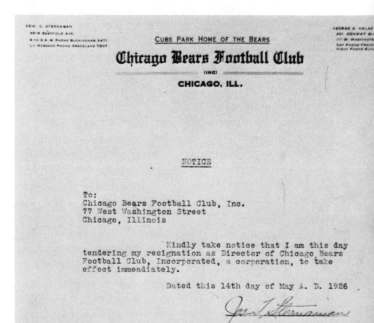

that with a total of 31 teams in its two circuits, professional football was dangerously over-extended.

Two events contributed substantially to the NFL's survival in 1926. The first of these involved Halas and Sternaman. The Chicago Bulls wanted to lure one of the NFL's best-known players—and one of pro football's biggest drawing cards—Paddy Driscoll of the Chicago Cardinals, over to their team. The Cardinals' owner, Chris O'Brien, faced a real dilemma. Playing in the small stadium they had been forced into, the Cardinals would not earn enough to afford paying Driscoll the same salary the Bulls could offer him. If the Cardinals couldn't meet his requirements, Driscoll would go over to the AFL, further jeopardizing the survival of O'Brien's own league.

At the same time, across town, Halas and Sternaman were in a predicament of their own. They were trying to put back together a team whose backfield was, to put it mildly, depleted. Their two best backs were gone, and one of them—Joey Sternaman—also happened to be their primary field-goal and extra-point kicker. Both Bear owners, being astute judges of talent and the needs of their team, quickly came to the conclusion that the only logical solution would be to acquire the league's top quadruple-threat, and their old nemesis—passer, running back, punter, and field-goal kicker Paddy Driscoll. So the Bears, flush with the new money they had banked from the Grange tours, bought Driscoll's contract from the Cardinals for $3,500 and then signed him to a Bear contract guaranteeing him $10,000 a year in salary. It was by far the highest amount yet paid by the Bears to a pro football player (with, of course, the exception of the previous year's arrangement with Red Grange).

The second factor that aided the National Football League in its confrontation with the AFL was the good fortune of the Duluth Eskimos, a new NFL franchise: they signed future Hall-of-Famer Ernie Nevers to a contract. The Eskimos extended themselves so much on his behalf—guaranteeing him $15,000 for the season—that they could only afford to carry a team that ranged over the season from 15 players down to as few as 13 players. And their schedule, it would turn out, included 13 regular season games plus a postseason tour of 16 exhibition games. They indeed earned the nickname "Iron Men from the North," given to them by sportswriter Grantland Rice. As Ernie Nevers later ruefully recalled, "The only mistake I made was that I forgot to ask how long the season was going to be." But the important thing was that Ernie Nevers, the second biggest name in professional football, was kept in the NFL, where his presence at that particular time was desperately needed.

Paddy Driscoll (center), with George Halas (left) and Dutch Sternaman, finally joined the Bears in 1926 and remained for the next five years as a player. The two Bear owners had tried to entice him away from the Chicago Cardinals back in 1922.
–Sternaman Collection

Ernie Nevers, in the uniform of the Duluth Eskimos, was one of the greatest backs ever to play professional football. During his career he had many occasions to remind the Chicago Bears of that fact—the most memorable was when he, as a Chicago Cardinal, entertained the Bears out at Comiskey Park in 1929. In that game, Nevers set an all-time NFL record, one still standing, by scoring all 40 points as the Cardinals demolished the Bears 40–6. –Pro Football Hall of Fame

Besides Red Grange and Joey Sternaman, the Bears also lost tackle Ralph Scott and back-up fullback Buck White to the AFL. On the other hand, they added Bill Senn, a rookie running back from little Knox College in Galesburg, Illinois, who would prove to be an outstanding running back over the next six seasons and who would take the starting halfback position away from veteran Laurie Walquist. Milt Romney was moved up from the reserves to replace Joey Sternaman at quarterback. Oscar Knop, at fullback, was the only returning back.

To accommodate the new players they had acquired, Halas and Sternaman took themselves out of the starting line-up for the first time in their pro careers. Link Lyman was now ensconced at one tackle and Ed Healey at the other; they were the most fearsome pair of tackles in the entire NFL. George Trafton was still the granite block at center, Duke Hanny and Verne Mullen started at ends, and Jim McMillen and Bill Buckler were the guards.

Link Lyman was signed by the Bears during the barnstorming tour of 1925 and stayed on to play seven seasons of football with them after it. At 6-feet-2 and about 250 pounds, Lyman was one of the bigger linemen of his day and proved to be one of the game's most awesome tackles. –Pro Football Hall of Fame

The face of the NFL itself had also changed for the 1926 season. Gone were the Rock Island Independents, Cleveland Bulldogs, and Rochester Jeffersons; and making their maiden appearance in the NFL were the Hartford Blues, Brooklyn Lions, a new Racine Legion, and two teams that played only road games, the Los Angeles Buccaneers and the Louisville Colonels, both of them based in Chicago. The total number of franchises in the league for 1926 was 22, an all-time high.

The NFL teams would no longer be able to pull off a stratagem like the one the Bears had in whisking Red Grange from the college football field to the professional sod in the same season. The outcry from college coaches and officials over that particular act had been loud and vitriolic, and it had not died down. To mollify them and to enable the NFL to peacefully co-exist with the college football establishment, George Halas, who with his partner had very questionably recruited Red Grange the year before, introduced a new rule at the league's post-season meeting prohibiting any NFL team from acquiring a college player whose class had not yet graduated. The rule was quickly approved by the other owners and adopted by the league. The irony of the two Bear owners introducing this piece of league legislation would be compounded four years later, when they would be the first to be fined for violating the rule.

The Bears opened their season in Milwaukee against the Badgers on September 19 with a 10–7 victory. (The Badgers' manager had been suspended ''for life'' the previous year because he used high school players in a farcical 59–0 game they lost to the Cardinals and assured that team the NFL title.) The Bears traveled to Green Bay the next week, where the Packers held them to a 6–6 tie. As the season moved along, it became quickly apparent that the Bears could get by without the services of Red Grange and Joey Sternaman. With the fine rushing of Bill Senn and the running, passing, and kicking of Paddy Driscoll, the

CHICAGO BEARS
FOOTBALL CLUB
SEASON 1926 TENDERS TO SEASON 1926
Mr.
The Courtesy of the Cubs Park
EDW. C. STERNAMAN 420 GEO. S. HALAS

Senn tore around end and broke loose for 62 yards and a Bear touchdown. Driscoll dropped back to kick the extra point, and as the ball left his toe he saw the now-familiar face of Guy Chamberlin, who slapped the ball back at him again. It was this defensive play that prompted a Chicago sportswriter to comment: "The Bears would have won had Chamberlin been content merely to coach." The Bears, with a comfortable 6–0 lead and only a few minutes remaining, kicked off deep, and the Yellow Jackets took over on their own 25-yard line. Behind the passing of tailback Hust Stockton, the Yellow Jackets marched all the way down to the Bears' 27-yard line. Then with only a minute and a half left, Stockton threw a pass into the end zone where the smallest man on the field—5-foot-5, 144-pound Two Bits Homan—was waiting. Tex Hamer kicked the extra point, and the Yellow Jackets won 7–6.

George Trafton (right), the Chicago Bears' captain of 1926, shakes hands with the Pottsville Maroons' captain, Charlie Berry, before the two teams met that season. The Bears emerged a winner that afternoon, 9–7. –Pro Football Hall of Fame

Bears won 10 of their next 11 games, being held to a scoreless tie in the other at the traditional Thanksgiving Day game with the Cardinals. But then they had to leave Chicago and the friendly confines of Wrigley Field, as the newly enlarged Cubs Park was now called, and travel east to face Guy Chamberlin and his Yellow Jackets at Shibe Park in Philadelphia. The Frankford Yellow Jackets had won 12 games, lost only one, and tied one. They were very much in contention for the league title, as were the Pottsville Maroons, with a 10–1–1 record. The Bears would face the Maroons, led by the fine end and kicker Charlie Berry, eight days later.

As it turned out, it was the Bear-Yellow Jacket game that decided the 1926 NFL championship. That Saturday afternoon in early December was a typical one for Philadelphia—wet, blustery, and cold. The first half was dominated by the two teams' awesome defenses. So was the third quarter, and when that period came to an end, the game was still scoreless. The only scoring threat had been a fourth-down field-goal attempt by Paddy Driscoll from Frankford's 24-yard line, but Chamberlin had come roaring in from the side and blocked it. Then in the fourth quarter, Bill

Dutch Sternaman tries right end in this 1926 game against the Canton Bulldogs, but he can't elude the clutches of the immortal Jim Thorpe. The Bear coming up behind Thorpe and looking as if he is contemplating throwing a colossal clip is end George Halas. Thorpe was 38 years old that year and played in only one more pro football season after it (as a Chicago Cardinal in 1928). –UPI

The following week the Bears beat the Pottsvile Maroons 9–6, then were tied by the Packers 3–3 in the final game of the year. The Bears had an impressive 12–1–3 record. But it was only good enough for second place, behind the Yellow Jackets, who ended the 1926 season with a sterling record of 14–1–1.

Paddy Driscoll had lived up to all expectations and ended the season as the NFL's top scorer, with 86 points to his credit, which included four touchdowns rushing and 14 extra points kicked. Second in the league was Ernie Nevers, with a total of 71 points. Driscoll also led the league in touchdown passes, with six; and field goals, with 12. And Bill Senn was eighth in total points, with 44. His seven touchdowns rushing accounted for 42 of the points, and only two players rushed for more touchdowns: Barney Wentz of Pottsville (10) and Nevers of Duluth (8).

In key games during the season, however, the AFL substantially outdrew the NFL. The important, title-deciding game between the Bears and the Yellow Jackets, for example, brought out only 10,000 fans to the same Philadelphia stadium where the week before 22,000 had watched the AFL's Philadelphia Quakers defeat Red Grange's New York Yankees. When the Bears played the Cardinals on October 17 at Normal Park, 12,000 people showed up. The same day, about four miles north of there, Grange brought his Yankees to Comiskey Park to face the Chicago Bulls and almost

The list of complimentary season passes to the Chicago Bear games of 1926 included such notables as:
   William Wrigley
   William Veeck
   A. E. Staley
   Grover Cleveland Alexander
   Warren Brown
   Abe L. Marovitz
   Chief Collins (Chief of Police)

Among the lesser knowns on the list, their occupations or services duly recorded just as they appear here, were:
   O. F. Nelson—"Alderman, 46th Ward"
   William Callahan—"Chicago traffic cop"
   Jack Smith—"Brings bear to games" (the live bear that was the team mascot back then)

Even by 1931, season passes were distributed somewhat cavalierly, as suggested by this note written by Florence Sternaman, Dutch's wife, on a scrap from a brown paper bag:
   John Manneon
   1929 N La Crosse Ave.
   Please put this in 1931 Passes. Game pass for this boy at Carson's Wholesale.
   He helped me get my package.

twice the number of spectators turned out for that game. But it was all small change compared to the 111,000 paying customers who showed up for the Army-Navy game in Chicago's brand-new Soldier Field that same year.

Over the season, however, the AFL teams as a whole did not fare very well at all. Red Grange was the only one of their players, it turned out, who could attract the paying customers. A few of the other franchises—the Chicago Bulls and the Philadelphia Quakers, for example—were almost breaking even, but as the season wore on, one after the other began to drop out of the AFL because they could no longer afford to play. By the end of their season, in fact, only four teams remained active in the league. Then insult was added to injury when the AFL champions, the Philadelphia Quakers, took on the NFL's seventh-place New York Giants in a post-season exhibition game on a snowy, bitterly cold afternoon in December at the Polo Grounds, and managing only one first down were summarily trounced 31–0. With that, the first American Football League folded.

The year had been bad for most of the NFL teams as well. Competition from the AFL had resulted in smaller crowds than had been anticipated, while operating costs reached new heights. The Bears, on the other hand, actually showed a small profit for the year, which was no doubt attributable to their acquisition of Paddy Driscoll and the excitement he and the team generated as they came so close to winning the NFL championship.

By 1927, the NFL had, out of necessity, pared itself down from a record high of 22 teams to 12 teams, the smallest number since the league was formed back in 1920. Among the better-known teams to drop out of

| 1926 SEASON | .923 | |
| Won 12 Lost 1 Tied 3 | | |
George Halas, Dutch Sternaman—Coaches	Bears	Opponents
Milwaukee Badgers	10	7
Green Bay Packers	6	6
Detroit Panthers	10	7
New York Giants	7	0
Chicago Cardinals	16	0
Duluth Eskimos	24	6
Akron Pros/Indians	17	0
Louisville Colonels	34	0
Chicago Cardinals	10	0
Milwaukee Badgers	10	7
Green Bay Packers	19	13
Chicago Cardinals	0	0
Canton Bulldogs	35	0
Frankford (Pa.) Yellow Jackets	6	7
Pottsville (Pa.) Maroons	9	7
Green Bay Packers	3	3
Totals	216	63

the league that year were the Canton Bulldogs (newly formed in 1925), Detroit Panthers, Akron Indians, Milwaukee Badgers, Hammond Pros, and Columbus Tigers. Added to the league were two new franchises, one picking up the secondhand name Cleveland Bulldogs and the other being the only holdover from the AFL to survive, C. C. Pyle's New York Yankees. The NFL owners now felt they would need the Yankees, with Red Grange, as opponents to bring paying spectators out to their ball parks.

The 1927 football season was an exercise in anticlimax. It began just after 20 million people were able to listen for the first time to a coast-to-coast radio broadcast of the World Series, to hear Graham McNamee and J. Andrew White describe the action as Miller Huggins's New York Yankees—with Babe Ruth, Lou Gehrig, and Tony Lazzeri—demolished the Pittsburgh Pirates in four straight games. This was the dawning of a new era in sports reporting, one that would not touch pro football in 1927 but would eventually lead to the phenomena of instant replays and Monday Night Football.

The year 1927 was in fact an incredible one in every respect. Charles Lindbergh made the first solo trans-Atlantic airplane flight, from New York to Paris. Al Jolson appeared in the world's first talking motion picture, *The Jazz Singer*. Babe Ruth hit 60 home runs in the regular season, more than any other *team* in the American League that year. (Two of the homers were hit off Ernie Nevers, who in the pro football off-season pitched for the St. Louis Browns.) And at

EDWARD C. STERNAMAN GEORGE S. HALAS

COMPLIMENTARY CHICAGO BEARS FOOTBALL CLUB INC.

Issued to

ADMIT ONE ONLY *Date*

NOT TRANSFERABLE

MANAGER

Charles C. Pyle

808 SOUTH WABASH AVENUE · CHICAGO

May
Twenty-fifth,
1 9 2 7

Messrs. Halas and Sternamann,
The Chicago "Bears",
Chicago, Ill.

Gentlemen:

This will acknowledge receipt of One Thousand
and Fifty Dollars ($1,050), being settlement in
full on all deals made between you and myself.

I further agree to pay the attorneys fees in the
Detroit settlement matter.

Yours very truly,

Chas C. Pyle

Chas. C. Pyle

CCP
FEB

ACCEPTED:

Geo S Halas

Edw C Sternaman

C. C. Pyle's personal letterhead was as flamboyant as his personal appearance and his sense of promotion. After the demise of the American Football League and the break-up of the New York Yankees, Pyle removed himself from the business of professional football. This letter closed out his dealings with the Chicago Bears. –Sternaman Collection

Soldier Field, Gene Tunney knocked out Jack Dempsey in the famous "long count" match to retain the heavyweight boxing title he had won the year before. There was really nothing pro football could do in the 1927 season to top the exciting sports events that had preceded it during the year. It was a tough billboard of acts to follow.

For the Bears of 1927, there were only two real changes in the line-up. Joey Sternaman came back and quickly regained his first-string spot at quarterback. Fullback Buck White also returned and took that starting position away from Oscar Knop. But now that pro football had gained some stature in terms of respectability, new stars were popping up all over the place. Besides such standards as Grange, Nevers, Chamberlin, and Driscoll, fresh names like Cal Hubbard, Steve Owen, Benny Friedman, August ("Iron Mike") Michalske, and Johnny Blood (christened John McNally) were now being talked about around the pro circuit.

The Bears managed to get off to a fine start that year, winning their first five games in a row. The third game in the Bears' win streak was against the New York Yankees, who made their Wrigley Field debut and lured the largest football crowd to that stadium since Red Grange had played there in a Bear uniform back in 1925. More than 30,000 fans showed up on a beautiful fall afternoon in mid-October to watch Grange take on his old team. With the Yankees losing 12–0 in the final minutes of the game, Grange was reaching for a forward pass when he collided with George Trafton, the Bear center. Grange went down, his knee a hunk of twisted and torn ligaments and tendons. He bore no grudges; on the contrary, he told members of the press who had gathered around him in the locker room that "it was one of the cleanest football games I ever played in."

After the injury, Grange missed the next four games but came back to play near the end of the season, even though his knee was not fully healed and was still very painful. (Knee surgery was not the recourse in those days.) He found, to his amazement, that the loyalty of the fans is often about as stable as leaves caught up in the autumn winds. The response when he returned to what was now his hometown to face the New York Giants was duly recorded for posterity in this article:

"New York, Dec. 4 (Special)—Red Grange, the hero of many a hard-fought football game and the idol of a nation, realized today as he lined up behind the retreating Yankees on the snowy, wind-swept field at the Polo Grounds, that fame is futile and the wages thereof is the razzberry.

"Even though Grange played every minute of the game against the Giants and did his best with a bad leg, it was not he who was cheered by the crowd. . . . All Grange got was the Bronx cheer, a prolonged boo, which must have fallen strangely on the ears of one who has known nothing but the approving roars of many a multitude."

Quarterback Joey Sternaman takes off up the middle with the ball in a 1927 game against the Frankford Yellow Jackets at Wrigley Field. It was his first year back in a Bear uniform after his one-year sojourn with the Chicago Bulls in the ill-fated American Football League. –Sternaman Collection

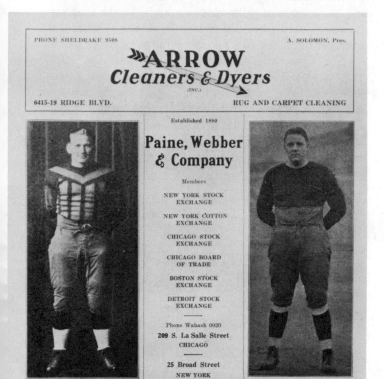
These Yankee fans were, perhaps, the ancestors of the "Boo Birds" who would take nest in Soldier Field about 45 years later and gain a league-wide reputation for making their displeasures with the home team loudly heard.

Even though Grange did come back to complete the 1927 season, his injury turned out to be more serious than he thought. It was bad enough to keep him on crutches for more than six months and to force him to miss the entire 1928 football season. "That injury ruined my career," Grange said later. "I never could run or cut again. I was just another halfback."

True, his days as the game's most dazzling broken-field runner were over. But he would return in 1929 with the team he had always been most comfortable with, the Bears, and he would still be a very good running back and prove to be one of the finest defensive backs in the game.

The Bears' march toward the title after five straight wins in 1927 was set back temporarily when they were held to a scoreless tie by the Providence Steam Roller, now led by Jimmy Conzelman, who had signed with them to play and coach after the demise of the Detroit Panthers at the end of the 1926 season. Then two days later, an inferior New York Yankees team—without the running abilities of Red Grange—somehow blew the Bears out of Yankee Stadium 26–6.

Another loss, this one three weeks later to the Cardinals at Wrigley Field (3–0), still did not put the Bears out of the race for the NFL Championship.

EDW. C. STERNAMAN
4708 N. Lincoln Street
Ravenswood 7377

GEORGE S. HALAS
111 W. Washington Street
Franklin 6040

Chicago Bears Football Club, Inc.

Wrigley Field, Home of the Bears

Addison and Clark Streets   CHICAGO, ILL.

The Bear calling card of the late 1920s. –Sternaman Collection

In 1927 an aging Joe Guyon (34) was in the backfield for the New York Giants. As he faded back for a pass, George Halas (then 32), the Bears' right defensive end, burst through. Guyon's back was to Halas, a perfect set-up for a blind-side hit, maybe a fumble, but if nothing else a reminder that the game of football was a rough one. At the last second, however, Guyon unloaded the pass and wheeled around to greet the charging Halas with his knee. It broke several of Halas's ribs. Guyon shook his head at the grimacing Chicago Bear on the ground. "Come on, Halas," he said. "You should know better than to try to sneak up on an Indian." And making Halas even more miserable, the referee called him for clipping and marched off 15 yards against the Bears.

Instead, it set the stage for a climactic showdown that turned into one of the hardest-fought defensive football games ever played. The Bears went to the Polo Grounds on November 27 to face the league-leading New York Giants, who had lost only one game and tied one in the 10 games they had played.

The game brought face to face the two best lines in professional football. Five of the linemen—George Trafton, Ed Healey, Link Lyman, and the Giants' Steve Owen and Cal Hubbard—would be inducted into the Pro Football Hall of Fame. And two others—Jim McMillen of the Bears and Century Milstead of the Giants—were equally deserving of that honor, many believe. The Giants' defense was so good in 1927, in fact, that when the season was over only 20 points had been scored against the team in 13 league games. Ten times their opponents failed to put a score of any kind on the board.

The field on that chilly November afternoon was muddy from an early morning rain, which also was a factor in keeping the crowd down to about 10,000. The first half was uneventful, except for two drives that were stifled when each team held off the other in desperate goal-line stands. Then in the third quarter, the Giants drove to two touchdowns, both scored by fullback Jack McBride. The Bears came back with a touchdown late in the fourth quarter when Joey Sternaman caught a pass thrown by Laurie Walquist, but time ran out, and the Giants clinched the NFL title for 1927 with their 13–7 victory. As Steve Owen put it much later: "It was the toughest, roughest football game I ever played."

With a final record of 9–3–2 for the season, the Bears slipped into third place. Paddy Driscoll was once again the Bears' highest scorer, and tied for third

highest in the NFL as well, with a total of 45 points—five touchdowns rushing, two field goals, and nine extra points. Bill Senn rushed for four touchdowns, and Buck White added three more. But it was another of those frustrating and disappointing seasons of coming close but not quite close enough. These seasons, however, would look good in comparison to what was about to befall the Chicago Bears in the next two years.

For Chicago Bear fans, then or now, the 1928 season was one that is eminently forgettable. It was lackluster from beginning to end, and the Bears were never in contention for the title. The team still had Paddy Driscoll, but he was 33 years old now and beginning to think seriously of retiring. Dutch Sternaman, 33, felt the aches and pains of age and gave up a

---

1927 SEASON   .750

Won 9   Lost 3   Tied 2

George Halas, Dutch Sternaman—Coaches	Bears	Opponents
Chicago Cardinals	9	0
Green Bay Packers	7	6
New York Yankees	12	0
Cleveland Bulldogs	14	12
Dayton Triangles	14	6
Providence (Mass.) Steam Roller	0	0
New York Yankees	6	26
Pottsville (Pa.) Maroons	30	12
Green Bay Packers	14	6
Chicago Cardinals	0	3
New York Giants	7	13
Frankford (Pa.) Yellow Jackets	0	0
Frankford (Pa.) Yellow Jackets	9	0
Duluth Eskimos	27	14
Totals	149	98

In the late 1920s, Bear center George Trafton took up boxing to supplement his income. But that career ended for all practical purposes in 1930, when he was knocked out in the first round by Primo Carnera, who won the world heavyweight championship a few years later. Trafton's 13-year career with the Bears was much more illustrious, and he is acknowledged as the finest center of his time. –Pro Football Hall of Fame

on a football field. "In his forties and musclebound, Thorpe was a mere shadow of his former self," wrote a sports reporter covering the game. He was describing the man who in two 1950 Associated Press polls would be named the "greatest football player" and the "greatest male athlete" of the first half of the 20th century.

In the third game of the season, the Bears beat the defending champion New York Giants 13–0, which was the season's high point, even though the Giants, like the Bears, were on the downslide.

Benny Friedman, with his great passing (he threw 11 touchdown passes in 1928, two less than his NFL record of 13 the year before) and rushing, led the Detroit Wolverines to two wins over the Bears (6–0 and 14–7, both at Wrigley Field). And the Green Bay Packers, behind the league-leading scorer of 1928, tailback Verne Lewellen, also defeated the Bears twice at Wrigley Field (16–6 and 6–0), and held them to a tie in Green Bay (12–12). The Frankford Yellow Jackets handed the Bears their fifth loss in the last game of the season (19–0). The Bears ended up in fifth place in the 10-team NFL of 1928, with a record of 7–5–1.

Meanwhile, former Chicago Bear Red Grange, who was sitting out the season because of his knee problems, managed to keep his name in the news in other ways. His contract with C. C. Pyle had expired at the end of the 1927 season, and with Grange's football future questionable and Pyle's New York Yankees about to go under, neither of them talked about renewing it. Pyle and Grange were still good friends, however. They had, as Grange explained later, a mutual respect for each other. Besides their football

playing role to devote all his time to coaching, scouting, and administering the team. George Halas, his 33-year-old partner, wanted to eke out one more season on the field, even though he knew most of it would be spent on the bench.

The NFL was reduced from 12 to 10 teams for the 1928 season. One of the teams that dropped out was the Cleveland Bulldogs, and their star player, Benny Friedman, joined the Detroit Wolverines, the only new franchise that year. Friedman's passing arm would hurt the Bears when the two teams clashed during the season. The Duluth Eskimos also folded, but their great fullback and coach, Ernie Nevers, decided to leave pro football; he returned to Stanford, his alma mater, as an assistant coach.

The Bears opened their season with a 15–0 win over the Cardinals, a game both sad and memorable. It was the game in which Jim Thorpe, now wearing a Cardinal uniform, made a brief and final appearance

1928 SEASON   .583
Won 7   Lost 5   Tied 1

George Halas, Dutch Sternaman—Coaches	Bears	Opponents
Chicago Cardinals	15	0
Green Bay Packers	12	12
New York Giants	13	0
Green Bay Packers	6	16
Detroit Wolverines	0	6
New York Yankees	27	0
Dayton Triangles	27	0
Pottsville (Pa.) Maroons	13	6
Chicago Cardinals	34	0
Detroit Wolverines	7	14
Frankford (Pa.) Yellow Jackets	28	6
Green Bay Packers	0	6
Frankford (Pa.) Yellow Jackets	0	19
Totals	182	85

Friedman Will Play Here Nov. 25

Expect Crowd of 25,000 Will Watch Famous Benny

For the second time this year Benny Friedman will lead his Detroit Wolverines into the lair of the

Tickets on Sale Tuesday At the Hub For Detroit Game

Bears Vow They Will Defeat Detroit Team

Individually and collectively the Bears vow they will get revenge on Friedman and his Wolverines next Sunday. Here's a few of the pledges made by the boys:

—Sternaman Collection

FOOTBALL

Benny Friedman's Detroit Wolverines

vs.

Chicago Bears

Sunday, Nov. 25th

Kickoff 2:15 P. M.

Benny Friedman
World's Greatest Forward Passer

Reserved Tickets on sale at

THE HUB
235 S. State St.

Tuesday, Wednesday, Thursday, Friday and Saturday

WRIGLEY FIELD

Sheffield, Addison & Clark Sts.   Take Northwestern Elevated to Addison St.

ventures, they had been into and out of a whole series of business enterprises in the past two years. With Pyle as his manager, Grange had made two movies (*One Minute to Play* in 1926 and *Racing Romeo* in 1927; another, *The Galloping Ghost*, would be released in 1929). During the filming of one of these, a situation arose in which Pyle showed his true business ingenuity, according to Grange. They were shooting the picture in June in Hollywood, with the temperature above the 90-degree mark. For a major scene, they needed a crowd of about 2,000 extras to populate the stadium where Grange was supposed to be playing a game. There were actually two problems—an extra in those days had to be paid a salary of $15 to $20, and the scene was supposed to depict a nippy autumn afternoon in the Midwest, not a broiling summer day in California. Pyle solved both problems by taking out a $25 ad in a Los Angeles newspaper announcing that Red Grange was to play in an exhibition football game. Anyone who would wear a coat and a hat and keep them on throughout the game would be admitted to the stadium free of charge. More than 3,000 warmly clad people showed up to perspire through the staged game, and Pyle saved the producers some $30,000 to $40,000 in salaries for the day.

Grange went along on another venture with Pyle in 1928. On this one, he traveled luxuriously in a specially built "land yacht" that paced 241 runners who were taking part in a 3,400-mile transcontinental race from Los Angeles to New York. It was the Pyle-sponsored "Bunion Derby," after which "Cash and Carry" Pyle was dubbed "Corn and Callous" Pyle by some members of the nation's press.

Somewhere in the middle of all this, George Halas, who had kept in touch with Grange, suggested that maybe Red might like to take up the game of football again. He would, Grange decided, and he signed a contract with the Bears for the coming 1929 season.

But 1929 was not the best of years for anyone, not for the "Bears" on the stock market or the football Bears of Chicago. Disaster struck both. With the great

When Red Grange returned to Chicago in 1929, the Bears announced it to their fans with a simple question. –Pro Football Hall of Fame

stock-market crash in October, investors were reported to be leaping out of windows on Wall Street and LaSalle Street; the response to the collapse of the Chicago Bears around the same time that year was fortunately nothing quite so dramatic.

There were other changes on the 1929 Bear roster besides the return of Red Grange. George Halas ended his playing days. The Bears also signed Red's younger brother, Garland, or "Gardie," as the Illinois alumnus was usually called. Luke Johnsos, from Northwestern, whose name would be very familiar to Bear fans for the next 30 years, first as a player and then as a coach, joined the team and so did Walt Holmer, also from Northwestern, one of the more highly regarded college fullbacks of the day. Another addition to the squad was Joe Kopcha, a fine guard from the University of Chattanooga.

Elsewhere in the league, change was also occurring, and nowhere more notably than up at Green Bay. The Packers, under coach Curly Lambeau, who at 31 still listed himself as a player even though he saw very little action, acquired three future Hall-of-Famers to add to an already impressive team. Joining the Pack were Cal

Hubbard, the huge (for those days) 250-pound tackle from the New York Giants; Johnny Blood, ace running back from the now-defunct Pottsville Maroons; and guard Iron Mike Michalske from the New York Yankees, another recently deceased team.

On the East Coast, Tim Mara in effect merged the Detroit Wolverines, who despite a good season the year before could not stay in business, with his New York Giants. The most notable acquisition in the deal was tailback Benny Friedman. One other running back who would eventually leave his indelible mark on the game of pro football, Ken Strong, entered the league that year too. Fresh from New York University, he signed with the newly franchised Staten Island Stapletons, who were also known around the league as the Stapleton Stapes.

The Bears actually got off to a decent enough start. At the end of six games, they had won four, lost only one (to Green Bay, 23–0), and tied another (with the Chicago Cardinals, 0–0). But then, like the stock market's Black Tuesday, the Bears had their Black Sunday and the collapse began—they lost eight of their next nine games and tied the other.

One of the 1929 Bear losses was a memorable chapter in the story of professional football, although the game is one most Bear fans would just as soon forget. It occurred Thanksgiving Day, November 28. The Bears took themselves out to Comiskey Park on Chicago's South Side to face their long-time rivals, the Cardinals, who had moved back there that year, and who had a losing record at this point in the season (4–5–1). The Cardinals also had a new man on their

1929 SEASON .308
Won 4 Lost 9 Tied 2

George Halas,
Dutch Sternaman—Coaches

	Bears	Opponents
Minneapolis Red Jackets	19	6
Green Bay Packers	0	23
Minneapolis Red Jackets	7	6
Buffalo Bisons	16	0
Chicago Cardinals	0	0
Minneapolis Red Jackets	27	0
New York Giants	14	26
Green Bay Packers	0	14
Frankford (Pa.) Yellow Jackets	14	20
New York Giants	0	34
Buffalo Bisons	7	19
Chicago Cardinals	6	40
Frankford (Pa.) Yellow Jackets	0	0
Green Bay Packers	0	25
New York Giants	9	14
Totals	119	227

Red Grange (left) and Paddy Driscoll, two of the biggest names in the game, pose with the Bears' mascot in 1929. Despite their presence on the team, the Bears endured the worst season in their 10-year history. –Sternaman Collection

squad, Ernie Nevers by name, whom they had coaxed back to the pro game as a player/coach. Running behind the blocks of the most famous black player of those years, tackle Duke Slater, and a guard who would later be inducted into the Hall of Fame, Walt Kiesling, Ernie Nevers had the most productive day any player has ever had on a professional football field. He scored all 40 points (an NFL record still standing)—rushing for six touchdowns (also still a record, but one that has been tied twice, by Dub Jones and Gale Sayers) and kicking four extra points—as the Cardinals humiliated the Bears 40–6.

Curly Lambeau's Green Bay Packers went undefeated to win the NFL championship that year, 12–0–1, although the New York Giants threatened them all the way to the last game and ended their season with an impressive 13–1–1 record. Ernie Nevers led the league in scoring, with 85 points, and in the number of touchdowns rushing, 12. Benny Friedman of the Giants broke his old season record of 13 touchdown passes with a then phenomenal 19.

As for the Bears of 1929, their 4–9–2 record dropped them to ninth place in the 12-team NFL, by far the worst season they had had in their 10-year history. George Halas and Dutch Sternaman both realized they would have to come up with a drastic remedy if a repetition of this sad season was to be avoided.

RALPH JONES AT THE HELM

DURING THE 1929 SEASON, a growing dissension was surfacing between the two owner/coaches, George Halas and Dutch Sternaman. Both men had devoted their lives to the game of football since adolescence; both had had their own ideas about how the game should be played. In the first eight or nine years they had worked together, their opinions were much the same. Lately, however, they had seldom been in agreement about how the team should be coached. And it had a bad effect on their relationship and on the team itself. As one player from the 1929 team put it: "Halas and Dutch Sternaman weren't getting along. We had two offenses, one devised by George and one by Dutch. Nobody knew what to expect on any play. People were running into each other on the field."

But after the horrendous 1929 season, Halas and Dutch Sternaman agreed on one thing. For 1930 they needed *one* coach for the team, and they further agreed that at this point in time it should not be either one of them. So they hired Ralph Jones, who was head coach at Lake Forest College, a small school located in a suburb north of Chicago. Jones had also coached both Halas and Sternaman at the University of Illinois, where he had been an assistant coach under Bob Zuppke from 1913 to 1920.

Ralph Jones, a short man with a glistening bald head that barely reached the shoulders of his players, possessed an outstanding mind for football strategy.

He was an innovator as well as a shrewd judge of talent. In an age of the single-wing, double-wing, and Notre Dame box, he would take the Bears' out-of-style T formation, split the ends, and send a man in motion, thus developing the modern form of the T, which would dominate pro football in the decades to come. The split-T formation, as it was called, would be refined over the years, but it got its beginning with the Bears and Ralph Jones in 1930.

Paddy Driscoll, now 35, did not return for the 1930 season. Still around were some other very familiar Bear names: George Trafton, Joey Sternaman, Link Lyman, and Laurie Walquist, but they too were all in their 30s. The Bears needed some new faces. And they recruited two significant ones. From the University of Florida, the Bears brought up Carl ("Brummy") Brumbaugh, a halfback who, Ralph Scott knew, was also a fine passer. And they signed a giant of a man from the University of Minnesota, who would one day be as famous as Red Grange or anyone else, for that matter, in the world of sports. "They got a one-man football team by the name of Bronko Nagurski," is the way one Chicago sportswriter put it.

By autumn 1930, the effects of the Great Depression were beginning to be felt. Many people had lost their jobs, money was scarce, and goods were not selling. And it was going to get worse before it got better. The Bears of 1929 suffered through both the depressed economy and a disastrous season. Although crowds still came out to the ball park, they weren't as large as they had been before 1929. Money was just not very plentiful. Fortunately for the Bears, their basic equipment wasn't terribly expensive either. In a ledger of expenses for 1930, the Bears listed such items as football pants, $2; athletic supporter, 50¢; helmet, $6; jersey, $4.85; shoulder pads, $4; and a regulation football, $9.35. In fact, the Bears' total expenditure for equipment that year was only $1,245.13.

Gone too was the $10,000 salary of Paddy Driscoll. Now the highest-paid player on the team was newcomer Bronko Nagurski, with a salary of $5,000 for the season. Behind him were Red Grange, still and forever hampered by a bad knee ($4,000); Walt Holmer, who took home the same salary as Grange; and Joey Sternaman, who received $3,300 for his quarterbacking services. The other players' pay ranged from about $1,450 to $2,500. The biggest single salary for the Bears was the $7,500 paid to coach Ralph Jones.

Ralph Jones was hired as head coach of the Bears in 1930 when George Halas and Dutch Sternaman decided some new ideas from the bench might help turn the team around after their dismal 1929 season. During his three years as head coach, Jones did just that, posting a record of 30–11–8—including pre-season and post-season games—and crowned his career with an NFL championship in 1932. –Pro Football Hall of Fame

Recruiting 1930 Style

In the spring of 1930, Dutch Sternaman received the following letter:

> Iowa City, Iowa
> March 31, 1930
>
> *Dear Mr. Sternaman,*
>
> *I am somewhat interested in playing football next fall, but am undecided as to where I want to go.*
>
> *Of course the thing that makes me undecided is the money. I have a chance to coach and also play some pro ball, but the terms are not satisfactory as yet.*
>
> *I weigh 180 pounds, am 5-feet 11-inches tall, and am ineligible for further collegiate competition. . . .*
>
> *I can pass, but am not so hot in the kicking department. But used the quick kick last year and I am fair at that type. I can placekick; getting five good ones out of six attempts last year (at U. of Iowa).*
>
> *I do not have a full length picture of myself in football togs, so am sending the next best. . . .*
>
> *Very truly yours,*
> *Oran H. Pape*

Within a week, Dutch Sternaman responded for the Bears. "In reply to your letter of March 31st, I wish to say that we would like to have you play with us next fall. With our new coach Mr. Jones and the men we already have we should have a winner of a club. We could offer you $115 a game. Inasmuch as we play from 15 to 17 games a season I think you could make some money here with us. . . . We do not pay any of the boys anything but traveling and hotel expenses. We hope this would be satisfactory with you. Would like to have your approval so that I can mail you some contracts."

Oran Pape, as it turned out however, did not take the Bears up on their offer, choosing instead to sign with the Minneapolis Red Jackets, to whom apparently he had also written.

The debut of the Bears' new split-T formation in the opening game of the season against the Brooklyn Dodgers—a new franchise that year—was less than spectacular. Even with two of the most famous names in football history in their backfield, Grange and Nagurski, complemented by two other highly respected backs, Joey Sternaman and Bill Senn, the Bears didn't score a point, and the game ended in a scoreless tie. Near the end of the game, Sternaman was hurt and Carl Brumbaugh was brought in to quarterback the team. This would be the last game in which little Joey Sternaman, now 30, would start. Except for part of the

1923 season, when he was player/coach of the Duluth Kelleys, and 1926, when he played with the AFL's Chicago Bulls, Sternaman had been the Bears' starting quarterback since 1922.

By mid-season the Bears were still unimpressive, with a 3–3–1 record, and it looked as if the season might be as disappointing as the preceding one. After all, they still had to face the undefeated and untied Packers two more times, as well as an array of other topflight opponents like the New York Giants, the Frankford Yellow Jackets, and the Portsmouth (Ohio) Spartans. A new entry in the league, and a team that also happened to be a title contender, the Spartans, under George ("Potsy") Clark, had already beaten the Bears during the first half of the season.

But then things began to happen. The man in motion was confusing defenses; the split-T was beginning to work. The team that had been manhandled so

In the year 1930, two of the game's true immortals were matched up in the Chicago Bears' backfield—Red Grange, a veteran pro of four seasons then, and Bronko Nagurski, a rookie out of the University of Minnesota. –Pro Football Hall of Fame

A Chicago Bear ledger page from 1930. This one gives an accounting of various salaries and expenses that were part of the Bears' trip to Green Bay that year. –Sternaman Collection

badly the season before won six of their last seven games, and the one they lost was a tightrope thriller that went to Green Bay 13–12. But the Bears avenged this defeat in the last game of the season by routing the reigning NFL champion Packers 21–0 before 22,000 people, the biggest crowd to watch a football match in Wrigley Field that year.

Green Bay still took the championship, with a 10–3–1 record. Right behind the Pack were the New York Giants, at 13–4–0, and the Bears, with a 9–4–1 record. Not only had the split-T proved a success, but Bronko Nagurski had shown he was definitely worth the top salary he was getting. The powerful back rushed for five touchdowns, and playing brutal defense effectively intimidated every team he played against. As the Giants' tackle and later their coach, Steve Owen, said of Nagurski, he was "the only back I ever

Clarence Spears, the coach at the University of Minnesota who recruited Bronko Nagurski, often told the story of how he did it. "I went up to International Falls to look at another kid named Smith, who was supposed to be a good prospect. Just outside town I saw this young kid pushing a plow. There was no horse or anything else, just the kid pushing the plow. I asked where I could find the Smith kid, and the other boy—who happened to be Bronko—just picked up the plow and pointed in the direction. I decided then and there to get the kid with the plow for Minnesota."

Red Grange's name was still a drawing card in 1930, as this poster amply illustrates. –Sternaman Collection

saw that ran his own interference. . . . There's only one defense that could stop him—shoot him before he leaves the dressing room.''

It was in 1930 also that the Bears tried to stretch the NFL rule George Halas himself had championed in 1926 to prohibit pro teams from signing a player before his college class graduated. The recruit in this case was Joe Savoldi, Notre Dame's top running back.

Savoldi arrived at the Bears' office in Chicago a day or two after the college season ended in mid-November. It seemed, he explained, that he had been unceremoniously ousted from school because he had secretly gotten married, which was against Notre Dame's rules in those days. Now he needed a job, and he wanted to play pro football—right away. Halas and Sternaman checked out the details, and officials at Notre Dame corroborated Savoldi's story. The Bears'

The Chicago Bears' hometown opener of the 1930 season against the Brooklyn Dodgers, which was also their debut under new head coach Ralph Jones. But it was not at Wrigley Field. The game was played at Mills Stadium on September 21, in a park on Chicago's North Side, because Wrigley Field was not available until the Chicago Cubs finished up their season. The only identifiable Bear in this picture is Joey Sternaman, running interference in front of the ball carrier. The game, incidentally, ended in a 0–0 tie. –Sternaman Collection

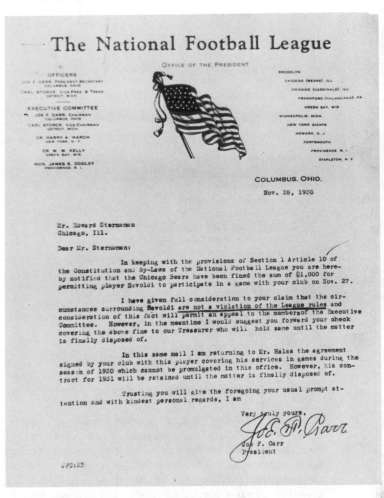

The National Football League

OFFICE OF THE PRESIDENT

OFFICERS
JOE F. CARR, PRESIDENT-SECRETARY
COLUMBUS, OHIO
CARL STORCK, VICE-PRES. & TREAS.
DETROIT, MICH.

EXECUTIVE COMMITTEE
JOE F. CARR, CHAIRMAN
COLUMBUS, OHIO
CARL STORCK, VICE-CHAIRMAN
DETROIT, MICH.
DR. HARRY A. MARCH
NEW YORK, N. Y.
DR. W. W. KELLY
GREEN BAY, WIS.
HON. JAMES E. DOOLEY
PROVIDENCE, R. I.

BROOKLYN
CHICAGO (BEARS), ILL.
CHICAGO (CARDINALS), ILL.
FRANKFORD (PHILADELPHIA), PA.
GREEN BAY, WIS.
MINNEAPOLIS, MINN.
NEW YORK GIANTS
NEWARK, N. J.
PORTSMOUTH
PROVIDENCE, R. I.
STAPLETON, N. Y.

COLUMBUS, OHIO.
Nov. 28, 1930

Mr. Edward Sternaman
Chicago, Ill.

Dear Mr. Sternaman:

In keeping with the provisions of Section 1 Article 10 of
the Constitution and By-Laws of the National Football League you are hereby notified that the Chicago Bears have been fined the sum of $1,000 for
permitting player Savoldi to participate in a game with your club on Nov. 27.

I have given full consideration to your claim that the circumstances surrounding Savoldi are not a violation of the League rules and
consideration of this fact will permit an appeal to the members of the Executive
Committee. However, in the meantime I would suggest you forward your check
covering the above fine to our Treasurer who will hold same until the matter
is finally disposed of.

In this same mail I am returning to Mr. Halas the agreement
signed by your club with this player covering his services in games during the
season of 1930 which cannot be promulgated in this office. However, his contract for 1931 will be retained until the matter is finally disposed of.

Trusting you will give the foregoing your usual prompt attention and with kindest personal regards, I am

Very truly yours,

Joe F. Carr
President

JFC:KE

Joe Savoldi, a fullback at Notre Dame in 1930, signs a Chicago Bear contract in November, as co-owners Dutch Sternaman and George Halas look on. It was a violation of NFL rules to "tamper" with a college player before his class had graduated, but it did not apply in this case, the Bear management claimed, because Savoldi had been kicked out of school. NFL president Joe Carr, however, viewed the situation differently, as this letter from him explains, and he fined the Bears $1,000. –Sternaman Collection

owners concluded that if he was no longer a student—after all, he had been removed from the rolls by the university—the 1926 rule didn't apply to Savoldi.

As Halas saw it, "Any team that would turn Savoldi aside wouldn't know its business. . . . Because of the extraordinary circumstances surrounding this case we do not feel that we are making any encroachment upon college football, nor does this set any precedent of jeopardizing the amateur standing of any college player, as Savoldi is no longer classed as a college player." And, Halas went on, "We are happy and proud to announce that Joe Savoldi will appear in uniform as one of our regular players to participate in our big game next Thanksgiving morning against the Cardinals."

Halas summed up his statement to the press: "His coming to us was somewhat of a miracle." Joe Carr, NFL president, did not see the miraculousness of it, however, and wrote a letter to the Bears announcing that he was fining the club $1,000 for violating the NFL's "Constitution and By-Laws."

Savoldi played a total of three games with the Bears at the end of the 1930 season. He also appeared in a post-season exhibition match against the Cardinals. (This, incidentally, was the first football game ever held indoors. It was played at the Chicago Stadium on an 80-yard-long field, with a complicated formula used for advancing the 100 yards needed to score.) With fullback Bronko Nagurski and a back-up runner like Dick Nesbitt on the squad, the Bears decided against signing Savoldi for the following year, and he retired from the game to become a professional wrestler.

Red Grange, with 37 points, was the Bears' high scorer in 1930, rushing for four touchdowns, catching two touchdown passes, and kicking one extra point. End Luke Johnsos caught four touchdown passes, second highest in the league that year.

The Bears, on the mend and despite the Depression, were able to show a year-end profit of $1,695.93 on a gross income of $155,294.69—nothing to raise the flag about, but better than practically any other team in the league. In fact, two of the franchises awarded in 1929 had to drop out of the league, which brought the NFL membership down to only 10 teams again for the 1931 season, and some of those remaining were on very shaky ground.

1930 SEASON .692
Won 9 Lost 4 Tied 1

Ralph Jones—Coach	Bears	Opponents
Brooklyn Dodgers	0	0
Green Bay Packers	0	7
Minneapolis Red Jackets	20	0
New York Giants	0	12
Chicago Cardinals	32	6
Portsmouth (Ohio) Spartans	6	7
Frankford (Pa.) Yellow Jackets	13	7
Minneapolis Red Jackets	20	7
Green Bay Packers	12	13
New York Giants	12	0
Chicago Cardinals	6	0
Portsmouth (Ohio) Spartans	14	6
Green Bay Packers	21	0
Chicago Cardinals	9	7
Totals	165	72

This 1930 gathering brought together owners or representatives of all NFL teams at the Seaside Hotel in Atlantic City, New Jersey, for their annual scheduling meeting. For the Bears, there were Dutch Sternaman (squatting, far right) and George Halas (standing just to the left of him). Other notables in the picture are Joe Carr, NFL president (squatting, far left), Dr. David Jones, owner of the Chicago Cardinals (squatting, fourth from the left), Jimmy Conzelman (standing, third from the left), and Curly Lambeau (standing, sixth from the left). –Pro Football Hall of Fame

The 1931 season began with Halas and Sternaman still feuding behind the scenes, although their disagreements were no longer affecting the team's play. Ralph Jones was well in charge of the operation on the field. Joey Sternaman retired to spend all his time selling cast-iron pipe and a little real estate on the side. One of the Bears' acquisitions that year was Keith Molesworth, a small (5-feet-9, 165 pounds) running back from tiny Monmouth (Ill.) College. Grange and Nagurski were still, of course, the power of the Bear running game.

The Bears got off to a mediocre start, winning only four of their first seven games, but they were ready to turn it all around when they traveled to New York to face the Giants under that team's new head coach, Steve Owen. The Giants, still led by tailback Benny Friedman, were coming off a four-game winning streak, with their appetites for the 1931 title now well whetted. And their confrontation with the Bears was to be a crucial swing game in that bid, they felt.

More than 30,000 people showed up for the game at the Polo Grounds on Sunday afternoon, November 15. Westbrook Pegler wrote about two of the more special ones in the *Chicago Tribune* the next day, describing them in his own inimitable way.

"Al Smith's brown derby popped up in the first row of the field boxes, accompanied by Mr. Smith himself, and the faithful rose and saluted the New York crown, with great respect. His honor the Mayor, Mr. Walker, made a more formal entrance, walking half the length

The National Football League
UNIFORM PLAYER'S CONTRACT

The CHICAGO BEARS FOOTBALL CLUB, INC. ....herein called the Club,

and EDWARD J. KAWAL ...., of CICERO, ILLINOIS. ....
herein called the Player.

The Club is a member of **The National Football League.** As such, and jointly with the other members of the League, it is obligated to insure to the public wholesome and high-class professional football by defining the relations between Club and Player, and between Club and Club.

In view of the facts above recited the parties agree as follows: 1931

1.   The Club will pay the Player a salary for his skilled services during the playing season of 192X.., at the rate of $ 100.00 per game.   As to games scheduled but not played the player shall receive no compensation from the Club, other than actual expenses.

It is further understood that the first game shall be played without compensation, other than necessary hotel and traveling expenses.

2.   The salary above provided for shall be paid by the Club as follows:

Seventy-five per cent (75%) after each game and the remaining twenty-five per cent (25%) at the close of the season or upon release of the player by the Club.

3.   The Player agrees that during said season he will faithfully serve the Club, and pledges himself to the American public to conform to high standards of fair play and good sportsmanship.

4.   The Player will not play football during 192X31 otherwise than for the Club, except in case the Club shall have released said Player, and said release has been approved by the officials of **The National Football League.**

5.   The Player accepts as part of this contract such reasonable regulations as the Club may announce from time to time.

6.   This contract may be terminated at any time by the Club upon six (6) days' written notice to the Player.

7.   The Player submits himself to the discipline of **The National Football League** and agrees to accept its decisions pursuant to its Constitution and By-Laws.

8.   Any time prior to August 1st, 192X31, by written notice to the Player, the Club may renew this contract for the term of that year, except that the salary rate shall be such as the parties may then agree upon, or in default of agreement, such as the Club may fix.

9.   The Player may be fined or suspended for violation of this contract, but in all cases the Player shall have the right of appeal to the President of **The National Football League.**

10.   In default of agreement, the Player will accept the salary rate thus fixed or else will not play during said year otherwise than for the Club, unless the Club shall release the Player.

11.   The reservation of the Club of the valuable right to fix the salary rate for the succeeding year, and the promise of the Player not to play during said year otherwise than with the Club, have been taken into consideration in determining the salary specified herein and the undertaking by the Club to pay said salary is the consideration for both the reservation and the promise.

12.   In case of dispute between the Player and the Club the same shall be referred to the President of **The National Football League,** and his decision shall be accepted by all parties as final.

13.   Verbal contracts between Club and Player will not be considered by this League. in the event of a dispute.

Signed this 26th day of May........................., A. D. 19X31..

CHICAGO BEARS FOOTBALL CLUB, INC.
(Club)

Witnesses:
                                                  By _Geo Halas_

....   By _JT Sternaman_

....

Original copy to be held by Club Management

                                                  Edward J Kawal

A typical NFL player's contract from 1931. Players and team owners of the early 1930s were dealing with salaries in the area of $100 to $150 a game, not the complex multi-year contracts of today involving hundreds of thousands, sometimes even millions, of dollars in salary and other benefits. –Sternaman Collection

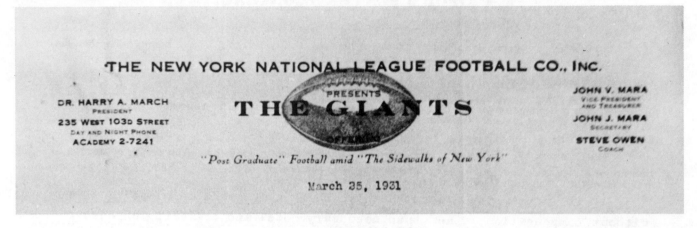

The New York Giants of 1931 claimed in their letterhead to offer "Post Graduate" Football amid "The Sidewalks of New York."
–Sternaman Collection

of the field, attended by several policemen wearing side arms. He raised his hat several times, developing a slight crease in one sleeve and two secretaries tore for the phones to summon his valets. However, two dozen pants pressers jumped out of nearby seats to smooth things out and a critical situation in the affairs of the local state was averted.

"A bit of scandal occurred when the mayor entered the governor's box to sit through the game with him. People had understood that they were sore at each other . . . and their apparent amity during the game gave rise to ugly rumors of a reconciliation which, to the adherents of each, would be a discredit to both.

"The mayor . . . and Mr. Smith fell to sparring during the first quarter, but no blows were struck and it developed that Mr. Walker was merely demonstrating the favorite punch of his favorite prize fighter, Max Rosenbloom."

The combat on the field of play was much less refined. As most of the Chicago Bear—New York Giant games of that era were, this one was a bruising, grind-it-out defensive match. The Giants made the first real move. Late in the second period, they launched a sustained 95-yard drive, with Benny Friedman finally plunging into the end zone from the 3-yard line. The kick for the extra point was wide.

The Bears went to their passing attack in the second half. With completions from Carl Brumbaugh to Luke Johnsos and Red Grange, the Bears moved to the Giants' 8-yard line. But there the Giants' defense, spearheaded by rookie center Mel Hein, held. On an 8-yard, goal-to-go fourth down, the Bears shunned the field goal and Brumbaugh threw a pass, which was batted away. The Bears marched again in the same quarter. And this time, at the Giants' 25-yard line, reserve back Joe Lintzenich took a pitch-out from

Brumbaugh and threw a perfect pass to Johnsos in the end zone. Mel Hein broke through and blocked Brumbaugh's extra-point try, to keep the game tied at 6–6.

In the fourth quarter, the Bears drove all the way to the 1-yard line, but the Giants' defensive line was impregnable and the Bears had to turn the ball over. The Giants marched back up the field into Bear territory. But time was running out, and so was the Giants' good fortune—a Friedman pass was picked off by Bear tackle Link Lyman. Then, in a finish more typical of one engineered by a Johnny Unitas or a Ken Stabler, Carl Brumbaugh threw two quick passes to move the Bears back into Giant territory. With only 12 seconds remaining, he lofted a 28-yard pass into the hands of Gardie Grange, who raced with it into the end zone to give the Bears a 12–6 victory and dash the title hopes of the Giants.

1931 SEASON .615		
Won 8 Lost 5 Tied 0		
Ralph Jones—Coach	Bears	Opponents
Cleveland Indians	21	0
Green Bay Packers	0	7
New York Giants	6	0
Chicago Cardinals	26	13
Frankford (Pa.) Yellow Jackets	12	13
Green Bay Packers	2	6
Portsmouth (Ohio) Spartans	9	6
New York Giants	12	6
Brooklyn Dodgers	26	0
Chicago Cardinals	18	7
Portsmouth (Ohio) Spartans	0	3
Green Bay Packers	7	6
New York Giants	6	25
Totals	145	92

But even in his moment of glory, Gardie Grange, like so many other younger brothers throughout history, couldn't escape his brother's shadow. A Chicago newspaper carried this headline the next day: "Red Grange's Brother Beats Giants on Pass."

The Bears went on to defeat the Green Bay Packers, the two-time NFL defending champions, a few weeks later, 7–6, before 15,000 people in Wrigley Field. But losses to the Portsmouth Spartans and to the Giants, who came to Wrigley Field for revenge in the last game of the season, left the Bears with a third-place 8–5–0 record. Curly Lambeau's Packers won their third straight league title (12–2–0), with Portsmouth right behind them (11–3–0).

Red Grange ran for five touchdowns during the year, caught two touchdown passes, and again led the team in scoring, with 42 total points. He ranked fifth in the league after four other Hall of Fame backs—Johnny Blood (of the Green Bay Packers), Ernie Nevers (Chicago Cardinals), Earl ("Dutch") Clark (Portsmouth Spartans), and Ken Strong (Staten Island Stapletons).

In Chicago Bear legend, the 1930s belong to Bronko Nagurski. Stories and reminiscences about him—most true, some no doubt exaggerated—abound.

"Here's a check for $10,000, Nagurski," said Dick Richards, owner of the Detroit Lions, in 1934. "Not for playing with the Lions, because you belong to the Bears, but just to quit and get the hell out of the league. You're ruining my team."

In one game, head down, charging like a bull, Nagurski blasted through two tacklers at the goal line as if they were a pair of old-time saloon doors, through the end zone, and full speed into the brick retaining wall behind it. The sickening thud reverberated throughout the stadium. "That last guy really gave me a good lick," he allegedly said to an ashen-faced Coach Halas after he trotted back to the bench.

Cal Hubbard, of the Green Bay Packers, himself one of the most punishing tackles in the pro game, remembers, "One time Bronko hit me from behind and I thought a grandstand had collapsed on me."

Everyone who played against Bronko Nagurski recalls the experience with pain, awe, or simply recurrent nightmares. Red Grange, who played only with him, never against him, said many years later: "He was the best player I ever saw. He had the power of Larry Csonka, but was faster, and he was equal to or better than [Dick] Butkus on defense."

By 1932, Bronko Nagurski was a fixture in the Bear backfield on offense and as a linebacker on defense. Teamed with him was Grange, whose running abilities

were diminished only in comparison to how he had carried the ball before damaging his knee. Grange was still an excellent receiver and passer too, and probably the finest defensive back in the game. The other running back slot was filled alternately by Dick Nesbitt and by Johnny ("Big Train") Sisk, who had just come to the Bears from Marquette University. Keith Molesworth was now sharing the starting quarterback position with Carl Brumbaugh. In his last year of play, George Trafton, for the first time since the Staley/Bear team began back in 1920, was not starting at center. Signed to replace him was Charles ("Ookie") Miller, from Purdue. For 1932 the Bears also added one of the finest ends they would ever acquire, future Hall-of-Famer Bill Hewitt, who came from the University of Michigan and was always recognizable on the field because he declined to wear a helmet. Joe Kopcha, who had returned from retirement and was at the same time studying to be a physician, and Zuck Carlson were excellent guards. The starting tackles now that Link Lyman had announced his retirement were Lloyd Burdick and Paul ("Tiny") Engebretsen. Luke Johnsos was back once again at the end opposite Hewitt. It was Ralph Jones's third year as head coach, his last chance to fulfill the promise he had made to Halas and

Another Bear intimidator of the 1930s was Dutch Clark, shown in action here, who played first for the Portsmouth Spartans and later for the Detroit Lions. A single-wing tailback and true triple-threat, he was the NFL's top scorer in 1932, 1935, and 1936 and led the Lions to their first NFL title in 1935. –Pro Football Hall of Fame

Bronko Nagurski, one of the most awesome players in the history of football, spent his entire professional career with the Bears. He was enormous, powerful, fast, and equally adept at tackling, blocking, or carrying the ball. When a person is inducted into the Pro Football Hall of Fame, which Nagurski was as a charter member, a ring is given as a symbol of the honor. Nagurski's turned out to be the largest that Josten's Inc. has ever had to make, and they produce more than a million rings a year. The size was 19½ (the average man's ring size is 10).
–Pro Football Hall of Fame

Sternaman when he was hired—to bring the Bears a championship within three years.

The league itself reached an all-time low in 1932. The Great Depression was at its worst, and its disastrous effects were felt everywhere, from the dust bowl of Oklahoma to the bread lines on a Chicago street. There were only eight teams in the NFL that year: the Bears, Green Bay Packers, Chicago Cardinals, New York Giants, Brooklyn Dodgers, Portsmouth Spartans, Staten Island Stapletons, and a new franchise called the Boston Braves (after the baseball team whose field they shared). Part owner of the Braves was George Preston Marshall, who also owned a chain of laundries in Washington, D.C. Marshall was an erstwhile actor and politician, later a newspaper publisher, and forever a promoter whose elegance of dress and dramatic presence would often stir memories of the redoubtable C. C. Pyle. With his innovative ideas and managerial skills, Marshall would become one of the great contributors to the success of the National Football League and a charter member of the Hall of Fame. His stormy relationship with George Halas over the years, marked by feuds and friendship, mutual respect and fierce competition, would also become a legendary part of NFL history.

The Green Bay Packers, winners of the last three NFL titles, were the team to beat in 1932. But the Portsmouth Spartans, with their great tailback Dutch Clark and bulldozer-like running back Leroy ("Ace") Gutowsky, were a formidable threat too, as both the Bears and the Packers would find out. Green Bay still had a fortress-like line headed by Cal Hubbard and Iron Mike Michalske, and the superb running and pass catching skills of Johnny Blood. But two new stars were added to round out the Packer backfield that year. Clarke Hinkle from Bucknell, an unusually powerful fullback, had been signed up after Curly Lambeau saw him play in the East/West Shrine game at the end of the previous college season. The other newcomer, at least to the starting line-up, was Arnie Herber, a resident Green Bay boy who had played at the University of Wisconsin and Regis College and for two years had served as back-up tailback to Verne Lewellen on the Packers. These five men gave the Packers the distinction of having five future Hall of Fame members on their 1932 starting team. (One of these players, Cal Hubbard, would also be enshrined in baseball's Hall of Fame—honored as an umpire—the only man to earn this accolade in both sports.)

The Bears showed that they too were in contention when they traveled up to Green Bay for the first game of the season and played the favored Pack to a scoreless tie. But then the Bears went to New York and were themselves held to a 0–0 tie by the league's weakest team, the Staten Island Stapletons. From there, it was back to Chicago and Comiskey Park, where they met the Cardinals—now without the services of Ernie Nevers, who had retired—and ended up in yet another scoreless tie. After the Bears' home opener on October 16 against the Packers, they were *still* relegated to that awful limbo of the scoreless, but this time, even with Nagurski and Grange in their backfield, they suffered their first loss of the season as well. The final score was Green Bay 2 and the Bears 0. Their fans were beginning to ask, with reason, if the Bears had any kind of offensive attack at all. Never in their 12-year history had they gone four straight games without posting one point on the scoreboard. It took the most supreme optimist to find consolation in the fact that the Bears' defense had not allowed a single offensive score in any of the four games either.

When the Stapletons arrived at Wrigley Field the following Sunday, the Bears proved that worries about their offense were groundless. In the first half, the proverbial ice was broken when on a fourth-down play quarterback Keith Molesworth laid a perfect pass into the waiting arms of Red Grange in the end zone. A taste of it was enough to get the Bears going; they went on to score 21 more points and chalk up their first win of the year, 27–7. The Bears did not lose another game, which paved the way for a classic showdown with the Packers on the last day of the season. The Packers, at this point, could hope only to be spoilers in the Bears' bid for the league title. The Portsmouth Spartans had ended their season the Sunday before by handing the Pack their second defeat of the year, 19–0. In those days, tie games were totally disregarded in figuring the winning percentages, so Portsmouth's record of 6–1–4 eliminated Green Bay, then with a 10–2–1 record, no matter what happened in the Bear-Packer game. If the Packers won, they would end in second place and the Bears would drop to third. But if the Packers lost, the Bears, with a 6–1–6 record, and the Spartans would be in a tie for first place—their win percentage .857 to the Packers' .769.

It had snowed the night before and most of the morning in Chicago on December 11, and it was still coming down when the Packers and Bears lined up for the kickoff at Wrigley Field that afternoon. Great banks of snow had been plowed along the sidelines, and the wind whipped the loose flakes into icy twister-like clouds. With the temperature only a few degrees above zero, it was not a fit day for player, spectator, or sled dog. By the middle of the first half, neither the players nor the officials could see the yard markers. The weather was miserable enough to keep the crowd down to 5,000 brave and dedicated souls who came fortified with long underwear, huge coats and mufflers, and a wide array of bootleg liquor carried in hip flasks.

The first half was a comic ballet of slip and slide over a snow-packed field, and neither team came close to a scoring threat. In the fourth quarter, however, the Bears managed to get down to the Packers' 14-yard line, where Tiny Engebretsen kicked a field goal. The Bears then held the Pack, and when they took over, Bronko Nagurski thundered off tackle and somehow raced through the snow 56 yards for a touchdown. The Bears won 9–0 and had themselves a tie for first place in the NFL.

In 1932, the first playoff game to decide the NFL title was played indoors at the Chicago Stadium on an 80-yard-long field that was the first ever to employ hashmarks. More than 11,000 people paid about $15,000 to sit snugly inside instead of outside where the temperature was below zero and the ground a mass of snow and ice. They watched Bronko Nagurski lob a short pass into the end zone to Red Grange to break a 0–0 tie late in the game and give the Bears the 1932 NFL championship. –Pro Football Hall of Fame

It was decided to have a playoff game to determine who should own the league title for 1932. This first playoff in NFL history was scheduled for the following Sunday at Wrigley Field.

Chicago might just as well have been in the Arctic Circle the week between the Bear-Packer game and the NFL championship game. The snow continued on and off, and the temperature sank below the zero mark. Even if they succeeded in keeping the snow off the field, the playing surface there would have the character of precast concrete. Halas and Sternaman were quick to see that even though the NFL title was at stake, they would not be able to entice anyone to Wrigley Field—except for a few Roman stoics and a handful of other masochists. So Halas contacted Joe Carr at the NFL office (which was in Columbus, Ohio, in those days) and the management of the Portsmouth team and got their approval to play the game *indoors*, at the Chicago Stadium. The Bears had done that once before, in an exhibition game back at the end of the 1930 season, and it had worked . . . with certain modifications.

The modifications for the 1932 game included a field only 80 yards long, with a single goal post that had to be moved up to the goal line. The playing field could only be 145 feet wide (a normal field was 160 feet). The wall separating the spectators from the field would only be a few feet from the sideline, so it was agreed that any ball downed within 10 yards of a sideline or one that went out-of-bounds would be brought 10 yards inbounds for the next play. And that really was the beginning of inbounds-marking, or hashmarks, in pro football.

The Bears and the Spartans were fortunate in that a circus had performed in the stadium the week before and a six-inch bed of dirt remained on the cement floor of the arena. All they had to do was lay down some sod and they had a fine outdoor-type field, infinitely softer than the frozen one beneath the snow at Wrigley Field.

More than 11,000 people paid to watch the now-famous indoor championship game, and they were exposed to the violence of professional football in a way that spectators in outdoor stadiums never were. In the enclosed stadium, the sounds of impact when players blocked or tackled each other resounded through the acoustically controlled hall. "It was the difference," one sportswriter noted, "between sitting ringside at a heavyweight fight or in the last row of the upper deck; all the awful sounds of human beings smashing other human beings were right there and very real." Another observer recalled that the stadium "was a little too aromatic, what with the horses and elephants that had traipsed around there a few days before the game."

Besides having to improvise and adapt for the game itself, the Portsmouth Spartans ran into another, and much more serious, problem. Their tailback and kicker, Dutch Clark, who had led the league in scoring that year (55 points), had to report to his off-season job as basketball coach at Colorado College before the title game was to be played. (When he signed his contract to coach, he had had no idea the season would be extended a week.) So Dutch Clark was on his way to Colorado Springs when his teammates were embarking for Chicago. Ace Gutowsky was moved from fullback to tailback for the game.

The first three quarters of the game was all defense, with several goal-line stands providing the only excitement. Red Grange was knocked out on one play after gaining 15 yards on an end run and had to be carried from the field. He would be back, however, to the chagrin of Portsmouth.

In the fourth quarter, Portsmouth was deep in its own territory when Gutowsky flipped a short pass that was picked off by the Bears' defensive back, Dick Nesbitt, who ran it back to the Spartans' 7-yard line. On first down, Bronko Nagurski burst through for 5 yards, but on the next two downs he could not get more than a foot or two. With fourth down and goal to go, the Spartans massed at the line of scrimmage, certain that the mighty Bronk would try once more to break through. It appeared they were right when

1932 SEASON .889*

Won 8 Lost 1 Tied 6

Ralph Jones—Coach	Bears	Opponents
Green Bay Packers	0	0
Staten Island Stapletons	0	0
Chicago Cardinals	0	0
Green Bay Packers	0	2
Brooklyn Dodgers	13	0
Staten Island Stapletons	27	7
Boston Redskins	7	7
New York Giants	28	8
Portsmouth (Ohio) Spartans	13	13
Brooklyn Dodgers	20	0
Chicago Cardinals	34	0
Portsmouth (Ohio) Spartans	7	7
New York Giants	6	0
Green Bay Packers	9	0

NFL Championship

	Bears	Opponents
Portsmouth (Ohio) Spartans	9	0
(Played indoors on 80-yard field)		
Totals	173	44

*All statistics include title game

The 1932 Championship Bears. Top row: Dr. J. F. Davis, Charles Tackwell, John Sisk, John Doehring, Bill Buckler, Paul Franklin, Tiny Engebretsen, Andy Lotshaw, Ralph Jones. Middle row: Charlie Bidwill, George Trafton, Don Murry, Lloyd Burdick, Gil Bergerson, Bronko Nagurski, Luke Johnsos, Bert Pearson, George Halas. Bottom row: Dick Nesbitt, Bill Hewitt, Carl Brumbaugh, Keith Molesworth, Red Grange, George Corbett, Ookie Miller, Jules Carlson, Joe Kopcha. –Pro Football Hall of Fame

Nagurski surged forward and took the handoff from Carl Brumbaugh. But instead of smashing straight into the struggling mass of humanity before him, he stopped, backpedaled a few steps, and lobbed the ball over the bodies flailing about on the goal line. Red Grange was alone in the end zone waiting for it.

The Spartans' coach, Potsy Clark, flew off the bench, shrieking at the official who was standing at the goal line with his arms held straight up signifying a touchdown. The pass was illegal, Clark screamed. In 1932, as in all the years before, a forward pass could not be thrown from anywhere less than five yards behind the line of scrimmage. Clark, who by this time was out in the middle of the field, stomped, gestured, and shouted that Nagurski was nowhere close to the minimum five yards back when he threw the ball. It was a judgment call, however, and like so many other coaches and players over the years, Clark found that no matter how vehement his objections, the official was not going to change his decision. When they finally got Potsy Clark off the playing field, Tiny Engebretsen kicked the extra point. A few minutes later Mule Wilson, the Portsmouth fullback, fumbled in his own end zone and the ball rolled out of it for an automatic safety and a 9–0 win for the Bears. Coach Ralph Jones had fulfilled his promise to George Halas and Dutch Sternaman. He had led the Bears to their first NFL title since 1921, the year they had won the first officially-recognized championship.

The 1932 season was the first for which the NFL attempted to compile individual statistics. From what was recorded that year—the statistics include the playoff game—Cliff Battles of the fourth-place Boston Braves was the leading rusher (576 yards, a 3.9 average), Arnie Herber of Green Bay the leading passer (37 completions out of 101 passes thrown), and Luke Johnsos of the Bears the leading receiver (24 for 321 yards).

For the Bears, the "also-ran" years were over. The powerhouse Bears who would cause people to start referring to them as the "Monsters of the Midway" were about to make their entrance as the dominant factor in the game through most of the next decade and a half.

HALAS GOES IT ALONE

CHAMPIONS OR NOT, the Chicago Bears' 1932 season was a dreadful failure at the box office. The Depression had hit pro football as it had every other way of earning a living in America. And at the end of the season the Bears showed a deficit of $18,000. It was the only year they lost money, with the exception of the $71.63 they had dropped back in 1921. In the cash-tight economy of 1932 a loss of $18,000 was indeed a devastating one.

George Halas and Dutch Sternaman were faced with the fact that they could not even pay out of their operating revenue all the salary commitments to their players much less the other assorted bills that come with the pleasure of owning a pro football team. They also agreed that it was now time for the Bears, as a team and an organization, to become a one-man show. The partnership was no longer a happy one for either man, and with the overwhelming financial problems that had cropped up, it seemed only feasible for one of them to step out. Which one, was the real question.

George Halas had always been center stage in the operations of the Chicago Bears, dealing with the public, the press, and the NFL organization. Dutch Sternaman was much more a behind-the-scenes administrator, more the businessman and coaching strategist than the promoter.

Neither man, up to this time, had implied that he might be willing to sell his holdings. To everyone, it was readily apparent that Halas wanted to keep the Bears. No one was really sure about Sternaman; he had other interests, in the oil business and in real estate. The two of them got together in private, thrashed around the idea of one buying the other out, and finally came to an agreement whereby Halas would purchase all of Dutch Sternaman's interests in the team for $38,000, to be paid in several installments over the next year. It shows perhaps how much Halas really wanted the Bears, because he did not have that much cash at his disposal then and it was no easy job digging up money for investment in the early 1930s. But he did it, borrowing money from a bank and persuading such people to invest as his mother, former Bear guard Jim McMillen, and George Trafton's mother. Another investor, a friend of Halas, was Charles W. Bidwill, who would shortly become the owner of the Chicago Cardinals and in the future a Hall-of-Famer.

The Chicago Bears of 1933, defending NFL champions with a roster of greats and near-greats and a pile of large debts, were faced with the dismal economic outlook for the country as well as the team and were now in need of a coach. Ralph Jones had resigned to go back to Lake Forest College as athletic director. The whole mixed bag—all the pleasures and problems that were the Chicago Bears—became George Halas's alone. He promptly hired himself back as coach—"For this year only!" he said to the press; when he recalled

WRIGLEY FIELD HOME OF THE BEARS

CHICAGO BEARS FOOTBALL CLUB
INCORPORATED

GEO. S. HALAS
PRESIDENT-TREASURER

J. W. McMILLEN
VICE-PRESIDENT

SECRETARY

TELEPHONES
DAY-FRANKLIN 6040
NIGHT-LONGBEACH 4433

111 WEST WASHINGTON STREET
CHICAGO

February 27, 1934.

Mr. Edward C. Sternaman,
c/o Public Service Petroleum Co.
2856 Diversey Blvd.
Chicago, Illinois.

Dear Sir:

I am enclosing my check #1794 in the amount of $10.05
covering balance due you. I was of the opinion that you
were to send me an itemized statement, but I guess it will
do if you will just receipt and return the enclosed bill.

I still have the note for $21.25 from the Planters Operating
Company and any time you are in the loop, I will be glad to
step across the street and see if we could collect on the
note.

Very truly yours,

Geo. S. Halas.

GSH:JG

Closing out the books on the Halas/Sternaman partnership. –Sternaman Collection

that statement years later, he added: "It turned out to be an awfully long year."

Up through 1932, success in pro football had been a combination of defense and well-executed running plays. Scoring was low, however, and ties were all too common. In fact, there was a total of 10 ties in the 48 games played in the 1932 season. Six of those ties involved the Chicago Bears. And the Bears, the highest-scoring team in the NFL in 1932, averaged only 11 points a game, against a mere three by their opponents. A lot of people around the NFL were thinking that the game could surely benefit from a little more excitement—higher scoring, wide-open offenses with more passing, a faster more unpredictable game, more games posted in the won-lost columns than as meaningless ties. Foremost among these people were George Halas, who was now the chairman of the NFL's

After a three-season absence, George Halas returned to the Bear bench in 1933, when Ralph Jones resigned as head coach. This would be Papa Bear's first season as the sole head coach of the team. He claimed at the time it would be "for this year only," but, of course, it wasn't. Halas remained as head coach all the way through the 1967 season, with only two brief interludes—1942-45, when he served in the U.S. Navy, and 1956-57, when he relinquished the head coaching duties to Paddy Driscoll. –Pro Football Hall of Fame

Rules Committee, and George Preston Marshall. Marshall had become full owner of the Boston franchise after the 1932 season, when it lost $46,000, and the first thing he did was to change the team's name to the Boston Redskins. In keeping with the Redskin motif, he hired an Indian coach, Will ("Lone Star") Dietz, and even went so far as to have each player dress for the team picture in war paint and an Indian headdress. Halas and Marshall conferred on what could be done to improve the game. At the February meeting of all NFL owners, they introduced three important rules changes, all of which were adopted. First, it would now be legal to throw a pass from anywhere behind the line of scrimmage, which would truly open up the passing game. Second, to encourage field-goal kicking (and increase scoring), the goal posts were to be moved up to the goal lines. Third, hashmarks, or inbounds-lines, would be chalked 10 yards in from each sideline and the ball would be placed there anytime it was downed within five yards of the sideline or when it went out-of-bounds. (The hashmarks were gradually brought in even more in the following years.)

Two of the rules changes, not so surprisingly, sounded like the unwritten ground rules used so successfully for the indoor championship game played some two months earlier. And, as Halas was quick to realize, the touchdown pass—legal or otherwise—in that same game had added excitement to a contest that up to then was all defense. Joe Carr, NFL president, said that the new rules "would make the game more spectacular and put the 'foot' back in football."

George Halas lost no time in taking advantage of the new rules. Immediately, the Bronko Nagurski fake plunge and jump pass became a standard in the Bears' playbook. Halas also signed up Jack Manders, an excellent field-goal and extra-point kicker from the University of Minnesota who, Halas knew, would be just that much better with the 10-yard end zone now clipped off the distance to the goal posts. He was right; "Automatic Jack" Manders, as he came to be called, would turn out to be one of the finest kicking specialists in the game. In one stretch, beginning with the opening game in 1933 and continuing through part of the 1937 season, he would kick 72 consecutive points after touchdowns.

The Bears also added a huge lineman, George Musso (6-feet-2, 257 pounds), from Milliken College, and Link Lyman returned from retirement to resume his position as one of the tackles. Bill Karr, from West Virginia, and Luke Johnsos traded off at the end opposite Bill Hewitt until Johnsos broke his ankle midway through the season. Karr had actually come to Chicago to see the Century of Progress exposition in

A pre-season warm-up, featuring Bill Hewitt (left) and Bronko Nagurski. The brawn of Nagurski and the sinew of Hewitt symbolize the Bears of 1933-34, a team many considered to be one of the greatest ever to play professional football. —Pro Football Hall of Fame

the summer of 1933, ran out of money, and decided to take up an earlier offer from Halas of a tryout with the Bears after he graduated. A fine back by the name of Gene Ronzani from Marquette University was also recruited to spell the aging Red Grange in the running department. For the first time, Halas, following the Cardinals' lead, took his players out of Chicago for pre-season training. He set up camp down on the Notre Dame practice field in South Bend, Indiana.

Three new teams came up with the $2,500 the NFL charged for a 1933 franchise, the Cincinnati Reds and two in Pennsylvania, where the blue laws had just been repealed—the Philadelphia Eagles and the Pittsburgh Pirates. The Eagles were owned by future Hall-of-Famer Bert Bell and Lud Wray; the Pirates by another Hall-of-Famer, Art Rooney, who it is said founded his team with the winnings from a big day at the racetrack. The Staten Island Stapletons folded, bringing the NFL to a total of 10 teams. That's when George Preston Marshall came up with the brainstorm to separate the league into two five-team divisions, with the winners of both to meet in an "official" championship game at the end of the season. Marshall's proposal was unanimously accepted by the other team owners. This was the first real face-lift of the league organization and one that would remain, evolving eventually into the divisional and conference playoffs and Super Bowl of today.

By 1933, only two small cities, Portsmouth and Green Bay, retained franchises in the NFL. But the Packers almost went out of business early in the season when a fan who fell out of their temporary stands sued the club and was awarded $5,000. The Packers' insurance companies couldn't pay this (they had gone broke), and the club went into receivership, only to be rescued at the last minute by a group of townsmen, calling themselves the "Hungry Five," who were dedicated to keeping pro football in Green Bay and who had saved the franchise from folding in 1923.

In the NFL's new alignment, both the Packers and Portsmouth Spartans were in the Western Division, along with the Bears, Chicago Cardinals, and Cincinnati Reds.

With Nagurski powering up the middle or faking and throwing little jump passes to Hewitt, Karr, or Johnsos, the precision kicking of "Automatic Jack" Manders, and a defense that was allowing an average of only 5.5 points a game, the Bears breezed through their first six games and appeared to be on their way to a third NFL title. The "also-ran Bears" were now being called the "storybook Bears," and George Halas was truly enjoying his return to coaching. The kind of football the Bears were playing was exemplified in an early-season win over the Cardinals. Losing 9–0, the Bears pulled this bit of chicanery: Hewitt on an end-around took a handoff from Carl Brumbaugh, and as the Cardinals moved in on him, lofted a long pass to Luke Johnsos in the end zone. It was a surprise "end-to-end pass play" that he and Johnsos had worked up in practice. Manders' extra point and a safety on the Cardinals' next set of downs tied the score. Then another Manders field goal in the last one-and-a-half minutes of the game brought victory.

The Bears climbed aboard the train in downtown Chicago to take their 6–0–0 record on a three-game eastern tour and found that their storybook had suddenly run out of pages. They were shut out 10–0 by a young Boston Redskin team, led by Cliff Battles, held to a 3–3 tie by what had appeared to be a threatless Philadelphia Eagles squad, and then beaten 3–0 by the New York Giants. It was an awakening to their mortality, but nothing more, as it turned out. When the Bears returned to Chicago they put their act back in order and won the remaining four games of the season. Their record of 10–2–1 was far and away the best in the NFL West (Portsmouth was a poor second, with six wins and five losses). The Bears would face the New York Giants in the first divisional NFL championship game. The Giants had won 11 of 14 games, but one of their three losses was to the Bears. Even so, they were rugged competition, fielding future Hall-of-

Famers like Ken Strong, Mel Hein, and Ray Flaherty, and All-Pro players like end Morris ("Red") Badgro and quarterback Harry Newman.

The NFL was now keeping official records, both individual and team, with separate statistics for regular-season and post-season games, which was not the case in 1932. The Giants' sensational rookie quarterback, Harry Newman, ran away with the league passing record (973 yards and 53 completions, 11 for touchdowns). Jack Manders of the Bears led the league in extra points (14) and tied for first place in field goals (six) with Glenn Presnell of the Portsmouth Spartans. Tailback Presnell, who had taken over for first-stringer Dutch Clark (he opted to stay on at Colorado) after sitting on the bench for two years, ended up tying for the league lead in total points scored (64) with the Giants' Ken Strong.

In Chicago on the day of the championship game, it was foggy, and a thin mist made being outside even worse. But in the damp cold and on a gradually muddying field, a game filled with strange and spectacular plays was about to keep 26,000 spectators on the edges of their wooden seats that Sunday afternoon in Wrigley Field. The attendance was only a little more than half the 40,000-seat capacity of the ball park, however. But pro football had come of age, one could say, because now there was a press box filled with writers from the Chicago papers and the wire services. And Bob Elson was there to announce the play-by-play action over WGN radio for the Chicago sports fans who decided not to sit in the rain that day.

The razzle-dazzle began right in the first period. In fact, the groundwork had actually been set before the game started, when the Giants' coach, Steve Owen, and center Mel Hein cornered the officials and explained a trick—but legal—play they were planning to spring on the Bears. Mel Hein, the star of this red-herring scenario, described it himself: "We put all the linemen on my right except the left end. Then he shifted back a yard, making me end man on the line, while the wingback moved up on the line on the right. Harry Newman came right up under me, like a T-formation quarterback. I handed the ball to him between my legs and he immediately put it right back in my hands—the shortest forward pass on record. [Newman instantly faded back as if to pass, then deliberately slipped and fell to attract all would-be tacklers.] The idea was that I would just stroll with the ball up in my shirt. Well, I got started walking down the field, but after a few yards I got excited and started to run, and the Bears' safety, Keith Molesworth, saw me and knocked me down. I got about 30 yards but I didn't score." This was probably the only "center-with-ball-hidden-under-shirt-keeper-play" in the history of the NFL.

The Bears scored in the first half on two field goals by Jack Manders, one a 40-yarder. But the Giants tied it up with a Newman-to-Badgro 29-yard touchdown pass and then took the lead on Ken Strong's extra point. In the third quarter, Manders added another field goal, and the Bears regained the lead, 9–7. Newman came right back and threw five consecutive completions, bringing the Giants to the Bears' 1-yard line, where Max Krause bulled in for the touchdown. Strong kicked the extra point. The Bears were also explosive. After the Giants' kickoff, the Bears pulled off a third-down 67-yard play, with halfback George Corbett passing to Carl Brumbaugh, who ran the ball to the Giants' 8-yard line. On the next play, Bronko Nagurski took the handoff from Brumbaugh and, reminiscent of his performance in the indoor championship game the year before, charged the line, then backed up and lobbed a short pass over the heads of the linemen and into the waiting hands of Bill Karr, just inside the end zone. Manders kicked the extra point, and the Bears were back in the lead, 16–14.

Newman, however, continued his dazzling display of passing, with four straight completions this time, and the ball was on the Bears' 8-yard line. Then came another Giant play right out of fantasyland. Unlike the center-sneak by Mel Hein though, this one was not pre-planned. Fullback Ken Strong, a central figure in the play, explained it this way: "Newman handed off to me on a reverse to the left, but the line was jammed up. I turned and saw Newman standing there [back at about the 15-yard line], so I threw him the ball. He was quite surprised. He took off to the right, but then he got bottled up. By now, I had crossed into the end zone and the Bears had forgotten me. Newman saw me wildly waving my hands and threw me the ball." Then, revealing a little about the football stadiums in those days, he added: "I caught it and fell into the first-base dugout." Strong kicked the extra point, and the score was Giants 21, Bears 16.

Time was running out in the fourth quarter now, but the Bears had penetrated to the Giants' 33-yard line. Nagurski took a handoff and rifled a short pass to Bill Hewitt, who started downfield. When Hewitt saw Ken Strong and a defensive halfback closing in, he whirled and flipped a lateral to Bill Karr, who was streaking out behind him. Gene Ronzani put the finishing touch to the play by taking out both Strong and the other Giant defender. "Well, I kind of got an angle on Strong, and I guess I must have thrown a pretty good block," Ronzani later said, "because those two fellows there, I knocked them right on their cans."

Karr raced untouched along the sideline for a Bear touchdown. The kick for the extra point was good, and the Bears led 23–21.

When the Giants got the ball again, there were only seconds remaining in the game. Newman faded back and threw his 12th completion for the day (of 17 attempts) to wingback Dale Burnett, who was open in the Bears' secondary. Racing a few steps behind Burnett was Mel Hein, ready to take a lateral if necessary. Only one man was between Burnett and the Bears' goal line—Red Grange. Burnett knew that when Grange hit him, all he had to do was lateral the ball off to Hein, who would go all the way with no one left to stop him. Unfortunately for the Giants, Grange knew that too. "I could see he wanted to lateral," Grange said afterward, "so I didn't go low. I hit him around the ball and pinned his arms." Both men went down in a heap, the ball safely wedged between their bodies by Grange's bear-hug tackle. As Tim Mara, the owner of the Giants, put it, "Red Grange saved the game for Chicago . . . that quick thinking prevented a score on the last play." George Halas was not as subdued in his assessment: "That play Grange made was the greatest defensive play I ever saw," he said.

And so the Bears slogged off a muddy field in Chicago, NFL champions for the second year in a row. Each player's share of the title game gate was $210.34; each of the losers took $140.22 with him back to New York City—a long way from the $15,000 that a Super Bowl winner in the 1970s would pick up for playing in a championship game.

Even though their NFL season was over, the Bears would play eight more games; these and four others

This is the famous lateral from Bill Hewitt (he never wore a helmet) to end Bill Karr, who then took the ball in for the Bears' game-winning touchdown against the Giants at Wrigley Field in the NFL's first divisional championship game, held December 17, 1933. The final score: the Bears 23, the Giants 21. –Pro Football Hall of Fame

1933 SEASON	.833	
Won 10 Lost 2 Tied 1		
George Halas—Coach	Bears	Opponents
Green Bay Packers . . . .(A)	14	7
Boston Redskins . . . .(H)	7	0
Brooklyn Dodgers . . . .(A)	10	0
Chicago Cardinals . . . .(H)	12	9
Green Bay Packers . . . .(H)	10	7
New York Giants. . . . .(H)	14	10
Boston Redskins . . . .(A)	0	10
Philadelphia Eagles . . . .(A)	3	3
New York Giants. . . . .(A)	0	3
Portsmouth (Ohio) Spartans . . .(H)	17	14
Chicago Cardinals. . . . .(H)	22	6
Portsmouth (Ohio) Spartans . . .(A)	17	7
Green Bay Packers . . . .(H)	7	6
Totals	133	82
NFL CHAMPIONSHIP		
New York Giants. . . . .(H)	23	21

earlier were exhibition games. Their schedule had included pick-up and semi-pro teams before, and would continue to include them for years to come, but only in the 1925 season, which the Red Grange tours overlapped, did they play more games (28) than they did during and after the regular 1933 season (26). The Bears this time compiled a seemingly impressive 12–0 record against the non-league squads, though judging from some of the scores—60–0 (over the Cicero Boosters), 55–0 (over the Arizona All-Stars)—most of the teams they played could hardly be qualified as serious competitors.

The Chicago Bears who took the field the following year were as great a team as the all-time greatest, many have said, ranking up there along with the Bears of 1941; the 1950 Cleveland Browns, whose incredible roster consisted of future Hall-of-Famers Otto Graham,

The only picture known to exist of the 1933 NFL champion Chicago Bears (taken in Washington, D.C.). From left: Cookie Tackwell, Keith Molesworth, Bill Karr, Gil Bergerson, Bull Doehring, Bill Hewitt, Gene Ronzani, Dick Nesbitt, Ray Richards, George Corbett, Joe

Marion Motley, Dante Lavelli, Bill Willis, and Lou Groza, as well as Mac Speedie, Alex Agase, Abe Gibron, and Dub Jones; the Green Bay Packers of the last few Vince Lombardi years; and the undefeated Miami Dolphins of 1972.

The Bears added a new halfback in 1934, a young man from the University of Tennessee with the unlikely name, for a football player, of Beattie Feathers. At 5-feet-10 and 185 pounds, he was both an elusive runner and one with fine acceleration and power. George Halas, envisioning this explosive new runner carrying the ball behind the ferocious blocking of Nagurski, even brought back the single-wing to be used along with the Bears' split-T formation. The combination enabled Feathers to become the first runner to gain more than 1,000 yards in a single season (1,004 yards in 101 carries). In fact, his average gain that year of 9.94 yards per carry is to this day an NFL record, one that appears about as unbeatable as Joe DiMaggio's consecutive game hitting streak of 56. Second to Feathers in this particular record category, incidentally, though well behind him with an average of 6.87 yards per carry, is another Chicago Bear, quarterback Bobby Douglass, who managed that in 1972.

There were several innovations in the game in 1934. A new football was introduced, one that was reduced to a more slender, aerodynamic form by taking an inch off its girth, making it much more suitable to the forward pass. The "cantaloupe-shaped ball," as George Halas called it, was gone forever, and with it the drop-kick that had been so much a part of the Bears' offensive attack in the days of Joey Sternaman and Paddy Driscoll. To help the place-kickers, the use of a kicking tee, albeit one specified as dirt, was legalized. This probably made it possible for Jack Manders of the Bears to become the first person to kick 10 field goals in a season, a record that would

endure until 1950, when Lou Groza kicked 13. And it was the first time a quarterback threw a forward pass behind his back. John ("Bull") Doehring of the Bears arched one just that way *30 yards* to Luke Johnsos, who was so astonished that he dropped the ball in the end zone. It was also the year that the Bears would become the first team in NFL history to go through an entire regular season undefeated and untied.

But the biggest "first" of that year was the initiation of the College All-Star game. According to Dutch Sternaman, it was one of the four key developments in the early years of pro football. "The game in Arcola that was never played brought in the concept of recruiting," he once said. "Then, the meeting in Canton in 1920 gave the sport some organization. After that, the Red Grange tour with the Bears in 1925 introduced the sport to most of the country. And finally, the College All-Star game made people aware of just how good pro football and the men who played it really were. After that, no one could ever look on it as something less than the game played by the college boys."

The College All-Star game was the brainchild of *Chicago Tribune* sports editor Arch Ward. From 1934 through 1976, when it was discontinued, it would launch every pro football season except one; it was canceled in 1974 because of the NFL players/owners dispute of that year. All the proceeds from the game (millions of dollars over the years) were given over to charity, under the sponsorship of Chicago Tribune Charities. All the games were played at Soldier Field in Chicago, with the exception of two during World War II that were played 15 miles north of there in Northwestern University's Dyche Stadium. The Chicago Bears played in seven of these games; the only team to appear in more was Green Bay, with eight. The first All-Star game turned out to be the only one in the

Kopcha, Bronko Nagurski, Jules Carlson, Ookie Miller, George Musso, Jack Manders, George Halas, Red Grange, Carl Brumbaugh, Joe Zeller, Johnny Sisk, Link Lyman, Bill Buckler, Luke Johnsos. –Pro Football Hall of Fame

history of the pre-season classic that ended in a scoreless tie. The so-called powerhouse Bears couldn't post a single point, and the game was described as "deadly dull." Nevertheless, a crowd of 79,432 came out to watch it, substantially more than the 26,000 who had shown up for the NFL championship game the previous season. College football players, it seems, could still bring out the fans.

With that exhibition game out of the way, however, the Chicago Bears quickly went out and showed all skeptics just how good they really were. In their first nine games, no NFL opponent came within 13 points of the Bears. By the end of the regular season, the Bears had scored a total of 286 points in their 13 victories and held their opponents to a meager 86. Their 22-point average per game was almost double

Two stalwarts of the Chicago Bears of 1934, guard Joe Kopcha (left) and scatback Beattie Feathers. Kopcha played five seasons with the Bears and was an All-Pro three of them. Feathers' four years with the Bears were highlighted by a sensational rookie year (1934) in which he set two NFL records when he rushed for 1,004 yards and averaged 9.94 yards per carry. –Chicago Bears

Beattie Feathers has the ball here, hurdling Bear Bronko Nagurski (3), on his way to pick up a few yards against the Green Bay Packers in one of the two games the Bears beat the Packers in the 1934 regular season. The other Bears are Carl Brumbaugh (8), Joe Kopcha (29), Ed Kawal (19), Gene Ronzani (6), and George Musso (without the helmet). –Chicago Bears

Bull Doehring, one of the more unusual backs in Chicago Bear history. He could throw a pass behind his back as far and as accurately as an average player could overhand. In one game, he threw a 30-yard behind-the-back pass to Luke Johnsos, who was so bedazzled by it that he dropped the ball in the end zone. Doehring had an extraordinarily strong passing arm. It was said that he never threw the ball as far as he could because no receiver was fast enough to get that far downfield. –Pro Football Hall of Fame

what the 1932 championship Bears were able to tally. The last two of the Bears' games were against the second-place (10–3–0) Lions, the former Portsmouth Spartans franchise whose new owner had moved the team to Detroit that same year. The Lions, who had posted seven consecutive shutouts, again had the services of the team's former star, Dutch Clark. Only Jack Manders of the Bears scored more points (76) than Clark (73) in the league that season.

The Bears, undisputed champions of the NFL West, climbed aboard the New York Central to travel to Manhattan and take on the New York Giants, whose less-than-spectacular record of 8–5–0 had been enough to win the NFL East title that year. Two of the Giants' losses had in fact been to the Bears: 27–7 at Wrigley Field and 10–9 at the Polo Grounds. The Bears were a heavy favorite to win their third straight NFL crown.

But as George Halas so aptly put it many years later, "Looking back [to 1934] . . . I often wonder whether it isn't better to be lucky than good." The first star-crossed event had occurred near the end of the season, when the Bears were proceeding to maul the Cardinals out at Wrigley Field. Beattie Feathers, after a crushing tackle on the sideline by 6-foot-5, 230- pound tackle Lou Gordon, was led off the field with a shoulder separation, out for the remainder of the year. The second misfortune was caused by the weather at the Polo Grounds on the day of the title game.

Because of the bitter cold (9 degrees above zero), Steve Owen took his team out on the field early for warm-ups that day. The entire playing field was covered over with a hard, slick coating of ice, and everyone just kept skidding around. Finally, the Giants' captain, Ray Flaherty, suggested to Steve Owen, "Coach, why not wear basketball shoes?" He went on to explain that while he was playing college ball at

Gonzaga his coach once had the team wear sneakers on an icy field because of the traction they could provide. Owen thought it might work—anything would be an improvement—but he had no idea where he could come up with enough pairs of gym shoes on a Sunday afternoon. Gus Mauch, the Giants' trainer, had the answer. He was also the trainer for Manhattan College's basketball team and was sure there were plenty of sneakers in the lockers in that school's gym. Maybe the Giants could borrow them for the day. Steve Owen grabbed Abe Cohen, a tailor, old-time fan, and sometime clubhouse attendant, and dispatched him in a cab to the Manhattan campus. It has been variously reported over the years that he then broke all the lockers open with a hammer (Cohen's story) or was given a master key to open them (Mauch's story). But how he did it is really irrelevant; the important fact was that he managed to get nine pairs of the shoes and deliver them at half-time to Coach Owen. By then, the Bears had somehow skated to a 10–3 lead on a touchdown by Bronko Nagurski and the extra-point and field-goal kicks by Jack Manders.

Arch Ward, long-time sports editor of the Chicago Tribune *and early booster of the Chicago Bears, was instrumental in establishing the College All-Star football game which became a pre-season tradition in the NFL from 1934 through 1976. The Bears played in seven of the 42 All-Star games (won 5, lost 1, tied 1).* –Pro Football Hall of Fame

This action scene, with Bill Hewitt (56) in the foreground, is from the 1934 Bear-Lion game in Detroit. The identifiable Lions here are Glenn Presnell (3), Ox Emerson (20), Jack Johnson (16), and Dutch Clark (7, on the ground). No. 26 on the Bears is center Milford Miller. The Bears won that game 19–16, on the way to their first undefeated season and a Western Division title. –Pro Football Hall of Fame

Eight of the mighty Chicago Bears of 1933 rally for this promotional photo taken at the Polo Grounds a few days before they played the New York Giants in a regular-season game (one of the only two games the Bears would lose that year). Hurdling (from the left) are Bear backs Keith Molesworth, Jack Manders, Red Grange, and Bronko Nagurski; the linemen are George Musso, Bill Buckler, Ray Richards, and Link Lyman. This copy of the photo also carries the autographs of Grange and Nagurski.
–Pro Football Hall of Fame

The second half, however, was a different story. More than 35,000 spectators, chilled to the bone by this time, watched Manders put another three points on the board for the Bears. But in the fourth quarter, the Giants, keeping their hands on the ball and their gym-shoe-clad feet on the ground, came up with one of the most astonishing turnabouts in pro football history. Suddenly Ken Strong was running hard and the Bear defenders were sliding all over the place. He chalked up two touchdowns, one a 42-yard run. And a minute or so later, tailback Ed Danowski, who had passed for the Giants' first touchdown, ran another one in by himself. Four touchdowns in the last 10 minutes of the game, and the Bears, helpless on the ice, went down to their first defeat in 18 league games. The New York Giants had won their second NFL title, by a score of 30–13.

The Giant fans went wild and stormed the field. Their team could hardly get to the locker room. When they finally did get in out of the cold, reporters flocked to Ken Strong for quotes on how the amazing turn of events had come about. Strong just shook his head. "I'm no hero," he said, and pointed to the little elderly man, bundled in a heavy overcoat, sitting over in the corner. "Abe's the real hero of the game." And when the full story was told about the "Sneakers Championship," even the press agreed. The next day Lewis

The closest any team came to beating the Bears during the 1934 regular season were the New York Giants, who entertained them late in the season at the Polo Grounds. But with less than a minute to go in the game, Jack Manders kicked this field goal to give the Bears a 10–9 victory. The holder is quarterback Carl Brumbaugh; the Bears blocking (and watching the flight of the ball) are Ookie Miller (76), Zuck Carlson (20), Link Lyman (not blocking anyone), and Bill Hewitt, blocking the Giants' No. 36. –Pro Football Hall of Fame

Getting set to assault the New York Giants' line in the 1934 championship game is Bear fullback Bronko Nagurski, ready here to take what was called a shuffle pass in the 1930s—something midway between a handoff and a pitch-out that the Bears used to get the ball to Nagurski quickly. About to shuffle the ball to him is Bear quarterback Carl Brumbaugh. –Pro Football Hall of Fame

Teaming up to bring down Bronko Nagurski on an ice-covered field during the 1934 NFL championship game between the Bears and the New York Giants are Mel Hein (left) and Ray Flaherty. The Giants went on to win the title that day, 30–13, when they donned sneakers for the second half. –Pro Football Hall of Fame

Burton wrote in the *New York American:* "To the heroes of antiquity, to the Greek who raced across the Marathon plain, and to Paul Revere, add now the name of Abe Cohen."

For the Bears it was a sad finale to what had been their most glorious season. It also marked the end of the playing days of Red Grange, now 31, and Link Lyman, 36, two of the finest football players ever to wear pro uniforms. A few weeks later, in an exhibition game against the Giants that the Bears won 21–0, Grange would make one more run with the ball, only to be caught from behind by a lineman—unimaginable as that might have seemed at one time. He said about this later: "I realized before I reached midfield that I was through. My legs kept getting heavier and heavier. I knew I'd never reach the end zone, but that I had reached the end." And with him ended the Bears' first real dynasty. So too ended the era in pro football when the strategy of running with the ball and occasionally augmenting the attack with a forward pass was the standard. The new rule that allowed a pass to be thrown from anywhere behind the line of scrimmage, and the new streamlined football, had opened up the game, adding a different dimension to gaining yardage and scoring touchdowns.

1934 SEASON 1.000
Won 13   Lost 0

George Halas—Coach	Bears	Opponents
Green Bay Packers ....(A)	24	10
Cincinnati Reds..........(A)	21	3
Brooklyn Dodgers ....(A)	21	7
Pittsburgh Pirates...........(A)	28	0
Chicago Cardinals ....(A)	20	0
Cincinnati Reds............(H)	41	7
Green Bay Packers ....(H)	27	14
New York Giants...........(H)	27	7
Boston Redskins ....(A)	21	0
New York Giants...........(A)	10	9
Chicago Cardinals..........(H)	17	6
Detroit Lions..............(A)	19	16
Detroit Lions..............(H)	10	7
Totals................	286	86

NFL CHAMPIONSHIP

New York Giants...........(A)	13	30

THE ROLLER-COASTER YEARS

EVEN THOUGH THE BEARS lost the 1934 title game, they had never had a better regular-season record. But in professional football things can change quickly and dramatically.

In 1935 the Bears began the routine of conducting their pre-season training in Delafield, Wisconsin, on the grounds of St. John's Military Academy, a private school there. Bronko Nagurski was now suffering from a growth on his hipbone that would keep him out of the line-up for most of the season, and Beattie Feathers, with a nagging pain from his shoulder injury the year before and a variety of new ailments, would have a poor season when he did play. Bernie Masterson, a second-string quarterback from the year before, was moved up to replace Carl Brumbaugh, who had decided to retire.

At the end of August, George Halas brought his team down to Chicago to face the College All-Stars at Soldier Field. (It was more convenient and economically sound that year for the All-Stars to play the Bears rather than the titleholders, the Giants.) A crowd of 77,450 showed up to watch the Bears eke out a 5–0 victory over an All-Star team that had a tall, rangy end from the University of Alabama by the name of Don Hutson; a rugged center from Michigan, Gerald Ford by name, who even then was thinking about a career in politics; and a tough but articulate quarterback from North Dakota, Irv Kupcinet, who later as a result of his

column in the *Chicago Sun-Times* and his television talk show would come to be known as "Mr. Chicago." For 29 years (1948-76), Kup would also announce the Bear games on radio, with Bert Wilson, the former Chicago Cubs radio broadcaster, for the first five years, and the rest of the time, with Jack Brickhouse, for many years the voice of the Cubs on television.

In their first game of the 1935 season, the Bears learned just how good Green Bay rookie Don Hutson was. On his first play in the game, he faked a cut and then streaked past safety Beattie Feathers. Arnie Herber's long pass was right on the mark, and Hutson took it over his shoulder without even breaking stride, an 83-yard touchdown play that was enough to beat the Bears 7–0. To show that this wasn't just a fluke, a month later down at Wrigley Field, Hutson caught two touchdown passes in the last five minutes of the game to give the Pack a come-from-behind, 17–14 victory. Hutson would prove to be good enough to be chosen a charter member of the Hall of Fame.

The Bears also lost to the Giants (3–0) and to the Detroit Lions (14–2), who went on to win their first NFL championship. The Bears ended up with a 6–4–2 record, in third place in the NFL West behind both Detroit and Green Bay. It was a disappointing year. Even Jack Manders, the NFL field-goal record-holder, was able to come up with only one successful kick in eight attempts, the worst season "Automatic Jack"

Don Hutson arrived at Green Bay in 1935 and stayed around to wreak disaster in the Bear secondary for 11 long years. He scored his first NFL touchdown in the opening game of the 1935 regular season against the Bears up at Green Bay, one of 105 career touchdowns (99 of them on pass catches). Hutson—six-time All-Pro, five-time NFL scoring leader, eight-time pass-reception leader—became the most legendary end in the game's history. –Pro Football Hall of Fame

would ever have with the Bears. Joe Kopcha was named All-Pro for the third year in a row and was joined on the All-Pro team that year by tackle George Musso and end Bill Karr, but this was about the only plus of the season.

Bert Bell, whom George Halas once referred to as the "owner, coach, ticket seller, and head cheerleader with the Philadelphia Eagles," was also unhappy with the way things were going. His team, perennially in last or next-to-last place in their division, needed some rebuilding too. The problem was that some of the teams in the league just were not making a lot of money and couldn't afford to lure the best prospects into their camps; while the more prosperous clubs like the Bears, Giants, and Redskins had more money to lavish on the big-name stars. "Lavish" in the mid-1930s, it should be explained, meant a $5,000 salary for an established star. Salaries of $1,500 to $2,500 a year were more common.

Bert Bell wanted to even things out, which he felt would not only help the Eagles but also make the league itself more competitive and therefore more exciting. So, he proposed a "draft" of college players. The team that ended up a season with the worst record would have first choice of the graduating seniors of that year. The team with the next-worst record would have second choice, and so on until each team had a selection. This was the prototype of the college draft that is employed today by the NFL. Bell's proposal was adopted, and the annual draft was launched along with the 1936 season.

The Philadelphia Eagles had first choice in the new draft and selected Jay Berwanger, the nation's first Heisman Trophy winner and an All-American from the University of Chicago. But when they felt they could not meet the salary he would demand, they traded their rights to negotiate with him to the Bears. Halas could meet the salary demand, or at least he could bargain with the young man until a feasible figure was agreed upon. It didn't matter, however, because Berwanger chose not to play pro ball anyway. The Bears fared very well in the first NFL draft nonetheless. Their first pick was tackle Joe Stydahar, from the University of West Virginia, and their last was guard Danny Fortmann, from Colgate. Both young men would play key roles in the Bears' future, handling their jobs so well that they would both be enshrined in the Pro Football Hall of Fame. The Bears also drafted a halfback from Cincinnati, Ray Nolting, who would prove to be an important addition to the Bear backfield over the next nine seasons. Carl Brumbaugh came back from his one-year retirement, but Joe Kopcha was traded to Detroit, where he had asked to go so he could finish up his medical studies in that city.

1935 SEASON	.600	
Won 6 Lost 4 Tied 2		
George Halas—Coach	**Bears**	**Opponents**
Green Bay Packers . . . .(A)	0	7
Pittsburgh Pirates. . . . .(A)	23	7
Philadelphia Eagles . . . .(A)	39	0
Brooklyn Dodgers . . . .(H)	24	14
Green Bay Packers . . . .(H)	14	17
New York Giants. . . . .(A)	20	3
Boston Redskins . . . .(A)	30	14
New York Giants. . . . .(H)	0	3
Detroit Lions. . . . .(H)	20	20
Detroit Lions. . . . .(A)	2	14
Chicago Cardinals . . . .(H)	7	7
Chicago Cardinals . . . .(A)	13	0
Totals	192	106

The Chicago Bears, pictured here in whatever uniforms they could muster up, are lined up at a practice field the team used before the 1935 season while the Chicago Cubs were still occupying Wrigley Field. In the backfield (from the left) are Gene Ronzani, Bronko Nagurski, Carl Brumbaugh, and Keith Molesworth; the linemen are Bill Karr, George Musso, Madison Pearson, Ed Kawal, Zuck Carlson, Link Lyman, and Bill Hewitt. Brumbaugh, Pearson, and Lyman were not in the line-up when the regular season started. –Pro Football Hall of Fame

For the first time since the NFL was formed, all the teams would play the same number of games. There were no franchise shifts in 1936, but there was a new American Football League, which—even with players like Harry Newman, Ken Strong, and Red Badgro—would barely manage to survive for two seasons before it folded.

The Bears were clearly on the way back in 1936, winning nine games—the first six in a row—and losing only three. Jack Manders, back in stride, led the league in field goals for the third time. The Bears finished second in their division, behind the Packers. With a combined attack of passing from Arnie Herber to Don Hutson (34 receptions that year, a record, for eight touchdowns) and Clarke Hinkle's powerful running, Green Bay was devastating. The Packers were good enough to go on and win the NFL title that year by defeating the Boston Redskins, a squad that included future Hall-of-Famers Cliff Battles, Wayne Millner, and Glen ("Turk") Edwards, as well as Pug Rentner and Ed Justice. The Redskins' owner, George Preston Marshall, was so mad at the fans in their hometown and their apparent lack of interest in his team that he arranged to have the title game played in New York instead of Boston. And the following year he moved his whole team down to Washington.

There were a few new faces on the 1937 Bear roster—end Edgar ("Eggs") Manske had been acquired from the Eagles and Frank Bausch, a rugged center and linebacker, from the Redskins. The Bears' first-round draft pick was end Les McDonald, from the University of Nebraska, and another draft choice was end Dick Plasman, from Vanderbilt. Gone, however, was the familiar curly head of Bill Hewitt, whom Halas had traded to the Eagles for their first-round draft choice, fullback Sam Francis from Nebraska. The Bears would rue that trade, because Hewitt still had several All-Pro seasons left in him.

The Bears were an improved team in 1937, and easily won their first five games before being held to a surprisingly low-scoring 3–3 tie by the New York Giants. After that they were beaten decisively by the Green Bay Packers, 24–14, in front of the largest crowd that up to then had ever assembled in Wrigley Field to watch the Bears play football. Paid attendance was 44,977. The excitement that day, unfortunately for

---

1936 SEASON   .750

Won 9   Lost 3

George Halas—Coach		Bears	Opponents
Green Bay Packers	(A)	30	3
Philadelphia Eagles	(A)	17	0
Pittsburgh Pirates	(A)	27	9
Chicago Cardinals	(H)	7	3
Pittsburgh Pirates	(H)	26	7
Detroit Lions	(H)	12	10
Green Bay Packers	(H)	10	21
New York Giants	(A)	25	7
Boston Redskins	(A)	26	0
Philadelphia Eagles	(A)	28	7
Detroit Lions	(A)	7	13
Chicago Cardinals	(A)	7	14
Totals		222	94

staunch Bear fans, was generated mainly by the Pack's Herber-to-Hutson passing combination.

Shrugging off that setback, the Bears went on to win their last four games in a row and ended the season as champs of the NFL West, with a 9–1–1 record. The last game of the season was a 42–28 victory over the Chicago Cardinals that set a record for the largest number of points ever scored by two teams in an NFL regular-season game, even though the last few minutes of it had to be called off because of darkness. Bear heroics for the year would have to go to the fine running of Bronko Nagurski, Ray Nolting, and Jack Manders behind the line play of such All-Pros as Joe Stydahar, George Musso, and Danny Fortmann.

The Bears were now about to make the personal acquaintance of "Slingin' Sammy" Baugh, a product

of Texas Christian University and George Preston Marshall's first-round draft pick that year. Led by rookie Baugh, who was destined for charter membership in the Hall of Fame, the Washington Redskins had won their division title easily. Marshall had thought highly of Sammy Baugh from the moment he selected him to be a Redskin. Ever the showman, Marshall called Baugh on the telephone and told the 23-year-old Texan how he wanted him to report to Washington before pre-season training and said he was sending him an airplane ticket. Reporters, photographers, and newsreel cameramen would await his arrival at the Washington airport, Marshall went on, and then inquired as to whether Baugh had some Texas cowboy boots and a 10-gallon hat. He did not, Baugh replied. "Then go out and buy some," Marshall said. "I want you wearing them when you step off the plane here in Washington. I'll pay you for them when you get here." Marshall wanted his new acquisition to look like the quintessential Texan.

In 1936, Danny Fortmann was 20 years old, a Phi Beta Kappa from Colgate University, and the last-round selection of the Chicago Bears in the NFL's first college football player draft. For a guard who was required to play offense and defense in those days he was rather small (6-feet-0, 205 pounds), but despite his size he won All-Pro honors six times in an eight-year career. –Pro Football Hall of Fame

Joe Stydahar came to the Bears in 1936 from West Virginia University, their first pick in the first college football draft ever held. He stayed for nine seasons, broken into two segments by a two-year stint in the military during World War II. A great tackle, he was named All-Pro four consecutive times. Like end Bill Hewitt, Stydahar often played the game without a helmet in the early years of his career. –Pro Football Hall of Fame

This Bear pass from Beattie Feathers to Bill Hewitt was good for a touchdown, but the Chicago Cardinals beat the Bears 14–7 in that 1936 game at Wrigley Field. It would not be until after World War II, however, that the Cardinals would fully exploit their long-time rivalry with the Bears by consistently spoiling the Bears' chances for division titles. –Pro Football Hall of Fame

This 1936 action shot is one of those rare ones that show Bronko Nagurski (3) doing nothing detrimental to the opposing team. The Green Bay Packer coming over the top is Ade Schwammel. Bear No. 76 is center Ookie Miller. –Pro Football Hall of Fame

Baugh was, of course, one of the finest draft choices Marshall, or anyone else for that matter, ever made. He proved this in his first season by leading the league in pass completions (81) and total passing yardage (1,127). He would also prove to be one of the NFL's all-time great punters. The Bears would learn his worth in the championship game of 1937.

Wrigley Field on December 12, 1937, was arctic, with a temperature of 15 degrees above zero and a 12-mile-an-hour wind. The field was frozen solid and encrusted with a treacherous veneer of ice. All the ballyhoo that goes with a championship game could not attract more than 16,000 hardy fans to view the contest.

Both teams came out on the field wearing sneakers, obviously having learned a lesson from Steve Owen and his Giants in 1934. The Bears planned to rely on the power of their running attack—Nagurski and Manders up the middle and Ray Nolting around the ends. The Redskins were going to mix it up, depending on the running of Cliff Battles, who had led the league in rushing that year, and on the passing of Sammy Baugh.

Washington scored first on a 7-yard run by Battles, but the Bears came right back, marched down the field, and eventually scored on a 10-yard run by Jack Manders. When the Bears got the ball again, they

Clarke Hinkle, the Green Bay Packers' powerful running back, teamed with the great passing combination of tailback Arnie Herber and end Don Hutson to lead the Pack to the 1936 NFL title. But despite their efforts, the Bears beat them up at Green Bay, 30–3, in the opening game of the season. –Pro Football Hall of Fame

Order on Chicago Bears Box Office

Sunday, Oct. 25 1936 — **Chicago Bears vs. Detroit Lions**

PLEASE SELL TO BEARER

MR. ....

NOTICE This order must be **exchanged not later than 5:00 P. M.** on Saturday, Oct. 24th at Spalding's, 211 S. State Street.

ONE TICKET $1.65 Federal Tax and Service Charge **50c**

.... MANAGER

NOT EXCHANGEABLE AT WRIGLEY FIELD

surprisingly took to the air themselves, with Bernie Masterson throwing a 37-yard pass to Manders for another Chicago touchdown. At half-time, the Bears held a 14–7 lead. In the third quarter, however, Sammy Baugh countered with a 55-yard pass to Wayne Millner for a Redskin touchdown. Then the Bears came back with a 3-yard pass from Masterson to Eggs Manske, and Chicago regained the lead, 21–14. With the Redskins trailing by a touchdown in the fourth quarter, time was now a factor. But this didn't seem to bother Sammy Baugh. He tied up the game quickly with one spectacular 78-yard pass play to Wayne Millner, and then in the final moments he added another touchdown by flipping a 35-yard pass to Ed Justice. As sportswriter Shirley Povich put it: "From the stabbing efforts of Baugh's rapier-like heaves, the big bruising Chicago Bears, Champions of the West, reeled and stumbled and finally yielded to the Redskins 28–21." "Slingin' Sammy" ended the day with 18 completions (33 attempts), three of them for touchdowns, and a total of 335 yards. He showed everyone in the stadium and those who listened to the game on the radio that the forward pass as a weapon was here to stay.

The loss was a heartbreaker for the Bears, who thought they had come back to the glory days of 1933 and instead were again defeated by a team with a poorer season record (8–3–0) than theirs. George Preston Marshall, relishing his first NFL title, rubbed it in to his friendly enemy, George Halas, not knowing just how enormous and awful a revenge the Bears

---

At one point in the Bear-Redskin championship game of 1937, George Preston Marshall, owner of the Washington team, saw a Bear player take a punch at his prize quarterback Sammy Baugh. Enraged, he stormed down onto the playing field and began a violent argument with George Halas. Marshall's wife, movie star Corinne Griffith, in her book My Life with the Redskins, tells what happened next, which gives more than a little insight into the famous Halas/Marshall relationship:

Somehow, they had been pushed over to the Bear bench in front of our box. Halas was saying: "You dirty _____ , get up in that box where you belong. It's too bad it ain't a cage. Now laugh that off."

"You shut that _____ mouth of yours, or I'll punch those _____ gold teeth right down that red throat!"

One of the Bear players started for him. George [Marshall] seemed to think that a good time to leave. He stomped back to the box, snorted as he sat down and, of course, took it out on me.

"What's the matter with you? You look white as a sheet!"

"Oh, that was awful!"

"What was awful?"

"That horrible language. We heard every word."

"Well, you shouldn't listen."

"Oh, you. And right in front of ladies. . . . And as for that man Halas!" Every hair of George's raccoon coat bristled. "He's positively revolt——"

"Don't you dare say anything against Halas," George was actually shaking his finger under my nose. "He's my best friend!"

would wreak on the Redskins the next time they met to determine the NFL championship.

By 1938, Americans were sharing their worries about the economy with concern over the growing

---

Clarke Hinkle, great fullback for the Green Bay Packers during the 1930s, waged a continuing battle with the Bears' Bronko Nagurski. Collisions on the field between the two were often described in the same terms as head-on railroad crashes. Hinkle, who carries his own scars from them, once broke the Bronk's nose and a rib in one violent meeting. But George Musso remembers one game in which Hinkle, with the ball, ran past him in the line only to meet Nagurski, who hit Hinkle so hard he sent him backpedaling past Musso until he regained his balance and then surged by Musso again—"the only time I ever saw a back go by me three times on one play," Musso said. When Hinkle was inducted into the Hall of Fame in 1964, he had Bronko Nagurski serve as his official presenter.

Just as Bear center George Trafton took to the boxing ring in the late 1920s to earn extra money, Bronko Nagurski a few years later found a source of added income in professional wrestling. It made for a busy schedule. Chicago sportswriter Howard Roberts reported that in one 22-day period in 1937 Nagurski played in five Bear football games and wrestled in eight heavyweight matches, each in a different city—from Philadelphia and west to Los Angeles, from Vancouver (British Columbia) and south to Phoenix. –Pro Football Hall of Fame

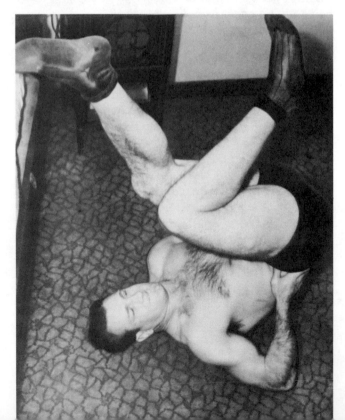

George Preston Marshall was never at a loss for ways to promote his Redskins, the team he founded in Boston and moved to Washington. His entanglements over the years with George Halas became legend, their relationship a wonderful mixture of feuds and friendship. –Pro Football Hall of Fame

threat of war in Europe. To add to the gloom among Chicago Bear fans, Bronko Nagurski retired, taking football's single most intimidating weapon back up to International Falls, Minnesota. Beattie Feathers, who had never repeated the running heroics of his 1,000-yard-plus season in 1934, was traded to the Brooklyn Dodgers, and Keith Molesworth departed to coach at the U.S. Naval Academy in Annapolis, Maryland. To bolster their now-weakened running attack, the Bears signed up Bobby Swisher, from Northwestern University, and Gary Famiglietti, from Boston, and acquired Joe Maniaci from the Brooklyn Dodgers in mid-season.

Nothing, however, went especially well for the Bears that year. Although Bernie Masterson ranked fifth in the league in passing, the running attack was noticeably weak and Jack Manders could only manage three field goals all season. After making a promising start by winning their first three games, the Bears ended up with a lusterless 6–5–0 record—their worst since 1929—in third place behind Green Bay and Detroit. There was one interesting development during the year, however, and it was the inspiration of Luke Johnsos, now a key assistant coach to George Halas. Johnsos thought he could get a better perspective of the action on the field by watching the game from an overall vantage point in the upper deck. It was a good idea, obviously, and one that would soon be adopted by all other teams. How to communicate with the coach down on the field, however, was another matter.

In the late 1930s, there were no walkie-talkie or telephone set-ups as there would be later. So the spotter had to relay what he observed in other ways. One method Johnsos used at Ebbets Field in Brooklyn was to write his notes on a piece of paper, wad it up, and drop it over the railing, which just happened to be above the rear of the Bears' bench. The Dodger fans, it is said, caught on to what he was doing and sabotaged his efforts by crumpling up their own notes and raining them down on the Bear bench along with those from Johnsos.

The year 1939 was a dramatic one everywhere—a year of ultimates. World War II broke out in Europe. The United States began quietly building for its possible involvement in the war. And at the opposite extreme, the fad of swallowing live goldfish spread

Rookie halfback Bobby Swisher (48) from Northwestern University moves out for the Bears here behind the interference of tackle Joe Stydahar (13). The game is against the Green Bay Packers in 1938. Swisher played for the Bears five years. –Pro Football Hall of Fame

Bronko Nagurski thunders off left end in the NFL championship game of 1937. He gained 15 yards on the play, but this game belonged to the Washington Redskins, who earned the NFL title that afternoon by defeating the Bears 28–21. Other Bears in the picture are George Wilson (30), Joe Stydahar (13), and Eggs Manske (18). The Redskins are Turk Edwards (17), Les Olsson (21), and Jim Barber (15). –Pro Football Hall of Fame

through college campuses across the nation. For the first time in 14 years Lou Gehrig, after playing in 2,130 consecutive games, finally sat one out on the bench. And sadly for the NFL, it was the year that future Hall-of-Famer Joe Carr, its president since 1921, died. Carl Storck was named acting president. It was also the year of the first Pro Bowl game, a public relations stratagem initiated by George Preston Marshall. The first game, played in January, pitted the Pro All-Stars against the 1938 NFL champions, the New York Giants, who won 13–10. Joe Stydahar was the only Bear starter in that first Pro Bowl game.

It was also a year for some revolutionizing behind the scenes by the Bears. George Halas, with the help of Clark Shaughnessy, who was in the words of Halas ''a sort of advisory coach,'' began to modernize the split-T formation. Both knew that the game of professional football was rapidly becoming one dominated by the forward pass. They had handled and tossed the new slenderized ball; they had seen and experienced what Don Hutson and Sammy Baugh could do to a team's defense. Halas and Shaughnessy felt that the most effective way of using the forward pass, however, could be from the T, which only the Bears used at that time—with some updating, that is. So they went to work devising new plays and blocking formations. Shaughnessy also developed a new signal-calling system to accompany the new plays. The Bears were on

PHILADELPHIA EAGLES
vs.
CHICAGO BEARS
Sunday, November 19, 1939
WRIGLEY FIELD · CHICAGO

the threshold of changing their image from a team whose offense was built around devastating runners—the memories still fresh of Grange, Nagurski, Feathers, and Nolting—to a team with a balanced offense, based on a strong passing attack complemented by a strong running game. Their modified split-T formation was to set the standard for all of professional football in the years to come.

What the Bears needed in 1939, however, was a quarterback. And the young man they wanted was finishing up at Columbia that year. His name was Sid Luckman. He played under Lou Little there, and had shown that he was both a fine runner and passer. Halas also knew that Luckman had a great football mind and therefore was the ideal candidate to engineer the Bears' newly streamlined and complicated split-T formation. But the Bears were not at the top of the list for the 1939 draft. Surely Luckman would go to another team before the Bears had a chance to get him, Halas feared. So Halas approached the Pittsburgh Pirates' owner, Art Rooney, whose team had the league's worst

Bear center Frank Bausch, who looks like he is about to throw a pass here, is in reality in the process of intercepting one in this 1939 game against the Green Bay Packers at Wrigley Field. Other Bears in the picture are Ray Bray (82) and Dick Bassi (35). No. 14 on the Packers is Don Hutson. The Bears won this particular game 30–27. –Pro Football Hall of Fame

1937 SEASON .900
Won 9   Lost 1   Tied 1

George Halas—Coach		Bears	Opponents
Green Bay Packers	(A)	14	2
Pittsburgh Pirates	(A)	7	0
Cleveland Rams	(A)	20	2
Chicago Cardinals	(H)	16	7
Detroit Lions	(H)	28	20
New York Giants	(A)	3	3
Green Bay Packers	(H)	14	24
Brooklyn Dodgers	(H)	29	7
Detroit Lions	(A)	13	0
Cleveland Rams	(H)	15	7
Chicago Cardinals	(A)	42	28
Totals		201	100

NFL CHAMPIONSHIP

Washington Redskins	(H)	21	28

1938 SEASON .545
Won 6   Lost 5

George Halas—Coach		Bears	Opponents
Chicago Cardinals	(H)	16	13
Green Bay Packers	(A)	2	0
Philadelphia Eagles	(A)	28	6
Cleveland Rams	(A)	7	14
Chicago Cardinals	(H)	34	28
Cleveland Rams	(H)	21	23
Detroit Lions	(H)	7	13
Green Bay Packers	(H)	17	24
Washington Redskins	(H)	31	7
Brooklyn Dodgers	(A)	24	6
Detroit Lions	(A)	7	14
Totals		194	148

1939 SEASON .727
Won 8   Lost 3

George Halas—Coach		Bears	Opponents
Cleveland Rams	(H)	30	21
Green Bay Packers	(A)	16	21
Pittsburgh Pirates	(A)	32	0
Cleveland Rams	(A)	35	21
Chicago Cardinals	(H)	44	7
New York Giants	(A)	13	16
Detroit Lions	(H)	0	10
Green Bay Packers	(H)	30	27
Detroit Lions	(A)	23	13
Philadelphia Eagles	(H)	27	14
Chicago Cardinals	(A)	48	7
Totals		298	157

A newcomer in 1939, and the man destined to launch the modernized T formation devised by George Halas and Clark Shaughnessy. —Pro Football Hall of Fame

A typical game-day scene at Wrigley Field in the mid-1930s. The best way to get to the ball park then was by streetcar, but there was also the El, the automobile, and even the double-decker buses of the day which stopped within a few blocks of the stadium. This picture was taken in October, 1935. –Chicago Transit Authority

record the preceding season, and worked out a trade for their first-round draft choice. Rooney selected Luckman and promptly sent him to the Bears.

The Bears' own first-round draft pick was running back Bill Osmanski, from Holy Cross, who rewarded them by becoming the league's leading rusher his very first year, grinding out a total of 699 yards with an average gain of 5.8 yards per carry. Osmanski would remain one of the best running backs in pro football, playing with the Chicago Bears for a total of seven

seasons, interrupted by two years in the Navy during World War II.

It took Sid Luckman and the Bears all of the 1939 season to experiment with and finally master the new T formation. In doing so, they recorded a respectable 8–3 record, but they ended up a full game behind the Green Bay Packers, who went on to win the NFL championship that year. But 1939 set the stage for an era of Chicago Bear domination, one of the most exciting in their entire history.

"THE PERFECT TEAM" OF 1940

ON DECEMBER 8, 1940, much of the world was in a rather gloomy state. Hitler's troops patrolled the streets of Paris and other European capitals, and Londoners cringed under the bombings of the German Luftwaffe. But in another world capital that day, at least outside government circles, the atmosphere was much less grim. Washington, D.C., was preparing for a football game. And not just an ordinary one. The Redskins, who in their brief four-year residency there, had captured the loyalty and pride of almost all Washingtonians, were playing the Chicago Bears that afternoon at Griffith Stadium for the NFL championship.

Pro football had come a long way by 1940, especially in Washington. The marching bands, assorted half-time entertainments, and other forms of pageantry that George Preston Marshall had injected into the Sunday afternoon shows in that city had paid off. Elsewhere too pro football had finally garnered the popularity it deserved. It was no longer the game that was frowned on in the 1920s for being mercenary and youth-corrupting; it was now perfectly respectable and looked on as a very exciting entertainment spectacle. For this championship game, which would pit the Bears' modern T formation against the long-time standard single-wing of the Redskins, more than 36,000 people would fill the seats and standing-room areas of Griffith Stadium. And hundreds of thousands of other fans would listen to Red Barber announce the game over the radio. This was the first time ever that a professional football game was to be broadcast on network radio, and the network had anted up $2,500 to beam the game to its 120 stations. College coaches, whose forerunners had so lustily condemned the professional game, now converged on the nation's capital to watch it and learn what they could from it. Lou Little came down from Columbia to see how his former protégé and single-wing tailback Sid Luckman would now handle a T-formation attack. Clark Shaughnessy of Stanford, master football tactician and co-formulator with George Halas of the Bears' modernized T, flew in from the Pacific Coast. Biff Evans and Glenn Presnell, coaches of the University of Nebraska, took time off from drilling their team for their upcoming Rose Bowl game to ride the train to Washington for the game.

The press box was filled with sportswriters from the wire services and major newspapers, many coming from other parts of the country. One of the columnists, Bob Considine, observed that they weren't the only ones traveling to the game that year. "We came down to the game from New York on the Lindy Institute Special. There couldn't have been a curbstone bettor left between Times Square and Columbus Circle," he wrote after seeing who his travel companions were. The gamblers who came were unwelcome guests to Messrs. Marshall and Halas, but it was impossible to

The starting quarterbacks of the 1940 title game, Sammy Baugh of the Washington Redskins (left) and Sid Luckman of the Chicago Bears. The two went head-to-head in a number of classic games. Besides being a great passer (he led the league in that category six times during his 16-year career) and punter (his lifetime average of 45.1 yards per punt is still an NFL record), Baugh was also a superb defensive back. —Left, Pro Football Hall of Fame; right, Chicago Bears

keep them away. They touted the game as a very close one, with the Bears about a 7-to-5 favorite. Not everyone agreed.

At the breakfast table in his Washington home on the morning of the game, George Preston Marshall said to his wife: "The so-called experts make us a slight underdog today . . . that's ridiculous. . . . We already beat them 7–3 [referring to the league game at Griffith Stadium against the Bears a few weeks earlier]. . . . Why, we only lost two games this year. . . . The bookmakers must be crazy."

At the hotel where the Bears were headquartered, George Halas and two of his assistant coaches, Hunk Anderson and Carl Brumbaugh, talked with a group of reporters. "Those guys [the odds-makers] must be crazy," said Halas, whose team had lost three of its games that year. "This game is an even-money game or nothing at all. Sure we've got power, but look at the Redskins—they have Sammy Baugh."

But Halas had been psychologically hyping the Bears for the game ever since he knew he would face Marshall's team for the NFL title. For the entire week preceding the game, the Bear locker room back in Chicago had been plastered with news clippings that Halas had hung everywhere possible. All of them contained the story of Marshall's comments after the Bears' 7–3 loss to his team earlier in the season. In the final seconds of that game, Bill Osmanski had gone up to grab a pass in the end zone but it bounced crazily off his chest. He always claimed that Redskin defender Frank Filchock had interfered with him. He yelled about it that afternoon too. And so did Halas, who raged out onto the field to add his protest because a penalty hadn't been called. But it was to no avail. And this prompted George Marshall, always delighted to give a wounded Halas the extra jab, to tell the press: "They're front-runners, quitters. They're not a second-half team, just a bunch of crybabies! They fold up when the going gets tough." Halas was furious when he first read about Marshall's remarks, and so were his players.

Now in the Bear locker room at Griffith Stadium, Halas brought out those same clippings and passed them out to the players waiting to go out on the field. "Gentlemen, this is what George Preston Marshall thinks of you," he reminded them. "*I* think you're a great football team, the greatest ever assembled. Go out on the field and prove it."

The day of the game was a beautiful one. The air was crisp, sunny, and clear. The temperature at game time was 39 degrees, and a two-mile-an-hour wind barely rustled the grass at Griffith Stadium. As the Bears took the field, the rabid hometown fans, accompanied by the Redskins' own marching band, went into

In the 1940 title game, the Bear defense was as awesome as the team's offense. Here Redskin fullback Jimmy Johnston gets a taste of it as he is ushered toward the sidelines and out-of-bounds at the hands of Sid Luckman. Other Bears converging to help out are Bill Osmanski (9), Joe Stydahar (13), George McAfee (5), Danny Fortmann (21), and John Siegal (6). –Pro Football Hall of Fame

a chorus of the Redskin fight song. Thousands of voices rang out with these somewhat unconventional lyrics:

> "Hail to the Redskins, Hail victory,
> Braves on the warpath, fight for old D.C.
> Scalp 'em, swamp 'em.
> We will take 'em big score,
> Read 'em, weep 'em,
> Touchdown, we want heap more."

In a box seat behind the Redskins' bench, an impeccably dressed George Preston Marshall sat with his wife and beamed at the enthusiastic crowd. It was a "perfect day for football," he observed to one of the Washington dignitaries who paid a visit to his box. He was delighted with the capacity turnout and boastful of his team, which besides Sammy Baugh included such greats of the 1940s as Ed Justice, Frank Filchock, Wayne Millner, Charlie Malone, Turk Edwards, "Wee Willie" Wilkin, and Steve Slivinski.

Across the field an equally optimistic George Halas stood by the Bears' bench and watched the officials gather the two teams' captains for the coin toss. One of the men in black and white, the head linesman, he knew well from Chicago, columnist Irv Kupcinet. The Bears won the flip, chose to receive, and precisely at 2:00 the game began.

Two and a half hours later, the Bears had amassed an incredible total of 73 points—to this day the most ever scored in *any* NFL regular-season, playoff, or championship game—and the Redskins had not posted a single one. When the final gun sounded, one reporter in the press booth turned to the man sitting next to him. "Marshall just shot himself!" he said.

It all began when the game was less than 55 seconds old. Bear fullback Bill Osmanski raced around left end for 68 yards and the Bears' first touchdown. George Wilson, who was known affectionately as "Quack-Quack" because he was so often used as a decoy on pass plays, threw a block that took out the last *two* Washington defenders, reminiscent of the great block thrown by Gene Ronzani to help the Bears win the 1933 NFL championship. The Bears posted 21 points in the first 13 minutes of the game, and the scoring frenzy would not end until, with less than three minutes left to play, Harry Clark crashed off right tackle for the Bears' 11th touchdown of the day. Ten different players contributed the 11 touchdowns, and six Bears added the team's seven extra points. Fifteen players in all each posted a score in the game.

Midway through the first half, the Redskin fans quit singing their battle song; a little later they stopped cheering. In the second half, the band stopped playing,

Bill Osmanski tries valiantly here to wrestle free of the clutches of Washington Redskin tackle "Wee Willie" Wilkin, but on this particular play he couldn't. It was, however, one of the few unsuccessful moments for the Bears on the afternoon they demolished the Redskins 73–0 in the 1940 NFL championship game. –Pro Football Hall of Fame

and George Preston Marshall was observed to be sitting there uneasily and uncharacteristically silent. When the score was 60–0, sportswriter Bob Considine noted, ". . . the most ill-advised announcement in the history of sport was made over the public address system. . . . 'Your attention is directed to a very important announcement regarding the sale of seats for the 1941 Redskin season.'" Those spectators who hadn't left the stadium suddenly broke their silence with a thunderous round of boos and then lapsed back into a state of dreary depression. It got so bad that when the next-to-last touchdown made the score 66–0, an official had to approach the Bear bench and ask Coach Halas if he would *not* try to kick any more extra points—so many balls had been booted into the stands already and confiscated by fans as souvenirs that the Redskins were down to their last football. Halas, always magnanimous with a 66-point lead in the fourth quarter, instructed his team to pass on the last two extra-point tries.

After the game, Bill Stern, famous radio sportscaster of that era, commented: "Some say . . . that George Marshall himself had nothing to say for a few minutes after the last whistle blew a merciful end to the slaughter." Marshall may have been speechless in the immediate moments after the debacle, but shortly thereafter he had plenty of words he wanted to dispose of. To the press, he said grumpily: "What can I say? Chicago was better than we expected. What else can I

The NFL Championship Game of 1940

Bears 73   Redskins 0

First Half

Bill Osmanski runs 68 yards for a touchdown.
Jack Manders kicks extra point.

Bears 7   Redskins 0

Sid Luckman scores on quarterback sneak, following an 80-yard drive.
Bob Snyder kicks extra point.

Bears 14   Redskins 0

Joe Maniaci runs 42 yards around end for score.
Phil Martinovich kicks extra point.

Bears 21   Redskins 0

Luckman passes to Ken Kavanaugh for 30-yard touchdown.
Snyder kicks extra point.

Bears 28   Redskins 0

Second Half

Hampton Pool intercepts Sammy Baugh's pass and runs 15 yards for touchdown.
Dick Plasman kicks extra point.

Bears 35   Redskins 0

Ray Nolting runs 23 yards for score.
Plasman misses extra point.

Bears 41   Redskins 0

George McAfee intercepts Roy Zimmerman's pass, runs it back 35 yards for touchdown.
Joe Stydahar kicks extra point.

Bears 48   Redskins 0

Bulldog Turner intercepts Zimmerman's pass, runs it back 20 yards for touchdown.
Maniaci's kick for extra point blocked.

Bears 54   Redskins 0

Harry Clark on double reverse goes 44 yards for score.
Gary Famiglietti misses extra point.

Bears 60   Redskins 0

Turner recovers muffed center snap on 2-yard line; Famiglietti bucks over for score.
Solly Sherman passes to Maniaci for extra point.

Bears 67   Redskins 0

Maniaci intercepts Frank Filchock's pass; Clark scores on 1-yard plunge.
Snyder's pass to Maniaci for extra point incomplete.

Bears 73   Redskins 0

George Halas, enjoying the situation to its fullest, later commented: "Some observers said the Bears were a perfect football team that day. I can't quite agree. Looking over the movies, I can see where we should have scored another touchdown."

say? We needed a 50-man line against their power. That's all there was to it. They won the championship, so what else can I say?" Sammy Baugh was more philosophical: "The teams were about equal. But after

Although this may look like a lateral to Bear tackle Joe Stydahar (13), in reality it is an airborne fumble from Redskin quarterback Sammy Baugh (33), the ball heading directly into the hands of Stydahar. This is a vivid illustration of how things were going for the Redskins in their 1940 championship match with the Bears. Also in the pile-up is Bear John Siegal (6). –Pro Football Hall of Fame

Statistics of the Championship Game

	Chicago Bears	Washington Redskins
First Downs	17	17
First downs rushing	13	4
First downs passing	3	10
First downs penalties	1	3
Yards Gained	501	245
Rushing	382	22
Passing	119	223
Passes Attempted	10	51
Passes completed	7	20
Passes intercepted by	8	0
Intercepted Passes Returned (yards)	117	0
Number of Punts	2	3
Average distance	46	41.3
Yards returned	28	4
Number of Penalties	3	8
Yards Penalized	25	70
Number of Fumbles	2	4
Opponents' Fumbles Recovered	1	1

we beat them once, we weren't quite as high as we should have been. They were higher than hell. . . ." And when Marshall had more time to think about the disaster that had just befallen him and his team, he found a few other things to say too: "We had the greatest crowd in Washington's history and we played our poorest game. I am mortified to think what we did to that crowd. . . . We were awful and you don't need to ask me if we are going to clean house. Some of the boys are going to be embarrassed when the time comes to make contracts for next year."

In the Bears' locker room, the scene was a mayhem-like mixture of jubilation and astonishment. As Eddie Gilmore, a reporter for the Associated Press, put it: "It was quite a scene. Thirty-three mastodons charging around a room 24 feet square, waving their huge arms and yelling like a pack of tarzans wired for amplification." George Halas, savoring every delectable moment of it, decided the most dramatic approach would be a subdued one: "It was just one of those days," he said. "Everything we did, we did right. Everything they did, they did wrong." But one sports

George McAfee (5), one of the string of great Bear halfbacks which began with Red Grange and extends up to Walter Payton, shows his dazzling style on this high-stepping run during the 1940 NFL championship game. Other Bears here are John Siegal (6), Bulldog Turner (66), and Danny Fortmann (21). Red Grange in 1940 called McAfee "the most dangerous man with a football in the game." –Pro Football Hall of Fame

commentator, not having to worry about sounding vainglorious, described the Bears that day as "the perfect football team . . . a team that did everything . . . with flawless execution. . . ."

In looking for a reason for the Washington catastrophe, Bernie Harter, sports editor of the *Washington Herald,* asked several of the pro coaches who were at the game—Curly Lambeau, Steve Owen, and Jimmy Conzelman among them—what had caused it. They all seemed to agree that a pass thrown by Sammy Baugh shortly after the Bears' first touchdown, which end Charlie Malone, all alone but blinded momentarily by the sun, had dropped on the Bears' 2-yard line, was the turning point. The Redskins were deprived of a sure game-tying touchdown early in the first quarter. Everything broke down after that, they suggested. Baugh was asked the same question later, which Bill Stern—among others—recorded for posterity:

" 'If Charlie had hung onto that pass near the end zone in the first quarter,' suggested Baugh's questioners, 'wouldn't it have been a different story?'

"Baugh grinned wryly. 'Yeah,' he said. 'It would have been 73–6.' "

Whatever—the Bears were the undisputed champions of 1940. And each Bear went back to Chicago

$873 richer as a result of his cut of the title game gate. And George Halas had his revenge on George Preston Marshall.

How did it all happen? It was basically rather simple. The Bears, as a result of their spectacular draft that year, were able to field one of the finest teams in pro football history. In that draft, they acquired the great open-field runner George McAfee, from Duke University, and center Clyde ("Bulldog") Turner, a Hardin-Simmons (Texas) alumnus whom Chicago sportswriter Howard Roberts later described with a war-year figure of speech as "fast as a featherweight, tough as a black-market steak and durable as iron." But that wasn't all; they added four other excellent rookies: end Ken Kavanaugh, from Louisiana State University, tackles Lee Artoe (Santa Clara) and Ed Kolman (Temple), and halfback Ray ("Scooter") McLean (St. Anselm's College in New Hampshire). Combining these newcomers with Sid Luckman, Bill Osmanski, Danny Fortmann, George Musso, Joe Stydahar, and Ray Nolting, the effect was tremendous. The Bears' starting line-up for the championship game contained five future Hall-of-Famers—Luckman, Fortmann, Stydahar, McAfee, and Turner—and several other players who may very well join them in that

After the Bears' annihilation of the Redskins in the 1940 title game, the post-game formality of congratulating the winner had to be a painful one. A still-stunned Redskin coach, Ray Flaherty (center), shakes hands with George Halas here, and team owner George Preston Marshall (right) manages a congratulatory word or two, but no one would believe his heart was truly in it. –Pro Football Hall of Fame

Bulldog Turner, a rookie in 1940, turned out to be one of the greatest Bear linemen of all time. On offense, as a center, he was named an All-Pro six times in his 13-year Bear career; on defense, he was a linebacker feared by running backs and pass receivers alike. –Pro Football Hall of Fame

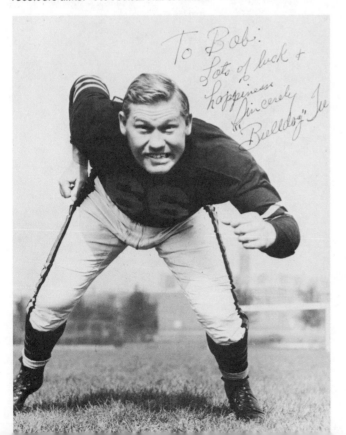

Bear fullback Bill Osmanski follows a block thrown by guard Danny Fortmann in this early regular-season game against Detroit in 1940. As a rookie the year before, Osmanski led the NFL in rushing, with 699 yards on an average of 5.8 yards per carry. He played on three Bear NFL championship teams (1940, 1941, and 1946). Osmanski's brother Joe joined the Bear backfield in 1946. –Pro Football Hall of Fame

prestigious honor one of these days. And, of course, the Bears had the new and devastating weapon devised by Halas and Clark Shaughnessy—the modern T, a formation that within five years would be adopted by practically all professional, college, and high school teams in the country.

The 73–0 rout of the Redskins was a spectacular end to a good, but less than exciting, year for the Bears. But they were in command of their division throughout the regular season, even though they did manage to lose three of their 11 games. Green Bay, the 1939 titleholder, could post only a 6–4–1 record for second place in the Western Division. One of the Bears' losses was to the third-place Detroit Lions, whose running star, Byron ("Whizzer") White (the future Supreme Court justice), led the league in rushing that year. A Rhodes scholar, White had also topped the league in rushing as a rookie with the Pittsburgh Pirates in 1938, but then left the game to study at Oxford.

George McAfee and Sid Luckman had both given hints during the season of what the future was to be like for them. In the Bears' opening game, against the Packers, McAfee, fielding his first kickoff in league competition, ran it back 93 yards for a touchdown; then he threw a touchdown pass to Ken Kavanaugh and finally scored again himself on a nine-yard run. Luckman set two Bear records during the season by completing a total of 48 passes for 941 yards. It was an excellent balance to the running attack that the Bears

1940 SEASON	.727		
Won 8 Lost 3			
George Halas—Coach		Bears	Opponents
Green Bay Packers	(A)	41	10
Chicago Cardinals	(A)	7	21
Cleveland Rams	(A)	21	14
Detroit Lions	(H)	7	0
Brooklyn Dodgers	(H)	16	7
New York Giants	(A)	37	21
Green Bay Packers	(H)	14	7
Detroit Lions	(A)	14	17
Washington Redskins	(A)	3	7
Cleveland Rams	(H)	47	25
Chicago Cardinals	(H)	31	23
Totals		238	152
NFL CHAMPIONSHIP			
Washington Redskins	(A)	73	0

launched with Osmanski, Nolting, McLean, and Famiglietti, as well as McAfee. Only two Bears, linemen Danny Fortmann and Joe Stydahar, were honored as All-Pros that year, however.

THE POWERHOUSE YEARS

NO ONE IN PROFESSIONAL FOOTBALL would soon forget the championship game of 1940, and when the 1941 season came around, the rest of the league approached the Bears with trepidation. George McAfee by now was the most feared breakaway runner in the league, dazzling from scrimmage as well as on punt and kickoff returns. The Bears had not had a running back like him since the Red Grange of 1925. Sid Luckman was among the smartest and most talented quarterbacks in the NFL. The team still had running backs like Bill Osmanski, Ray Nolting, Bob Swisher, and Gary Famiglietti. If that wasn't enough, two more fine ones, Norm Standlee and Hugh Gallarneau, both from Stanford University, were added. The only major change in the line was that Ray Bray, who would twice become an All-Pro, replaced an aging George Musso at guard.

To begin the season, more than 98,000 people jammed into Soldier Field in Chicago to watch the mighty Bears manhandle an upstart College All-Star team that featured Tommy Harmon and Forrest Evashevski, both of Michigan, 37–13. Tommy Harmon had been the Bears' first draft choice that year, but George Halas had been unable to sign him. Harmon opted to play with the New York Americans of the American Football League, which had sprung up the year before. (The third short-lived league with this same name, it would fold after the 1941 season.)

The year's statistics show just how awesome the Bears' offense was. The team led the league in total yards gained (4,265), with George McAfee and Norm Standlee ranking among the top five in rushing yardage. On their way to another Western Division title, with a record of 10–1–0, the Bears compiled a total of 396 points, an average of 36 a game and their highest ever, and allowed an average of only 13 points a game to be scored on them. Bears 53–Cardinals 7, Bears 49–Lions 0, Bears 34–Steelers 7, Bears 49–Eagles 14, so it went that wonderful season of 1941.

The Bears' only loss came midway through the season, when they stumbled before a fine Green Bay Packer team at Wrigley Field 16–14 (besides that game, the lowest the Bears scored all that year was 24 points). The Packers, in fact, were so good that they ended up the season with an identical 10–1–0 record, their only defeat inflicted on them by the Bears in the first game of the season (25–17). Coincidentally—because there had never been a divisional tie before—the NFL had taken care of just that possibility earlier in the year. The new by-law called for a playoff to determine the division winner and sudden death overtime if this game ended in a tie. (The NFL also decided that pro football needed a commissioner, like pro baseball had, instead of a president. Chosen for the post was Elmer Layden, one of the Four Horsemen and later coach and athletic director at Notre Dame.)

George McAfee, carrying the traditional white football with black stripes used in earlier College All-Star games, gains a few yards for the Bears before being tackled in this 1941 game at Soldier Field. The Bears won that game 37–13. –Chicago Bears

The Packers would have to face the Bears once again at Wrigley Field to determine who had the right to play the New York Giants, winner of the NFL East, for the league title. The Giants had ended the regular season with an 8–3–0 record. Green Bay came to town relying on the fabulous aerial combination of Cecil Isbell, an admirable replacement for Arnie Herber, who had retired during the season, and Don Hutson. Isbell was the league's top passer and Hutson the top receiver that year. To handle much of the running chores, as well as their field-goal kicking, the Pack still had Clarke Hinkle, who during the season had become the NFL's all-time leading ground-gainer. And a future Hall-of-Famer, rookie Tony Canadeo, "The Gray Ghost of Gonzaga," added another dimension to Green Bay's running game.

Despite the fact that the United States had gone to war the Sunday before and the temperature was a brittle 16 degrees in Chicago on December 14, more than 43,000 people squeezed into Wrigley Field to watch the Bear-Packer playoff game. The first period suggested it was going to be an exciting game. Clarke Hinkle put the Packers on the scoreboard early with a touchdown, but Hugh Gallarneau scored on an 81-

yard punt return to keep the Bears in the ball game. In the second quarter, the Bears were virtually unstoppable. Two touchdowns by fullback Norm Standlee, another by Bob Swisher, and a field goal by Bob Snyder gave the Bears a 30–7 lead at half-time. Green Bay was never in the game again. The final score was 33–14, and the Bears had won their second consecutive Western Division title.

The weather warmed up during the following week, and by game time on December 21, it was an unseasonable 47 degrees in Chicago. But that blessing from nature and the inherent drama of an NFL championship game were somehow not enough to bring very many fans out to Wrigley Field that day. Perhaps it was because of the crush of Christmas preparations or because people were suddenly more worried about the war and their own safety now that the tragedy of Pearl Harbor had sunk in, or perhaps it was the fact that the Giants were not supposed to be much of a threat or that it was all anticlimactic after the Green Bay game, but whatever the reason, only 13,341 spectators made it to the game, the smallest crowd to watch a title match since it became an NFL standard back in 1933. There were so many empty seats that after several calls

In 1941, the Chicago Bears introduced a new fight song, one that has remained with the team ever since. The name often listed as composer of the song, Jerry Downs, is a pseudonym. The words and music were actually penned by songwriter Al Hoffman, who perhaps is better remembered as the composer of "If I Knew You Were Coming, I'd Have Baked a Cake." To Bear fans, however, the words and music of "Bear Down, Chicago Bears" have become as familiar as those of the national anthem.

> Bear down, Chicago Bears,
> Make every play clear the way to victory.
> Bear down, Chicago Bears,
> Put up a fight with a might so fearlessly.
> We'll never forget the way you thrilled
>   the nation,
> With your T-formation.
> Bear down, Chicago Bears,
> And let them know why you're wearing
>   the crown.
> You're the pride and joy of Illinois,
> Chicago Bears, bear down.

bear down chicago bears

CHICAGO BEARS FOOTBALL CLUB
— INCORPORATED —
37 S. WABASH AVE., CHICAGO, ILL.

1941 SEASON TICKET PRICES

PRICE No. 1

$13.20

One choice seat for the 6 Chicago Bears' home games at Wrigley Field. Either the lower deck, close to the field of play, or the upper deck, from where you can see the intricate plays open up.

PRICE No. 2

$10.80

One reserved grand stand seat for the 6 Chicago Bears' home games at Wrigley Field. All grand stand seats are between the 30 yard lines. Your choice of upper or lower deck.

CHICAGO BEARS 1941 Schedule

Sept. 7 - N. Y. Giants Here
(NOT INCLUDED IN SEASON TICKET)

Sept. 28 - - - at Green Bay

Oct. 5 - - - at Cleveland

Oct. 12 - Cardinals Here

Oct. 19 - Detroit Here

Oct. 26 - Pittsburgh Here

Nov. 2 - Green Bay Here

Nov. 9 - Cleveland Here

Nov. 16 Washington Here

Nov. 23 - - - at Detroit

Nov. 30 - - - at Philadelphia

Dec. 7 - - - at Cardinals

Home Games Played at Wrigley Field

for doctors came over the public address system, one denizen of the press box said to the writer next to him: "A few more pages and he'll empty the ball park."

Those who stayed home didn't miss much. The Bears took the field, and the band struck up their brand-new fight song, "Bear Down, Chicago Bears." And the team proceeded to do just that, demolishing the Giants by a score of 37–9. Norm Standlee, who scored two touchdowns, gained more yards rushing that day (89) than the entire Giant team. George McAfee and Ken Kavanaugh each contributed a touchdown, and with three field goals by Bob Snyder, there wasn't much else the Bears needed to do. The players received $430 each from the meager gate receipts, less than half of what they had taken home from the championship game the year before.

The 1942 Bears, like all the other NFL teams, had to give up some of their best players to the war effort. Gone from the Bears' starting line-up were George McAfee, Norm Standlee, Ken Kavanaugh, and Dick Plasman; Joe Stydahar would leave late in the year, and more would follow. The Bears would also lose their coach midway through the season when Lieutenant Commander George Halas of the Naval Reserve would go on active duty. He would entrust the coaching duties to three of his assistants: Hunk Anderson, Luke Johnsos, and Paddy Driscoll. The administration

1941 SEASON .909 Won 10 Lost 1 Tied 0		
George Halas — Coach	Bears	Opponents
Green Bay Packers . . . .(A)	25	17
Cleveland Rams . . . .(A)	48	21
Chicago Cardinals . . . .(H)	53	7
Detroit Lions . . . .(H)	49	0
Pittsburgh Steelers . . . .(H)	34	7
Green Bay Packers . . . .(H)	14	16
Cleveland Rams . . . .(H)	31	13
Washington Redskins . . . .(H)	35	21
Detroit Lions . . . .(A)	24	7
Philadelphia Eagles . . . .(A)	49	14
Chicago Cardinals . . . .(A)	34	24
Totals	396	147

Divisional Playoff

Green Bay Packers . . . .(H)	33	14

NFL Championship

New York Giants . . . .(H)	37	9

One of the great Bear backfields of the 1940s. From the left: George McAfee, Bill Osmanski, Sid Luckman, Hugh Gallarneau.
–Pro Football Hall of Fame

Bear halfback Hugh Gallarneau follows Bulldog Turner through an immense hole in the Chicago Cardinal line during this game at Comiskey Park in 1941. The other Bears are Lee Artoe (on one knee) and Ray Nolting (in the background). The Bears won the game 34–24, and were on their way to the NFL championship. –Pro Football Hall of Fame

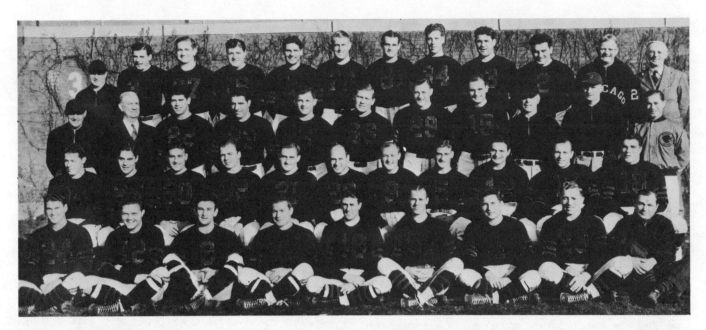

The Chicago Bears, NFL champions of 1941. Top row (from the left): Paddy Driscoll (asst. coach), Lee Artoe, Joe Mihal, George Musso, Joe Maniaci, Hampton Pool, Ken Kavanaugh, John Federovich, Joe Stydahar, Gary Famiglietti, Andy Lotshaw (trainer), Frank Halas (front office). Third row: George Halas (coach), Dr. John Davis (team physician), Norm Standlee, Aldo Forte, John Siegal, Bulldog Turner, Ed Kolman, Al Matuza, Hunk Anderson (asst. coach), Luke Johnsos (asst. coach), manager Cole. Second row: Dick Plasman, Ray Nolting, George Wilson, Ray Bray, Danny Fortmann, Bob Nowaskey, Bill Osmanski, George McAfee, Sid Luckman, Bob Snyder, Jack Manders. Front row: Bernie Hughes, Harold Lahar, Hugh Gallarneau, Young Bussey, Bobby Swisher, Scooter McLean, Harry Clark, Al Baisi, manager Rennie. –Pro Football Hall of Fame

of the Bears' organization he turned over to Ralph Brizzolara, who was named president in his absence.

Despite the departure of some of their key players, the Bears were still the dominant force in the NFL. Luckman was back at quarterback, and his primary receiver now would be Scooter McLean, who would lead the team in total points scored (54); Gallarneau, Osmanski, and Famiglietti would handle the running chores; Fortmann, Turner, Artoe, Bray, and George Wilson would populate the line; and rookie halfback Frank Maznicki, from Boston College, would handle the kicking duties.

The Bears made their first hometown appearance of the year before a record crowd of 101,100 at Soldier Field, where they made easy work of the 1942 College All-Stars. On the sidelines guiding the All-Stars was the one-time castigator of the pro game and the college coach of Halas (25 years earlier), the Sternaman brothers, and Red Grange—none other than Illinois's Bob Zuppke.

One of the Bear touchdowns in that 21–0 rout was a pass from back-up quarterback Young Bussey to Hampton Pool. It was Bussey's last professional football game. Shortly afterward, he went into the Navy and did not return, killed in January, 1945, during a landing battle in the Philippines. Bussey was the only Chicago Bear to lose his life in World War II. (A total of 638 NFL players—the count includes only those who

appeared in league games—were in military service before the war ended; 21 of them were killed.)

The regular season posed no more difficulty for the Bears than the College All-Stars had. The Bears won all 11 league games, four of them shutouts; in fact, no team came within 14 points of them. Once again their offense was overwhelming, piling up huge scores—this year for a total of 376 points, only 20 less than the record set the previous year, and an average of a little more than 34 points a game. And for the second year in a row, they led the league in total yards gained. The defense was equally impressive, giving up a total of only 84 points, considerably less than the year before. The Bears' opponents in the NFL championship game

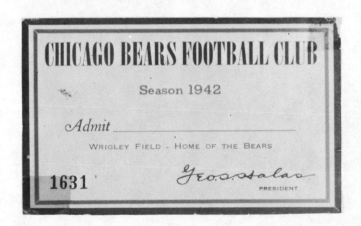

Football programs in the 1940s listed team rosters served up like this by Chesterfield and other advertisers of the day. This one gives the line-ups for the game held in January, 1942, between the Bears and the NFL All-Stars, which was the early form of today's Pro Bowl. This is the second "Pro Bowl" the Bears played in. —Pro Football Hall of Fame

season (2,021); his primary receiver, Don Hutson, adding three new NFL records by catching 74 passes for a total of 1,211 yards and 17 touchdowns; and the grand entrance of a 21-year-old running back with Pittsburgh, "Bullet Bill" Dudley, who led the league in rushing in this his rookie year. (The Pittsburgh franchise had been renamed the Steelers in 1941.)

Lieutenant Commander Halas, temporarily stationed at Norman, Oklahoma, was able to arrange a leave to watch his team play for the NFL championship in Washington, D.C., where they had so thoroughly embarrassed the Redskins two years earlier. Even though the Redskins had lost only one game during the season, the Bears were a 5-to-1 favorite, and many bookmakers would not take bets at any odds on the Bears because they felt a win was such a sure thing (the bookmakers in those days commonly took bets on the odds as well as on the point spread). Going into the title match the Bears had won 16 straight regular-season games—24 if pre-season and post-season games are included.

Despite George Preston Marshall's threat to clean house, the 1942 Redskins were pretty much the same team they fielded in 1940. Washington's coach, Ray Flaherty, a veteran of the 1940 disaster, remembered it only too well. He wanted his players to dwell on it also. In lieu of the customary locker room pep talk, he simply walked to the blackboard and chalked on it in large numerals "73–0."

would be a team hungry for revenge—the Washington Redskins. Washington's only loss that year had been to the New York Giants, who won 14 to 7 even though they made no first downs, gained exactly one yard rushing, and completed just one pass.

It was also an interesting year around the league, with Cecil Isbell of the Packers becoming the first player ever to pass for more than 2,000 yards in a

Carrying the ball for the Bears in the 1942 "Pro Bowl," played at the Polo Grounds in New York, is halfback Ray Nolting, following interference run by George McAfee. The All-Stars moving in on him are Pug Manders of the Brooklyn Dodgers (at the left) and Joe Kuharich of the Chicago Cardinals (88). The Bears won 35–24, with two touchdowns scored by McAfee, who was playing his last game before going into military service. —Pro Football Hall of Fame

The game began slowly. It wasn't until the second quarter, when Lee Artoe scooped up a Redskin fumble and carried it 50 yards for a Bear touchdown, that the first score of the day was registered. Unlike 1940, this time the Redskins came steaming back, and on their first set of downs marched into Bear territory where Sammy Baugh lofted a 38-yard pass to Wilbur Moore for their first touchdown. In the second half, the supposedly awesome offense of the Bears was nowhere to be found, except for one drive that culminat-

1942 SEASON 1.000 Won 11 Lost 0 Tied 0		
George Halas — Coach	Bears	Opponents
Green Bay Packers . . . .(A)	44	28
Cleveland Rams . . . .(A)	21	7
Chicago Cardinals . . . .(H)	41	14
New York Giants . . . .(H)	26	7
Philadelphia Eagles. . . . .(H)	45	14
Detroit Lions . . . .(H)	16	0
Brooklyn Dodgers. . . . .(A)	35	0
Green Bay Packers. . . . .(H)	38	7
Detroit Lions . . . .(A)	42	0
Cleveland Rams . . . .(H)	47	0
Chicago Cardinals. . . . .(A)	21	7
Totals.	376	84
NFL Championship		
Washington Redskins . . . .(A)	6	14

University of Illinois head coach Bob Zuppke, who had guided the college careers of Halas, the Sternamans, Red Grange, and a host of other Chicago Bears, poses here between two Bear stars of 1941—Sid Luckman (left) and George McAfee. The following year, Zuppke coached the College All-Stars when they faced the Bears at Soldier Field. –Pro Football Hall of Fame

Bear linebacker Bulldog Turner (66) charges downfield with an intercepted pass at Wrigley Field in 1942 to help the Bears defeat the Packers 38–7. Turner set a Bear record that year for the most interceptions in a single season, eight (tied later, then broken by Rosey Taylor's nine in 1963). Other Bears here are Lee Artoe (35), Ray Bray (82), Bob Nowaskey (20), Danny Fortmann (21), George Wilson (30), Ed Kolman (29), and Hugh Gallarneau (8). –Pro Football Hall of Fame

Bear fullback Gary Famiglietti moves out behind the block of rookie Len Akin in this 1942 game against the Cleveland Browns. Famiglietti led the Bears in rushing that year, with a total of 503 yards, and was selected for the All-Pro team. –Pro Football Hall of Fame

ed with Hugh Gallarneau plunging in for a touchdown only to have it called back because the Bear backfield had been in motion. The Redskins then put on a magnificent goal-line stand and stopped the Bears. The Redskins' single touchdown in the second half, a 1-yard power play by Andy Farkas, was enough to take the NFL championship away from an astounded Bear team—the final score, 14–6—that was favored to win by more than 20 points.

For the Bears, it was a grim repeat of what had happened to them back in 1934, the only other time they had recorded an undefeated, untied season. That year they had been upset in the title game when the New York Giants, with an 8–5–0 record, surprised them 30–13.

In describing the 1942 Bear-Redskin championship game, *Chicago Tribune* sports columnist Ed Prell wrote: "A football dynasty fell with a thud today on the frozen turf of Griffith Stadium." True. . . . but it would rise again.

Bear halfback Ray Nolting struggles for a few yards here against the Washington Redskins in the 1942 NFL title game. The defensive back he is dragging along is Andy Farkas, while Redskins Steve Slivinski (16) and Bill Young (37) give chase. The Bears lost that afternoon, and George Preston Marshall had the revenge he so dearly wanted since the Bears humiliated his team 73–0 two seasons earlier. –Pro Football Hall of Fame

HUNK, LUKE, AND PADDY TAKE OVER

FOR THE FIRST TIME since 1933, Bear owner George Halas would not hold the coaching reins when his team took to the field at the start of a new season. Hunk Anderson, Luke Johnsos, and Paddy Driscoll, who had taken over for him late in 1942, would handle the coaching chores for the next three seasons.

By 1943, vast numbers of NFL players had exchanged their football uniforms for those of the Army, Navy, or Marines. All teams were depleted of manpower, at least of experienced players, and the league was reduced to eight teams when the Cleveland Rams were allowed to suspend operations for the season (they would be back the following year) and the Philadelphia Eagles and the Pittsburgh Steelers were permitted to merge for this one year only. The Phil-Pitt Steagles, as they called themselves, divided their home games between the two cities.

The Chicago Bears had lost so many seasoned players that they thought it might be a good idea to solicit the services of Bronko Nagurski, who was running a farm up in International Falls, Minnesota. Nearing 35 and still in pretty good shape, Nagurski felt he was "just a little old for this kind of activity," as he put it. But he would give it a try, he told Ralph Brizzolara and Hunk Anderson, and reported to the Bears' training camp in Delafield, Wisconsin.

The Bronk was brought back into the line-up as a tackle, and his skill, he quickly proved, was hardly dimmed by his age. The Bears were in contention for the division title all the way, having won all but two of their games—a tie with the Packers in the season opener and a loss later to the Redskins. To clinch the title, however, the Bears had to beat the Chicago Cardinals in the last game of the season, otherwise they would fall into a tie with Green Bay and be forced into a divisional playoff game.

The Cardinals were the worst team in the entire NFL that year, going into the Bear game with a 0–9 record. They had one running back of note, Marshall Goldberg, who would later be a part of the Cardinals' "Dream Backfield," and Chet Bulger, a good tackle. But outside of those two players, the names of the 1943 Cardinals would leave little mark on NFL history. The deeply rooted crosstown rivalry, however, was apparently enough to stir them to extraordinary heights. By the end of the third quarter, they led the heavily favored Bears 24–14. But now one of the most memorable performances in NFL history was about to take place. In the fourth quarter, the Bears moved Nagurski back to fullback. What happened then has never been told better than the way novelist and screenwriter William Goldman did in his novel *Magic*.

"He's comin' in, The Bronko. The Bronko. And I sat there thinking omijesus, what a great spot for a legend to be in, coming back after so many years, one quarter

123

to play, the title on the line, and ten points behind . . .

"And then the crowd started screaming like nothin' you ever heard because on the bench he stood up. Nagurski. And he reached for his helmet. And he come onto the field . . .

"Well, everybody knew they were going to give the ball to Bronko . . . and if you're smart and everybody knows what you're going to do, well you don't do it, you fake it and do something else and when they came out of the huddle and when they lined up with Nagurski at fullback and Luckman at quarterback well it had to be a decoy thing, they had to pretend to give him the ball and then Luckman could throw one of his long passes . . . Only it wasn't no decoy . . . They gave it to him and he put it under his arm and just kind of ran slow, straight into the Cardinal line. They were all waiting for him. And Nagurski tried, you could see that, but they just picked him up, the Cardinals did, and for one second they just held him on their shoulders."

Chicago Bears in World War II

The following members of the Chicago Bears served in various branches of the United States armed forces during World War II. The only Bear to lose his life in the war was Young Bussey, killed at the battle of Lingayen Gulf in the Philippines, January 7, 1945.

Len Akin	Jim Logan
Lee Artoe	Joe Maniaci
Al Baisi	Phil Martinovich
Ray Bray	Al Matuza
Young Bussey	Frank Maznicki
Chet Chesney	George McAfee
Harry Clark	Monte Merkel
Stu Clarkson	Joe Mihal
Chuck Drulis	Frank Morris
John Federovich	Bob Nowaskey
Aldo Forte	Charlie O'Rourke
Danny Fortmann	Bill Osmanski
Hugh Gallarneau	John Petty
Bill Geyer	Dick Plasman
George Halas	Hamp Pool
Bill Hempel	John Siegal
Bill Hughes	Norm Standlee
Tony Ippolito	Bill Steinkemper
Ken Kavanaugh	Bob Steuber
Nick Keriasotis	Joe Stydahar
Adolph Kissell	Bob Swisher
Ed Kolman	Joe Vodicka
Hal Lahar	

Bears vs. Brooklyn

OFFICIAL PROGRAM 15¢

Sunday Oct. 24th—Wrigley Field

"And then they threw him down?"

"Not exactly, they all fell backwards and he gained four yards . . . He kind of got up and shook himself off and went back into the huddle and out the Bears come again and this Luckman, he hands the ball to Nagurski and he lumbers up and they're waiting, only this time he falls forward for eight more. First down . . . But it was starting to get a little eerie on the field. You could see all the Cardinal linemen slapping each other on the asses and the Bears come out again and this time they did fake and the pass was good for another first down and the next play was Nagurski kind of slipping down for six. He was like an ax hitting a tree. It doesn't matter how big the tree is, when the ax starts coming, you better look out.

"Now the Bears were inside the twenty. And there wasn't any doubt about what was gonna happen. It was gonna be the Bronko up the middle, and all these Cards, they bunched, waiting, and sure enough, here he comes, and they hit him and he hits them and for a second they did what they could but then he bursts through and he's doing five, six, eight, and then they knock him down and he's crawling—*crawling for the goal*, and everybody's screaming and there's a Cardinal on his back, trying to make him stop but he can't, he can't, and finally about six guys jump him at the one and stop him short of the TD. But they were scared now. They knew he was coming and they knew there wasn't anything they could do about it, and they waved their fists and tried to get steamed up but old Bronko, he just lined up behind the quarterback and the quarterback give him the ball and they're all waiting . . . and this old man starts forward and they're braced and he jumps sideways at them, the old man flies at them and they parted like water and he was through and the rest of the game was nothing, the Bears slaughter them behind the Bronko . . ."

It was true; the Bears went on to win 35 to 24. In that quarter alone, Nagurski carried 16 times for a total of 84 yards—and with the passing of Sid Luckman, it was enough to carry the Bears into their fourth consecutive NFL championship game.

Bronko Nagurski's memorable comeback notwithstanding, 1943 was really Sid Luckman's year. Late in the season, before a crowd of more than 56,000 people in the Polo Grounds, he led the Bears to a 56–7 victory over the New York Giants and set two NFL passing records in the process. He threw seven touchdown passes in that game and passed for a total of 433

The three Bears in this locker-room scene—from the left, Bronko Nagurski, George Musso, and Bob Snyder—show just how worry-free they were before the NFL championship game of 1943. Maybe they were clairvoyant, because the Bears easily handled the Redskins later that afternoon 41–21. –Pro Football Hall of Fame

yards (100 yards more than the existing record Cecil Isbell of the Packers had set the previous year). Luckman also captured the NFL season record in these same two categories. He racked up a total of 28 touchdowns and an aggregate passing yardage of 2,194 yards (an average of almost 20 yards per completion).

Luckman did not let up in the championship game either. The Washington Redskins, who had ended the

---

The Bears were moving toward a touchdown as time was running out in the first half during the NFL championship game of 1943 against the Washington Redskins. Ralph Brizzolara, acting president of the Bears while George Halas was in the Navy, looked down the Bear bench and suddenly noticed that the person sitting at the end of it was not wearing a Bear uniform. He was, in fact, dressed in an elegant raccoon coat and a homburg hat.

"My god, it's Marshall," Brizzolara shouted, as he stormed down to confront the owner of the Washington Redskins. George Preston Marshall began to explain that he had merely been on his way down to the Redskins' locker room and decided to pay a quick half-time visit to the Bears as well. Brizzolara, sure that Marshall was there for some nefarious reason, like stealing signals or listening in on the Bear coaches' instructions, summoned Jack Goldie, the team's equipment manager. "Physically remove Marshall from this area," he told him. Goldie clutched the fur-covered arm of the Redskins' owner and roughly escorted him back into the grandstand. There an usher demanded to see his ticket stub, which Marshall could not produce. The usher then called two policemen. Grasping Marshall by the arms, the lawmen were about to lead him from the ball park when he finally managed to convince them that he actually was who he said he was.

After the game, Brizzolara said: "I didn't want Marshall there eavesdropping. . . . A championship and a great honor were at stake. . . . That's the lowest way there can be of trying to win a game. . . . Yes, we threw him out—not invited him out."

Regarding the incident, Marshall said: "Fiddlesticks! It was a first-class bush-league trick." And then added: "You can say for me that Brizzolara is not a gentleman. And I'll never speak to him again!"

Later the following week, Elmer Layden, the NFL commissioner, also had something to say. He fined both Marshall and Brizzolara $500 each for "actions not reciprocal of the public confidence in the National Football League."

regular season in a 6–3–1 tie with the New York Giants, and then won their divisional playoff game 28–0, were once again the Bears' opponents, as they had been in two of the three previous NFL title games. This time, however, the game would be played at Wrigley Field in Chicago. George Halas took another leave from the Navy to watch the game from the grandstand, along with 34,320 other football fans. (Shortly after the first of the new year, Lieutenant Commander Halas would be on his way to the Pacific Theater of Operations, where he would serve for the duration of the war as a welfare and recreation officer for the forces under the command of Admiral Chester Nimitz. But even at that distance, he would keep in touch with the four men who were running his team.)

The game, as it turned out, was exactly the kind that Halas loved being a part of—the Bears were in complete control throughout and won easily, 41–21. Sid Luckman threw five touchdown passes, and Bronko Nagurski scored his final touchdown in the last game of an illustrious football career. George Halas came down to the jubilant locker room after the game and congratulated the team and coaching staff on what he considered the finest of going-away gifts. In the midst of it all, a reporter asked Nagurski why he had come back after a five-year retirement. "Halas wanted me to," he said, pointing at the man responsible. Would he be back for another year, the writer inquired. "No," a smiling Nagurski said, loud enough for his former coach to hear, "I can't go on taking care of Halas all my life."

Each Chicago Bear received $1,146 as his share of the title game receipts, the largest ever paid out up to that time (it was equal to about a third of the average player's full-year salary in 1943). The Bears' domination of the league, however, was at an end—at least it was taking a two-year vacation.

After the 1943 season, more and more players had to leave to serve the wartime needs of their country. Nineteen of the 28 members of the 1943 Bear championship team, in fact, would not return for the following season. To fill out the roster, the Bears had to bring back from retirement such relative oldsters as Gene Ronzani, then 35, and even Carl Brumbaugh, 37, who hadn't played in a pro game since 1938. But Brumbaugh found out at training camp that it really was too late for him and decided not to suit up for the 1944 regular season. Ronzani was used primarily as a back-up for Sid Luckman, who had been called to duty with the Merchant Marine, though he was able to join the team on Sundays. The Bears did add one notable newcomer whom Bulldog Turner had brought up with him from Texas to training camp. The young man had played at the same small college that Turner had, Hardin-Simmons. He was a guard named Ed Sprinkle, but his fame would be gained as an end during most of his 12-year career with the Bears.

Other teams in the league also lost players, of course, and they too added some new and some old faces. The Philadelphia Eagles picked up a rookie running back and future Hall-of-Famer, from Louisiana State, by the name of Steve Van Buren. The New York Giants went the other direction and brought back 38-year-old Ken Strong, 35-year-old Mel Hein, and former Packer great Arnie Herber, now 34 years old. Apparently it was the proper route to follow, because that year the New York Giants would win the NFL Eastern Division title.

Although the Eagles managed to find enough players to go it alone after the Phil-Pitt combine was dissolved, the Steelers were less fortunate. Both the Pittsburgh and Chicago Cardinal rosters were so depleted that at the NFL's request they agreed to a one-year merger, playing under the name Card-Pitt. Pooling their resources didn't help their performance, however. Before the season was over, the Card-Pitts, who ended up with an 0–10–0 record, were being called the "Carpets" because their opponents walked all over them—the Bears by scores of 34–7 and 49–7.

In 1944, the Bears moved their pre-season training camp to the campus of St. Joseph's College in Rensselaer, Indiana, where it would remain for the next 31 years—suitably out in the country where the only distractions, Halas thought, would be the cornfields and the quiet summer nights. A whole line of incorrigible roisterers over the next three decades would show

---

1943 SEASON   .889

Won 8   Lost 1   Tied 1

Hunk Anderson, Luke Johnsos,
Paddy Driscoll — Coaches

	Bears	Opponents
Green Bay Packers..........(A)	21	21
Detroit Lions ....(A)	27	21
Chicago Cardinals ....(H)	20	0
Phil-Pitt Steagles............(H)	48	21
Brooklyn Dodgers...........(H)	33	21
Detroit Lions ....(H)	35	14
Green Bay Packers..........(H)	21	7
New York Giants ....(A)	56	7
Washington Redskins ....(A)	7	21
Chicago Cardinals...........(A)	35	24
Totals..................	303	157

NFL Championship

	Bears	Opponents
Washington Redskins ....(H)	41	21

him that just wasn't so. When the Bears came to Chicago that year, they shrugged aside a College All-Star team 24–21, despite the efforts of Glenn Dobbs, Bill Willis, Lou Saban, and a junior from Georgia, future Hall-of-Famer Charlie Trippi (underclassmen were allowed to play because so many graduates had gone off to war). The coach of the All-Stars was Northwestern's Lynn ("Pappy") Waldorf. But the rest of the season was an exercise in mediocrity, and the Bears ended up in second place in the NFL West, with a 6–3–1 record. Green Bay, which now had Irv Comp passing to Don Hutson, won the division and the league championship.

The absence of McAfee, Gallarneau, Stydahar, Kavanaugh, and Osmanski had been felt with acute pain by the Bears. Connie Mack Berry and Al Hoptowit were moved up to the starting line-up, and Ed ("Special Delivery") Jones joined the team. And even though the war was now over in both Europe and the Pacific when the 1945 season got under way, the big-name Bear players and George Halas were still waiting to be discharged from military service.

Don Hutson, the Green Bay Packers' great end, doing what he did so often and so well, catching a pass. This one, despite the efforts of Bear defensive back Sid Luckman, was good for 20 yards in a game at Wrigley Field in 1944 that the Bears won 21–0. The other Bears are Jim Fordham (3), Gary Famiglietti (23), George Wilson (30), Bulldog Turner (66), Jake Sweeney (13), and George Zorich (14). –Pro Football Hall of Fame

CHICAGO BEARS
vs. DETROIT
WRIGLEY FIELD

Field Pass

CHICAGO BEARS

Sun., Oct. 22, 1944
2:00 P. M.

7

ADMIT ONE
No Tax
CHICAGO BEARS
vs. DETROIT
FIELD PASS
Sun., Oct. 22, 1944
WRIGLEY FIELD
7

This was also the year that *Chicago Tribune* sports editor Arch Ward, founder of the College All-Star game, began to lay the groundwork for the launching of another professional football league to compete with the NFL. The new organization was to be called the All-America Football Conference and it would get under way in 1946. The competition for players and spectators would indeed be a source of woe to the

NFL. George Halas was particularly upset because now a third professional football team, the Chicago Rockets of the AAFC, would take up residence in the Bears' hometown. It had been difficult enough to support two teams, as both he and the owners of the Chicago Cardinals had been especially aware of.

Among the less than momentous events of 1945 was a rule adopted by the NFL that required players to

1945 SEASON   .300

Won 3   Lost 7   Tied 0

Hunk Anderson, Luke Johnsos, Paddy Driscoll — Coaches	Bears	Opponents
Green Bay Packers . . . .(A)	21	31
Cleveland Rams . . . .(A)	0	17
Chicago Cardinals . . . .(H)	7	16
Cleveland Rams . . . .(H)	21	41
Detroit Lions . . . .(A)	10	16
Green Bay Packers . . . .(H)	28	24
Detroit Lions . . . .(H)	28	35
Washington Redskins . . . .(A)	21	28
Pittsburgh Steelers . . . .(H)	28	7
Chicago Cardinals. . . . .(A)	28	20
Totals.	192	235

1944 SEASON   .667

Won 6   Lost 3   Tied 1

Hunk Anderson, Luke Johnsos, Paddy Driscoll — Coaches	Bears	Opponents
Green Bay Packers . . . .(A)	28	42
Cleveland Rams . . . .(A)	7	19
Card-Pitt . . . .(H)	34	7
Detroit Lions . . . .(H)	21	21
Cleveland Rams . . . .(H)	28	21
Green Bay Packers . . . .(H)	21	0
Boston Yanks. . . . .(H)	21	7
Detroit Lions . . . .(A)	21	41
Philadelphia Eagles . . . .(A)	28	7
Card-Pitt . . . .(A)	49	7
Totals.	258	172

LIONS VS. BEARS

30

OFFICIAL PROGRAM 15¢

WRIGLEY FIELD · NOV. 11

wear long socks in all league games—the sight of hairy calves was apparently distasteful to the league office. In that year too, the Cleveland Rams, behind the running and passing of a rookie from UCLA, Bob Waterfield, won the NFL championship and managed to lose $50,000 while they were doing it. The Rams' owner, Dan Reeves, who would someday follow his star player, Waterfield, into the Hall of Fame, was granted permission to move his franchise to Los Angeles. With a team on the West Coast, the NFL in 1946 would be truly national for the first time.

For the Chicago Bears, the 1945 season was a veritable disaster. After their first eight games, they had compiled the worst record in their entire history, 1–7.

One of their losses—to the Chicago Cardinals—was especially embarrassing; it was the only game their South Side rivals won all year. By Thanksgiving morning, however, most of the players and George Halas had been discharged and were back on the field. The patsy that had been kicked around earlier in the season was no longer that. The Bears won their last two games, and showed their potential in the next-to-last game of the season when George McAfee, who had just returned from the armed services, managed to score three touchdowns, even though he played for only 12 minutes. The 1946 season, George Halas promised the Bear fans of Chicago, would be significantly different from the one they had just endured.

DOMINATION AND FRUSTRATION

WITH MOST of the Bear starters who had been mustered out of the service now back in the line-up, George Halas had every reason to expect a return to the glory years when the 1946 season rolled around. There would be a few new faces on the squad, but most of the players were veterans of the great 1941 team. And Halas himself would be handling the duties of head coach again.

The first postwar year brought some changes in the league. Elmer Layden resigned as commissioner of the NFL when his contract expired, and Bert Bell sold his holdings in the Pittsburgh Steelers franchise so he could take over that office. The AAFC was formally launched, with one-time Notre Dame star Jim Crowley at its head. The new league had eight solid teams: the Cleveland Browns, San Francisco 49ers, Miami Seahawks, Buffalo Bisons, Chicago Rockets, New York Yankees, Brooklyn Dodgers, and Los Angeles Dons—the last four of these in cities that had NFL franchises. And the creation of the new league caused just what NFL owners feared—large-scale defections by players and the equally crushing inflation of salaries to keep players in the NFL. The Bears were hurt sorely when they lost fullback Norm Standlee to the San Francisco 49ers, where he teamed up with another Stanford alumnus, Frankie Albert. A left-handed quarterback and among the first of the topflight scramblers, Albert had been the Bears' first draft pick back in 1942 but

chose not to sign with them. The Bears also lost tackle Lee Artoe and halfback Harry Clark, to the Los Angeles Dons, and Special Delivery Jones, to the Cleveland Browns.

The AAFC, besides luring a number of big names away from the NFL, also recruited some of the finest newcomers to the pro game. Cleveland, under a man destined to be enshrined in the Hall of Fame as one of the greatest coaches in pro ball, Paul Brown, in that first year of the AAFC had the makings of their football dynasty: Otto Graham, Marion Motley, Dante Lavelli, Mac Speedie, Bill Willis, and Lou Groza. Other top names in the AAFC included future Hall-of-Famer Elroy ("Crazy Legs") Hirsch, "Wee Willie" Wilkin, and Bob Hoernschmeyer, with the Chicago Rockets; Spec Sanders, Ace Parker, Frankie Sinkwich, Pug Manders, and Bob Masterson, with the New York Yankees, who also signed up former Washington Redskin coach Ray Flaherty; Glenn Dobbs and Dub Jones, with the Brooklyn Dodgers; Angelo Bertelli, with the Los Angeles Dons; and Bruno Banducci, with the San Francisco 49ers.

The Bears, as a result of the talent raids by the covetous AAFC, faced what could have been catastrophe. AAFC clubs were very seriously courting the nucleus of the team: Sid Luckman, George McAfee, and Bulldog Turner. George Halas, however, refused to let his team be stripped of its top players. He came

George Halas, back in civilian clothes after his tour of World War II duty, is flanked here by Admiral Chester Nimitz and General Dwight Eisenhower as they announce the beginning of the annual Armed Forces benefit football game. The first game of what was to become a pre-season tradition for the Bears was held at Wrigley Field September 1, 1946. (The Bears beat the New York Giants 19–0.) Proceeds of the games, held through 1970, were used to help needy war veterans and their families. –Pro Football Hall of Fame

up with the money to compensate the three, and they happily stayed at Wrigley Field.

Other returnees to the Bear line-up besides Luckman, McAfee, and Turner included Hugh Gallarneau, Joe Stydahar, Bill Osmanski, Ken Kavanaugh, and Ray Bray. Ed Sprinkle was switched from guard to end, when Halas, it was alleged, took a look at the 6-foot-1, 205-pound Sprinkle and said: "The big boys are coming back. We'd better move this kid out to end before he gets killed." Jim Keane, a rookie out of Iowa who would become one of the Bears' finest pass receivers over the next six seasons, was signed up. Also recruited were a ferocious tackle from the University of Alabama, Fred Davis, who would be a mainstay in the Bear line for the next six years, and a fullback named Joe Osmanski, Bill's younger but larger brother.

And the 1946 Bears put on the show that they were capable of. They breezed through the NFL West with an 8–2–1 record, tied by the Los Angeles Rams and losing only to the New York Giants and a revitalized Chicago Cardinal team. Sid Luckman led the league once again in passing yardage, accounting for a total of 1,826 yards. His 17 touchdown passes were only one less than those thrown by the league leader that year, Bob Waterfield of the Rams.

The New York Giants won the NFL East and would face off against the Bears at the Polo Grounds for the league crown. The "curbstone bettors of Damon Runyon's Broadway," as Bob Considine called them, were getting a little more flagrant now it seems. The night before the game, it was announced that two members of the Giants, quarterback Frank Filchock and fullback Merle Hapes, had been approached by a New York City gambler, who had offered them $2,500 in cash and promised to lay down a $1,000 bet for each and find off-season jobs for both if they would

1946 SEASON	.800	
Won 8 Lost 2 Tied 1		
George Halas — Coach	**Bears**	**Opponents**
Green Bay Packers . . . .(A)	30	7
Chicago Cardinals. . . . .(A)	34	17
Los Angeles Rams . . . .(H)	28	28
Philadelphia Eagles. . . . .(H)	21	14
New York Giants . . . .(A)	0	14
Green Bay Packers. . . . .(H)	10	7
Los Angeles Rams . . . .(A)	27	21
Washington Redskins . . . .(H)	24	20
Detroit Lions . . . .(H)	42	6
Chicago Cardinals . . . .(H)	28	35
Detroit Lions . . . .(A)	45	24
Totals.	289	193
NFL Championship		
New York Giants . . . .(A)	24	14

Frank Filchock, New York Giant quarterback, is going nowhere on this play during the 1946 NFL championship game with the Bears. Bulldog Turner (66) is the Bear bringing him down as Jim Keane (20) and Joe Osmanski close in. The picture sequence below shows another play in the same game—a pass from Sid Luckman that did not go the way Bear receiver Ken Kavanaugh (51) was expecting. Suddenly the Giants' Howie Livingston had the ball, and Kavanaugh was forced to play a little defense. It was only a minor setback, for the Bears won the game, 24–14. But it would be their last NFL title for a long 17 years. –Pro Football Hall of Fame

The 1946 Bears celebrate in their locker room at the Polo Grounds after beating the New York Giants out of the NFL crown 24–14. Identifiable are Sid Luckman (42), riding someone's shoulders, and, in the foreground, Rudy Mucha (16), Andy Lotshaw (with glasses), Al Baisi (21), Hugh Gallarneau (8), George McAfee (5), and Frank Maznicki (4). The locker-room scene below shows George McAfee's exuberant reaction to the Bears' win as he lays one on the cheek of Sid Luckman, while Scooter McLean settles for a mere handclasp with the quarterback. –Pro Football Hall of Fame

purposely play poorly—in other words, throw the game. When the story broke, the gambler was arrested, and NFL commissioner Bert Bell ruled that Hapes could not play in the title game because he had not reported the incident to his coach, Steve Owen, or to an NFL official. Filchock, for some unaccountable reason, was allowed to play in the game, but he was suspended later.

As it turned out, the scandal had no real bearing on the game. Filchock, despite having his nose broken early in the game, played hard and well. But the Giants were simply no match for the Bears that year, and went down to defeat 24–14. Sid Luckman threw a 21-yard touchdown pass to Ken Kavanaugh and ran 19 yards for another himself. Intercepting a pass, Dante Magnani raced 39 yards for a third touchdown, and Frank Maznicki added three points with a field goal, all of which was plenty to offset Filchock's two touchdown passes. The two New York extra points, incidentally, were kicked by 40-year-old Ken Strong, who was finishing up his 14th season (he missed four during the war years), and who still had no intentions of getting out of the game.

While George Halas was priming his postwar team, blending the veterans back from Europe and the Pacific with a fine crop of newcomers, across town Charles Bidwill, owner of the Cardinals and a long-time friend of Halas, was making some alterations in his line-up that would haunt the Bears over the next four years. The Chicago Cardinals, who in their 14-year existence in the NFL West had dwelled in the cellar there nine times and had an overall record during those years of 38–107–8, were on the verge of changing their entire image. In 1947, they acquired the most sought-after back in the nation, future Hall-of-Famer Charlie Trippi, who had just graduated from the University of Georgia. The AAFC—Dan Topping, owner of the New York Yankees, in particular—had wanted him dearly, but Bidwill wanted him more and proved it by offering Trippi a four-year contract for $100,000, up to then the largest ever awarded in NFL history (if Red Grange's profit-sharing arrangement of 1925 is not considered). Trippi had also been offered a lucrative contract by the Boston Red Sox baseball team but turned it down too. Now, along with Paul Christman, Marshall Goldberg, Pat Harder, and Elmer Angsman, the addition of Trippi gave the Cardinals what Bidwill called his "Million Dollar Backfield" but what the working press dubbed the "Dream Backfield." Jimmy Conzelman was also back as their head coach.

The team that the Bears had routinely demolished over the years—out of 53 regular-season games, since they first met back in 1920, the Bears won 37, lost 10, and tied six—would no longer be the pushovers they once were. George Halas had gotten a sampling of what was to come when he watched the Cardinals defeat his Bears 35–28 on that cold December afternoon the year before. For the city of Chicago, it was the beginning of the hardest-fought, most exciting intra-city football competitions they would ever see.

The revival of the Cardinals also brought about a divisiveness among the city's football fans like none Chicago had ever experienced. Unyielding in their devotion, Bear fans and Cardinal fans were about as compatible as a cobra and a mongoose and usually totally irrational when they spoke with each other about the team they loved or hated. In all of sport, the intensity of the intra-city rivalry between the Bears and Cardinals of the late 1940s and early 1950s has perhaps been equaled only by that between the baseball Yankees and Dodgers of the 1950s.

In 1947 the Bears were also about to enter a four-year period of frustration unlike any they had encountered in almost three decades of playing professional football. From that season through the 1950

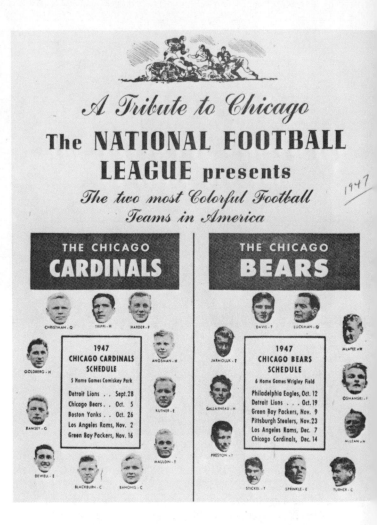

season, the Bears would post an aggregate record of 36–12–0, better than any other team in either division of the NFL. But they would not play in a single one of the NFL championship games during those years. The Cardinals, two-time winners of the NFL West, would have a record of only 31–16–1, and the Los Angeles Rams, who won the division title the other two years, could merely boast a 29–16–3 record. Even the top team in the NFL East, the Philadelphia Eagles—populated with the likes of Steve Van Buren, his fellow Hall-of-Famer Pete Pihos, Tommy Thompson, Bosh Pritchard, Al Wistert, Bucko Kilroy, and place-kicker Cliff Patton—who would win three divisional titles in those four years, came up with a record of only 34–13–1. Each year, the Bears' division title hopes would hinge on one game, and each year the Bears would lose that particular game.

The Bears' 1947 season began with a disillusioning 16–0 loss to the College All-Stars, who were coached by Frank Leahy from Notre Dame. Starters for the collegians, predominantly from the Midwest, included quarterback George Ratterman, fullback Jim Mello, and tackle John Mastrangelo, from Notre Dame; half-back Claude ("Buddy") Young and guard Alex Agase,

Bear fullback Joe Osmanski takes a screen pass from Sid Luckman in this 1947 game against the Philadelphia Eagles at Wrigley Field. His older brother Bill, on his knees, was playing out his last season that year. The Bears at the left are Fred Hartman and Ray Bray. The pursuing Eagles are Frank Kilroy (76) and Al Wistert (70). The Bears won this game 40–7. –Pro Football Hall of Fame

from Illinois; halfback Vic Schwall, from Northwestern; and guard Dick Barwegan, from Purdue. The unexpected loss to the All-Stars, perhaps a harbinger of what was to come for the Bears, was witnessed by an all-time record crowd of 105,840, at Soldier Field.

The regular season also began badly for the Bears. Two straight losses, one to the Packers at Green Bay and the other to the Cardinals out at Comiskey Park, were as mystifying as they were disappointing to the defending NFL champions. Once back at Wrigley Field, however, the Bears turned it all around. Beginning with a 40–7 mauling of a highly respected Philadelphia Eagle team from the NFL East, the Bears ran up an eight-game winning streak before they fell, 17–14, to the Los Angeles Rams, a team with the formidable Bob Waterfield, Tommy Harmon, and Kenny Washington in their line-up.

The Bears and Cardinals then queued up for the last game of the season at Wrigley Field. Each team had identical records of 8–3–0, and the division title was at stake. A crowd of 48,632 jammed the ball park, then the largest turnout in history for a Bear game at Wrigley Field.

It was a typically frigid Chicago day in mid-December. The Cardinals trotted out garbed in their distinctive white helmets, red jerseys, and white pants and with a special surprise that they planned to spring on the Bears. After studying scouting reports and some game films, coach Jimmy Conzelman was convinced

Don Kindt of the 1947 Bears being collared by Redskin Tom Farmer in a game played in Washington in which the Bears demolished the Redskins 56–20. Behind Farmer is teammate Eddie Saenz. –Pro Football Hall of Fame

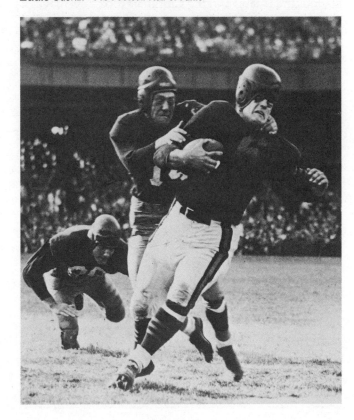

that if he sent fleet end Mal Kutner straight down the field, the Bears would put two defensive backs on him. Trailing Kutner from out of the backfield, however, would be halfback Boris ("Babe") Dimancheff, a good receiver as well as a fine runner. The only defender left to cover him, Conzelman reasoned, would be Bear linebacker Mike Holovak. Dimancheff, a fast back, would follow Kutner down the side then flare out across the field to catch Paul Christman's pass and out-race the slower defender, Conzelman concluded. During the days before the game, however, a problem cropped up. Dimancheff never showed up at a Cardinal practice to work on the play. His wife was in the hospital expecting a baby and Dimancheff spent his days with her. The only preparation he had before the game was a verbal explanation by Conzelman.

The Cardinals won the toss and chose to receive. The kickoff was downed in the end zone, and the Cardinals began from their 20-yard line. Dimancheff sprang Conzelman's surprise on the opening play. They would only have one chance to bamboozle the Bears with it, Conzleman knew, but what a way to start the game if it worked. And it worked, just as it had on paper. Dimancheff streaked away from Holovak, Christman laid the ball right in his hands, and he took off on an 80-yard journey to the Bears' end zone. The setback on the first play of the game was enough to stagger the Bears, and the Cardinals took advantage of this, coming up with three more touchdowns in the first half, two from Elmer Angsman and another on a pass from Christman to Kutner. Sid Luckman hit Ken Kavanaugh for a Bear touchdown, and at half-time the score was 27–7. The Bears rallied in the fourth quarter with two touchdowns, one on a pass from Luckman to end Jim Keane and the other on a sneak

by back-up quarterback Nick Sacrinty. But it wasn't enough. Pat Harder added a field goal, and the Bears went down to defeat, 30–21. When the game statistics were tallied, the Bears had out-rushed the Cardinals 155 yards to 82, had twice as many first downs (20 to 10), and gained 352 yards passing to the Cardinals' 247, but the Cardinals had the division championship. It was the first time since 1922 that the Cardinals had defeated the Bears twice in the same season. The Cardinals then went on to trounce the Philadelphia Eagles 28–21 for their first NFL title.

Sid Luckman passed for 2,712 yards in 1947, his 176 completions the second highest in the NFL. End Jim Keane led the league in pass receptions, with a total of 64 for 910 yards and 10 touchdowns. Only one player caught more touchdown passes that season, Keane's partner at the other end of the Bear line, Ken Kavanaugh, with 13. And Scooter McLean kicked more extra points (44) than anyone else in the NFL that year. But George McAfee, hampered by injuries for much of the season, rushed for only 209 yards (a 3.3-yard average).

The Bears placed three players on the 1947 All-Pro team: Luckman, Kavanaugh, and tackle Fred Davis. When the NFL team statistics for the year were toted up, it turned out that the Bears had topped the league in points scored (363 for a 30.3 average per game), in touchdowns passing (29), and in touchdowns rushing (21—tied with the Eagles in this cate-

On the Bear bench for a few minutes of rest during the 1947 season is Sid Luckman (without the helmet), flanked by Frank Minini (right) and Bill Milner and assistant coach Paddy Driscoll at the left. Luckman was the All-Pro quarterback of 1947 (the seventh time he was so honored). –Pro Football Hall of Fame

1947 SEASON .667		
Won 8 Lost 4 Tied 0		
George Halas — Coach	Bears	Opponents
Green Bay Packers...........(A)	20	29
Chicago Cardinals...........(A)	7	31
Philadelphia Eagles..........(H)	40	7
Detroit Lions...............(H)	33	24
Washington Redskins.........(A)	56	20
Boston Yanks...............(A)	28	24
Green Bay Packers...........(H)	20	17
Los Angeles Rams...........(A)	41	21
Pittsburgh Steelers..........(H)	49	7
Detroit Lions...............(A)	34	14
Los Angeles Rams...........(H)	14	17
Chicago Cardinals...........(H)	21	30
Totals..................	363	241

Coach George Halas talks a little sideline strategy here with the Bears' third-string quarterback of 1948, Bobby Layne. After the season, the Bears traded Layne to the New York Bulldogs, a move the Bears would painfully regret throughout the 1950s.
–Pro Football Hall of Fame

gory, 13 of whose 21 rushing touchdowns were contributed by Steve Van Buren).

Three veterans of the Bears' championship seasons earlier in the 1940s—Bill Osmanski, Hugh Gallarneau, and Scooter McLean—retired in 1948. At the same time, it was one of those cornucopia years for the Chicago Bears in the college player draft. Picked up were Johnny Lujack, from Notre Dame, and future Hall-of-Famer George Connor, also from Notre Dame, and Bobby Layne, from the University of Texas.

Sid Luckman was still performing well at age 31, but George Halas knew that he couldn't last forever. So he signed up the two best and most expensive quarterbacks that the college game had to offer. And it truly was a question of money because the AAFC was competing with heart and pocketbook for every major college player that year. Just as Halas would not let the AAFC tempt away Luckman, McAfee, and Turner back in 1946, he would not let the rival league get its hands on Lujack and Layne now. He came up with a reported $22,500 a year for three years for Bobby Layne, plus a $10,000 bonus for signing, to keep him from joining the AAFC's Baltimore Colts and $18,000 a year for

Lujack—considerably higher on the pay scale than the $6,250 that was enough to sign Sid Luckman 10 seasons earlier.

George Connor, 6-feet-3 and 240 pounds, would quickly distinguish himself in the Bear line, playing offensive and defensive tackle and linebacker. He

---

George Connor often tells the story of his initiation into that street-fighting arena which is more commonly known as the pro football line of scrimmage. As a rookie in 1948, Connor, at least in the pre-season, was used as a back-up tackle for Fred Davis. "When I raise my hand coming out of the huddle," Davis told him before their first exhibition game, "that means I need a rest. You come in on the next play."

Connor watched. When he saw the arm go up, he grabbed his helmet from the bench and when the play was over raced out onto the field. As soon as the ball was snapped on the next play, his face ran smack into the fist of the lineman opposing him. It was an especially unpleasant greeting in those days before face masks were routinely worn. Connor was startled but thought that maybe this was the typical welcome a rookie got to the more brutal game played by the pros.

Later in the same game, Davis raised his hand again, and Connor replaced him on the next play. This time he was lined up opposite a different lineman. But the reaction was the same. When play began, this lineman smashed him square in the face too. It was getting a little out of hand, Connor thought. After the game, he tried again to figure out why it was happening to him; perhaps they resented all the publicity he was getting for a rookie, or maybe it was because he came from Notre Dame—a lot of pro players were less than fond of Fighting Irish alumni in those days. He even asked a few other linemen about this so-called special greeting. They agreed that work in the line was violent as hell, but what was occurring to Connor did seem a little extraordinary.

It went on for several weeks. Then, one Sunday, it all became crystal clear. This time when Davis raised his hand, Connor for some reason kept his eyes on him rather than on the play itself. When the ball was snapped, he saw Davis lunge across the line, punch the opposing lineman in the face, and then trot off toward the Bear bench.

For the rest of that year, Connor announced himself to whoever the opposing lineman was when he lined up after coming into the game: "Connor in, Davis out." It made his life a lot easier the rest of that rookie year.

would play so well that during his eight years with the Bears he would be named All-Pro five times. What is more remarkable, however, is that three of these times he would be awarded that distinction on both the All-Pro offensive and defensive teams (the way selections would be made after 1950 when platoon football became the mode of operation). No other player in the history of the NFL would be named in the same year to both All-Pro squads three times. In fact, only one other player was ever accorded that honor in the same season: end Leon Hart of the Detroit Lions in 1951.

Sid Luckman was the starting quarterback in 1948. Lujack was the first back-up and Layne the second. During their brief appearances that year, Lujack managed to throw six touchdown passes during the season and Layne three. Lujack, who also excelled as a defensive back, came up with eight interceptions. And he was converted into an extra-point kicker—something he had never done at Notre Dame—ending the season kicking 44 of 46 points after touchdowns.

With their three excellent draft picks, the Bears really had an awesome team for 1948. Kavanaugh and Keane were among the best pass-catching ends in football, and Ed Sprinkle a top defensive end who had now come into his own. The line consisted of Bulldog Turner, George Connor, Fred Davis, Ray Bray, and Chuck Drulis. And to round out the Luckman-led back-

The "Three L's"—Sid Luckman, Johnny Lujack, and Bobby Layne, the Bears' quarterback corps of 1948. The following year, however, Layne would be gone. –Pro Football Hall of Fame

Bear passing star Sid Luckman showing that he could run when he had to. Here, he tries to outrace the Rams' great end Tom Fears in a game at the Los Angeles Coliseum in 1948. –Pro Football Hall of Fame

field were George McAfee, fully recovered from his various injuries, George Gulyanics, and Joe Osmanski.

The Bears got off to a good start, winning their first four games easily, one of which was a sweetly revengeful victory over the Cardinals, whom they beat 28–17 at Comiskey Park. Then they lost a squeaker to the potent Philadelphia Eagles, 12–7. After that, they powered their way through the next six games. In the last three of these, they crushed the Boston Yanks 51–17, the Redskins 48–13, and the Lions 42–14. Their record going into the last game of the season: 10–1. The Cardinals, whom they were to meet again, this time at Wrigley Field, had an identical won-loss record. A huge and rabid crowd assembled at Wrigley Field for what they knew would be the most bitterly fought game of the season. Among the spectators, watching his first professional football game, was a college senior from the University of Tulsa, who would one day be the chief operating officer of the Chicago Bears, Jim Finks.

Johnny Lujack had to replace an ailing Sid Luckman at quarterback, and he led the Bears to a first-half 14–3 lead. Then, as the fourth quarter got under way, Lujack threw a perfect bullet to back Don Kindt, who went in for the score, to give the Bears what appeared to be a commanding, 21–10, lead. But in the last six minutes of the game, their world caved in. Ray Mallouf came off the bench to replace Paul Christman at quarterback and promptly led the Cardinals on an

The Chicago Bears of 1948. Top row: Bear mascot, Ed Rozy (trainer), Ray Bray, Washington Serini, Thurman Garrett, Ken Kavanaugh, Jim Keane, Stu Clarkson, Alf Bauman, Hank Norberg, Andy Lotshaw (trainer), George Wilson (asst. coach). Third row: George Halas (coach), Gene Ronzani (asst. coach), George Connor, Fred Davis, Bulldog Turner, H. Allen Smith, Ed Cifers, Paul Stenn, Walt Stickel, Hunk Anderson (asst. coach), Luke Johnsos (asst. coach). Second row: Frank Halas (front office), Ed Sprinkle, Pat Preston, Bill Milner, Bobby Layne, Sid Luckman, Johnny Lujack, George McAfee, Joe Osmanski, Mike Holovak, Chuck Drulis, Paddy Driscoll (asst. coach). Front row: Don Kindt, Dick Flanagan, Fred Evans, J. R. Boone, Frank Minini, George Gulyanics, Noah Mullins, Al Lawler, Jim Canady, Bill DeCorrevont, Joe Abbey, manager Lembo. –Jim Keane Collection

85-yard scoring drive. After the ensuing kickoff, Lujack dropped back to pass and threw his first interception of the game. Vince Banonis, the Cardinal center, picked it off and carried the ball all the way to the Bears' 18-yard line. A 6-yard pass from Mallouf to Charlie Trippi was followed by a 12-yard slant off tackle by Elmer Angsman for the touchdown. Pat Harder converted his third extra point of the game, and the Cardinals again destroyed the Bears' bid for a division title, this time by the score of 24–21.

Bobby Layne had not been happy sitting on the bench most of that year. George Halas wasn't that happy about it either. As Bear end Jim Keane once put it, "Halas had absolute apoplexy every time he looked back at the bench and saw two $20,000 quarterbacks sitting there." So Halas sold Layne to the New York Bulldogs, reportedly for $50,000 and two draft choices. The Bulldogs' owner, Ted Collins, called it "the biggest player deal in the history of the National League." Whether or not it was the biggest is subject to some debate, but it was a deal that would come back to torment Halas later, when Layne would lead the Detroit Lions in the 1950s against a Bear team who had lost Sid Luckman because of age and Johnny Lujack due to an injury.

In 1949 the Bears would score their 10,000th point in pro competition, a statistic pointed out in the *Bear News* that year as "an all-time record for professional football." This was also the year in which they would score their 1,000th extra point, the year they would play before the largest crowd ever assembled for a regular-season NFL game (86,080, at the Coliseum in Los Angeles against the Rams), and the year they would make their debut on local television. Each week during the season on Channel 7, called WENR-TV in those days, the official movies of the Bear game the preceding Sunday would be shown, replete with commentaries by Red Grange and Bear assistant coach Luke Johnsos. The show was called simply "The Bears Quarterback Club."

1948 SEASON	.833	
Won 10 Lost 2 Tied 0		
George Halas — Coach	Bears	Opponents
Green Bay Packers . . . .(A)	45	7
Chicago Cardinals. . . . .(A)	28	17
Los Angeles Rams . . . .(H)	42	21
Detroit Lions . . . .(H)	28	0
Philadelphia Eagles. . . . .(A)	7	12
New York Giants . . . .(H)	35	14
Los Angeles Rams . . . .(A)	21	6
Green Bay Packers. . . . .(H)	7	6
Boston Yanks. . . . .(A)	51	17
Washington Redskins . . . .(H)	48	13
Detroit Lions . . . .(A)	42	14
Chicago Cardinals . . . .(H)	21	24
Totals.	375	151

To replace Bobby Layne on the bench, the Bears drafted a 21-year-old quarterback from the University of Kentucky, George Blanda. And halfback Julie Rykovich, a rookie from Illinois, would fill in much of the time for an aging and sometimes ailing George McAfee. Sid Luckman, who had to spend almost the entire season off the field because of a thyroid condition, was replaced as the starting quarterback by Johnny Lujack.

It was not the Cardinals who were the Bears' nemesis in 1949. This time it was a distinctly improved Los Angeles Rams team. Among an admirable crop of newcomers that owner Dan Reeves had acquired for 1949 were quarterback Norm Van Brocklin, from the University of Oregon, Elroy Hirsch, who had come over from the Los Angeles Dons of the AAFC, running backs Paul ("Tank") Younger, from Grambling, and Verda ("Vitamin") Smith, from Abilene Christian College. Clark Shaughnessy, coach of the Rams, intro-

When the Chicago Cardinals faced the Bears at Wrigley Field to determine the winner of the 1948 Western Division title, it was plays like this 10-yard gain by Charlie Trippi (62) that helped defeat the Bears. Trippi is being pursued here by Mike Holovak, George Connor, Washington Serini, and Bill Milner. The other Cardinals in the picture are Buster Ramsey (20), Pat Harder (34), Vince Banonis (32), and Chet Bulger (11). The Bears lost the game 44–21. –Pro Football Hall of Fame

George Blanda began his incredible 26-year professional football career in 1949 as a Chicago Bear. The leading scorer in Bear history, with a total of 541 points (88 field goals, 247 extra points, and five touchdowns rushing), he was better known as a place-kicker than a quarterback in his 10 years with the team. He scored in 83 consecutive regular-season games; the next closest Bear, Johnny Lujack, scored in 34. –Jim Keane Collection

duced that year the concept of a flanker back so he could get Elroy Hirsch in the starting line-up without losing either of his two fine ends, Tom Fears and Bob Shaw. It was another major innovation from football strategist Shaughnessy that, like the modernized split-T he had worked out with George Halas, would eventually be adopted by all teams in the NFL. Both Van Brocklin and Fears would join Hirsch and Ram quarterback Bob Waterfield in the Hall of Fame.

The Rams set the Bears down twice that year, 31–16 and 27–24. These two defeats, along with a 35–28 loss to the New York Giants at the Polo Grounds in October, were enough to strand the Bears in second place with a record of 9–3–0, a half game behind Los Angeles, who ended up 8–2–2 for the season. The highlight of this otherwise disappointing year was the last game of the season, when the Cardinals came to Wrigley Field. The Cardinals had spoiled the Bears' title hopes two years in a row and had beaten them three times in their last five meetings. But in this game, played before more than 50,000 fans, the Bears were able to work out all the frustrations the Cardinals had bestowed on them over the past few seasons. In a drizzling rain and on a slippery, muddied field, "with Johnny Lujack doing everything but taking tickets," as *Chicago Herald-American* sportswriter Jim Enright put it, the Bears beat the Cardinals 52–21. "A humiliating defeat" is the way Cardinal coach Buddy Parker described it. In the game, Johnny Lujack had the finest day in his pro football career when he passed for an NFL record of 468 yards. He threw six touchdown passes—only one short of the NFL record held

The expression on Bear halfback Jim Canady's face tells a little something about his problems with the Packer defense in this 1949 game. George Connor (81), unaware of Canady's dilemma, zeroes in on another Packer defender. The game was played at City Stadium in Green Bay, eight years before Lambeau Field was built. The Bears won this game 17–0. –Pro Football Hall of Fame

"Bullet Bill" Dudley of the Detroit Lions about to gather in a touchdown pass in a game against the Bears at Wrigley Field in 1949. A step behind him is Bear Bill DeCorrevont (36). Doing to Lion quarterback Frank Tripucka what he was notorious for doing to all opposing quarterbacks is Ed Sprinkle (7). No. 16 on the Bears is Ed Cody. The Bears won this game 27–24. –Pro Football Hall of Fame

The Great Intra-City Rivalry

In the late 1940s and early 1950s, Chicago football fans were treated to one of the most exciting series of intra-city competitions in professional sports—the Bears vs. the Cardinals. These were the rosters in the 1949 season.

Bears		Cardinals
Ken Kavanaugh	LE	Bill Dewell
George Connor	LT	Bill Fischer
Chuck Drulis	LG	George Petrovich
Bulldog Turner	C	Vince Banonis
Ray Bray	RG	Buster Ramsey
Fred Davis	RT	Chet Bulger
Jim Keane	RE	Mal Kutner
Johnny Lujack	QB	Paul Christman
George Gulyanics	LH	Charlie Trippi
George McAfee	RH	Elmer Angsman
John Hoffman	FB	Pat Harder

Others

Ed Sprinkle	Bob Ravensburg
Bill Milner	Jim Hardy
Bill DeCorrevont	Bill Blackburn
Paul Stenn	Bob Dove
Washington Serini	Corwin Clatt
Sid Luckman	Plato Andros
Don Kindt	Ray Apolskis
J. R. Boone	Vic Schwall
Julie Rykovich	Babe Dimancheff
George Blanda	Vinnie Yablonski

The Bears celebrating the day in December, 1949, when Johnny Lujack set an NFL passing record—468 yards gained on 24 completions. Lujack (32) accepts congratulations from George Halas, while the other Bears cheer his feat as well as their 52–21 butchery of the Cardinals that afternoon. Other identifiable Bears here are: George McAfee (shirtless), assistant coach Hunk Anderson (above Halas), Sid Luckman (42), Bulldog Turner to the right of him, Ray Bray (82), being bussed by Washington Serini, Chuck Drulis (21), directly above him and shirtless is Jim Keane, and right of him are Bill DeCorrevont and John Hoffman. –Pro Football Hall of Fame

1949 SEASON	.750		
Won 9 Lost 3 Tied 0			
George Halas — Coach		Bears	Opponents
Green Bay Packers . . . .(A)		17	0
Chicago Cardinals. . . . .(A)		17	7
Los Angeles Rams . . . .(H)		16	31
Philadelphia Eagles. . . . .(H)		38	21
New York Giants . . . .(A)		28	35
Los Angeles Rams . . . .(A)		24	27
Green Bay Packers. . . . .(H)		24	3
Detroit Lions . . . .(H)		27	24
Washington Redskins . . . .(A)		31	21
Detroit Lions . . . .(A)		28	7
Pittsburgh Steelers . . . .(H)		30	21
Chicago Cardinals . . . .(H)		52	21
Totals.		332	218

by his predecessor, Sid Luckman—two to Ken Kavanaugh, two to rookie back John Hoffman, and one each to McAfee and J. R. Boone. George Gulyanics added a seventh touchdown on a 2-yard plunge. George Blanda kicked a field goal, and Lujack had a perfect day with seven extra points.

Besides his single-game record, Johnny Lujack also led the league in passing for most yards (2,658), most completions (162), and most touchdowns (23). He also kicked 42 of 44 extra points. End Jim Keane also tied an NFL record of 14 pass receptions (for 193 yards) in a single game, still an all-time Chicago Bear record. Ironically, he did it in the game the Bears lost to the New York Giants. But guard Ray Bray was the only Bear named All-Pro that year.

With the close of the 1949 season, so ended the life of the All-America Football Conference. The financial losses to both AAFC and NFL teams as a result of the two leagues competing for top players as well as spectators over the past four years was calculated in the millions of dollars. The Bears did not lose money during those difficult years, even though there were three teams then playing in Chicago, but they were one of the few franchises that didn't. The folding of the AAFC, however, was not like that of the earlier leagues which had tried to compete with the NFL. People associated with the AAFC referred to its demise as a "merger" (and so did the NFL officially) because three teams—the Cleveland Browns, San Francisco 49ers, and Baltimore Colts—became a part of the NFL. But diehards from the NFL looked on it less as a merger and more as a usurpation of the better teams from a league that couldn't make it on its own. Either way, it resulted in the restructuring of the NFL. To accommodate the league's expansion to 13 franchises, there would now be a National Conference with seven teams and an American Conference with six.

Along with the Bears in the National Conference were the Baltimore Colts. George Preston Marshall had bitterly opposed the Colts coming into the NFL, fearing they could become strong competition for his Washington Redskins, even though Baltimore won only one game in 1949. According to the *New York Times*, "Marshall revealed he had cleared the way for Baltimore's admission [to the NFL] by waiving his territorial rights for a 'nominal fee'." The "nominal fee" turned out to be $150,000. And on top of all that, the Redskins ended up in the American Conference.

"Movie Stars" of the late 1940s, among them Sid Luckman of the Chicago Bears. –Pro Football Hall of Fame

The demise of the AAFC also made available a large pool of quality players from which the NFL teams could choose, over and above the ordinary college draft. Four franchises from the AAFC were now legitimately extinct, and their rosters were laid open to the NFL. A special draft was held, and the 13 NFL teams beefed up their squads with seasoned pros. Partly as a result of this abundance of talent, the rule allowing free substitutions, that had been in effect during World War II, was reinstated, opening the way for the two-platoon system, which then became the prevailing mode of operation for all NFL teams. After 1950 only a rare few players, like George Connor of the Bears and another future Hall-of-Famer, Chuck Bednarik of the Eagles, would continue to excel as "two-way," or "60-minute," men, as the game of pro football evolved into one of almost pure specialization.

For the Bears, the 1950 season followed three years of unhappy surprises, last-minute falterings, and shattered hopes. The powerful postwar team that had been practically everyone's choice to ride off with a string of NFL titles had somehow been derailed. The villains who denied the Bears the reality of their championship dreams had been the Cardinals and the Los Angeles Rams. For three straight years, those two teams had jolted the Bears out of contention, just when George Halas and his players thought they had the NFL crown a short step from their team trophy case. The 1950 season was about to become the quintessence of that situation.

Once again the Bears had conducted a successful draft, enlisting running backs Chuck Hunsinger, from the University of Florida, and Fred ("Curley") Morrison, from Ohio State, as well as two future All-Pro linemen—guard Dick Barwegan, who had played with the Baltimore Colts when that team was in the AAFC, and sometime tackle Bill Wightkin, a product of Notre Dame.

The Bears started strong and moved smoothly through the season. By the next-to-last game of the season, they had compiled a record of 8–2–0 and were a half game in front of the Los Angeles Rams, whose 8–3–0 record, incidentally, included two losses to the Bears. But then Halas and company had to take their act out to meet the Cardinals at Comiskey Park. Nostalgic fans who watched games out there in those days still remember the aromatic waftings of Chicago's famed stockyards that so often arrived on the southwesterly winds and took a fan's mind off the sports event he was watching.

The Cardinals were now playing under a new coach, Curly Lambeau. The guiding force at Green Bay for 31 years, Lambeau had been hired to try to

The Chicago Bears of 1950. Top row: Frank Halas (front office), George Connor, W. D. Garrett, Alf Bauman, Stu Clarkson, Frank Dempsey, Bill Wightkin, John Hoffman, Washington Serini, John O'Quinn, Andy Lotshaw (trainer). Third row: George Halas (coach), Paddy Driscoll (asst. coach), Paul Stenn, Gerry Weatherly, Bulldog Turner, Jim Keane, Ray Bray, Luke Johnsos (asst. coach), Hunk Anderson (asst. coach), Ed Rozy (trainer). Second row: Fred Davis, Ed Sprinkle, Dick Barwegan, Johnny Lujack, George McAfee, Sid Luckman, Curley Morrison, Julie Rykovich, George Gulyanics, Wayne Hansen, Ken Kavanaugh. Front row: Fred Negus, Steve Romanik, Chuck Hunsinger, J. R. Boone, Al Campana, Harper Davis, Ed Cody, George Blanda, Don Kindt, Joe Bernardi (manager).
–Pro Football Hall of Fame

Bear halfback Julie Rykovich gains a few yards in this game against the San Francisco 49ers in 1950. The Bears beat the 49ers twice that year. Other Bears in the picture are Washington Serini (wearing face mask), John Hoffman (29), and George Connor (81, blocking). –Pro Football Hall of Fame

revitalize the faltering Cardinal team. But so far he had not been successful. The Cardinals of 1950 were an unimpressive collection of good football players who somehow could not get it all together. When they entertained the Bears on December 3, they did so with a 4–6–0 record, languishing in next-to-last place in the American Conference. But the Cardinals always took a special relish in serving as spoilers to the Bears' ambitions in those years. And they did not let this splendid opportunity pass by. Behind the quarterbacking of Jim Hardy, who had replaced Paul Christman, and the running of Charlie Trippi, Elmer Angsman, and Pat Harder, the Cardinals won 20–10 and thrust the Bears into a tie with the Rams for the National Conference title.

The conference playoff was scheduled for the week before Christmas. The Bears left the snow and ice of Chicago for the sun of southern California, traveling with an air of confidence that year because of the two defeats they had handed to the Rams during the regular season (24–20 and 24–14). At the same time, however, they knew they could not discount the explosiveness of a team that had two passers like Bob Waterfield and Norm Van Brocklin, a pair of receivers like Elroy Hirsch and Tom Fears, and a contingent of runners that now included Glen Davis (Doc Blanchard's old running mate from Army), Vitamin Smith, Dick Hoerner, Dan Towler, and Tank Younger.

Bear quarterback Johnny Lujack (32) lofts this pass to fellow Notre Dame alumnus, rookie Bill Wightkin (53) in a game against the New York Yanks at Wrigley Field in 1950. The Bears won the game 28–20. Other Bears here are: Jim Keane (lower left), Paul Stenn (35), and Bulldog Turner (66). –Pro Football Hall of Fame

Pat Harder (34), Chicago Cardinal fullback, starts out on a sweep around left end against the Bears here after taking a pitch-out from quarterback Jim Hardy (21). Among the Bears pursuing him in this 1950 encounter at Wrigley Field are Ed Cody (16), and at the top Fred Davis (24), Don Kindt (6), and Bill Wightkin (53); running interference for Harder is George Petrovich (18). Harder gained only two yards on the play, and his team lost that day 27–6. –Pro Football Hall of Fame

In 1950, a football card, with painted portrait on the front (left), and with vital statistics and biography on the back, like this one of Bear end Jim Keane, could be had for 1¢ with a slab of odorous bubble gum thrown in too. –Jim Keane Collection

A crowd of 83,501 showed up at the Coliseum on a balmy, 83-degree Sunday afternoon to watch the two teams compete for the first National Conference title. In Cleveland, 2,500 miles east, the Browns were meeting the New York Giants in another playoff game to decide who would represent the American Conference in the NFL championship match.

Norm Van Brocklin started for the Rams, but when he couldn't get anything going—completing only two out of 10 passes—Bob Waterfield replaced him. The Bears held a tenuous 7–3 lead in the second quarter on a 23-yard touchdown run by Al Campana. But Waterfield, who had been in bed with the flu most of the week, was to be at his golden best that afternoon. First, he hit Tom Fears with a 43-yard touchdown pass, then came right back on their next possession with a 68-yarder to the same receiver, giving the Rams a 17–7 lead at the half. In the third quarter, he found Fears again, this time with a 27-yard touchdown pass. Waterfield kicked all three extra points as well as the 43-yard field goal in the first period. The Bears managed another touchdown in the fourth quarter on a 4-yard plunge by Curley Morrison, but it was too little and too late. As a result of their 24–14 win over the Bears, the Rams went to the NFL championship game, where they lost to Cleveland 30–28, the outcome decided in the final 20 seconds by a 16-yard Lou Groza field goal. It was the Browns' maiden year in the NFL.

Johnny Lujack had been playing hurt throughout the 1950 season. A shoulder injury affected his passing, and he was not the threat he had been the year

1950 SEASON   .750

Won 9   Lost 3   Tied 0

George Halas — Coach		Bears	Opponents
Los Angeles Rams	(A)	24	20
San Francisco 49ers	(A)	32	20
Green Bay Packers	(A)	21	31
Chicago Cardinals	(H)	27	6
Green Bay Packers	(H)	28	14
New York Yanks	(A)	27	38
Detroit Lions	(A)	35	21
New York Yanks	(H)	28	20
San Francisco 49ers	(H)	17	0
Los Angeles Rams	(H)	24	14
Chicago Cardinals	(A)	10	20
Detroit Lions	(H)	6	3
Totals		279	207

Conference Playoff

Los Angeles Rams	(A)	14	24

before. Still he managed to complete 121 of 254 passes for 1,731 yards, score 11 touchdowns rushing, and kick 34 of 35 extra points and was named to the All-Pro team that year. Jim Keane led the Bears in receptions for the fourth year in a row, with 36 for 433 yards. George Gulyanics was the leading rusher on the team—571 yards on 146 carries for a 3.9 average. And linemen George Connor and Dick Barwegan also received All-Pro honors in 1950.

After the season, in January, the first Pro Bowl as we know it today, a game between all-star teams representing each conference, was played. There hadn't been a Pro Bowl game since 1942, and those earlier ones had been between the league champion playing against a team made up of pro all-stars from both divisions. In the first of the new Pro Bowl games, seven players from the Bears were selected to represent the National Conference team—Lujack, Connor, Barwegan, Bulldog Turner, Ed Sprinkle, Fred Davis, and Ray Bray.

Four years had now come and gone, with the Bears in each one just a wisp of good fortune away from first place. Those who witnessed it could only sit back in wonder at the fates that had waylaid such a fine team. The story of the Bears from 1947 through 1950 was one of disillusionment and frustration. Going back to the revelry in the Bear locker room after they had won the NFL championship of 1946, it would have indeed been difficult to convince those mighty champions—the incredible cast of Luckman, McAfee, Turner, Kavanaugh, Osmanski, Gallarneau, Keane, Sprinkle, Bray, and Davis among them—that the team would not win another NFL championship during the next four years, not to mention that the long-respected and feared Bear name would not harvest such an honor for another 17 years.

CLIMBING OUT OF THE SKIDS

TO SAY THAT THE EARLY 1950s were a rather lackluster segment of Chicago Bear history is not an overstatement. Even the "Bear Historical Highlights," chronicled in the annual *Official Chicago Bears Media Guide*, which usually has something noteworthy to report for each year or at least every other one, shows no entries for that period. But these years were not without their excitement. There were great performances by memorable players: George Connor at his best, Rick Casares, Harlon Hill, Dick Barwegan, Stan Jones, Larry Strickland, Willie Galimore, J. C. Caroline, George Blanda, Doug Atkins, and Ed Brown, among many others.

Despite the ups and downs of the team during that period, the fans remained as loyal and optimistic as ever. The newly formed Bear Alumni Fan Club, with one of the most famous of Bear names, Red Grange, as titular head and group-gathering toastmaster, held luncheons during the season for its members and sponsored an annual trip to a Bears' away game. The first of these excursions, in 1951, carried 800 Bear fans to Cleveland to watch the Bears in their first regular-season encounter with the Browns. For about $30, a fan would receive railroad transportation, hotel accommodations for one night, a ticket to the game, meals en route, and transportation between railroad terminals, hotel, and the ball park. And it only cost $2 to join the fan club.

Besides all that at such a bargain price, those fans who traveled the 345 miles to Cleveland also saw a spectacular record-tying performance. Unfortunately, it was on the part of the Browns' 6-foot-4, 205-pound halfback Dub Jones, who scored six touchdowns in the game, equaling the record set by Ernie Nevers back in 1929, also in a game against a Bear team. In addition, they saw Don Shula of the Browns intercept a Bear pass and run 94 yards with it for a touchdown, only to have it called back because of a penalty. The Bears were victimized 42–21 that afternoon by a Cleveland Brown team that not only had won the 1950 crown in their first NFL season but would end up leading the American Conference seven out of their first eight years in the league.

But in 1951, the Bears did give their fans something to get excited about. They were a distinct contender in an especially competitive six-team conference. (The Baltimore Colts, who closed their first NFL season with a 1–11–0 record, had folded.) When the season was over, in fact, three teams were within a single game of the conference champion Los Angeles Rams (8–4–0): the Detroit Lions and San Francisco 49ers (both 7–4–1) and the Bears at 7–5–0.

Before the season got under way, however, there were a lot of comings-and-goings in the Bears' organization. Sid Luckman, George McAfee, and Ken Kavanaugh retired, taking with them the memories of their

When he had to, linebacker George Connor could throw a mean stiff arm, as he does here after he had intercepted a Ram pass in a game played at the Los Angeles Coliseum. –Pro Football Hall of Fame

Johnny Lujack could do just about everything on a football field and do it exceptionally well: pass, carry the ball, kick, and play superb defense. On this occasion he decided to run with the ball but is necktied by Duke Iversen of the New York Yanks in a 1951 game. –Pro Football Hall of Fame

contributions to some of the best Bear teams ever. Also gone was assistant coach Hunk Anderson. He had been offered the head coaching job with the Redskins by George Preston Marshall, but Halas would not release Anderson from his Bear contract unless Washington sent their star tackle Paul Lipscomb to Chicago as compensation. Marshall wouldn't do it, hired another coach, and Hunk Anderson, at least formally, dropped out of football coaching altogether.

Added to the Bear roster was a fine running back in John ("Kayo") Dottley, from the University of Mississippi, who ended up as the Bears' leading rusher in his rookie year, with a total of 670 yards and an average gain of 5.3 yards a carry. Other rookies of note included end Gene Schroeder, from Virginia, and halfback Billy Stone, from Bradley.

The Bears were in the race for the conference title all the way to the last game of the season. But this was a game the Bears had to win if they were to have any chance at all. Then they had to hope that the Detroit Lions would lose to the 49ers out in San Francisco and that the Rams would lose to the Green Bay Packers in Los Angeles. If the Rams and the Bears both won, there would be a conference playoff because they would end up with identical records.

But the Bears were hosting their perennial menace from the city's South Side, the Cardinals, who had hurt the Bears mortally in three of the last four years. The Cardinals were only 2–9–0 going into the season's last game, but they had beaten the Bears earlier for one of their two wins (28–14 out at Comiskey Park in the second game of the season). Even so, the Bears were heavy favorites when the Cardinals brought their famous crimson and white uniforms up to a snow-covered Wrigley Field on December 16.

It was the Bears' "homecoming" game, and 75 veterans of the Bears' glory years were guests of the management. But only about 15,000 other fans showed up that day because the temperature was below zero at game time.

Early on, Fred Davis recovered an Elmer Angsman fumble on the Cardinals' 16-yard line. The Bears moved to the 1-yard line but were stopped on three successive efforts at moving the ball in for a score. But as the second quarter was coming to a close, Johnny Lujack unleashed a pass to end Gene Schroeder who took it in for a 75-yard touchdown. The second half, however, was all Charlie Trippi. When he came out onto the frozen field he lined up as a tailback in a single-wing formation that the Cardinals adopted espe-

In this 1951 game, San Francisco 49er halfback Strike Strzykalski stumbles over Bear end Ed Sprinkle. Coming over the top is George Blanda (22), who had been switched to fullback that year and also played on the defensive unit. Other Bears converging on the ball-carrier are Ed Neal (58) and Ray Bray (82).–Pro Football Hall of Fame

cially for the game. And out of the single-wing, Trippi ran for two touchdowns and passed for another. All told for the day he piled up a rushing total of 145 yards and threw nine passes for another 106 yards. Steve Romanik threw a pass to Schroeder for a Bear touchdown in the third quarter, but it wasn't enough.

When the game ended and the Bear alumni headed over to the Edgewater Beach Hotel for a reunion party and the other bone-chilled fans made their way to their homes, favorite saloons, or other places of warmth, it no longer mattered what happened out on the West Coast. The Cardinals had done it to the Bears once again, shattering their title hopes with a bitter-tasting 24–14 defeat.

George Halas, however, attributed an earlier event in the season as the key to locking the Bears out of the NFL title game, which he recounted in an article in the *Saturday Evening Post* in 1956: "It was Elroy Hirsch, of the Los Angeles Rams . . . with the most spectacular catch I've ever had the misfortune to witness. We had piled up a 14–0 lead in the first eight minutes and had the Rams in the hole. . . . Quarterback Bob Waterfield faked a handoff to Tank Younger, held the ball behind his hip for a one-two-three count, then retreated to the goal line and arched a long pass. Hirsch made a

leaping grab on the Rams' 44 and raced another 56 yards for a touchdown—a 91-yard scoring play. There was no holding the Rams after that. They stunned us 42–17."

The Rams also went on to surprise a powerful Cleveland Browns squad (11–1–0 for the season), beating them for the NFL title that year in the first championship game that was nationally televised. The DuMont television network had paid $75,000 for the rights of what was to become an institution in television scheduling for the years to follow.

Johnny Lujack, who because of his ailing shoulder had never regained his former passing prowess, retired after the season. But even though he wasn't up to par physically, he led the 1951 squad in total points scored, in passing yardage, in touchdowns rushing, and in touchdown passes. When the All-Pro team was selected after the season, George Connor was named at both offensive and defensive tackle and Dick Barwegan was selected at guard.

The Bear quarterbacking would now be shared by George Blanda and Steve Romanik. To try to help the running game, Babe Dimancheff, who had so often stung the Bears in the past when he was with the Chicago Cardinals, came to play out his last season of pro football. The Bears did have a fine college draft in 1952, but the benefits wouldn't be felt until later. Their first-round draft pick was end and flanker back Jim Dooley, from the University of Miami. They also added future All-Pro linebacker and Hall-of-Famer Bill George, from Wake Forest, end Bill McColl, from Stanford (who at 6-feet-4 and 230 pounds was structured more like the tight ends of the 1970s than the receivers of the 1950s), and tackle Bill Bishop, who played his college games at North Texas

1951 SEASON	.583		
Won 7 Lost 5 Tied 0			
Goerge Halas — Coach		Bears	Opponents
Green Bay Packers . . . .(A)		31	20
Chicago Cardinals. . . . .(A)		14	28
New York Yanks . . . .(H)		24	21
San Francisco 49ers . . . .(H)		13	7
Detroit Lions . . . .(A)		28	23
Washington Redskins . . . .(A)		27	0
Detroit Lions . . . .(H)		28	41
Green Bay Packers. . . . .(H)		24	13
Cleveland Browns. . . . .(A)		21	42
Los Angeles Rams . . . .(H)		17	42
New York Yanks . . . .(A)		45	21
Chicago Cardinals . . . .(H)		14	24
Totals.		286	282

OFFICIAL PROGRAM • TWENTY-FIVE CENTS

CHICAGO BEARS
vs
CHICAGO CARDINALS

DECEMBER 14, 1952 • WRIGLEY FIELD, CHICAGO

touchdown. Blanda then kicked the extra point and the Bears won, 24–23. It was one of only three losses suffered by the Lions that year.

The Bears finished the season ahead of only the Dallas Texans, whose lone win that year among 11 losses was over the Bears before a meager gathering of 3,000 at Akron, Ohio. The Texans, who had just entered the league and had to play at various cities on

1952 SEASON .416		
Won 5 Lost 7 Tied 0		
George Halas — Coach	Bears	Opponents
Green Bay Packers..........(A)	24	14
Chicago Cardinals...........(A)	10	21
Dallas Texans..............(H)	38	20
San Francisco 49ers.........(H)	16	40
Los Angeles Rams...........(A)	7	31
San Francisco 49ers.........(A)	20	17
Green Bay Packers..........(H)	28	41
Los Angeles Rams...........(H)	24	40
Detroit Lions...............(H)	24	23
Dallas Texans..............(A)	23	27
Detroit Lions...............(A)	21	45
Chicago Cardinals ....(H)	10	7
Totals..................	245	326

State. The Bears' second draft choice that year was a landmark in a way: Eddie Macon from College of the Pacific became the first black ever to play on the Chicago Bears, and he distinguished himself as a rookie by averaging 6.5 yards on 30 carries. The Bears also drafted back Dick Kazmaier, from Princeton, who was the Heisman Award winner, but he chose not to play pro ball. Elsewhere around the league, it was surely a year to draft great backs. The 49ers signed up Hugh McElhenny, the Giants added Frank Gifford, and the Chicago Cardinals welcomed Ollie Matson.

But from a very real contender in 1951, the Bears dropped to fifth place in their conference, with a record of 5–7–0, in 1952. The Bears played their best and certainly most exciting game of the year in the first of their two meetings with the Detroit Lions. With only a minute and a half left in the game, it appeared the Lions had pulled it out when future Hall-of-Famer Jack Christiansen, their great defensive back and punt-return specialist, raced 79 yards with a Bear punt for a touchdown, giving the Lions a 23–17 lead. After the following kickoff, however, George Blanda moved the Bears from their own 32-yard line to the Detroit 2, with passes to Billy Stone and Curley Morrison. Then, with only nine seconds left and the Bears out of time-outs, Blanda flipped a short pass to Ed Sprinkle, who was far more famous as a defensive player, for the tying

the road because they could not attract enough fans into the Cotton Bowl in their hometown, folded at the end of the season. This would be the last time a team dropped out of the NFL.

If 1952 was the year for bringing top running backs to the pro game, the following year was the one to invite great linemen and linebackers. Drafted into the NFL in 1953 were Joe Schmidt, Jim Ringo, Roosevelt ("Rosey") Brown, Ray Wietecha, Gene ("Big Daddy") Lipscomb, Dick Modzelewski, and Doug Atkins (who signed with the Browns and would join the Bears in 1955). The Bears, however, added no one notable that year. And Bulldog Turner did not suit up for the first time after 12 years in a Bear uniform, but he did stay on as an assistant coach.

For the Bears, the season was even more of a disaster than the previous year's, at least record-wise (3–8–1), although they did land in fourth place, ahead of the Baltimore Colts—a completely new franchise that year—and the Green Bay Packers. In their entire history, however, the Bears had lost eight games in a single season only one other time, and that was back in 1929.

The highlight of that otherwise forgettable season for the Bears came when they finally got back at the Los Angeles Rams by reversing roles and knocking them out of the conference title race with a 24–21

1953 SEASON   .273

Won 3   Lost 8   Tied 1

George Halas — Coach	Bears	Opponents
Baltimore Colts..............(A)	9	13
Green Bay Packers...........(A)	17	13
Baltimore Colts ....(H)	14	16
San Francisco 49ers ....(H)	28	35
Los Angeles Rams ....(A)	24	38
San Francisco 49ers ....(A)	14	24
Green Bay Packers...........(H)	21	21
Washington Redskins ....(A)	27	24
Detroit Lions ....(H)	16	20
Los Angeles Rams ....(H)	24	21
Detroit Lions ....(A)	7	13
Chicago Cardinals ....(H)	17	24
Totals..................	218	262

During the 1952-53 Bear recession, not one of the running backs rushed for more than 400 yards. Curley Morrison led the team both years, but his best effort was 367 yards, with an average carry of 3.9 yards. In 1953, George Blanda led the league in number of pass completions, with 169, one of the few praiseworthy statistics of that period. On the other hand, he set a Bear record for the most pass attempts in a season (362) and threw 24 interceptions, in what turned out to be his only full year as the Bears' starting quarterback. George Connor, however, was still honored as the standout he truly was on both the offensive and defensive teams of the Bears. He had now switched to linebacker on the defensive unit, and in both 1952 and 1953 he made All-Pro at that position as well as at offensive tackle.

In 1954 the Bears began their journey up from the valley they had skidded into. It was a rebuilding year, and it was an effective one, foremost being the acquisition of an end from tiny Florence State Teachers College in Alabama named Harlon Hill. There were two new quarterbacks—Zeke Bratkowski, from the University of Georgia, and Ed Brown, from San Francisco. They also latched onto several fine linemen, such as tackle Stan Jones, from Maryland, center Larry Strickland, from North Texas State, and defensive end Ed Meadows, an All-American out of Duke.

defeat. That year too, the Bear Alumni Fan Club, 300 strong, went up to Detroit to lounge around the Sheraton-Cadillac Hotel and then sit through the Bears' second loss of the season to the Lions, this one 13–7. As for those in the Bears' front office, they had to be feeling a certain pain as they watched the young man they had traded away just a few years earlier, Bobby Layne, lead the same Lions team to their second straight NFL championship.

Frank Gifford, the New York Giants' great running back and receiver of the 1950s and early 1960s, moves through the Bear defense with ease (left) in this Armed Forces benefit game in 1954. The Bear defenders are S. J. Whitman (22) and Bill Bishop (73). Harlon Hill (right), one of the finest ends in Bear history, grabs the head of a New York Giant who broke up a pass play in that same game. Watching the action is the Giants' Tom Landry (49), the future head coach of the Dallas Cowboys. The Bears won the game 28–24, but Gifford won the Eisenhower Trophy as the outstanding player. –Pro Football Hall of Fame

WRIGLEY FIELD
NOVEMBER 28, 1954

CHICAGO BEARS vs. **LOS ANGELES RAMS**

The year 1954 also saw the initiation of an NFL rule requiring all players to wear face masks, "making it no longer possible to determine the quality of a player by the number of teeth he was missing," as one writer of the day put it.

The Bears' season began as if it were going to be a shambles, a repeat of the preceding two years. In the first game of the season, Bobby Layne led his Detroit Lions in a thorough drubbing of the Bears, 48–23. The Bears won their next two games but then dropped two cliff-hangers (to the 49ers 31–24 and the Rams 42–38). After these three losses, however, the Bears won six of their last seven games.

One of those wins turned out to be among the most exciting storybook endings in all Bear history. The game was against the 49ers out at Kezar Stadium in San Francisco. With about 45 seconds left and the score tied at 24 to 24, Gordie Soltau kicked a field goal for the 49ers that appeared to clinch a victory for them. Sportswriter Seymour Korman set the mood of the moment: "It was near total darkness, the wind was blowing, the lights were glowing on top of the surrounding hills, and the crowd was edging toward the exits as Soltau readied for the kickoff."

The kick was short and it was grabbed by end Ed Sprinkle, who quickly stepped out-of-bounds to stop the clock with 35 seconds remaining. It was obvious to everyone that the Bears would pass, and most probably to their brilliant rookie, end Harlon Hill, who had already caught three touchdown passes that afternoon. And sure enough, on the first play, Hill streaked downfield, but at the same time the two Bear guards pulled and quarterback George Blanda pitched out to Ed Brown, who had lined up at halfback. Brown followed the two guards and fullback Chick Jagade on what appeared to be a routine end run. Then suddenly Brown turned, faded back, and launched a perfect bomb that traveled 40 yards through the darkness into the hands of Hill, who never lost a step as he raced along the sideline and into the end zone with the game-winning touchdown, the final score, 31–27.

Another savorful victory was over the Lions, 28–24, before a capacity hometown crowd at Wrigley Field in the last game of the season, getting even for the opening-day embarrassment they had suffered at the hands of the Detroit team. The Bears ended up with a record of 8–4–0, in second place behind the Lions, who chalked up their third straight conference title.

The key to the Bear attack in 1954 was the superb pass-catching abilities of Harlon Hill, whom many Chicagoans were already ranking with such great Bear ends of the past as Bill Hewitt, Bill Karr, Ken Kavanaugh, and Jim Keane. Hill led the NFL that year in touchdown receptions, with 12, and caught 45 passes for a total of 1,124 yards—his yardage total was a new Bear record, 214 yards more than Jim Keane's 910, set back in 1947. He also led the league in average yards gained per reception (25). And rookie Hill was the only Bear named to the All-Pro team. Pitching to him in tandem was a trio of quarterbacks who became known around town as the "Three B's"—Bratkowski, Blanda, and Brown.

1954 SEASON .667		
Won 8 Lost 4 Tied 0		
George Halas — Coach	Bears	Opponents
Detroit Lions . . . .(A)	23	48
Green Bay Packers. . . . .(A)	10	3
Baltimore Colts . . . .(H)	28	9
San Francisco 49ers . . . .(H)	24	31
Los Angeles Rams . . . .(A)	38	42
San Francisco 49ers . . . .(A)	31	27
Green Bay Packers. . . . .(H)	28	23
Cleveland Browns . . . .(H)	10	39
Baltimore Colts. . . . .(A)	28	13
Los Angeles Rams . . . .(H)	24	13
Chicago Cardinals. . . . .(A)	29	7
Detroit Lions . . . .(H)	28	24
Totals.	301	279

The Bears' rookie fullback, Rick Casares, takes a pitch-out here from quarterback George Blanda (16) in this 1955 game in which the Bears mauled the Baltimore Colts 38–10. The other Bears here are Bobby Watkins (45), Stan Jones (78), and Bill Wightkin (72). –Pro Football Hall of Fame

George Connor had had to sit out much of the season with an injury; thus for the first time in four years two All-Pro positions were open to other aspiring linemen. Fullback Chick Jagade, whom the Bears had acquired from the Cleveland Browns, led the team in rushing with 498 yards. All told, it was a year that one Chicago sportswriter defined as "hope-inspiring" and another referred to as "emerging from the pits."

By 1955, George Halas had been associated with the Bears for 35 years—from the earliest days when they were the Staleys down in Decatur, through the Red Grange barnstorming tour, the Nagurski era, and the championship days of the Luckman/McAfee teams. During those years, the Bears had racked up seven NFL championships, eight division titles, and one division title tie—more than any other NFL team up to that time. His Bear teams had won the most games, scored the most points and the most touchdowns, tallied the most first downs and the most consecutive wins, and gained the most total yards of any team in the overall history of professional football. Now he was thinking about retiring from coaching. His wife, Minnie, once said: "He promised he'd retire when he was 55. But when he got there, he changed it to 60." True at least to his second promise, he announced that the 1955 season would be his last as head coach; he would

retire to the duties of the front office. He told his coaching staff, which in 1955 consisted of Paddy Driscoll, Luke Johnsos, Clark Shaughnessy, Bulldog Turner, and Phil Handler, that the team was a rebuilt one now, that the nucleus of a winner was there. Perhaps he could retire with a championship.

The nucleus Halas was talking about was substantially reinforced by four inspired acquisitions for 1955, one by a trade and three through the draft. Doug Atkins, 6-foot-8, 255-pound defensive end, was picked up from the Cleveland Browns, and out of the college draft the Bears plucked fullback Rick Casares, from Florida, halfback Bobby Watkins, from Ohio State, and linebacker Joe Fortunato, who was an alumnus of Mississippi State.

Zeke Bratkowski went off to the armed services, breaking up the "Three B's" of the quarterbacking department, and Bob Williams came back after two years in the Navy to fill in for him. George Blanda, who had injured his shoulder in the preceding season, was still suffering somewhat, and the Bears were forced to use only his talents as a kicker in 1955. The starting quarterback position was handed over to Ed Brown.

As the season began, however, it appeared that Halas had overestimated the Bears. They traveled to Baltimore to face the Colts in the league opener.

Heavy favorites to beat the team who ended up last in their conference the year before, the Bears were rudely introduced to a fullback playing his first regular season NFL game, Alan ("The Horse") Ameche. The young man from Wisconsin carried the ball 21 times for a total of 194 yards, including a 79-yard touchdown on his very first carry in the game and led Baltimore to a 23–17 victory.

The Bears followed that loss with two more, both to teams they had expected to beat—the Packers and the 49ers. But then like so many other solid Bear teams of the past, they turned around full circle. They won eight of their remaining nine games.

Before the tenth game of the season, the Bears were in first place in their conference just ahead of the Los Angeles Rams. The Detroit Lions, from the lofty heights of their three successive conference titles and two NFL crowns, had plummeted to last place. Their 3–9–0 final record was the result of Bobby Layne having to play with a severely injured shoulder and the loss of their mainstay on defense, Les Bingaman, who had retired.

The Chicago Cardinals, with an unimpressive 3–5–1 record, awaited the Bears in Comiskey Park, thirsting after another chance to undo the Bear plans for a division crown. The Cardinals, under new coach Ray Richards—he replaced Joe Stydahar after the former Bear great was fired the year before when the team won only two games—had been rebuilding. Along with halfback Charlie Trippi, who was playing out his last year of pro ball, the Cardinals had future Hall-of-Famer Dick ("Night Train") Lane in their defensive backfield. They also had Ollie Matson, feared as a punt and kickoff-return specialist, and a fine running back from scrimmage. Against the Bears, coming out to meet them after a six-game winning streak, they were substantial underdogs. Only they didn't know it.

As so often happened in the Bear-Cardinal games of those earlier years, Chicago's winter weather made itself felt in the most brutal of ways. A snowstorm began during the game and soon reached almost blizzard intensity. And the result of the action on the field was just as unhappily typical for the Bears. George Strickler of the *Chicago Tribune* summed it up best: "Being of sound and disposing mind and memory, I hereby make, publish and declare the following to be the truth, the whole truth and nothing if not astounding: The Chicago Cardinals, who a week ago could not get out of their own way against the Washington Redskins, yesterday whipped, humbled and humiliated the mighty Chicago Bears 53–14." It was the largest number of points scored against the Bears in their

Fred Williams (75) and an unidentified Bear team up to bring down Chicago Cardinal running back Ollie Matson (33) in this 1955 game (top) at Comiskey Park. A snowstorm began during the game, but Bear fullback Chick Jagade (30) found more than the elements working against him (bottom). The Cardinals demolished the Bears 53–14 that day. Other Bears shown are Harry Hugasian (48), George Connor (71), Ralph Jecha (69), and end Doug Atkins (81). –Pro Football Hall of Fame

35-year history, and with the defeat went the Bears' chances for a conference title.

The Bears beat the Lions and the Philadelphia Eagles in their remaining two games and ended their season with a record of 8–4–0, the same as the year before. The Rams, finishing with a record of 8–3–1, went to the NFL title game, where they were demolished by the Browns in what was Otto Graham's final

1955 SEASON .667		
Won 8 Lost 4 Tied 0		
George Halas — Coach	Bears	Opponents
Baltimore Colts. . . . .(A)	17	23
Green Bay Packers. . . . .(A)	3	24
San Francisco 49ers . . . .(H)	19	20
Baltimore Colts . . . .(H)	38	10
San Francisco 49ers . . . .(A)	34	23
Los Angeles Rams . . . .(A)	31	20
Green Bay Packers. . . . .(H)	52	31
Los Angeles Rams . . . .(H)	24	3
Detroit Lions . . . .(A)	24	14
Chicago Cardinals. . . . .(A)	14	53
Detroit Lions . . . .(H)	21	20
Philadelphia Eagles. . . . .(H)	17	10
Totals.	294	251

game. And just so the Cleveland fans would not forget him too quickly, the 34-year-old quarterback passed for two touchdowns and ran for two others that afternoon.

But the Bears had proven that they were again a team who could not be discounted. They ended the season in second place, just one game away from the conference title, which was captured by a Los Angeles team they had decisively beaten twice during that year (31–20 and 24–3). Rick Casares had an impressive rookie season, leading the league in average yards per carry, 5.4. And he rushed for a total of 672 yards, the most a Bear had gained on the ground since Bill Osmanski had picked up 699 back in 1939. In fact, the only other Bear to rush for more yardage in a single season up to that time besides Osmanski had been Beattie Feathers, with his record-setting 1,004

Doak Walker of the Detroit Lions is tripped up in this 1955 game by two great Bear linebackers, Bill George (only his helmet and shoulder are visible) and Joe Fortunato (31). Moving in to help are Bill Bishop (73) and Ray Gene Smith (20). The Bears won the game on Detroit's home ground 24–14. –Chicago Bears

yards in 1934. Casares even managed to throw a touchdown pass that year as well. The Bears' three key receivers caught passes for a total of 1,606 yards—Harlon Hill (789), Bill McColl (502), and Gene Schroeder (315). And Ed Brown had an impressive completion percentage of 52%. As a team, the Bears led the entire NFL in rushing yardage (2,388), average per rush (4.9), and number of first downs (235).

Alan Ameche, a fellow rookie, was the only running back to outshine Rick Casares that year, leading the league in rushing with 961 yards (a 4.5 average). Casares, however, would even the score next year. Otto Graham ended his career topping the league in pass completion percentage (53%), but a future Chicago Bear name, Jim Finks, quarterback of the Pittsburgh Steelers, threw the most completions in the NFL (165 to Graham's 98) and gained the most yardage passing (2,270 to Graham's 1,721). One rookie who went nowhere in 1955 was a quarterback from the University of Louisville named Johnny Unitas. Drafted by the Steelers, he was cut the same year.

The rejuvenated Bears placed five players on the All-Pro team in 1955: Harlon Hill at an end; Bill Wightkin, an offensive tackle; Stan Jones, who that year had been switched to offensive guard; middle guard Bill George (the first of eight times he would be so honored); and the familiar name there of George Connor, this time singled out as a linebacker.

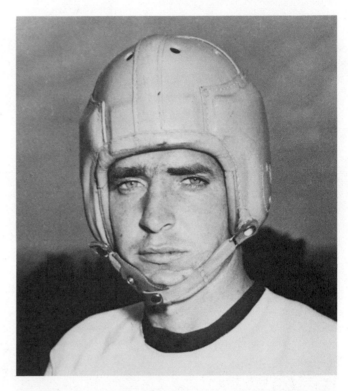

The Chicago Bears would not be able to claim Jim Finks until 1974, but the Pittsburgh Steelers had him from 1949-55. He played first as a defensive back and then as a T-formation quarterback. In 1955 Finks led the NFL in passing, with 165 completions for a total of 2,270 yards. –Pittsburgh Steelers

PADDY ALMOST BRINGS IT OFF

AT THE CLOSE of the 1955 season, George Halas, still 60 years old, at least for another month or so, and true to the promise he made to his wife, resigned as head coach of the Bears. As his replacement he chose a long-time friend, former teammate, and associate, Paddy Driscoll.

One of the first changes Driscoll made was to enlarge the coaching staff from five assistants to seven. Returning in that capacity were Clark Shaughnessy, Luke Johnsos, Phil Handler, and Bulldog Turner. Driscoll now added Sid Luckman to tutor the quarterbacks and Chick Jagade to work with the running backs. To coach the linemen, he hired George Connor, who had decided to retire from playing after an eight-year career that would assure him a place in the Pro Football Hall of Fame.

In 1956 Lenny Moore came into the league with the Baltimore Colts and Howard ("Hopalong") Cassady was a top draft pick of the Detroit Lions. And the Colts made an 80-cent telephone call to free agent Johnny Unitas, who had been playing semi-pro ball for $6 a game, offering him a tryout at quarterback. The only notable addition made by the Bears that year was J. C. Caroline, who had been a fine running back at Illinois and in fact had broken several of Red Grange's records there. The Bears would turn him into one of the best defensive backs in the league. Gone from the roster, however, was Ed Sprinkle, who had decided

to retire after 12 years of intimidating offensive teams of all types and sizes.

George Halas had been correct. The Bears were now of championship caliber. They bulldozed their way through the first three-quarters of the season, with an offense that was finally running up some formidable scores, 38 and 37 points against the Packers, 38 and 31 in defeating the 49ers, and 58 points against the Colts. The starting quarterback for the Colts in that lopsided (58–27) win of the Bears was George Shaw. When he was injured in the game, with Baltimore ahead 21–20 at that point, Johnny Unitas came off the bench, and the first pass he threw was intercepted by J. C. Caroline. The rest of the game was all downhill for the rookie quarterback, but it was the beginning of a brilliant 17-year career with the Colts that would eventually see him enshrined in the Hall of Fame.

After the first nine games of the season, the Bears had rung up a record of seven wins, one loss, and one tie, averaging almost 34 points a game, and resting happily if not securely in first place, a half game ahead of the Detroit Lions. Two of their remaining three games, however, were against those Lions.

A key game in the Bear season of 1956 ironically was their one tie. Trailing the Giants 17–3 late in the fourth quarter, it looked as if the Bears were about to suffer their second loss of the season. Only the Bears saw it differently. Ed Brown pitched out to Bill McColl on an end-around, who in turn lofted a bomb to Harlon Hill for a 78-yard touchdown. Then, with only a few seconds left in the game, Brown threw a long pass to Hill, who made a diving, juggling, rolling catch in the end zone for a 56-yard touchdown. George Halas called it "one of the most spectacular catches I've ever seen." And the Bears turned an apparent defeat into a tie—one that would enable them, as it turned out, to earn the conference title that year.

The first game with the Lions was at Detroit, and over 57,000 fans jammed into Briggs Stadium for this seemingly decisive match. Apparently George Halas couldn't take it anymore in the grandstands and was down on the field that afternoon, manning the Bear telephone alongside his appointed coach. But it didn't help. Bobby Layne, who always seemed to rise to a Bear occasion, had one of his better days of the year, passing for two touchdowns, running for another, and kicking six extra points as the Lions proceeded to demolish the Bears 42–10. The Bears sank a half-game into second place in the Western Conference.

Despite the mauling they had just taken, the Bears were not disheartened. J. C. Caroline said after the game: "They have a good ball club, but they're not *that* good." And George Halas was heard to say that "the race is still in our hands, still in our hands."

But the Bears also had to face the Cardinals, who so often before had thwarted their quest for a division crown. And there was still that other game with the Lions. This was not to be a spoiler year for the Cardinals, however, although they tried—no one could deny them that. Future Hall-of-Famer Ollie Matson raced 65 yards in the first quarter and 83 yards in the third quarter for touchdowns that were nullified by Cardinal penalties. The Bears could come up with only a field goal and a three-yard touchdown by J. C. Caroline, who, because of injuries to other backs, was switched from the defensive backfield to a running back that day. Caroline also saved the game when he caught up with Night Train Lane after a 75-yard run, bringing him down at the Bears' 10-yard line in the last play of the game. The Bears won 10–3.

The next week the Lions showed up. Two weeks earlier, the game between these two bruising teams had erupted into a brawl, and there was reason to believe it would be even worse this Sunday. The mood was set by a huge banner that stretched along a portion of the upper deck at Wrigley Field; it read:

WE WANT LION BLOOD!!!

To prevent the Bears from getting their wish, the Lions brought along four Detroit policemen to guard their bench and Chicago added 10 of their own, just in case. And true to all premonitions, the violence that after-

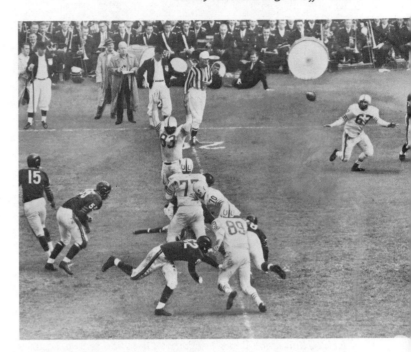

Ed Brown (15) throws to Harlon Hill (87) in a 1956 game against the Baltimore Colts. From this angle, it looks like a sure interception, but it wasn't. Everything turned out so well for the Bears that they won 58–27, accumulating the most points they had ever scored in a regular-season game. The other Bears are Larry Strickland (55), Kline Gilbert (62), and Stan Jones (78). The Colts are Gino Marchetti (89), Art Donovan (70), Tom Finnin (77), Don Joyce (83), and Doug Eggers (67). –Pro Football Hall of Fame

An altercation between the Bears and the Chicago Cardinals at Wrigley Field in 1956. Harlon Hill (87) does battle with Cardinal Pat Summerall (later a well-known TV announcer), while Bill McColl (83) holds on to George Blanda (16). Fred Williams (75) leaps into the thick of it, and Bill George (61) and Jack Hoffman (82) move up to help. The fight may have ended in a draw, but the Bears did win the game, 10–3. –Pro Football Hall of Fame

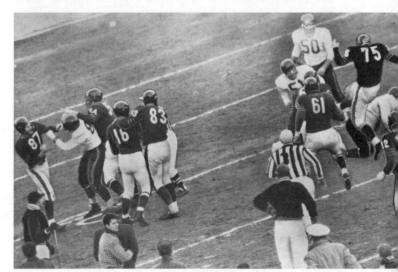

Better known as a defensive back, J. C. Caroline could also play offense when he had to. Here he plunges into the end zone for a score during the Bears' last game of the 1956 season, against the Detroit Lions. Their win (38–21) in this game gave the Bears their chance to play in the NFL championship that year. Bear No. 43 is end and future coach of the team, Jim Dooley. The Lions are Ray Krouse (70), Jim David (25), Sherwin Gandee (85), and Joe Schmidt (56). –Pro Football Hall of Fame

noon went from minor fistfights to a full-scale riot at the end of the game that involved not only the players on both teams but several hundred fans as well.

It was a brutal game all the way around, as Bobby Layne knew better than anybody. In the second quarter he was hit so hard from the blind side by defensive end Ed Meadows that he left the field with a concussion. After the game, Lion coach Buddy Parker fumed and accused: "We heard rumors all week that the Bears would be out to get Layne, but we didn't think they would be so open about it." Halas said the charges were "ridiculous"; rough play was just one of the occupational hazards of professional football, he explained. Whether Layne's injury was the result of a motivated act or simply an accident is a moot point, but it did hurt the Lions because they were never in the game after the incident. The Bears wreaked their revenge on the Lions 38–21 that afternoon and with it they took the Western Conference title. Rick Casares had the finest day of his career in this game, rushing for 190 yards on 17 carries, one of them a 68-yard touchdown run.

The Bears would now face the Giants for the NFL championship at Yankee Stadium in New York, and the confrontation would prove to be in many ways a repeat of that historic championship match-up between the same two teams back in 1934, which has become known as the "Sneakers Game."

In 1956 the New York turf was just as frozen as it had been 22 years earlier. But despite the freezing temperatures, almost 57,000 people came out to watch the favored Giants. This was a team with an impressive roster of names. Besides backs like Charlie Conerly, Alex Webster, Mel Triplett, and future Hall-of-Famer Frank Gifford, there were star-quality players like Roosevelt ("Rosey") Grier, Sam Huff, Dick Modzelewski, Jim Katcavage, Ray Wietecha, Kyle Rote, Ben Agajanian, Emlen Tunnell, Andy Robustelli, and Rosey Brown—the last three also in the Hall of Fame.

When the Giants found the field slick with ice, true to tradition, they came out wearing flat-soled sneakers. The Bears obviously did not remember vividly enough their slip-and-slide defeat of 1934, and they wore rubber-soled shoes with short cleats. These didn't work especially well for them, and they changed to sneakers in the second half. But it was to little avail. As some racehorses take to mud, the Giants in title contention apparently took to ice. They were invincible that chilly Sunday afternoon and by half-time had run up a 34–7 lead. The Bears were thoroughly demoralized by then, and when it was all over the score stood at an embarrassing 47–7. It was a most unhappy end to the Bears' most successful season since they had defeated the Giants for the NFL title 10 years earlier.

The individual players' purses for the championship game had risen. Each of the Giants was $3,779 wealthier after the game and each Bear received $2,485 as the loser's share (about $500 more than they took home as winners back in 1946).

In looking back over the year, the Bears did have some prideful memories, both as individuals and as a team. Rick Casares led the league in rushing and set an

---

1956 SEASON .818

Won 9   Lost 2   Tied 1

Paddy Driscoll — Coach	Bears	Opponents
Baltimore Colts. . . . .(A)	21	28
Green Bay Packers. . . . .(A)	37	21
San Francisco 49ers . . . .(H)	31	7
Baltimore Colts . . . .(H)	58	27
San Francisco 49ers . . . .(A)	38	21
Los Angeles Rams . . . .(A)	35	24
Green Bay Packers. . . . .(H)	38	14
Los Angeles Rams . . . .(H)	30	21
New York Giants . . . .(A)	17	17
Detroit Lions . . . .(A)	10	42
Chicago Cardinals . . . .(H)	10	3
Detroit Lions . . . .(H)	38	21
Totals.	363	246

NFL Championship

New York Giants . . . .(A)	7	47

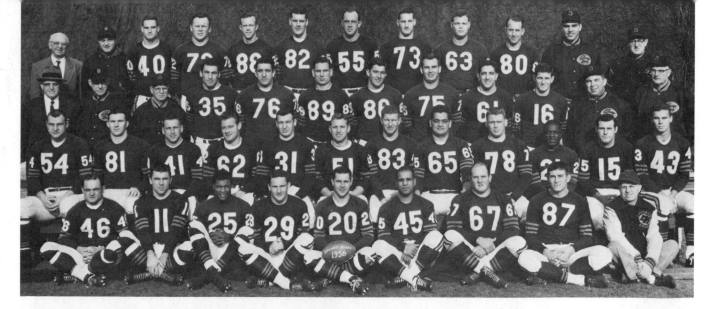

The Bears of 1956. Top row (from the left): Frank Halas (front office), Sid Luckman (asst. coach), Stan Wallace, Bill Wightkin, Gene Schroeder, Jack Hoffman, Larry Strickland, Bill Bishop, M. L. Brackett, John Helwig, George Connor (asst. coach), Ed Rozy (trainer). Third row: George Halas (front office), Clark Shaughnessy (asst. coach), Paddy Driscoll (coach), Rick Casares, John Mellekas, John Hoffman, Ed Meadows, Fred Williams, Bill George, George Blanda, Phil Handler (asst. coach), Luke Johnsos (asst. coach). Second row: Dick Klawitter, Doug Atkins, Harland Carl, Kline Gilbert, Joe Fortunato, Wayne Hansen, Bill McColl, Herman Clark, Stan Jones, Perry Jeter, Ed Brown, Jim Dooley. Front row: Don Bingham, Jim Haluska, J. C. Caroline, McNeil Moore, Ray Gene Smith, Bobby Watkins, Tom Roggeman, Harlon Hill, Joe Bernardi (manager). –Pro Football Hall of Fame

In this sequence, Rick Casares (35) is shown bulling his way to the Bears' only touchdown during the 47–7 trouncing they took from the New York Giants in the 1956 NFL championship game. Handing off to him is Bear quarterback Ed Brown (15). The Bear blockers are Bill Wightkin (72), Bill McColl (83), Kline Gilbert (62), and Stan Jones (78) to his left; the Giants include Rosey Grier (76), Emlen Tunnell (45), Bill Svoboda (30), and Harland Svare (84). –Pro Football Hall of Fame

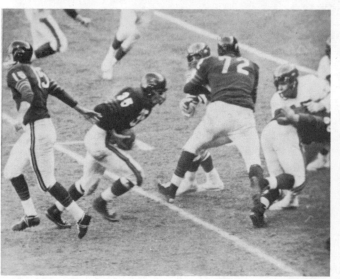

Here, in a game against the San Francisco 49ers, Rick Casares is going in for one of his 14 touchdowns (12 rushing, two receiving) that set a Bear record in 1956. Other Bears in the picture are Bill Wightkin (72), Herman Clark (65), and clutched between two 49ers at the right is Bobby Watkins. The Bears won the game handily, 31–7. –Pro Football Hall of Fame

all-time Bear record when he ground out a total of 1,126 yards (122 more than Beattie Feathers rushed for back in 1934 and only 20 yards short of the NFL record held by Steve Van Buren of the Philadelphia Eagles). He also led the league in touchdowns rushing, a total of 12. Harlon Hill caught 47 passes for 1,128 yards and had a league-leading average of 24 yards per reception. In three years now, Hill had caught 32 touchdown passes and gained 3,041 yards with his pass receptions. No other Bear receiver has ever come close to that three-year accomplishment. Ed Brown led the NFL in passing, with a 57% completion average (96 of 168) and a total of 11 touchdown passes.

As a team, the Bears had the most devastating offense in the NFL, leading the league in four categories—most points scored, 363 (an average per game of 30.3); most yards rushing, 2,468 (an average of 206 per game); most touchdowns rushing, 22; and the highest average yardage per passing attempt, 8.77. They also had the most first downs rushing (140) and most points after touchdowns (45). And five Bears were named to the All-Pro team that year: Rick Casares, Bill George, Harlon Hill, Stan Jones, and Larry Strickland.

The year 1957 was an especially lucrative one in terms of college talent moving into the NFL. The draft produced Jim Brown for Cleveland, Paul Hornung and Ron Kramer for Green Bay, Jim Parker for the Colts, John Brodie for the 49ers, Sonny Jurgensen for the Eagles, and Len Dawson for the Steelers, though he would make his mark in the AFL later rather than the NFL. The Bears were not left out of the rich pickings either. They added two fine tackles in Earl Leggett, from Louisiana State, and Bob Kilcullen who had done his playing at Texas Tech. But the real find for the Bears that year was a young running back from tiny Florida A & M and, as the story goes, assistant coach Phil Handler had heard about him from a jockey at Hialeah Racetrack in Miami. The halfback was Willie Galimore, who would prove that the jockey indeed had a very keen eye for football talent. The Bears slipped him in as a late-round draft choice. As one observer put it: "Galimore was one of the last great steals before pro scouting and recruiting became so sophisticated."

Perhaps because of rising costs and the success of the preceding season, the Bears raised their ticket prices in 1957 to $4.50 for a box seat and $3.50 for a reserved grandstand seat—and season tickets were readily available that year at $27 and $24 respectively.

Expectations for the 1957 season were high, but the Bears of 1957 hardly resembled the team that had won the NFL West title the year before. The players were pretty much the same, the results of their efforts were not. Three straight losses at the outset of the season dropped them into last place in their division. In the fourth game, Willie Galimore became a starter and shot some excitement into Wrigley Field when he ran for four touchdowns and rushed for a total of 153 yards against the Los Angeles Rams. His performance prompted *Chicago Tribune* reporter George Strickler to write: "A new meteor flashed across the football horizon in Wrigley Field yesterday," and the comparisons to McAfee and Grange were flooding in.

From that point on, it was a matter of trading wins with losses for the rest of the year, and the Bears ended

Pay scales in 1957 were hardly what they would come to be in the 1970s. The Bears that year were the third-highest paying team in the league. The following list is from a report prepared by the NFL and submitted to the Anti-Trust Subcommittee of the U.S. House of Representatives in July, 1957.

Team	Total Salaries	Individual Salary Range
Cleveland Browns	$368,031	$6,000 – 19,000
Los Angeles Rams	352,958	5,500 – 20,000
Chicago Bears	*342,525*	*6,500 – 14,200*
San Francisco 49ers	332,614	5,600 – 20,100
Detroit Lions	330,375	5,500 – 20,000
New York Giants	324,258	5,200 – 16,000
Chicago Cardinals	318,441	5,500 – 20,000
Baltimore Colts	294,392	6,000 – 17,500
Philadelphia Eagles	283,483	5,750 – 13,500
Green Bay Packers	277,642	5,000 – 18,500
Pittsburgh Steelers	276,875	5,250 – 12,250
Washington Redskins	275,942	5,000 – 14,000

This is the way the more innovative end-zone inhabitants shagged extra points at Wrigley Field during the 1950s. –Pro Football Hall of Fame

the season with a disheartening record of only five wins against seven defeats. Two of the Bears' losses were to the Baltimore Colts, led by a Johnny Unitas who in his first full year as a starter topped the league in total

1957 SEASON   .417
Won 5   Lost 7   Tied 0

Paddy Driscoll — Coach	Bears	Opponents
Green Bay Packers...........(A)	17	21
Baltimore Colts.............(A)	10	21
San Francisco 49ers.........(H)	17	21
Los Angeles Rams...........(H)	34	26
San Francisco 49ers.........(A)	17	21
Los Angeles Rams...........(A)	16	10
Green Bay Packers...........(H)	21	14
Baltimore Colts.............(H)	14	29
Detroit Lions...............(A)	27	7
Washington Redskins.........(H)	3	14
Chicago Cardinals...........(A)	14	6
Detroit Lions...............(H)	13	21
Totals.................	203	211

passing yardage (2,550) and touchdown passes (24). The only team the Bears beat twice were the Rams.

Rick Casares ended up as the league's second leading rusher that year with a total of 700 yards and a 3.4 average per carry, behind Jim Brown, a Cleveland rookie destined for the Hall of Fame, who showed the entire NFL just what he had in store for them during the next eight seasons. Ed Brown did most of the passing that year, but his completion average was only 45%. The leading receiver on the team was Jim Dooley, who caught 37 passes for 530 yards, while Harlon Hill, hampered by injuries for a good part of the season, caught only 21 passes for 483 yards. The Bear defense, surprisingly enough, gave up fewer points to the opposition in 1957 than they had the year before when the Bears won their division.

But the Bears who had almost reached the summit in Paddy Driscoll's first year as head coach ended this season in next-to-last place, leaving everyone—especially the Bears—wondering at the erratic course they seemed to be careening up and down on.

HALAS COMES BACK

WHEN THE 1957 SEASON was mercifully over, George Halas decided he couldn't take it anymore spending his days behind a desk and merely handling the team telephone during games. He promoted coach Paddy Driscoll to a vice-president in the front office and demoted him to an assistant coach on the field. He took back the head coaching chores himself, for the third time.

Chuck Mather, who had been head coach at the University of Kansas, was signed on as an assistant, a job he would hold for the next eight years. Also hired was George Allen, an end coach from the Rams, who like Hunk Anderson before him would learn later just how strongly his employer regarded the unassailability of a written contract. And beginning his 10-year career with the Bears was Johnny Morris, a running back and receiver drafted from the University of California at Santa Barbara. Another newcomer to the Bears, although not to the NFL, was 32-year-old guard Abe Gibron, acquired from the Philadelphia Eagles.

Ed Brown continued to hold down the primary quarterbacking job in 1958, relieved part of the time by Zeke Bratkowski, who had returned from military service the year before. Harlon Hill was still plagued with injuries; so too was Willie Galimore.

The Bears changed course in 1958 almost as abruptly as they had the year before, but this time it was for the better. In fact, by the eighth game of the season the Bears were only a game out of first place in the NFL West, with a 5–2–0 record. But then, unfortunately, they met the first-place Baltimore Colts, led by Johnny Unitas and his two favorite receivers and fellow Hall-of-Famers, Ray Berry and Lenny Moore. More than 48,500 fans jammed into Wrigley Field to watch the Bears suffer their first shutout since 1946. The 17–0 loss virtually removed the Bears from contention that year, even though they won three of their remaining four games, and they ended the season with a respectable record of 8–4–0, tied for second place in their conference with the Los Angeles Rams.

Offense was the problem for the Bears. The defensive team, led by linebackers Bill George and Joe Fortunato and linemen Doug Atkins, Fred Williams, and Bill Bishop, had been excellent, except for two games which they and the Bear fans would as soon forget (the Colts scored 51 points against them in the second game of the season and the Rams hit them for 41 later in the year).

How a good defense can stymie even the best offense was illustrated in the playoff between the Cleveland Browns and the New York Giants for the Eastern Conference title that year. Jim Brown, who rushed for a record 1,527 yards (and 17 touchdowns) during the season, was held to just eight yards, and the total Cleveland offense to only 86 yards, in that game. The Giants, though, lost to the Colts in a dramatic

Flanker back Johnny Morris tries to turn on some of the speed he was known for to evade the Philadelphia Eagles closing in on him. Drafted by the Bears in 1958, he was co-holder of the world's record for the 50-yard dash (5.2 seconds). Morris was the Bears' all-time leading pass receiver (a total of 356 passes for 5,059 yards). When his playing career ended, he became a television sports announcer in Chicago. –Chicago Bears

sudden-death championship game, the first time in NFL history that the title was decided in overtime.

One plus for the Bears' offense during 1958 was the performance of Johnny Morris, who proved to be among the best kickoff and punt-return specialists in the league. The season, George Halas said, offered some hope: from 5–7–0 and fifth place to 8–4–0 and second place in one year was encouraging.

1958 SEASON   .667

Won 8   Lost 4   Tied 0

George Halas — Coach	Bears	Opponents
Green Bay Packers . . . .(A)	34	20
Baltimore Colts . . . .(A)	38	51
San Francisco 49ers . . . .(H)	28	6
Los Angeles Rams . . . .(H)	31	10
San Francisco 49ers . . . .(A)	27	14
Los Angeles Rams . . . .(A)	35	41
Green Bay Packers . . . .(H)	24	10
Baltimore Colts . . . .(H)	0	17
Detroit Lions . . . .(A)	20	7
Pittsburgh Steelers . . . .(A)	10	24
Chicago Cardinals . . . .(H)	30	14
Detroit Lions . . . .(H)	21	16
Totals.	298	230

A surprise that year, but only in retrospect, was the horrendous 1–10–1 record posted by the Green Bay Packers, the worst in their entire history. And it was a team, granted a rather young one, with players whose names were to become legend: Paul Hornung, Jerry Kramer, Jim Ringo, Max McGee, and Dan Currie and future Hall-of-Famers Jim Taylor, Bart Starr, Len Ford, Forrest Gregg, and Ray Nitschke. Because of the Packers' abysmal showing that year, the powers in Green Bay were looking for a new coach and they found one in the assistant coaching ranks of the New York Giants. Vince Lombardi would begin his career in Green Bay in 1959, and the Packers would change their ways considerably—change so dramatically, in fact, that their new coach would also be enshrined in the Hall of Fame.

For 1959 the Bears bolstered their defense by adding linebacker Larry Morris (no relation to flanker back Johnny Morris), who came to them from the Redskins, and by drafting future All-Pro safety Richie Petitbon, from Tulane. And in 1959 there was a new "Three B's" quarterback combo when Rudy Bukich,

THE 1958 BEARS

acquired from the Washington Redskins, joined the club to serve along with Brown and Bratkowski. Gone, however, was place-kicker and sometime quarterback George Blanda, who after 10 years with the Bears was supposedly close to the end of the line as a pro, but, one could say, was actually just beginning his pro football career, for there were 16 good years of playing time still ahead of him. Among the all-time NFL records he garnered in his long career were most field goals (335) and most extra points (943) kicked, most total points scored (2,002), and most pass completions in a single game (37, with the Houston Oilers in 1964). And Blanda still holds the Bear record for most points scored (541) and most points after touchdowns (247).

Because of their better-than-average showing the year before, everyone expected great things from the 1959 Bears, but it was not what the Bears were about to give them, at least at the beginning of the season. The Green Bay Packers of lowly last place the two previous years, beat them in the season opener. After that surprise, the Bears proceeded to lose three of their next four games. The one game they won was over the Baltimore Colts, who would go on to win the NFL title that year. Their fans began to steel themselves for the frustrations and disappointments of another losing season. Some of them began to question whether

An All-Pro eight times in his 14-year Chicago Bear career, Bill George, running down Jim Taylor in this game in Green Bay, was the first of the great middle linebackers. Only Bobby Joe Green and Doug Buffone have played in more Bear games than George. And a little-known fact about him is that at one time in his early years with the team he kicked four field goals and 14 extra points. –Pro Football Hall of Fame

Summer camp at Rennselaer, Indiana, 1959. Willie Galimore (28) follows guard Abe Gibron through the motions during a workout session. The Bears used the facilities at St. Joseph's College in Rennselaer as their summer camp for 31 years until they moved to Lake Forest College, in Lake Forest, Illinois, in 1957. Gibron played only two seasons with the Bears but later served seven years as the team's assistant coach and another three as head coach. Galimore, an electrifying open-field runner, ranks fourth in all-time rushing for the Bears. –Pro Football Hall of Fame

Halas should remain at the helm; others wondered what it would be like to have an awesome offense; still others wondered how the team's performance could be so amazingly unpredictable.

And perhaps just to keep the fans guessing, the Bears of 1959 turned around and won their last seven games in a row, ending up in second place with a record of 8–4–0, only one game behind the conference champion Baltimore Colts. Chicagoans scratched their heads and shrugged their shoulders all the way into the 1960 season. By now they could hardly imagine what to expect.

The 1960 season brought with it a new American Football League, one that would last longer than the three which had come and gone since 1926. The AFL, which would pose a threat to the NFL for a number of years and eventually merge peacefully and successfully with it, launched itself with eight franchises—none, to the good fortune of the Bears, in the city of Chicago. The teams that took the field that first year, split up into two divisions, were the Houston Oilers, Buffalo Bills, Boston Patriots, and New York Titans; and the Oakland Raiders, Denver Broncos, Los Angeles Chargers, and Dallas Texans. There would be name changes and moves among them, but none would fold.

There were also a number of changes in the NFL. The owners of the Cardinals felt they could no longer survive in Chicago, so they were allowed to move the franchise to St. Louis, ending what had become a Chicago institution. The Cardinals, under various names and owners, including Hall-of-Famer Charles W. Bidwill, Sr., a former vice-president of the Chicago Bears, had played football in Chicago off and on for 61 years—continuously as a professional team since 1918. Another change in the NFL was the granting of a

The "Three B's" of the Bears' 1959 quarterbacking department: from the left, Rudy Bukich, Zeke Bratkowski, and Ed Brown. Bukich, who put in more time on the field in the 1960s, is third on the Bears' list of all-time leading passers; Brown is fifth, and Bratkowski 13th. –Pro Football Hall of Fame

new franchise to the Dallas Cowboys, raising the number of teams to 13 in 1960. The NFL also needed a new commissioner because Bert Bell, who had guided the league since 1946, had died of a heart attack while watching the Philadelphia Eagles/Pittsburgh Steelers game the year before. A 33-year-old named Pete Rozelle was selected for the post.

The Bears entered the 1960 season with a seven-game winning streak behind them. They added an eighth win quickly by setting down a much improved Lombardi-coached Packer team 17–14. For the first time in several years, it looked to many Bear fans as if their team could finally handle the Baltimore Colts, the league's powerhouse of the late 1950s; and if they could, the divisional title they had been lusting after might be theirs once again. But the Bears found out that the Colts had other ideas. In the second game of the season, they welcomed the Bears to Baltimore and overpowered them 42–7.

When the Colts came to Chicago, the Bears were still in contention (so were the Packers, however). Almost 49,000 people sat in Wrigley Field to watch the Bears rise to the occasion. With 17 seconds remaining in the game, the score 20–17, and the Colts facing a fourth down and 14 yards to go back on the Bears' 39-yard line, it looked like a sure Bear win. But then in professional football one cannot discount the fates in

1959 SEASON .667		
Won 8 Lost 4 Tied 0		
George Halas — Coach	**Bears**	**Opponents**
Green Bay Packers . . . .(A)	6	9
Baltimore Colts. . . . .(A)	26	21
Los Angeles Rams . . . .(H)	21	28
Baltimore Colts . . . .(H)	7	21
San Francisco 49ers . . . .(A)	17	20
Los Angeles Rams . . . .(A)	26	21
Green Bay Packers . . . .(H)	28	17
San Francisco 49ers . . . .(H)	14	3
Detroit Lions . . . .(A)	24	14
Chicago Cardinals. . . . .(A)	31	7
Pittsburgh Steelers . . . .(H)	27	21
Detroit Lions . . . .(H)	25	14
Totals.	252	196

the person of a Johnny Unitas. Declining to go for a field goal, which if successful would have tied the game, Unitas faded back to pass. There was plenty of pressure from the Bear line, especially from end Doug Atkins, who had bloodied Unitas's forehead, nose, and mouth a few plays earlier. Unitas just barely got the pass off. Down at the 5-yard line, Lenny Moore and Bear defender J. C. Caroline were racing side by side, their eyes on the ball spiraling toward them. Then suddenly they collided. Caroline went crashing to the ground, and Moore careened into the end zone, where the ball fell perfectly into his hands. The Bears looked for a penalty flag at the point of the collision. But what they saw was a referee standing there with his arms raised in the signal for a touchdown. The kick for the extra point was good, and Chicago lost 24–20.

The Bears came right back, however, winning their next two games in a row. They were only a half game out of first place, because the Colts had lost their next two games. Now the team to beat were the Packers, who had not beaten the Bears in Wrigley Field since 1952. And there Green Bay illustrated all too graphically how well Vince Lombardi had succeeded in building up the team in that small Wisconsin town. The Pack annihilated the Bears 41–13.

Paul Hornung was only one of the day's heroes. Scoring 23 points—two touchdowns, two field goals, and five extra points—he broke the single-season NFL scoring record of 138 set in 1942 by another Packer, Don Hutson. (By season's end, Hornung would have a total of 176 points, a record that still stands in the NFL.) But that day there was also Jim Taylor, who rushed for 121 yards in 24 carries, not to mention Bart Starr, who threw two touchdown passes and guided the team with brilliancy. The Packers went on to win their first divisional title since 1944. In seventh place were the Dallas Cowboys, who under coach Tom Landry posted a first-season record of 0–11–1.

The loss to the Packers was the beginning of the end for the Bears, in 1960 anyway. They folded miserably after that, shut out 42–0 by the Cleveland Browns and 36–0 by the Detroit Lions in their last two games. It was a dismal 5–6–1 record and a fifth-place finish for a team that was actually in contention three weeks before the regular season was over—hardly the way to start a new decade of NFL football.

In the early years of the 1960s, it was not uncommon in the senior Halas household for the telephone to ring suddenly in the dead of night. Stirred from sleep, George Halas would answer it, to hear at the other end a deep if somewhat disjointed voice cussing, berating, and otherwise unpleasantly addressing him. It was the voice of the only Chicago Bear who would have dared to do this, Halas's premier defensive end, Doug Atkins. The topics that Atkins chose to air at those odd hours would vary, but inevitably included complaints about his meager salary, the way the team was being coached, training rules, and other football-oriented problems. An angry Halas would respond by giving it back to Atkins as profanely as he received it, and before hanging up would urge him in impolite terms to "go sober up."

Colorful personalities were part of that era in professional football before the inflow of the really big money from television, larger crowds, and expanded schedules would convert the young men who played the game into the player/businessman types we know today. The pro football milieu of the early 1960s was one in which players spent more time on pranks or raising a little hell or hazing rookies than they did reading the *Wall Street Journal* or taking acting lessons or weighing the comparative values of a Mercedes-Benz 450 against those of a Ferrari.

1960 SEASON	.455		
Won 5 Lost 6 Tied 1			
George Halas — Coach		**Bears**	**Opponents**
Green Bay Packers	(A)	17	14
Baltimore Colts	(A)	7	42
Los Angeles Rams	(H)	34	27
San Francisco 49ers	(H)	27	10
Los Angeles Rams	(A)	24	24
San Francisco 49ers	(A)	7	25
Baltimore Colts	(H)	20	24
Detroit Lions	(H)	28	7
Dallas Cowboys	(H)	17	7
Green Bay Packers	(H)	13	41
Cleveland Browns	(A)	0	42
Detroit Lions	(A)	0	36
Totals		194	299

Doug Atkins, in his inimitable way, was perhaps the most graphic symbol of the time. At 6-feet-8 and with a playing weight that varied between 240 and 280 pounds, he was as strong and as powerful on the field as the ruggedest players in Bear legends, a peer of Bronko Nagurski, George Connor, and Dick Butkus. "Trying to throw over [Atkins was] like trying to throw over a mountain," Bart Starr once said. And off the field, Atkins could take his place in anyone's Hall of Fame for rowdyism and roistering.

Despite all their post-game shenanigans, Doug Atkins and the other Bears were in Chicago to play football. George Halas would have it no other way.

The man who received all those calls from Atkins in the middle of the night referred to him as "the best defensive end I've ever seen," and Halas had seen quite a few.

To even up the two NFL conferences into seven teams each, a franchise had been awarded to the twin cities of Minneapolis-St. Paul. The new team, called the Minnesota Vikings, joined the Bears in the Western Conference, and the Dallas Cowboys moved over to the Eastern Conference. Beginning in 1961, the regular-season schedule was increased to 14 games, following six league exhibition games.

After the erratic seasons following the Bears' 1956 division title, Halas conceded that it was time to seriously rebuild his team. The defense was clearly not the problem. The Bears had three of the best linebackers in the business in Bill George, Joe Fortunato, and Larry Morris. The defensive backfield was also outstanding, especially when rookies Roosevelt ("Rosey") Taylor, from Grambling, and Dave Whitsell, from Indiana, were added to the corps that included Richie Petitbon and J. C. Caroline. The defensive line was healthy and strong, spearheaded by Doug Atkins, Bob Kilcullen, and Fred Williams. It was the offense, however, that needed shaping up. So Halas traded with the Rams for quarterback Bill Wade, then added the first of the really great tight ends and the Bears' first-round draft choice, Mike Ditka, from Purdue. Another major acquisition was center Mike Pyle, a Chicagoan who did his college playing out east at Yale.

The Bears of 1961 not only had to rebuild their offensive attack, they literally had to rebuild their front office. A fire broke out in the downtown building where they made their home and virtually destroyed all of the Bear business offices. Tragically, along with furniture and other nonessentials, a wealth of photographs, written records, memorabilia, and other irreplaceable items were lost forever. The staff then moved to another building a block east on Madison Street in the heart of Chicago's Loop.

The 1961 season opener was an astounding one for the Bears. The expansion team from Minnesota devastated them 37–13 in a game they had expected to win easily. The Vikings introduced their quarterback, rookie Fran Tarkenton, who showed that he could pass with the best. In his first regular-season game, he threw four touchdown passes, among 17 completions out of only 23 attempts. And he raised scrambling—which would become his trademark—to a new art when he ran for a fifth touchdown. Defensive end Jim Marshall was also in the line-up for the Vikes that afternoon, and his pro football career, like Tarkenton's, would endure for almost two decades.

Ray Sons, sports editor of the Chicago Sun-Times, once wrote: "Doug Atkins stories are something like the legends of Beowulf, Siegfried and St. George. They aren't quite believable." There are, however, quite a few people still around, telling them with the faith and conviction of confirmed fundamentalists.

One story reveals more than a little about the personality of the enormous end. It is told by Blanton Collier, who was an assistant coach at Cleveland the year Atkins broke in with the Browns and among whose duties was "looking after" the free-wheeling rookie. At a lunch counter one day after a morning practice session, Atkins offhandedly asked Collier if his wife was in town.

Collier shook his head negatively: "I'm batching it," he said.

"Are you behaving yourself, coach?" Atkins asked.

"Of course I am."

"It's hell, ain't it coach?" sighed Atkins.

Then there was the day he came onto the practice field late, clad only in shorts, T-shirt, and a helmet. He raced up and down the field several times before the mystified eyes of his fellow players and the coaching staff and then trotted back into the locker room. Asked later what he had been doing, he replied: "Just breaking in a new helmet."

Bill Bishop, a tackle who played alongside Atkins, once said about him: "If he'd had the temperament of Ed Sprinkle, they would have had to bar him from football." They also tell the story of the time Atkins had a martini-drinking contest with tackle Fred Williams. "I drank 21," Williams said, "same as Atkins. But he beat me. I figured because he drove me home and carried me in that he must have won."

And, of course, there are the incidents involving the pit bulldog named Rebel he kept in his dormitory room at the Bear training camp in Rensselaer, Indiana. The dog was trained to kill on command—at least that's what Atkins had all the other players convinced of. No guest would attempt to leave the room or pass by Rebel, even to go to the bathroom, it has been told, unless it was sanctioned by the dog's master.

Tom Fears, one of the Los Angeles Rams' leading pass receivers and later coach of the New Orleans Saints, said of Atkins: "When they made Doug, they threw away the mold . . . there'll never be another like him in professional football."

The season for the Bears that year could not be called a success—a record of eight wins and six losses was only good enough for a third-place tie, with the

Colts, in their conference. But there was evidence that this was a team to be reckoned with, as the Vikings discovered when they lost to the Bears 52–35 in the last game of the season.

One highlight of 1961 was the day the Bear defense stopped cold the revolutionary "shotgun offense" of the San Francisco 49ers that had scored 49, 35, and 38 points respectively in the three games before they met the Bears. And this was done so effectively—the final score was Bears 31, 49ers 0—that San Francisco went back to using the T formation.

Willie Galimore had his finest season as a running back in 1961, gaining 707 yards on an average carry of 4.6 yards. The most spectacular play of his career also came that year. In the final quarter against the Baltimore Colts, he caught a short screen pass from Ed Brown, and in a dazzling display of running carried it 84 yards for the touchdown that won the game for the Bears. George Strickler, writing for the *Chicago Tribune,* said: "Galimore's run stamped him as one of football's all-time great open-field runners."

Quarterback Bill Wade had an exceptional year in his debut with the Bears—throwing 22 touchdown passes, gaining 2,258 yards in the air, and registering a completion percentage of 56%. In addition to Galimore, he had very worthy receivers in Mike Ditka and Johnny Morris. Ditka, an almost unanimous choice for NFL Rookie of the Year, led the team with 56 pass receptions for 1,076 yards. His 12 catches for touchdowns were only one short of the all-time Bear record set back in 1947 by Ken Kavanaugh. Johnny Morris had been converted from a running back to a flanker, and this was his first real year as a receiver He showed that he was not only a threat on long passes, because

Quarterback Bill Wade lets go with a pass here against the Minnesota Vikings in 1961. It was his first year with the Bears, having been acquired from the Los Angeles Rams. Wade is the only Bear quarterback to have passed for more than 2,000 yards in a season three times. –Chicago Bears.

Rick Casares puts a move on Clancy Osborne (31) of the Vikings in this 1961 game. The Bears beat Minnesota 52–35 at Wrigley Field that day. No. 58 on the Vikings is Rip Hawkins. –Chicago Bears

1961 SEASON	.571	
Won 8 Lost 6 Tied 0		
George Halas — Coach	Bears	Opponents
Minnesota Vikings............(A)	13	37
Los Angeles Rams ....(A)	21	17
Green Bay Packers...........(A)	0	24
Detroit Lions ....(A)	31	17
Baltimore Colts ....(H)	24	10
San Francisco 49ers ....(H)	31	0
Baltimore Colts..............(A)	21	20
Philadelphia Eagles...........(A)	14	16
Green Bay Packers...........(H)	28	31
San Francisco 49ers ....(A)	31	41
Los Angeles Rams ....(H)	28	24
Detroit Lions ....(H)	15	16
Cleveland Browns ....(H)	17	14
Minnesota Vikings............(H)	52	35
Totals................	326	302

A rare picture that shows Willie Galimore (28) and Bo Farrington (84) of the Bears in action together. It was taken during a game against the Baltimore Colts in 1961 that the Bears won 21–20. Both young men were killed in an automobile accident in 1964. Galimore had played for the Bears seven years, Farrington four. –Chicago Bears

of his great speed (a sprinter in college, he was co-holder of the world's record for the 50-yard dash—5.2), but he also excelled at short passes thrown into highly congested defensive areas. He would go on to catch more passes for more total yardage than any other receiver in Bear history.

This was also the year in which end John ("Bo") Farrington tied an all-time Bear record and tied what was then a league record by taking a pass 98 yards for a touchdown to help the Bears defeat a tough Detroit Lion team, 31–17. And in the second Lion game of the season, Bear place-kicker Roger Leclerc also tied what was then an NFL record and set a Bear record when he kicked five field goals in the game. Only Ernie Nevers and Bob Waterfield had accomplished that before. Unfortunately for the Bears, however, Leclerc's field goals accounted for all of their points, and they lost 16–15.

Bear rookie Ronnie Bull (29) finds the awesome Green Bay defense converging from all sides in this 1962 game at Wrigley Field. Among the Packers are Hank Gremminger (46), Willie Wood (24), and Henry Jordan (74). Bull ranks fifth on the list of all-time Bear rushers, with 2,871 total yards. –Chicago Bears

Green Bay back Paul Hornung reverses his normal role, going after Bear defensive back Bennie McRae (26), who has just intercepted a Packer pass. The Bears lost this game to the team that won the 1962 NFL crown. Looking on from the sidelines is Bear John Johnson (76). –Vernon Biever

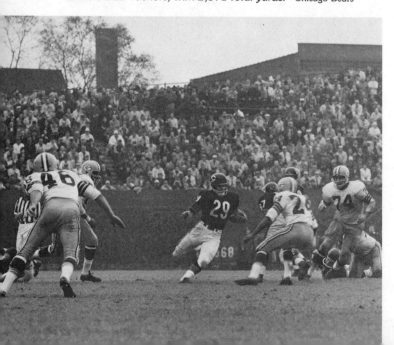

In 1962 the Bears added defensive end Ed O'Bradovich, from the University of Illinois. Bennie McRae, from Michigan, joined the already outstanding Bear defensive backfield. The offense, however, still faced some rather serious problems. Both Rick Casares and Willie Galimore, who together had contributed almost 1,300 yards rushing the year before, were injured and would spend much of the season on the sidelines. The loss of Galimore was especially disheartening because he was well on his way to a superlative season, gaining 181 yards rushing in the opening day victory (30–14) over the San Francisco 49ers. He was injured the following week. With Casares and Galimore out of the line-up, the rushing responsibilities fell to the Bears' first-round draft choice that year, Ronnie Bull, from Baylor, and Joe Marconi, a fullback the Bears acquired from the Rams. Another noteworthy addition to the Bear roster in 1962 was Bobby Joe Green, traded to them from the Pittsburgh Steelers. He would handle the Bears' punting responsibilities over the next 12 years.

The Green Bay Packers, who had breezed through the Western Conference the year before and then crushed the New York Giants 37–0 in the NFL championship game, were clearly the team to beat in 1962. Accomplishing that, however, was another matter. The Bears, after winning their first two games, visited Green Bay and were trounced 49–0.

When they faced the Detroit Lions for the first time that year, the Bears had lost only one game besides the Packer debacle and had come up with four wins.

Bear fullback Joe Marconi (34), acquired from Los Angeles in 1962, attracts a horde of his former teammates during this game against the Rams. Marconi led the Bears in rushing that year. The other identifiable players are quarterback Bill Wade (9) and tight end Mike Ditka (89) of the Bears, and Ram defenders Jack Pardee (32), Ed Meador (21), Lindon Crow (41), Mike Henry (53), and Merlin Olsen (74). –Pro Football Hall of Fame

Detroit had an identical 4–2–0 record; both teams were two games behind the undefeated Packers. The Bears, however, dropped into third place as the Lions squeezed out an 11–3 win at Detroit. And that is as high as the Bears could rise that season. They ended

Bear end Mike Ditka leaps high for this touchdown pass from Bill Wade in a 31–30 win over the Minnesota Vikings at Wrigley Field in 1962. Wade set an all-time Bear record by passing for a total of 3,172 yards that year. Other Bears in the picture are Herman Lee (70), Bob Wetoska (63), Mike Pyle (50), Ted Karras (67), and Rick Casares (35). The Vikings are Jim Prestel (79), Paul Dickson (76), Clancy Osborne (31), John McCormick (51), and Ed Sharockman (45). –Pro Football Hall of Fame

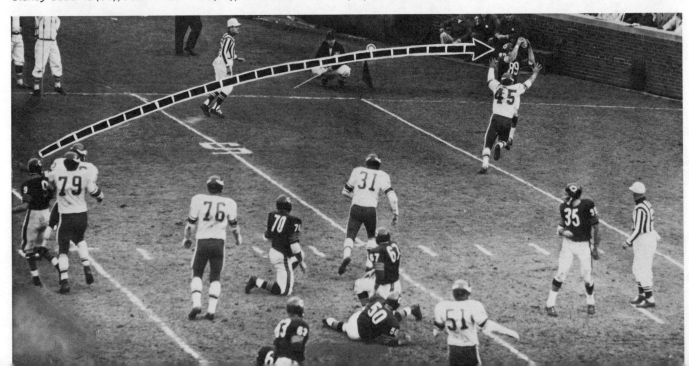

up with a 9–5–0 record, definitely respectable when compared with the Vikings' 2–11–1 and the Rams' 1–12–1. The Packers, who lost only one of 14 games, went on to defeat the Giants again for the NFL championship, this time by a score of 16–7.

Quarterback Bill Wade topped his 1961 performance by setting two new Bear records: most total passing yardage, 3,172, and most pass completions, 225. In pass completions—18 of them for touchdowns—he also topped the league. Mike Ditka and Johnny Morris each had 58 pass receptions, tied for fifth among NFL receivers that season. And Ronnie Bull was named Rookie of the Year.

One of the highlights of the 1962 season was a dramatic win over the Vikings. With less than half a minute to go and Minnesota in possession of the ball, Fran Tarkenton was thinking of nothing other than running out the clock on their narrow but seemingly controllable two-point lead. "Why I didn't call a quarterback sneak, I'll never know," Tarkenton said later. But he didn't. Instead he handed off to fullback Doug Mayberry who fumbled the ball. When they peeled all the bodies off the squirming pile of humanity on the Vikings' 20-yard line, a fetal-positioned Ed O'Bradovich was on the bottom with the ball securely cradled in his arms. A few moments later, Roger Le-

clerc kicked a field goal, and the Bears won, 31–30.

After the Bears had annihilated the Colts 57–0 later in the season, a sports columnist who covered the game wrote: "A football team on the way up met one on the way down here today." And that proved to be an understatement.

1962 SEASON .643		
Won 9 Lost 5 Tied 0		
George Halas — Coach	Bears	Opponents
San Francisco 49ers . . . .(A)	30	14
Los Angeles Rams . . . .(A)	27	23
Green Bay Packers. . . . .(A)	0	49
Minnesota Vikings. . . . .(A)	13	0
San Francisco 49ers . . . .(H)	27	34
Baltimore Colts . . . .(H)	35	15
Detroit Lions . . . .(A)	3	11
Green Bay Packers. . . . .(H)	7	38
Minnesota Vikings. . . . .(H)	31	30
Dallas Cowboys . . . .(A)	34	33
Baltimore Colts. . . . .(A)	57	0
New York Giants . . . .(H)	24	26
Los Angeles Rams . . . .(H)	30	14
Detroit Lions . . . .(H)	3	0
Totals.	321	287

Flanker back Johnny Morris leaps for the football in this 1962 game at Baltimore, bobbles it, and shaking off Colt defender Bobby Boyd (40) grabs it again for an 18-yard gain. The Bears handed the Colts the worst defeat (57–0) in their 10-year history that day. –Pro Football Hall of Fame

THE TRIUMPH

ALTHOUGH THE 1962 SEASON had been interesting, even encouraging, there was little reason to believe that the Bears could challenge the Green Bay Packers in 1963 for the conference title. In 1962 the Bears had lost their two games with the Packers by a combined score of 87–7. But as the 1963 season approached, George Halas, now 68 years old and beginning his 44th year of association with the Bears and his 36th year as head coach, was filled with anticipation. The Bears had won five of their last six games in the 1962 season, losing only a squeaker to the champs of the NFL East, the New York Giants, 26–24. The Packers meanwhile had encountered a setback when star back Paul Hornung was suspended for having placed some bets on his team (as was defensive tackle Alex Karras of the Detroit Lions). And when the seemingly invincible Packers lost to the College All-Stars at Soldier Field 20–17, they showed very real traces of mortality.

As it would turn out, the anticipation that Halas harbored was well justified. The year 1963 was about to become one of the most tumultuous and exciting in all Bear history. Close games, dramatic comebacks, brilliant plays, a conservative ball-control offense coupled with what some described as a miracle defense, and a title race that went down to the final minute of the final game of the regular season were all to be part of the 1963 season for the Chicago Bears.

The Bears were fielding basically the same team in 1963 as they had the year before. In fact, the only notable differences were that Stan Jones was moved over from an offensive guard to a defensive tackle and a new end and extra-point kicker was added in rookie Bob Jencks from Miami University of Ohio. Along the sidelines, signed on as an assistant coach, was Jim Dooley, who had been a pass receiver for the Bears for nine years during the 1950s and early 1960s.

In the first game of the season, the Bears were scheduled to meet the NFL defending champion Packers up in Green Bay. George Halas had said before the season: "If we're going to win this thing, we're going to have to beat Green Bay twice." The Bears met half of this requirement that day in mid-September. By a score of 10–3, they stopped a confident Green Bay team they hadn't beaten since the opening game of the 1960 season, and a team that had to admit to only one defeat the year before, a team, in fact, that in the preceding two years had dropped only four games while winning a total of 26 (two NFL championships among them).

The Bears went on to win their next four games before running up against the last-place, 0 and 5 San Francisco 49ers—a squad, according to Bear assistant coach Chuck Mather, "the press was talking about as the worst pro football team in the history of the game." But the 49ers won that day 20–14. The unexpected

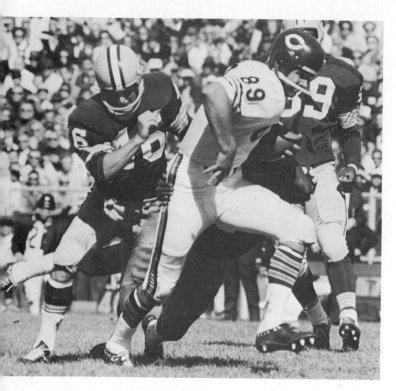

Mike Ditka, the Bears' great tight end during the early and mid-1960s, shows here some of the running power he combined with his pass-catching abilities. The Bears surprised the NFL defending champs that day in the opening game of the 1963 season at Green Bay by beating the Packers 10–3. The Packers here are Hank Gremminger (46) and Dave Robinson (89). –Vernon Biever

defeat dropped the Bears into a first-place conference tie with Green Bay, who had won all their games since meeting the Bears.

The loss to the lowly 49ers surprised the Bears but it didn't sidetrack them; they came right back to beat the Eagles, the Colts, and the Rams, due primarily to the efforts of their defensive unit, who allowed only two touchdowns in those three games. A feeling of competition had developed between the defensive and offensive units that year, some might even have called it a rivalry. The defense looked down on the offense, even though the latter had run up some respectable scores, like 52 points against the Rams, 37 against the Lions, and 28 in a win over the Vikings. Ed O'Bradovich remembers that when the two groups of players passed each other coming on and off the field the defensive team would often taunt the offensive team with the ultimate insult: "We'd just say, 'Hold 'em.'"

The Packers like the Bears continued to win, and when they met in Wrigley Field on November 17, the two teams were still tied for first place in the NFL West.

The game was totally sold out. Because all NFL home games were blacked out in those years, only the lucky 45,000 or so fans who had tickets for seats or

standing-room areas would be able to watch the game in Chicago. Everyone else in town would have to listen to the description of the action by Jack Brickhouse, Irv Kupcinet, and Vince Lloyd on the radio.

One group of almost 400 fans who couldn't get tickets worked it out their own way. They chartered railroad cars on the Santa Fe and traveled to Galesburg, Illinois, 180 miles away and well beyond the TV blackout area. They had made arrangements to watch the game on a large-screen television in the Grand Ballroom of the Custer Hotel in Galesburg.

Besides the absence of Paul Hornung in the lineup, the Packers when they came to Chicago were also without the services of Bart Starr, who was relegated to the sidelines with a broken hand. The quarterbacking chores were turned over to John Roach, who would be spelled from time to time by one-time Bear Zeke Bratkowski. He had come to Green Bay in mid-season by way of the Los Angeles Rams. Nonetheless, the Packers were confident of avenging their earlier loss that season. But they never came close. More than a decade and a half later, fans still talk about J. C. Caroline's devastating tackle on the opening kickoff that showed Herb Adderley, Green Bay's return man, and everyone else in Wrigley Field that day just what the tenor of the game would be. The Bear defense was magnificent, allowing only a single touchdown and that one not until the fourth quarter when the Bears already had a 26–0 lead. The Bear offense contributed two

Roger Leclerc of the Bears strides into a field-goal kick during this 1963 game against the Los Angeles Rams, but moving in to bat the ball right back at him is Ram linebacker and future Bear head coach Jack Pardee (32). Holding for the kick is Dave Whitsell and blocking for the Bears are Doug Atkins (81) and Joe Fortunato (31). No. 21 on the Rams is Ed Meador. –Pro Football Hall of Fame

The Pro Football Hall of Fame in Canton, Ohio, was officially opened in 1963. Seventeen charter members were enshrined, three of whom were from the Chicago Bears—George Halas, Red Grange, and Bronko Nagurski. (For a list of all the Bears in the Hall of Fame, see Appendix.)

Charter Members	**Principal Affiliation**
Sammy Baugh	*Washington Redskins*
Bert Bell	*NFL Commissioner*
Johnny Blood	*Green Bay Packers*
Joe Carr	*NFL President*
Dutch Clark	*Detroit Lions*
Red Grange	*Chicago Bears*
George Halas	*Chicago Bears*
Mel Hein	*New York Giants*
Pete Henry	*Canton Bulldogs*
Cal Hubbard	*Green Bay Packers*
Don Hutson	*Green Bay Packers*
Curly Lambeau	*Green Bay Packers*
Tim Mara	*New York Giants*
George Preston Marshall	*Washington Redskins*
Bronko Nagurski	*Chicago Bears*
Ernie Nevers	*Chicago Cardinals*
Jim Thorpe	*Various early teams*

touchdowns running—one a 27-yard jaunt by Willie Galimore, the other a five-yard rollout around right end by Bill Wade—and four field goals by Roger Leclerc. The Bears wiped the Packers out 26–7 that joyful afternoon in Wrigley Field. And when the contest was over, the game ball was handed to offensive line coach Phil Handler.

Green Bay had no complaints, but were more than a little surprised that they were actually never in the game. As their coach, Vince Lombardi, summed it up afterwards, "The Bears were terrific. . . . They beat us up front where it counts—and both ways." Then he added, "I'm happy for Papa George. He's a helluva guy."

Five days after the game, the nation was stunned by President John F. Kennedy's assassination on that dark Friday in Dallas, Texas.

The nation went into mourning, but the NFL football season went on. Pete Rozelle, in one of his more controversial decisions, announced that the games scheduled for Sunday would not be postponed. It was not the ideal day for playing a football game. TV and radio were covering the events in Washington, where the president's body lay in state, and had declined to carry the day's football games. As the Bears' bus was pulling up to Forbes Field, in Pittsburgh, the players heard on the bus radio that alleged assassin Lee

Willie Galimore scores a touchdown here on a spectacular 27-yard run against the Green Bay Packers in 1963, a play that helped the Bears to win that afternoon at Wrigley Field and take sole possession of first place in the NFL West. In the sequence, he vaults over Bear end Mike Ditka (89), then races past the key block of Bo Farrington (84), and steps into the end zone as Johnny Morris (47), sidelined because of an injury, leaps for joy. –Pro Football Hall of Fame

Harvey Oswald had just been shot and killed in the Dallas jail. George Halas turned the radio off and told the team to concentrate, for the next few hours anyway, on the game they had to play. Out on the field two hours later, with all flags flapping at half-mast, the singing of the national anthem was an especially solemn moment.

The Bears were a definite favorite that afternoon, but Buddy Parker's Pittsburgh Steelers still had a mathematical if somewhat far-fetched chance for their division title. Halas was not taking the game lightly.

And the Bears came as close to losing it as any team possibly could. In fact, they would have, if it were not for what George Halas later called "one of the greatest individual efforts I have seen in 40 years of football." He was referring to Mike Ditka's now-legendary 63-yard gain late in the fourth quarter which set up a field goal that enabled the Bears to eke out a 17–17 tie and hang tenuously in first place by half a game.

Losing 17–14, and with time running out, the Bears had the ball on their own 22-yard line. It was second down and a distant 36 yards for a first down. The game had been a rugged one, and by that time everyone on the field was tired—Mike Ditka especially; he said later that he felt the weariness "down through his muscles all the way to the bone." But when the ball was snapped, he raced out about five yards beyond the line of scrimmage and ran a quick hook pattern. Bill Wade hit him with a short, quick pass, and Ditka rolled out toward the goal line. A defensive back had a shot at him but missed. A linebacker bounced off him. At about the 50-yard line, three Steelers—linebacker Myron Pottios and defensive backs Glenn Glass and Clendon Thomas—all hit him at just about the same moment. But unbelievably the only person moving after the crunching encounter was Ditka, still plowing toward the goal. Some observers among the Bears said that at least six players had their hands on him at one

This is the scene of the action so many Bear fans remember with deep nostalgia—Wrigley Field, the team's home for 50 seasons—from 1921 to 1970. This photograph was taken during the Bear-Packer game of 1963, which the Bears won 26–7. The portable stands on the far side of the field are the same ones that were moved to the end zone of Soldier Field and used until they were condemned after the 1978 season. –Pro Football Hall of Fame

Among the first greats in the NFL at the new position of tight end was Mike Ditka of the Bears. In his six-year Bear career he led the team in receiving three times, in scoring twice, and was named to the All-Pro team four times. –Vernon Biever

time or another during the run; others, like assistant coach Luke Johnsos, were convinced that as many as 10 players had a chance at him. Thomas, who had gotten up after Ditka knocked him down back at the 50, caught up with an exhausted Ditka and wrestled him to the ground at the 15-yard line.

"I lost my legs," Ditka said after the game. "They were completely dead. I'd just run three pass patterns on the three previous plays and now suddenly I found myself in the clear with the ball. But my legs felt paralyzed. I never had a feeling like that before. I kept looking for somebody to lateral to, but nobody showed up." Of the approximate 36,000 people who watched Ditka's run that day, none had ever seen one quite like it. Roger Leclerc kicked the field goal a few moments later, and the Bears were spared the loss that, as it turned out, would have deprived them of the undisputed conference crown.

The next week the Bears played host to the Minnesota Vikings, and in one of their poorest showings of the year they had to make up a 14-point deficit in the second half to salvage a tie. The final score ended up the same as the week before, 17–17.

These tie games, however, didn't count against the Bears because in those days divisional titles were still determined strictly by won-loss percentages, with ties totally disregarded in the rankings. As a matter of fact, after their second victory over the Packers the Bears could clinch the conference championship even if they tied all four of their remaining games. When the Detroit Lions came to Wrigley Field for the last game of the season, if the Bears won or tied, they would have their first conference title since 1956. But if the Bears lost, the Packers would be conference champions for the fourth year in a row.

After wasting several scoring opportunities in the first half, the Bears trailed 7–3. Then, in the third quarter, Johnny Morris made the key play, catching Bill Wade's short pass at the Lions' 40-yard line as a Detroit defender slipped. Morris outran three other Lions to the goal line to complete a 51-yard scoring play that gave the Bears a 10–7 lead. The Bears recovered a Lion fumble on the next possession, and 3½ minutes later Wade connected with Mike Ditka on a 22-yard touchdown pass to pad the Bears' lead.

Early in the fourth quarter, a Detroit touchdown made the score 17 to 14. When the Lions got the ball for their final possession in the last two minutes of the game, it was one more challenge for the superb defense that had carried the Bears so far that memorable year of 1963. With approximately 35 seconds left to play, the Lions were 65 yards from the Bear goal. Now only a desperation bomb could destroy the Bears' title hopes. The Lions' quarterback, Earl Morrall, went for his end Gail Cogdill on a sideline pass. With Cogdill, however, was Bear cornerback Dave Whitsell. To everyone's surprise, in this situation anyway, Whitsell chose to gamble by going for the interception. Flashing in front of Cogdill, he picked off the pass cleanly and raced down the sideline. Whitsell sprinted 39 yards to the Detroit goal, carrying the conference title with him as 46,000 yelling fans pummeled each other deliriously. When he crossed the goal line with the final touchdown of the 1963 regular season, he flipped the ball joyfully in the air in the second before he was mobbed by his teammates. The final score was 24–14. After the game, Whitsell admitted he had taken a chance. "It was a gamble," he said. "I decided we needed the ball."

And just so the prescience of Coach George Halas is not overlooked, it truly had been necessary for the Bears to beat the Packers twice in 1963, because those were the only two losses Green Bay recorded that year. And when it was all over, they were a mere half-game behind the Bears.

Two legendary Chicagoans, Mayor Richard J. Daley (left) and George Halas, along with the Bears' quarterback Bill Wade (right), join up to provide a little hype for the upcoming Bear-Giant 1963 NFL championship game at Wrigley Field. –Pro Football Hall of Fame

In the NFL East, the New York Giants were again the winner. For three years in a row now, five times in fact in the preceding six years, the Giants had won their division. Their great wealth of talent was aging by 1963. Y. A. Tittle was 37, Andy Robustelli 38; Hugh McElhenny 35, Frank Gifford 33, and Rosey Brown 31. But what all these future Hall-of-Famers lacked in youth they made up for in football knowledge and experience. (Tittle led the league in touchdown passes that year, with a total of 36.) The Giants had to travel out to Wrigley Field, a plus for the Bears. It was the first championship game Chicagoans had been treated to in Wrigley Field since 1943, a long 21 years in the past.

The Bears had not even been in an NFL championship game since 1956, the year they lost to the Giants in Yankee Stadium. Six of the Chicago Bears who would be on the field for the 1963 title match—Doug Atkins, Bill George, Joe Fortunato, Stan Jones, Fred Williams, and J. C. Caroline—had been there in New York seven years earlier. Another Bear, Rick Casares, who could not play that Sunday because of an injury suffered in a game against Green Bay six weeks earlier, had also been on the 1956 team.

More than 45,800 fans squeezed into a wintry Wrigley Field on December 29 to watch the Bears try for their eighth NFL championship. Thousands of others gathered at McCormick Place, the Coliseum, and the Amphitheater to watch it under much warmer conditions on closed-circuit television (the only way it could be shown within a 75-mile radius of Chicago back then).

The oddsmakers, according to *Newsweek* magazine, saw the Giants as a 10-point favorite. But when Bart Starr, who had faced the Bear defense, was interviewed by the magazine, he predicted the Bears would win by three points.

Game time was at 12:05, and when that moment arrived the thermometers at Wrigley Field registered 9 degrees above zero. Heating units with air blowers had been used all week to keep the playing field in a relatively thawed condition, but it was still slippery when the opening kickoff landed in the arms of Bear halfback Billy Martin. By the benches, other hot-air blowers enabled those players not on the field to find some semblance of warmth, but for the bundled-up fans who faced Chicago's notorious winds up in the stands, there was no protection from the cold.

The hearts of the Bear fans were not especially warmed in the early minutes of the game either. In the first quarter, it appeared that Y. A. Tittle was going to intimidate the Bears. He put the Giants on the scoreboard on their first ball possession with a 14-yard touchdown pass to Frank Gifford. From then on, however, the day belonged to the Chicago Bear

defense. Five crucial times the Bear defenders came up with pass interceptions. Two of these set up the Bears' only touchdowns of the afternoon, and one ended the Giants' last-ditch chance as time ran out.

Trailing 7–0 in the first period, the Bears got a break when the Giants' wide receiver, Del Shofner, dropped a Tittle pass in the end zone. They took advantage of it on the next play when linebacker Larry Morris picked off a pass from Tittle and ran it back 61 yards to the Bears' 5-yard line. Two plays later, Bill Wade carried it in for the score from the 2. Don Chandler, however, put the Giants back out in front 10–7 with a 13-yard field goal before the first half ended. In the third quarter, defensive end Ed O'Bradovich came up with another key interception when he anticipated a Tittle screen pass at the Giants' 24-yard line and carried the ball back to the 14. On third and 9, Wade passed up the middle to Mike Ditka, and on the following play carried it in on a quarterback sneak for the score. The defense simply would not let the Giants go anywhere either in the air or on the ground. And as the fourth quarter drained away, it appeared that the Bears' two touchdowns and the

Bear linebacker Larry Morris (33) races 61 yards with a Y. A. Tittle pass he picked off in the first quarter of the 1963 NFL title game against the New York Giants. Moments later, the Bears posted their first touchdown of the day, to even the score at 7–7. –UPI

Bear defensive end Doug Atkins (81) puts the rush on Y. A. Tittle (left) in the 1963 championship game. At this point in the third quarter, the Giants were leading 10–7. The other Bear defensive end, Ed O'Bradovich (87), anticipates Tittle's screen pass and intercepts it (right), carrying the ball down to the Giants' 14-yard line and setting up what turned out to be the game-winning touchdown for the Bears. –UPI

two extra points that had been contributed by Bob Jencks would be enough.

In the final 10 seconds of the game, however, the Giants, on the Bears' 39-yard line, had one last chance. As their fleet receiver Shofner, always a threat, raced downfield, Tittle faded back and let fly with a long, looping bomb. Shofner was nearing the Bear end zone, but he was surrounded by Bear defenders, and the pass was overthrown. Bear defender Richie Petitbon was standing in the end zone and caught the football as if he were fielding a punt, wiping out whatever hopes had flickered in the Giants during those last seconds. Dave Condon wrote the next day in the *Chicago Tribune:* "That catch was payday at the mill, Christmas at home, the kiss from the best gal, a double shot of 100 proof. This was the fuse that put the Bear fans into orbit."

Y. A. Tittle left the game physically and emotionally exhausted and did not watch the last play as Bill Wade fell to the ground with the ball, allowing the last two seconds on the clock to run out; he just sat there on the Giants' bench, wrapped in a parka, his head in his hands, weeping openly at the frustration and sadness of the day for the Giant team. On paper, the Giants, it seemed, should have won: they gained more yards rushing (128 to 93) and more yards passing (140 to 129) and chalked up more first downs (17 to 14) than the Bears. But in reality and in the record book the Bears had won, by a score of 14 to 10, and the NFL championship was theirs. In many respects, it was a typical game for the opportunistic Bear defense, which had produced a remarkable 54 turnovers during the regular season.

After the game, an exhilarated Bear team quickly forgot the freezing cold they had just left and enjoyed the very real warmth that comes with victory. In the locker room turned madhouse, somehow above the noisy congratulations and the raucous backslapping linebacker Joe Fortunato was heard shouting the announcement that the game ball was being awarded to defensive coach George Allen. Over in a corner, a beaming George Halas told several members of the press, "I just hope the All-Stars go easy on us next summer." And outside, Chicago's Mayor Richard J. Daley, as he was leaving his box seat, announced to other reporters that a special session of the city council would be held the next day to honor the Bears and their coach George Halas. The jubilant mayor said that there would be a band at city hall and he would pass out mementos of the victory to the players and the coaches, and the entire city was welcome to attend the celebration, if they wanted to.

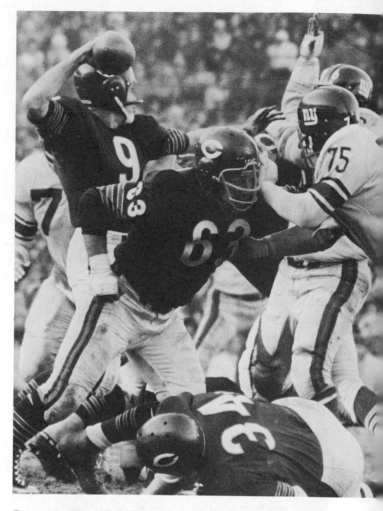

Bear quarterback Bill Wade (9) throws under pressure here in the 1963 NFL title game against the Giants. Blocking for him is tackle Bob Wetoska (63), and on the ground is fullback Joe Marconi (34). Wade's two quarterback sneaks were enough to give the Bears the championship by a score of 14–10. –UPI

The following morning, the news of the Bears' accomplishment was carried on the front pages of both the city's morning newspapers, the *Tribune* and the *Sun-Times*—not the front page of the sports section either, but *the* front page of the papers. The Bears had journeyed a long way from those days back in the early 1920s when their exploits were not even covered by Chicago's newspaper writers, when the three or four paragraphs that sometimes did appear were paid for and personally delivered to the newspaper offices by George Halas and Dutch Sternaman.

When the gate receipts for the 1963 championship game were divvied up, each Chicago Bear received $5,899, the highest paid out up to that time. And when the year's statistics were calculated, the Bear defense led the league in 10 of 19 categories and were second in eight others. They were first in the fewest average

1963 SEASON	.917		
Won 11	**Lost 1**	**Tied 2**	
George Halas — Coach		Bears	Opponents
Green Bay Packers	(A)	10	3
Minnesota Vikings	(A)	28	7
Detroit Lions	(A)	37	21
Baltimore Colts	(H)	10	3
Los Angeles Rams	(A)	52	14
San Francisco 49ers	(A)	14	20
Philadelphia Eagles	(H)	16	7
Baltimore Colts	(A)	17	7
Los Angeles Rams	(H)	6	0
Green Bay Packers	(H)	26	7
Pittsburgh Steelers	(A)	17	17
Minnesota Vikings	(H)	17	17
San Francisco 49ers	(H)	27	7
Detroit Lions	(H)	24	14
Totals		301	144

NFL Championship

New York Giants	(H)	14	10

points allowed per game (10.1); the fewest yards allowed rushing (1,442, for a 103-per-game average); the fewest touchdowns allowed rushing (7); the fewest yards allowed passing (2,045, for a 146-per-game average); the most pass interceptions (36); and the highest percentage of interceptions (10.2).

Rosey Taylor led the league in pass interceptions with nine, which was also an all-time Bear record. And six Chicago Bears were named to the 1963 All-Pro team, the most in their entire history. Only one player was from the offensive unit, end Mike Ditka, who had caught 59 passes during the season, eight of them for touchdowns. The other five were Doug Atkins, Bill George, Joe Fortunato, Richie Petitbon, and Rosey Taylor. And the Associated Press, the United Press, and the *Sporting News* all named George Halas the Coach of the Year.

The Chicago Bears, NFL champions of 1963. *Top row:* Joe Stydahar (asst. coach), Phil Handler (asst. coach), Frank Halas (front office), Jim Dooley (asst. coach), Herman Lee, Bob Jencks, Bob Wetoska, John Johnson, Maury Youmans, Doug Atkins, Ed O'Bradovich, Richie Petitbon, Jim Cadile, Fred Williams, Bill George, Chuck Mather (asst. coach), Earl Leggett. *Third row:* Sid Luckman (asst. coach), Paddy Driscoll (asst. coach), George Allen (asst. coach), Mike Ditka, Angelo Coia, Mike Rabold, Bob Kilcullen, Roger Leclerc, Joe Fortunato, Larry Morris, Bill Wade, Val Keckin, Rick Casares, Ed Rozy (trainer), Luke Johnsos (asst. coach), George Halas (coach). *Second row:* Willie Galimore, Joe Marconi, Rudy Bukich, Bo Farrington, Ronnie Bull, Bennie McRae, Stan Jones, Mike Pyle, Ted Karras, Steve Barnett, Roger Davis, Charlie Bivins. *Front row:* manager Martell, Bobby Joe Green, Dave Whitsell, Johnny Morris, Bill Martin, Rosey Taylor, J. C. Caroline, Larry Glueck, Tommy Neck, ——Schulte, Tom Bettis. –Chicago Bears

ON THE ROLLER-COASTER AGAIN

WOULD GEORGE HALAS retire now with the glory of an NFL championship as the culmination of his long career, a newspaperman asked him after the 1963 title game. "Where else is a 68-year-old going to get another job in these times," he replied, and then went about preparing to defend his NFL title in 1964.

Before the Bears would play another game, however, the spirit and the emotions of the players on that championship team were dealt a horrible blow. It happened on a warm July night at about 10:30 on a country road some two and a half miles from the Bear training camp in Rensselaer, Indiana. Halfback Willie Galimore and end Bo Farrington were driving back to the Bear camp to make the 11:00 curfew when their car missed a curve, skidded off the road, and catapulted into a farm field. The two Bear players were thrown from the auto and killed instantly. To a tightly woven team of young men who had lived, worked, and suffered together, shared well-earned glories and heartbreaking defeats in that way unique to a football team, the news hit with a tremendous impact. The loss was felt by everyone associated with the Bears, from the players to the secretaries in the front office. The next day, Halas told the assembled team: "I know we all share the same sad feelings. It's going to take a great deal of will power to carry on, but I know you can do it. The greatest honor we can bestow on Willie and Bo is if you players would dedicate the season to them."

It was the first and most tragic misfortune to strike the 1964 Chicago Bears. Injuries would come later in plentitude and destroy the once indomitable Bear defense. Doug Atkins, Bill George, and Ed O'Bradovich were out for a good part of the season, and Joe Fortunato and Larry Morris missed a number of games.

The Bears picked up a fine defensive lineman when they drafted Dick Evey, from Tennessee, added a back-up quarterback in Larry Rakestraw, from the University of Georgia, and traded with the Los Angeles Rams to get breakaway back Jon Arnett. And for the first time in Bear history, a second generation Bear player joined the team when John Sisk, a defensive back from the University of Miami in Florida, was signed up. He was the son of halfback Johnny Sisk, who had played for the Bears from 1932 through 1936. Late in the season, to help their running game, the Bears picked up a back named Andy Livingston, who even though he was 6 feet and weighed 234 pounds was said to be able to run the 100-yard dash in less than 10 seconds. He had never played college football; in fact, he did not reach his 20th birthday until midway through the 1964 season.

As George Halas had hoped, the College All-Stars were not too rough on his Bear team. On that All-Star squad, coach Otto Graham was blessed with a few players who would later leave their marks in the pro game, like Paul Warfield, Mel Renfro, Wally Hilgen-

The Chicago Tribune Charities, Inc. *presents its*
31ST ANNUAL ALL-STAR FOOTBALL GAME

COLLEGE ALL-STARS/CHICAGO BEARS

Soldiers' Field, August 7, 1964   Official Program 50¢

berg, and George Seals, but his team never made a game of it. The Bears triumphed easily 28–17.

Once again the Bears opened their season at Green Bay, but this year the outcome was different. The Packers, with Paul Hornung and Bart Starr back, beat them 23–12. Then two weeks later, the Bears were humiliated by the Baltimore Colts 52–0. In the locker room after that particular game, Doug Atkins, who in his own way was trying to console Coach George Halas, said to him: "Well, at least we proved we've got some togetherness." An incredulous Halas answered, "What the hell do you mean—togetherness." Atkins shrugged: "Now the defense is just as horseshit as the offense."

The truth of the matter, however, was that the defense was riddled with injured players, and it had a noticeably harmful effect. The defense that had allowed the opposition to score a total of just 144 points for an average of only 10.1 points a game the year before gave up 379 for an average of 27 in 1964. And the Bears lost almost twice as many games as they were able to win, ending up with a record of 5–9–0 and dropping to sixth place in the NFL West ahead only of the San Francisco 49ers, who managed to lose 10 games that year.

The quarterbacking for the year was shared by Bill Wade and Rudy Bukich. Despite the team's record, the two passers actually did quite well. Wade gained 1,944

yards passing, completing 182 passes for a 56% average, while Bukich led the NFL in that latter category with an impressive completion average of 62%. Johnny Morris was their prime receiver, and he led the league and set two all-time Bear records by catching 93 passes (29 more than Jim Keane had back in 1947) for a total of 1,200 yards. Morris was also one of three players whose 10 touchdown receptions topped the league that year. His 93 pass receptions in one season was then an NFL record. Mike Ditka, with 75 catches, was second to Morris in the league, and their combined receiver total of 168 was also a league record.

George Halas knew at the end of that disappointing season that he needed some new bodies and spirits to replace the now aging and often ailing men who had brought him the NFL title in 1963. The Bears had three first-round draft choices, so this would be a good year for rebuilding his team. But there were problems associated with the draft in 1965. The American Football League, wealthier than it had ever been, was bidding strongly for the same players as teams in the NFL were. Salaries and bonuses to top players were skyrocketing because of it. The New York Jets, for example, signed up Alabama quarterback Joe Namath for a yearly salary reported to be $400,000.

The Bears lost one of their three first-round choices, Steve DeLong, a top-ranked lineman from Tennessee, to the San Diego Chargers. They were unable to come to terms with a later-round draft pick, fullback Jim Nance, who then signed with the Boston Patriots and went on to become one of the finest fullbacks in the AFL. But George Halas did not lose the Bears' first two draft choices that year—linebacker Dick Butkus, from

1964 SEASON	.357	
Won 5 Lost 9 Tied 0		
George Halas — Coach	Bears	Opponents
Green Bay Packers . . . .(A)	12	23
Minnesota Vikings. . . . .(A)	34	28
Baltimore Colts. . . . .(A)	0	52
San Francisco 49ers . . . .(A)	21	31
Los Angeles Rams . . . .(H)	38	17
Detroit Lions . . . .(H)	0	10
Washington Redskins . . . .(A)	20	27
Dallas Cowboys . . . .(H)	10	24
Baltimore Colts . . . .(H)	24	40
Los Angeles Rams . . . .(A)	34	24
San Francisco 49ers . . . .(H)	23	21
Detroit Lions . . . .(A)	27	24
Green Bay Packers. . . . .(H)	3	17
Minnesota Vikings. . . . .(H)	14	41
Totals.	260	379

Illinois, and running back Gale Sayers, from the University of Kansas. He wanted both young men just as earnestly as he had wanted Red Grange back in 1925, and Sid Luckman in 1939, and Bulldog Turner and George McAfee in 1940, and Bobby Layne and Johnny Lujack in 1948. And so he came up with the money to secure them, reportedly in the vicinity of $150,000 for each, plus a bonus for signing—a bargain by most standards, because both players would perform so well that each would be elected to the Pro Football Hall of Fame in his first year of eligibility for that honor.

That year the Bears also drafted end Dick Gordon, from Michigan State, and fullback Ralph Kurek, from Wisconsin. Abe Gibron, whose face and rotund figure would be familiar around the Bear bench for the next 10 years, was added to Halas's coaching staff.

The 1965 Chicago Bear team was a rather unique blend of noteworthy elders and outstanding newcomers. Both Doug Atkins and Joe Fortunato were now 35, and Bill George was only a year younger, as were

Having to crouch to crunch, 6-foot-8 Bear end Doug Atkins (81) goes to work from the left on Green Bay Packer quarterback Bart Starr, while Bear tackle Dick Evey (79) adds a shot from the right. One of the finest defensive ends in the team's history, Atkins was a three-time All-Pro in his 12-year career. –Chicago Bears

George Halas confers on the sidelines during the 1964 Pro Bowl game with Terry Barr (41) and Ray Berry (82). –Pro Football Hall of Fame

quarterbacks Bill Wade and Rudy Bukich. But the rich draft and the acquisition of lineman George Seals from the Redskins offered the hope of some new life.

The season's start, however, was a disaster apparently left over from the year before. The Bears went out to San Francisco and were overwhelmed by the previous year's cellar-dwelling 49ers, 52 to 24. It was an unhappy surprise and it would take the Bears several weeks to recover from it. The next week, just down the Pacific Coast from San Francisco, the Bears took on the Rams. Going into the fourth quarter they had a 28–9 lead, only to watch it dwindle away until Los Angeles had a 30–28 win on a touchdown pass in the final minute. This was the game, by the way, in which Gale Sayers scored the first of his 56 career touchdowns for the Chicago Bears. It came on an 18-yard run, a play that had been planned as an option pass or run.

The third game of the season brought first despair (the first half) and then a resurgence of hope (the second half). The Bears went up to Green Bay to face the Packers, who had won their first two games. The roster of greats and near-greats that Vince Lombardi had put together was overwhelming: Bart Starr, Jim Taylor, Paul Hornung, Carroll Dale, Max McGee, Boyd Dowler, Marv Fleming, Ray Nitschke, Lee Roy Caffey, Dave Robinson, Herb Adderley, Willie Wood, Forrest

Gregg, Jerry Kramer, Fred ("Fuzzy") Thurston, Willie Davis, Lionel Aldridge, Henry Jordan, and Ron Kostelnik, among the most prominent. At the end of the first half the Bears were losing 20–0.

In the second half, Rudy Bukich replaced Bill Wade at quarterback and the passing game began to take shape. Gale Sayers and Andy Livingston suddenly got the Bear running game going. Even the most critical of spectators saw that it was not the same team that had gone into the locker room at half-time. The Bears completely dominated the second half. Two touchdowns were contributed by Sayers, and the Bears out-scored the Packers 14–3 during that time period. Another touchdown, a pass from Bukich to Johnny Morris, was nullified by a holding penalty. As a result of their second-half showing, the Bears actually out-gained the Packers 413 yards to 299 and amassed a total of 192 yards rushing to the Pack's 78. All of this was of little consolation, however, because the final score remained Green Bay 23, the Bears 14, and at

that point in the season the Bears were all alone in the basement of the NFL West, winless and with six teams ahead of them in the standings. But the Bears' performance in the second half was enough to prompt George Halas to say: "I'll tell you one thing, this could be the real beginning of a good ball club. We've got that offense going now, and the defense is taking shape."

He was right. When the Bears came back to Wrigley Field, Sayers, in his first appearance in Chicago in a regular-season game, ran 80 yards for a touchdown with a screen pass and threw a 26-yard pass for another score as the Bears breezed to a 31–6 victory over the Los Angeles Rams.

The game at Minnesota the following week was one of the wildest and most exciting of the 1960s. The Bears led 17 to 13 at the half, and the lead see-sawed back and forth all the way through the second half. Sayers caught touchdown passes of 18 and 25 yards in the second half, but the Vikings scored with just over two minutes left to take a 37 to 31 lead. Sayers took

Bear rookie Gale Sayers electrified Bear fans with his dazzling running performances. In his rookie year alone, he set an NFL record by scoring 22 touchdowns and tied the single-game record with six of them in one game. –Pro Football Hall of Fame

the following kickoff at the 4-yard line, and starting up the middle, then veering sharply to the sidelines, ran 96 yards for the touchdown that tied the game. The conversion put the Bears ahead. Dick Butkus then intercepted a Viking pass and returned it to the Minnesota 9. Sayers burst up the middle, broke several tackles, and dove into the end zone with his fourth touchdown of the day to clinch a 45 to 37 victory.

The Bears had begun a streak that would produce nine victories in 10 games. The only loss was to the Western Conference champs of the year before, the Baltimore Colts, and that was on a controversial play. Ray Berry caught a pass in the Bear end zone, bobbled the ball, and then dropped it when he was hit by Bear defender Dave Whitsell. The officials, however, ruled that he had possession of it long enough and awarded the Colts what turned out to be the crucial touchdown in their 26–21 win over the Bears.

While the Bears were winning in 1965, Gale Sayers was establishing himself as one of the greatest runners ever to play the game, and Dick Butkus was in the process of creating his reputation as a ferocious and talented linebacker and a very worthy replacement for the all-time great Bill George, who was still sidelined with a knee injury. At the same time, Rudy Bukich, who had kept the starting quarterback position since that second half up in Green Bay, was having a fine year passing.

The season's singular highlight, however, came on December 12, a day that endures in the NFL and Chicago Bear record books. It was the Sunday that Gale Sayers scored six touchdowns in one game. Only two other players had ever done it before, both, ironically, against the Bears: Ernie Nevers of the Chicago Cardinals back in 1929 and Dub Jones of the Cleveland Browns in 1951. Now Gale Sayers did it on a muddy gridiron before a wildly cheering hometown crowd at Wrigley Field as the Bears wreaked a heavy vengeance for their opening-day embarrassment out in San Francisco by crushing the 49ers 61–20.

Four runs from scrimmage, a screen-pass play, and a punt return were the vehicles Sayers used that day to post his six touchdowns. His combined total yardage for the day was 336—113 yards on nine rushes (an average of 12.5 yards per carry), 134 yards on punt returns, and 89 yards on two pass receptions. The last of Sayers' six touchdowns in the game was his 21st of the season, breaking the NFL record of 20 set by Lenny Moore in 1964 (which had been tied the week before, incidentally, by Jim Brown of Cleveland). It came on an 85-yard punt return in the final period. Sayers made one of his dazzling cuts against the grain, leaving defenders flat-footed; there wasn't one within

At Wrigley Field on December 12, 1965, rookie Gale Sayers tied an NFL record by scoring six touchdowns in a single game, as the Bears defeated the San Francisco 49ers 61–20.

How He Did It

80-yard screen-pass play (from Rudy Bukich)
21-yard run from scrimmage
7-yard run from scrimmage
50-yard run from scrimmage
1-yard run from scrimmage
85-yard punt return

What They Had to Say about It

Y. A. Tittle, 49ers assistant coach: "I just wonder how many that Sayers would have scored if we hadn't set our defense to stop him."

George Halas: "It was the greatest performance ever by one man on a football field; I never saw such a thing in my life."

Gale Sayers: "I had real good blocking on every play."

15 yards of him from midfield to the end zone. He might have scored a seventh touchdown that day if he hadn't slipped making one of his patented cuts on another punt return, which he carried 32 yards as it was. And taken out late in the game, he watched from the bench as Jon Arnett plunged over from the 2 for the Bears' last touchdown of the day. Sayers also broke a Bear all-time season scoring record that afternoon, moving ahead of the previous mark of 109 points set by Johnny Lujack in 1950.

In that day's endeavor, two other Bear records were set: the most points scored and the most touchdowns in a regular-season game (post-season games are not included in official NFL statistics). The 61 points they put on the board were three more than the 58 they had scored against the Colts in 1956. And their nine touchdowns of the day were one more than the total they had recorded four times previously.

The Bears had a slight chance to win their conference title going into the last game of the season. For that to happen the Colts and Packers would both have to lose, but neither did. The season ended for the Bears with a surprising but now meaningless loss to the Minnesota Vikings 24–17 and a record of 9–5–0.

The excitement and hope that had melted away in 1964 were restored, however, with the feats of Sayers and Butkus. Both rookies were named to the All-Pro team that year, along with Joe Fortunato. Sayers, who added his 22nd touchdown of the year in the last game of the season, now held the NFL record in that category, and it was one that would stand until 1975, when Chuck Foreman of the Vikings tied it and O. J. Simpson of the Buffalo Bills broke it, with 23.

Gale Sayers led the Bears in rushing his rookie year, with 867 yards and an impressive average of 5.2 yards per carry (three runs from scrimmage were for 61, 50, and 45 yards and touchdowns). He also returned 21 kickoffs for 660 yards (one for 96 yards and another for 86 yards) and 16 punts for 238 yards (one for 85 yards) and caught 29 passes for another 507 yards (including two that were 80-yard plays). His total of 132 points scored that season was also an all-time Bear record. But what transcended even those impressive statistics was the explosiveness he showed as a runner, the dazzling cuts, the great moves, the incredible elusiveness in the open field. A defensive back for the 49ers that year, George Donnelly, aptly described Sayers the ball carrier: "He looks no different than any other runner when he's coming at you, but when he gets there he's gone."

To no one's surprise, Gale Sayers was named the NFL Rookie of the Year.

Rudy Bukich, the principal Bear quarterback of the mid-1960s, eyeing the action on the other side of the gridiron in a game at Wrigley Field. –Chicago Bears

1965 SEASON .643		
Won 9 Lost 5 Tied 0		
George Halas — Coach	Bears	Opponents
San Francisco 49ers . . . .(A)	24	52
Los Angeles Rams . . . .(A)	28	30
Green Bay Packers. . . . .(A)	14	23
Los Angeles Rams . . . .(H)	31	6
Minnesota Vikings. . . . .(A)	45	37
Detroit Lions . . . .(H)	38	10
Green Bay Packers. . . . .(H)	31	10
Baltimore Colts . . . .(H)	21	26
St. Louis Cardinals . . . .(H)	34	13
Detroit Lions . . . .(A)	17	10
New York Giants . . . .(A)	35	14
Baltimore Colts. . . . .(A)	13	0
San Francisco 49ers . . . .(H)	61	20
Minnesota Vikings. . . . .(H)	17	24
Totals.	409	275

Rudy Bukich also had a good year in 1965, completing 176 passes for 2,641 yards, with an impressive completion average of 56%. Once again Johnny Morris led the team's receivers, picking up 846 yards on 53 receptions.

The offensive unit had an exceptional season, scoring a total of 409 points. This was the first and only time in their history that the Bears went over the 400 mark, topping the 396 points tallied by the NFL championship squad of 1941.

The expectations for the next season that had been generated by the team's performance in 1965, however, did not carry over into 1966, or 1967 for that matter. Sayers was still spectacular on offense and Butkus was masterful and punishing on defense, but the passing game faded away, and the team that had shown great promise sank back to mediocrity. It was the roller-coaster syndrome all over again.

The biggest news in 1966 occurred off the field. The NFL and the AFL agreed to merge. Their teams would play separate schedules until 1970, but beginning in 1967 they would conduct a common draft, bringing down what owners in both leagues looked on as outlandish salaries and bonuses that they were forced to shell out to sign a player. (In 1966, the Green Bay Packers spent $1 million to sign rookie running backs Donny Anderson and Jim Grabowski— thereafter known as the "Gold Dust Twins"—in a bidding contest with the AFL.) And before the start of the regular 1967 season all NFL and AFL teams would meet in a schedule of inter-league exhibition games. Also agreed upon was an "NFL–AFL World Championship Game" to be played between the victors of each league, with the first one held at the end of the

Bill George on Butkus: "I've never seen anybody who was such a cinch. I'd been having trouble recovering from a knee operation, and the day Dick showed up in camp I knew I was out of a job."

Jim Dooley on Butkus: Explaining the linebacker's ferocity on a given Sunday afternoon, Dooley said that it was something Butkus worked himself up to days before a game. "He's very seldom happy during the week before a game. Maybe one day a week I'll see him smile. The rest of the time he goes around angry. He builds himself up mentally for the game, so by the end of the week he's really mad."

Butkus on Butkus: "Everybody gets the wrong impression about me. They think I hate everybody and that I eat my meat raw. But I can talk and read and write like ordinary people do, and actually I like to have my meat cooked."

1966 season. The name "Super Bowl" for this post-season classic would be applied later.

The Atlanta Falcons became the 15th team in the NFL in 1966, joining the Eastern Conference. A franchise was also granted to the New Orleans Saints, but they would not begin play until the next year.

Off the field for the Bears, things were stirring as well. Late in 1965 assistant coach George Allen, with two years remaining on his Chicago Bear contract, had sought out the vacant head-coaching job with the Los Angeles Rams. When the Rams said they wanted him, he, as was contractually required, asked Halas to allow him to talk with Los Angeles Rams' owner Dan Reeves about the job, even if it was a little after the fact. Halas reportedly told Allen that he was free to talk with Reeves if the subject of the conversation was to tell him that he was *not* available until his contract with the Bears expired in 1968. Allen argued unsuccessfully; then Reeves announced that Allen was accepting the offer of the Rams anyway. Halas referred to this act on the part of the Rams' owner as "a flagrant case of tampering with a coach under contract," and said he would not release Allen. NFL Commissioner Pete Rozelle was asked to intervene officially, which he chose not to do. But he let it be known where his sympathies were when he said: "It has been traditional with the NFL and throughout sports that assistant coaches are permitted to take advantage of opportunities for advancement."

It was a legal matter, Halas maintained, one that extended beyond the jurisdiction of the NFL. He would take it to court before he let Allen out of the contract. And in a Chicago court, early in 1966, the contract was ruled to be valid. But as soon as that point was made, Halas withdrew his suit and freed Allen to go to the Rams. The validity of the contract was the point that Halas wanted made, and it was. The court's decision was to have an important bearing in disputes and similar situations that would confront the NFL office and various teams in later years.

Departing from the Bears that year too were Bill George, who was traded to Los Angeles, and Larry Morris, who went to the Falcons, the expansion team down in Atlanta.

Johnny Morris, the Bears' great pass catcher over the past nine years, was hurt early in the season and spent most of his time on the bench. The Bears added a young linebacker from the University of Louisville, Doug Buffone, who alternated throughout the year with aging Joe Fortunato. Other newcomers included Frank Cornish, an enormous (6-feet-6, 270 pounds) defensive tackle from Grambling College; Randy Jackson, an offensive tackle from Florida; and running back Brian Piccolo, whom the Bears had obtained the year before but who could not suit up because of an injury suffered before an early-summer all-star game. Free agent Piccolo, whose first coach at Wake Forest was Bear great Beattie Feathers, had led the nation in rushing and scoring in 1964.

Nothing helped much, however. And the Bears, who had looked so challenging the year before, careened through an erratic season, winning some games but losing more. At the end of it, they had sunk to fifth place with a record of 5–7–2, far behind the Green Bay Packers, who lost only two of their 14 games and won their conference, the NFL championship (by beating the Dallas Cowboys 34–27), and the

1966 SEASON   .417

Won 5   Lost 7   Tied 2

George Halas — Coach	Bears	Opponents
Detroit Lions . . . .(A)	3	14
Los Angeles Rams . . . .(A)	17	31
Minnesota Vikings. . . . .(A)	13	10
Baltimore Colts . . . .(H)	27	17
Green Bay Packers. . . . .(H)	0	17
Los Angeles Rams . . . .(H)	17	10
St. Louis Cardinals . . . .(A)	17	24
Detroit Lions . . . .(H)	10	10
San Francisco 49ers . . . .(H)	30	30
Green Bay Packers. . . . .(A)	6	13
Atlanta Falcons. . . . .(H)	23	6
Baltimore Colts. . . . .(A)	16	21
San Francisco 49ers . . . .(A)	14	41
Minnesota Vikings. . . . .(H)	41	28
Totals.	234	272

Rain, mud, or snow never deterred a healthy Gale Sayers—in fact, some of his finest performances were in bad-weather games. Here, he moves out in the mire of Wrigley Field as Coach George Halas (hands on hips) looks on sternly from the sideline. But Sayers' running was one of the few things Halas did not have to worry about in the mid and late 1960s. Sayers was named All-Pro five years in a row (1965-69). –Chicago Bears

football world's first Super Bowl (by manhandling the Kansas City Chiefs 35–10). To illustrate the improved economies of the newly merged leagues, each of the Packers received $15,000 for his Super Bowl efforts and each of the Chiefs took home $7,500.

In this otherwise uneventful season, Gale Sayers gave the fans the only thing they had to cheer about. He led the league in rushing, with a total of 1,231 yards, averaging 5.4 yards per carry. It was the first time a halfback had taken the rushing crown since Steve Van Buren did it back in 1949. Sayers also caught the most Bear passes that year, 34 for 447 yards; ran back 23 kickoffs for 718 yards (his average of 31 yards per return was the highest in the NFL that year and so were his two touchdowns); and earned another 44 yards on six punt returns. It all added up to a new NFL record for combined net yardage—2,440, 12 yards more than Timmy Brown of the Philadelphia Eagles, who had tallied 2,428 in 1963. Sayers was the only Bear named All-Pro that year.

When the New Orleans Saints joined the NFL in 1967, bringing the total number of teams to an even 16, the structure of the league was reorganized. To add more playoff life to the league, and more excitement to the season, each of the NFL conferences was divided into two four-team divisions. The Bears were placed in

the Central Division of the Western Conference along with Green Bay, Detroit, and Minnesota; competing for the conference title would be the Coastal Division, comprising the Los Angeles, Baltimore, San Francisco, and Atlanta franchises.

Before the 1967 season got under way, quite a few changes were made in the Bear roster. Bill Wade, having spent most of the last two seasons on the bench, retired at 36. Rudy Bukich, the same age as Wade, stayed on but his best days were now behind him, so George Halas traded Mike Ditka to the Philadelphia Eagles for their back-up quarterback, Jack Concannon. Doug Atkins, now 37, and Herman Lee went to the New Orleans Saints in exchange for offensive guard Don Croftcheck. The only remaining starting lineman or linebacker from the legendary defensive team of 1963 was Ed O'Bradovich. Rudy Kuechenberg was brought up from the Bears' ready-reserve unit to join linebackers Dick Butkus and Doug Buffone. Joe Taylor, from North Carolina Agricultural and Technical State University, was drafted for the defensive backfield, and Mac Percival of the Dallas Cowboys was signed on to handle the kicking chores.

The Bears of 1967 were somewhat better than the previous year's team, but it was another up-and-down year and they were no match for Vince Lombardi's

Packers. By winning two and tying one of their last three games, the Bears eked out a 7–6–1 record, good enough for second place in their division.

Again the highlights of the season were the running of Gale Sayers and the defensive savagery of Dick Butkus, both of whom were selected All-Pros that year. Sayers, hampered part of the season by an ankle injury, managed to gain a combined net yardage of 1,689, but dropped to third in rushing in the NFL. End Dick Gordon emerged as the Bears' best pass receiver in 1967, and Brian Piccolo traded off with Ronnie Bull as Gale Sayers' tandem running back. Jack Concannon threw 92 passes for 1,260 yards, but his 49% completion average was evidence that the Bears had not yet solved their quarterbacking problems.

The Green Bay Packers won the Central Division, then beat the Coastal Division's Rams for the Western Conference title. They played the Dallas Cowboys for

Jack Concannon became the Bears' first-line quarterback in 1967, and led the team in passing four consecutive years (1967-70). Also in this picture, taken during a game in the late 1960s, is Bear fullback Ronnie Bull (29). –Chicago Bears

Two of the more highly regarded defensive linemen in Bear history move out here in pursuit of one of the game's greatest flanker backs, the Baltimore Colts' Lenny Moore. They are Ed O'Bradovich (87), who played from 1962-71, and Stan Jones (78), from 1954 through 1965. –Pro Football Hall of Fame

1967 SEASON		.538	
Won 7	**Lost 6**	**Tied 1**	
George Halas — Coach		**Bears**	**Opponents**
Pittsburgh Steelers . . . .(A)		13	41
Green Bay Packers. . . . .(A)		10	13
Minnesota Vikings. . . . .(A)		17	7
Baltimore Colts . . . .(H)		3	24
Detroit Lions . . . .(H)		14	3
Cleveland Browns. . . . .(A)		0	24
Los Angeles Rams . . . .(H)		17	28
Detroit Lions . . . .(A)		27	13
New York Giants . . . .(H)		34	7
St. Louis Cardinals. . . . .(H)		30	3
Green Bay Packers. . . . .(H)		13	17
San Francisco 49ers . . . .(A)		28	14
Minnesota Vikings. . . . .(H)		10	10
Atlanta Falcons. . . . .(A)		23	14
Totals.		239	218

the NFL championship in that now famous "Arctic Bowl" game at Green Bay, when the temperature was 13 degrees below zero and the wind-chill factor calculated at 40 below. This was the game that Bart Starr won with a quarterback sneak behind what has turned out to be one of the most famous blocks ever thrown, when Jerry Kramer blew Jethro Pugh out of Starr's path. The mighty Packers went on to win their second straight Super Bowl, this time handily beating the Oakland Raiders 33–14.

There were changes coming in the NFL's Central Division, however. The first one would affect the Bears' long-time rivals up in Green Bay. Right after his Packers won their third straight NFL title and second Super Bowl, Vince Lombardi unexpectedly announced his retirement as the team's head coach. There were also going to be some major changes in store for the Chicago Bear franchise.

Friendly bench-side combatants of the 1960s, George Halas and Vince Lombardi chat here before a Bear-Packer game. A classic in the history of pro football, the Bear-Packer rivalry has been sustained since the Chicago Staleys beat the Pack at Cubs Park in 1921. Through the 1978 season, the teams had met in 119 regular-season games, the Bears winning 63, losing 50, tying 6. But during the Lombardi era (1959-67), the Pack beat the Bears in 13 of 18 regular-season encounters. –Vernon Biever

THE DOOLEY-GIBRON ERA

ON MAY 27, 1968, George Halas called a press conference in the old Bear offices over on Madison Street. Sportswriters from all the Chicago newspapers showed up, so did representatives of the Associated Press and the United Press and the radio and television industries. Papa Bear had celebrated his 73rd birthday a few months earlier, and almost every newsman who came had an inkling of what he was going to tell them.

A full 48 years had elapsed since that spring day back in 1920 when George Halas went down to Decatur to meet the cornstarch maker A. E. Staley, 48 years since he and Dutch Sternaman took on the job of recruiting a group of recent college grads to work in the Staley plant during the week and play football under the company's sponsorship on the weekends. It had been almost half a century, and a lot had happened during those years. Prohibition had long since come and gone, so had the Great Depression and a world war. The Space Age had begun, and many things only dreamed about back in the 1920s were rapidly becoming the realities of modern times.

The sport of professional football that Halas had helped to found had also changed considerably. The game that might on an average day draw 2,000 people out to Cubs Park in the early 1920s now attracted audiences of nearly 50,000 to each Sunday home game at Wrigley Field; the tickets that were practically given away in the early days were, by 1968, next to impossible to obtain by anyone who was not an established season-ticket subscriber. The greats had come and gone from the game—Thorpe, Grange, Lambeau, Nevers, Nagurski, Hutson, Baugh. Halas was the only one of that select company to remain all the way to 1968.

He told the assembled writers: "The time has come for me to retire as head coach of the Bears. It's a decision I've made with considerable reluctance but with no regrets." Later he said with characteristic humor, "I knew it was time to quit when I was chewing out an official and he walked off the penalty faster than I could keep up with him." It was the third time Halas resigned, the fourth time he placed the team in the hands of others. Back in 1930, he let Ralph Jones handle it for three years. And Hunk Anderson, Luke Johnsos, and Paddy Driscoll had to take over while he was in the Navy during World War II. Paddy Driscoll got a chance at the reins for a short two years in the mid-1950s. Except for those brief interruptions, Halas had always been the ruler on the Bear sidelines. But everyone who was in the Bear offices that day, including George Halas, knew that this time his retirement was for real.

During the almost five decades that he had presided over the Bears, he coached 716 regular-season, pre-season, and post-season games, winning 480 of them, losing 201, and tying 35. He personally coached

When George Halas retired as head coach before the 1968 season, he and his teams had literally glutted the record books with their achievements in all phases of the sport of professional football. Besides these and an overall coaching record of 480 wins, 201 losses, 35 ties, six NFL championships, and nine divisional titles, he left behind a remarkable series of "firsts" in the NFL. His Bears were the first to:
- *Hold daily practice sessions*
- *Take game films to study their play and that of their opponents*
- *Play their games in a major league baseball park*
- *Have a team fight song*
- *Take their team on a national tour*
- *Have their games broadcast on radio*
- *Use a tarpaulin to protect their playing field*
- *Utilize a field announcer*
- *Publish and distribute a club newspaper*
- *Organize an alumni association*
- *Hold a "homecoming game" and a dinner for their former players each season*

six NFL championship teams and won eight division titles. It was the most impressive coaching record in pro football history.

The day after his official retirement, George Halas named 38-year-old Bear assistant coach Jim Dooley as his successor. Dooley, an end with the Bears for nine seasons, had coached the Bear offensive unit from 1963 through 1965 and then guided the team's defense for the next two years.

Dooley kept the same coaching staff that Halas had handpicked, with only one change. Paddy Driscoll, member of the Pro Football Hall of Fame and the tailback Halas had coveted so much back in the earliest days of the game and who later was so much a part of the Bears as a player and a coach, had died that summer at the age of 72.

Dooley's first season as head coach was a very interesting one. It was also the last relatively successful one before the Bears would begin a descent into the darkest years of their history. Mike Hull, a fullback from Southern California, was the first draft choice that year, but he would carry the ball only 12 times during the season and gain only 22 yards. The Bears added a fourth quarterback when they drafted Virgil Carter, from Brigham Young. They also signed defensive lineman Willie Holman, from South Carolina State, and wide receiver Cecil Turner, from California State Polytechnic College, who would eventually replace Gale Sayers as the Bears' kickoff-return specialist.

The Bears won four of their five pre-season games in 1968 but the debut of Coach Dooley in the NFL regular season was less than inspiring. The Bears lost their first two games to teams who had lost more games than they had won the year before and who had finished lower in divisional standings than the Bears of 1967—the Washington Redskins and the Detroit Lions. The loss to Detroit was especially embarrassing; the score was 42–0. In the third game they faced the Minnesota Vikings, a team led by quarterback Joe Kapp and so far undefeated. The Bears, playing the best game of their otherwise disillusioning season, managed to defeat the Vikings that day 27–17, but it was a costly victory. First, starting quarterback Jack Concannon left the game with a broken collarbone. Then his replacement, Rudy Bukich, was lost for the season with a shoulder separation. Third-string quarterback Larry Rakestraw came off the bench to finish the game for the Bears.

Rakestraw was given the job of leading the Bear offensive attack in the next two games, but after two shattering losses to the Baltimore Colts and the Lions he was benched, and rookie Virgil Carter took over.

With a 1–4–0 record, the Bears went to Philadelphia to face the Eagles, one of only two teams who had a record worse than the Bears, having lost all five of their games. Carter threw a touchdown pass to Cecil Turner, and the Bears won that Sunday. But the key factor in the 29–16 victory was the five field goals contributed by Mac Percival, who tied the Bear record for most field goals in a single game which Roger Leclerc had set back in 1961.

The next week the Bears beat the Vikings for the second time. Percival kicked four field goals in that game, one of them a 47-yarder with three seconds left in the game to give the Bears a 26–24 victory. And up in Green Bay the following week, there was another reason to cheer. The Bears again won on a Mac Percival kick; in fact, it was a real rarity, a 43-yard free kick in the last minute of play which the Bears had earned on a fair catch of a Packer punt. The final score was 13–10. In that game, Gale Sayers set a Bear single-game rushing record when he gained over 200 yards—205, to be precise, and eight more than the record of 197 he had set two years earlier against the Minnesota Vikings.

Then came San Francisco. The 49ers, behind the superb passing of John Brodie (he would lead the league in completions and yards gained passing that year) and the powerful rushing of Ken Willard (who would gain just short of 1,000 yards in 1968), were a strong team that year. In the second quarter the Bears were leading 14–0, the result of a seven-yard keeper and a one-yard sneak by Virgil Carter. Sayers, the NFL's leading rusher going into that game, was not having one of his better days; he had carried the ball 11 times for a total of only 32 yards; even so, the 49ers' defense was keying on him on practically every play. And then disaster struck. Carter pitched out to Sayers, who was sweeping wide. Breaking through the wave of blockers, 49er defensive back Kermit Alexander caught Sayers with a low blocking tackle just as the Bear halfback was about to make his cut. Sayers leaped up from the collision, but his leg gave way and he crumpled back to the Wrigley Field turf before the horrified eyes of some 47,000 spectators. All the ligaments in his right knee were torn. He was helped from the field. Dr. Ted Fox, the Bears' long-time physician, would operate on the knee later that day, and Gale Sayers was through playing football for 1968.

It was a brutal blow to the Bears. Sayers had been on the way to one of his best seasons ever. His combined net yardage had already totaled 1,463. He had rushed for a total of 856 yards up to the time of the injury, and his average carry of 6.2 yards was a career high, as well as the league record that year. At the time of the injury, he had, in fact, raised his career rushing average to 5.3 yards, an all-time NFL record for backs with more than 750 carries.

The Bears went on to win the game that Sunday, 27–19, and were locked into a tie with Minnesota for first place in their division. But Bear fans went home that evening wondering fretfully if one of the most exciting backs in pro football history would ever return to the gridiron, and, if he did, would he be the same Gale Sayers that they had had the joy of watching over the past 3½ seasons. They didn't know that they would never again see a great breakaway run by Gale Sayers in a regular-season game.

It was a dark moment in Bear history when this tackle cut down Gale Sayers. The day was November 10, 1968, and the Bears were hosting San Francisco. On the play, Sayers took a pitch-out from Virgil Carter but 49ers' defensive back Kermit Alexander (39) burst through and his shoulder caught Sayers in the knee just as he was making his cut—the moment this picture was taken. It was the first of Sayers' knee injuries, and it kept him out for the rest of the season. –UPI

The Bears' bad luck continued. The next week, in a game against the Atlanta Falcons, Virgil Carter suffered a broken ankle and joined the ranks of Bear starters out for the season. The depleted Bears lost to the Falcons, and the following week to the Dallas Cowboys.

Jack Concannon came back from his collarbone injury, and even though he could not function at a full 100% the Bears defeated the New Orleans Saints. Then, by a single point, they slipped by a highly favored Los Angeles Rams team now coached by former Bear assistant coach George Allen. The win was tainted somewhat by the controversy surrounding an error by the officials in the waning minutes of the game. Somehow they managed to turn the ball over to the Bears after the Rams had only had three official downs. They still had a fourth down coming (with long yardage), but the Ram coaches did not protest and the game proceeded. The Bears ran out the clock and had themselves a win. As a result the Rams were denied their chance at the Coastal Division crown, while the Bears with a record of only 7–6–0 were still very much in the running for the Central Division title. Pete Rozelle, NFL commissioner, suspended all six officials for the rest of the season when the case was brought before him. But that didn't help the Rams. When the Packers came to Wrigley Field for the last game of the season, the Bears were tied with the Vikings for first place in their division. If they won that Sunday, the Bears would be awarded the title, because they had defeated the Vikings in both their encounters earlier in the season.

But the beleaguered and wounded Bears were not up to it that day. Losing through most of the game, they put on a magnificent comeback in the fourth quarter and scored two touchdowns which brought them within a point of the Packers, but that is where the game ended. The Packers upset Chicago's dream of a berth in the playoffs of 1968, 28 to 27, and the Vikings had their first division title.

The Bears, despite the physical debris made of its personnel, had salvaged a successful season, and there was good reason to look forward to the next year. They had won under Virgil Carter, even though his passing added up to only a 45% completion average. Gale Sayers, it was claimed, would be back and in top shape. Mac Percival had led the NFL with 25 field goals and boasted a 100% extra-point average (25 for 25). Ronnie Bull and Brian Piccolo had rushed for a respectable 472 and 450 yards respectively. And Dick Butkus, still the most awesome defensive player in the entire NFL, was named All-Pro for the third time in his four-year career. Gale Sayers was named to the All-Pro team for the fourth consecutive year.

1968 SEASON	.500		
Won 7 Lost 7 Tied 0			
Jim Dooley — Coach		Bears	Opponents
Washington Redskins . . . . (H)		28	38
Detroit Lions . . . . (A)		0	42
Minnesota Vikings. . . . . (A)		27	17
Baltimore Colts. . . . . (A)		7	28
Detroit Lions . . . . (H)		10	28
Philadelphia Eagles. . . . . (A)		29	16
Minnesota Vikings. . . . . (H)		26	24
Green Bay Packers. . . . . (A)		13	10
San Francisco 49ers . . . . (H)		27	19
Atlanta Falcons. . . . . (H)		13	16
Dallas Cowboys . . . . (H)		3	34
New Orleans Saints. . . . . (A)		23	17
Los Angeles Rams . . . . (A)		17	16
Green Bay Packers. . . . . (H)		27	28
Totals.		250	333

Eight NFL teams had worse records than the Bears' 7–7–0 in the 1968 season, among them the Green Bay Packers, so formidable in 1966 and 1967. No one really had any reason to suspect what was about to transpire in the 1969 season.

Two quarterbacks who would later take their turns trying to get the Bear offense moving, Bobby Douglass (14) and Virgil Carter (15), watch a 1969 game against the St. Louis Cardinals—one of 13 the Bears lost that year. –Pro Football Hall of Fame

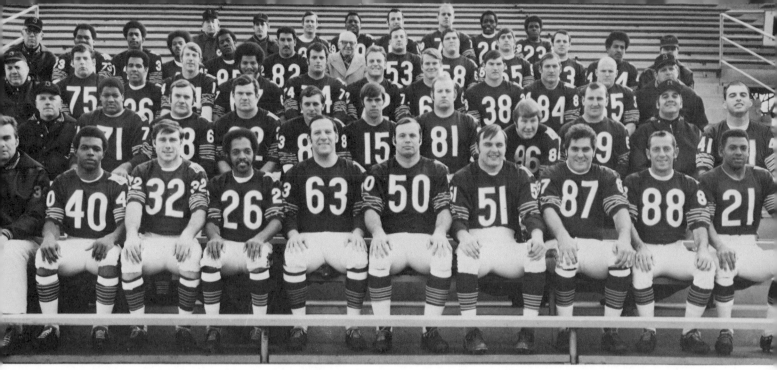

The Chicago Bears of 1969. Top row: Ed Rozy, Fred Caito, Ronnie Bull, Bob Wallace, Jack Concannon, Dick Evey, Joe Taylor, Dick Daniels. Fourth row: Bob Shaw, Frank Cornish, George Youngblood, Dick Gordon, Willie Holman, Emilio Vallez, Frank Halas, Dave Martin, Jim Ferguson, Doug Buffone, Mike Hull, Garry Lyle, Bill Martell. Third row: Abe Gibron, Dave Hale, Ron Copeland, Bobby Douglass, George Seals, Wayne Mass, Jim Cadile, Randy Jackson, Ray Ogden, Austin Denney, Joe Aluise, Jim Ringo. Second row: Ed Cody, Rufus Mayes, Howard Mudd, Ross Montgomery, Mac Percival, Virgil Carter, Marty Amsler, Loyd Phillips, Rudy Kuechenberg, Jim Carr, Brian Piccolo. Front row: Jim Dooley (coach), Gale Sayers, Ralph Kurek, Bennie McRae, Bob Wetoska, Mike Pyle, Dick Butkus, Ed O'Bradovich, Bobby Joe Green, Cecil Turner. –Pro Football Hall of Fame

In that year Rudy Bukich, now 38, retired, and Larry Rakestraw did not return. The Bears, however, drafted Bobby Douglass, a 6-foot-3, 215-pound quarterback from the University of Kansas. He was known to be a fine runner and possess a powerful passing arm, and the Bears hoped he would serve as a strong back-up to Jack Concannon and Virgil Carter. Gale Sayers was back in uniform, and he and his doctors said his knee was in excellent shape. Indeed it was. The first time he touched the ball in the exhibition season, he ran 69 yards on a kickoff return. That kind of dazzling run, however, he would not be able to repeat in the regular season.

Concannon had won the starting position at quarterback, but the Bears could not get going, and they lost their first four regular-season games. Coach Dooley then benched Concannon and, to everyone's surprise—especially Virgil Carter—started rookie Bobby Douglass. That didn't help either. The Bears lost their next three games. Their record was 0–7–0 when the Pittsburgh Steelers came to town. The Steelers had won their first game of the year and then lost the next six. One Chicago sportswriter conjectured about the game: "The big question here is: Which team will extend its losing streak?" As it turned out, Pittsburgh did. The Bears demolished them 38–7. That win, ironically, would come back to haunt the Bears after the season. How? The Bears lost the rest of their

Bear fullback Brian Piccolo picks up a few tough yards in this 1969 game against the Pittsburgh Steelers at Wrigley Field. Behind him is his roommate Gale Sayers (40). A week later, Piccolo took himself out of the game against the Falcons; it was his last game. A little more than seven months later, Brian Piccolo died of cancer. –Chicago Bears

games in 1969. So did the Steelers. Both ended the season with appalling records of 1–13–0. Had the Bears lost the game to Pittsburgh they would have qualified for the first choice in the upcoming college player draft. But as a result of having beaten Pittsburgh, that choice would have to be decided by a coin toss. Which it was, and the Steelers won it. They selected the most sought-after college player of the day, the quarterback (which the Bears so sorely needed) from Louisiana Tech, Terry Bradshaw.

The Bears in 1969 had developed a game of musical quarterbacks, and it had not worked. The frustration of it culminated in the next-to-last game of the season in one of the more sorry incidents of Bear memorabilia. The Bears were meeting the Green Bay Packers at Wrigley Field, and Virgil Carter was given the starting assignment. He had replaced Bobby Douglass in the previous week's game and had become the team's third quarterback to start that year. Against

Green Bay, however, he had a most depressing first half, completing only two of 17 passes. Dooley replaced him in the second half with Douglass, but the Bears still lost, 21–3. When the game was over Carter blew up in the Bear dressing room. He called his coach "a liar" because, he claimed, Dooley had promised *not* to take him out; no matter what, he was supposed to be given his chance in a full game. Then he said he hoped the Bears' organization would not be so "chicken-shit" (which the press changed to "chicken-bleep") as to deprive him of playing out his option. With that, George Halas stepped in. He suspended Carter for the rest of the season—actually the last game of the year—and then traded him to the Cincinnati Bengals.

The press was not taking the Bear problems lightly. If the football reporting of the day were likened to a shotgun, one barrel was zeroed in on Jim Dooley and the other on George Halas. The Carter incident only heightened the sportswriters' dissatisfaction with what

Things did not go especially well for Jim Dooley in his four years as the Bears' head coach. Witnesses to his frustrations are Gale Sayers (top left), Bear assistant coach Sid Luckman (above), and Bobby Douglass (left). –Vernon Biever (top left); Pro Football Hall of Fame

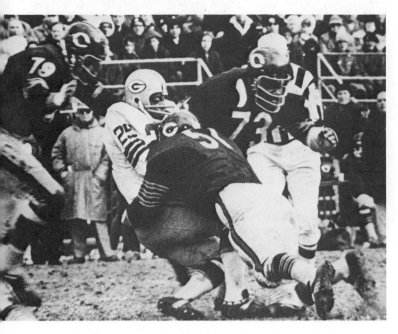

No one could tackle harder than Dick Butkus, as Green Bay Packer back Dave Hampton learns here at Wrigley Field in 1969. The other Bears are Dick Evey (79) and Frank Cornish (73). –Pro Football Hall of Fame

Dick Butkus (51) and fellow linebacker Doug Buffone (55) team up here to show Detroit Lion back Mel Farr how it feels to be squeezed between the jaws of a vise. The photo is from a 1969 game in Chicago. –Pro Football Hall of Fame

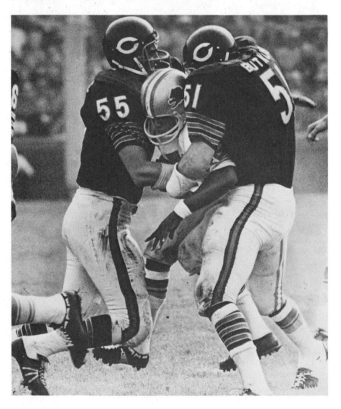

was going on in the Bears' organization. An example of the tone of what was being written came from the typewriter of Ed Stone of *Chicago Today*: "Once the most proud and mighty franchise in pro football, the Halas operation has fallen into disgrace under the weight of its own incompetence." George Halas had never cottoned to criticism. Responding to all the reporters who were dissecting him, his coach, and his team, Halas showed that at 74 he still had not lost one scintilla of his feistiness. "Ninety-seven percent of what you read last week was bull," he said. Then he told the collective world of sportswriters with no uncertainty where he thought they could deposit their criticisms. "I didn't need them for 48 years and I don't need them now," he added.

The 1969 season had been the bleakest in Chicago Bear history. No Bear team had ever posted a record as bad as the Bears of 1969. The offense had averaged only 15 points a game, while the defense gave up an average of 24.2 points. The only decent note in the entire season was the fact that Gale Sayers had recovered sufficiently from his knee injury to lead the league in rushing with a total 1,032 yards. It was a remarkable achievement for a football team with a 1–13–0 record. But still, some of the magic was gone. Sayers' longest run from scrimmage was only 28 yards; his longest pass reception, a mere 25-yard gain; his longest kick return, 52 yards; and his average carry of 4.4 yards rushing was the lowest of his career up to that time.

That year a tragedy of different proportions took place away from the playing field. It was enacted in a Chicago hospital where the doctors discovered that the cough that had been plaguing running back Brian

1969 SEASON   .071

Won 1   Lost 13   Tied 0

Jim Dooley — Coach		Bears	Opponents
Green Bay Packers	(A)	0	17
St. Louis Cardinals	(A)	17	20
New York Giants	(A)	24	28
Minnesota Vikings	(H)	0	31
Detroit Lions	(A)	7	13
Los Angeles Rams	(H)	7	9
Minnesota Vikings	(A)	14	31
Pittsburgh Steelers	(H)	38	7
Atlanta Falcons	(A)	31	48
Baltimore Colts	(H)	21	24
Cleveland Browns	(H)	24	28
San Francisco 49ers	(A)	21	42
Green Bay Packers	(H)	3	21
Detroit Lions	(H)	3	20
Totals		210	339

The American Football League merged with the National Football League in 1970, and the expanded NFL was divided into two conferences of 13 teams each—the number of franchises in operation at that time. The following list also reflects the changes that have been made since then.

American Conference	National Conference
Eastern Division	**Eastern Division**
Baltimore Colts	Dallas Cowboys
New England Patriots*	New York Giants
Buffalo Bills	Philadelphia Eagles
Miami Dolphins	St. Louis Cardinals
New York Jets	Washingon Redskins
Central Division	**Central Division**
Cincinnati Bengals	Chicago Bears
Cleveland Browns	Detroit Lions
Houston Oilers	Green Bay Packers
Pittsburgh Steelers	Minnesota Vikings
	Tampa Bay Buccaneers†
Western Division	**Western Division**
Denver Broncos	Atlanta Falcons
Kansas City Chiefs	Los Angeles Rams
Oakland Raiders	New Orleans Saints
San Diego Chargers	San Francisco 49ers
Seattle Seahawks†	

*The New England Patriots were called the Boston Patriots until 1971.
†Seattle and Tampa Bay joined the NFL in 1976.

Piccolo was the result of lung cancer. His season ended in November when he left the team to undergo surgery in New York City.

For the National Football League, 1970 was a significant year. This was the year that the NFL and the AFL truly became one. The 26 teams from both leagues were incorporated into an American Conference and a National Conference, each with an Eastern, Central, and Western Division. The name National Football League, which George Halas came up with so many years before, was retained. Three former NFL teams—the Baltimore Colts, Cleveland Browns, and Pittsburgh Steelers—moved over to play with the former AFL teams now in the American Football Conference. The Bears remained in the Central Division, which did not change; it became part of the National Football Conference.

It could also be said that 1970 was the year in which the great largesse of television was fully bestowed on professional football. ABC-TV worked out an arrangement with the NFL to televise 13 games in prime time on a week night during the regular season. Monday Night Football and Howard Cosell became an inte-gral part of the pro football scene. The network paid $8 million for the privilege, and that when added to a beefed-up budget for regular football broadcasting contributed an annual munificence of approximately $1.7 million to each NFL team. Before the season got under way, CBS and NBC contracted to televise the other regular season and all post-season games, and ABC's Monday night schedule was later expanded.

With the new two-conference alignment, it was agreed to appoint a president for each. George Halas was elected to the post in the NFC, and Lamar Hunt, owner of the Kansas City Chiefs, received the appointment in the AFC.

In order to avoid another disastrous showing like the one the year before, the Bears traded liberally for the 1970 season. They had given up their first two draft choices that year and had acquired linebacker Lee Roy Caffey, center Bob Hyland, and running back Elijah Pitts from the Packers; running back Craig Baynham

Courage . . .

In May, 1970, Gale Sayers flew to New York to accept the George Halas award for the Most Courageous Athlete of the Year because of his comeback from a serious knee injury to lead the NFL in rushing. But when George Halas handed him the trophy, Gale Sayers told the large group of people gathered that evening at the Professional Football Writers dinner that a mistake had been made. The award should have been given to his friend and former Bear roommate, Brian Piccolo. With deep emotion, he told them:

"Think of Brian and his courage and fortitude shown in the months since last November, in and out of hospitals, hoping to play football again but not too sure at any time what the score was or might be. Brian Piccolo has never given up.

"He has the heart of a giant and that rare form of courage that allows him to kid himself and his opponent—cancer. He has the mental attitude that makes me proud to have a friend who spells out the word courage twenty-four hours a day, every day of his life.

"You flatter me by giving me this award, but I tell you here and now that I accept it for Brian Piccolo. Brian Piccolo is the man of courage who should receive the award. It is mine tonight. It is Brian Piccolo's tomorrow.

"I love Brian Piccolo and I'd like all of you to love him. When you hit your knees to pray tonight, please ask God to love him, too."

from the Cowboys; defensive back Ron Smith from the Rams; and quarterback Kent Nix from the Steelers (to fill in for the departed Virgil Carter). The Bears also drafted end George Farmer, from UCLA, and linebacker Ross Brupbacher, from Texas A & M.

In June the Bear players received the news they had dreaded but had known was inevitable—26-year-old Brian Piccolo had died of cancer.

"State Street Jack" Concannon, as he was now being called (some said in the hope that it would help him emulate the artfulness on the field of "Broadway Joe" Namath), once again won the now dubious honor of starting at quarterback.

At the beginning of the 1970 regular season, the Bears appeared to be a rejuvenated team. They won their first two games. Then, disaster struck again. Gale Sayers suffered another knee injury and would not be back for the remainder of the season.

Four straight losses followed, and memories of the preceding year's debacle were coming back with distasteful intensity. After one win and then two more losses, Coach Dooley once again became disenchanted with Concannon and sent Bobby Douglass in to face the Buffalo Bills and O. J. Simpson. Douglass threw four touchdown passes in that game as the Bears pounded the Bills 31–13, and the fans at Wrigley Field loved it. But in the effort, Douglass broke his wrist and joined Sayers on the sidelines for the rest of the year. "State Street Jack" came back to finish out the season.

The next-to-last game of the season was against Green Bay, and it was noteworthy because it would be

This early-season game of 1970 against the Philadelphia Eagles was played at Northwestern University's Dyche Stadium, in Evanston, thought of then as a possible new home for the Bears, who were contemplating a move from Wrigley Field. The residents of the Chicago suburb were less than fond of the idea, so the Bears chose Soldier Field the following year. The Bears beat the Eagles that afternoon 20–16, aided by the field goal kicked here by Mac Percival at the right. –Pro Football Hall of Fame

the Bears' last appearance in Wrigley Field. The following year, they would move to Soldier Field.

Fifty football seasons had elapsed since George Halas and Dutch Sternaman had signed that first agreement with William L. Veeck, Sr., back in 1921 to lease the Cubs' ball park for Chicago Staley football games. Since then, the Bears had known no other home. The nostalgia of the place was tremendous. It was the field where ardent fans once sat on wooden benches to watch Joey Sternaman and Paddy Driscoll drop-kick field goals, where Red Grange made his professional debut that famous Thanksgiving Day back in 1925, where Ed Healey and George Trafton battered opponents, where Bronko Nagurski exploded through enemy lines and George McAfee and Gale

Wrigley Field—A Fan Remembers

Wrigley Field, one of the most intimate baseball stadiums in the country, was once one of the most intimate football stadiums. The conversion from one sport to another was accomplished with the simple construction of temporary east stands in front of the right-field bleachers. They enlarged the seating capacity of the park, but they also enabled the gridiron to be laid out with all front-row seats very close to the sidelines and endlines. The south end zone was practically in the dugout, and the north end zone was up against the left-field bleacher wall. It actually was somewhat of a hazard for the players on plays in the deeper parts of the end zone, and the proximity of wall and dugout to end line may have inspired the famous Bronko Nagurski story about "that last guy really gave me a good lick," when he hit the wall head-on.

Bear fans in Wrigley Field may or may not have been any more enthusiastic than those who watch the Bears in Soldier Field, but there is no doubt that they certainly sounded louder. The roar of the crowd would reverberate against the lower and upper deck roofs and bounce around, magnifying itself. There were times in the big games when the stands literally shook with the noise. The less than 50,000 who could squeeze into Wrigley Field actually sounded louder than the 80,000 or 100,000 in some other stadiums.

In Soldier Field, with most front-row seats far removed from the sidelines, and with the stands spreading out at a very low angle of elevation, the roar of the crowd does not seem nearly as loud and is usually gone instantly in the wind. That never happened at Wrigley Field. How we do miss you.

—Richard Youhn

Sayers streaked to touchdowns, where Sid Luckman and Johnny Lujack threw wonderfully exciting passes, where Dick Butkus terrorized opposing runners and passers alike, where George Halas stalked the sidelines and the officials, where the Chicago Bears met the Chicago Cardinals on days that always seemed to be the most bitterly cold of the season. For the Bear fans whose heritage goes back to the pre-1970s, Wrigley Field holds many memories.

And the Bears went out of Wrigley Field just as they had come into it back in 1921. They began their stay with a win over the Rochester Jeffersons, and they left on the same note. The Bears beat the Packers 35–17 that day. And while they were so doing, Jack Concannon had his best game ever as a Chicago Bear, throwing four touchdown passes and running another one in himself.

The Bears also won their last game of the season down at New Orleans, 24–3, and ended the year with a record of 6-8-0, a third place in their division, but at least offering a bit more hope for the future than they had at the end of the previous year. Dick Gordon had the best season of his career and led the NFL in number of pass receptions, with 71. He also led the league in touchdown catches, 13, which also tied an all-time Bear record set by Ken Kavanaugh in 1947. Cecil Turner proved to be an admirable replacement for Gale Sayers at kickoff returns. His four touchdowns returning kickoffs that year tied the NFL single-season record set by Travis Williams of Green Bay three years earlier. He also led the National Conference that year with a 33-yard kickoff-return average. But with Gale Sayers injured, the team's rushing attack suffered. The leading rusher that year was Ross Montgomery, with a

1970 SEASON   .428

Won 6   Lost 8   Tied 0

Jim Dooley — Coach	Bears	Opponents
New York Giants . . . .(A)	24	16
Philadelphia Eagles. . . . .(H)	20	16
Detroit Lions . . . .(A)	14	28
Minnesota Vikings. . . . .(H)	0	24
San Diego Chargers . . . .(H)	7	20
Detroit Lions . . . .(H)	10	16
Atlanta Falcons. . . . .(A)	23	14
San Francisco 49ers . . . .(H)	16	37
Green Bay Packers. . . . .(A)	19	20
Buffalo Bills. . . . .(H)	31	13
Baltimore Colts. . . . .(A)	20	21
Minnesota Vikings. . . . .(A)	13	16
Green Bay Packers. . . . .(H)	35	17
New Orleans Saints. . . . .(A)	24	3
Totals.	256	261

total yardage of only 229. Both Dick Butkus and Dick Gordon were named to the 1970 All-Pro team.

The Bears brought their temporary stands with them from Wrigley Field and set them up in the end zone of Soldier Field. Their new home would have a seating capacity of over 55,000, approximately 6,000 more than Wrigley Field.

It quickly became apparent that because of his knee problems Gale Sayers would not be able to run with anywhere near the proficiency he once had. So the Bears drafted running back Joe Moore, from the University of Missouri, and acquired another rusher in Cyril Pinder from the Eagles.

The momentum that the Bears had going for them by winning their last two games of the 1970 season carried over into 1971, as both Coach Jim Dooley and George Halas had hoped. Somehow the Bears of 1971 came up with clutch plays in close games. They managed to win six of their first nine games, several of these in a most unusual manner, like their home opener in Soldier Field.

In this first game of the season, against the Pittsburgh Steelers, the Bears trailed 15 to 3 with just four minutes left. Pittsburgh had the football and appeared to be in complete control of the game. The fans were filing out of the stadium when Ed O'Bradovich made a jarring tackle that knocked the ball from the hands of the Pittsburgh runner. Linebacker Ross Brupbacker picked up the ball and ran 30 yards for a touchdown to put the Bears back in the game. The Steelers, however, managed a first down several plays after the kickoff, and it looked like they could run-out the clock. Then Dick Butkus, who had already intercepted two passes in the game, blitzed into the Pittsburgh backfield and ripped the ball loose from halfback Warren Bankston. O'Bradovich recovered it at the 18-yard line. The Bears moved to a first down inside the 10, and then, with less than a minute left, back-up quarterback Kent Nix, who had replaced Concannon, threw the winning touchdown pass.

The following week, Nix again relieved Concannon, this time with the Bears trailing 17 to 3 in the last quarter against the Minnesota Vikings. One of his first passes was deflected up in the air by a Viking defender, but it was caught by wide receiver Dick Gordon, who sprinted in for a touchdown. The Bears added a field goal and then won the game in the final two minutes with another Nix-to-Gordon touchdown pass.

The Bears moved to Soldier Field after the 1970 season. They had appeared there before in many College All-Star, Armed Forces, and other exhibition games. Soldier Field is almost as old as the Bears themselves (it was dedicated in 1926). It has been the site of many special events, including sports spectacles, but it is not considered the ideal stadium for watching football today. Soldier Field has a capacity of more than 57,000 for Bear games. –Bill Smith

When both Nix and Concannon were injured later in the season, the Bears went back to Bobby Douglass for their quarterback. Coach Dooley announced that he was moving into Douglass's bachelor apartment to insure an intensified preparation for the game against the Detroit Lions, allowing the Chicago press, capitalizing on Neil Simon's famous play, to have a wonderful time with all kinds of "Odd Couple" references. Douglass responded with perhaps the finest passing game of his career, as the Bears beat Detroit 28 to 23. The following week, against the Dallas Cowboys, the Bears were thoroughly outplayed, but somehow they managed to beat Dallas, 23 to 19. (The Cowboys, incidentally, were to go on to defeat the Miami Dolphins in the Super Bowl that year.)

In the ninth game of the season, the Bears found a new way to win—with Dick Butkus as a pass receiver! They were playing the Washington Redskins, whose new coach that season was George Allen. The Bears trailed 15–9 late in the fourth period until halfback Cyril Pinder tied it up by breaking loose on a 40-yard run up the middle for the only touchdown of the game. The snap from center for the game-winning extra point was high, and holder Bobby Douglass could only bat the ball down. Douglass picked it up and scrambled to his left. There was no opening to run it in, however, so Douglass in desperation lobbed the ball into the end zone just over the heads of several Redskins. Butkus, who had been in the backfield to block for the kick, had rumbled into the end zone after the snap misfired. Now, in the midst of several Redskins, he leaped up and crushed the ball to his chest. It was his first NFL point, and it gave the Bears the lead 16 to 15.

This improbable contest still wasn't over, however. The Redskins, who had already kicked five field goals in the game, got close enough to try a long 46-yarder with several seconds left. The kick had plenty of distance and looked as if it would be good, but the swirling winds of Soldier Field caught the ball and blew it just wide of the left upright. The eight field goals —three by the Bears—in that 16 to 15 contest set an NFL record for a single game.

Then it was back to reality, and the Bears collapsed. They not only lost their last five games, but in the first three of them they didn't post a single touchdown. The Bears were out-scored collectively in those five games 126 to 29. George Halas, who for years had denied speculation by the press that he had exerted any influence on Jim Dooley's coaching decisions, was unhappy and said so for the first time.

Kent Nix had done much of the quarterbacking during the first half of the season, and his overall record of pass completions for the year was a very disappoint-

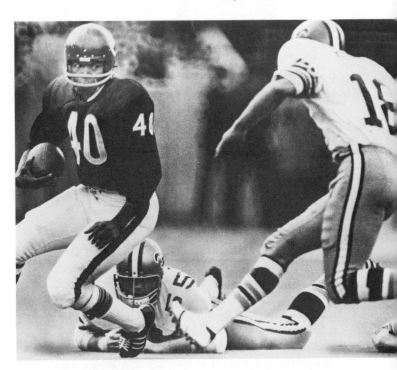

One of Gale Sayers' last appearances in a Bear game. Here he is running against the New Orleans Saints at Soldier Field in 1971. He would carry the ball 13 more times before his damaged knee forced him to retire. The Saint defenders are Jim Flanigan (55) and Hugo Hollas (18). –Pro Football Hall of Fame

If he couldn't blast or crush his man, he could always grab him, which is what Dick Butkus (51) is doing here to Hoyle Granger of the New Orleans Saints. Moving in to help is Bear defensive lineman Willie Holman (85). The Bears won this 1971 game at Soldier Field by the tidy score of 35–14. –Chicago Bears

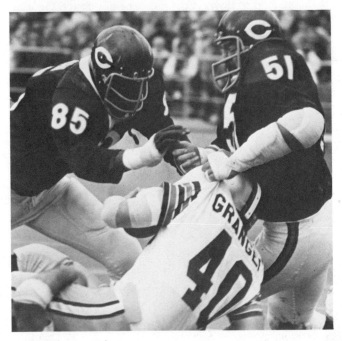

ing 37%. Bobby Douglass, who was brought in at mid-season, was not much better, ending up by completing 40% of his passes. And without Gale Sayers, the running game had suffered. He had tried to come back, but his knee was too damaged for him to play. He carried the ball 13 painful times and picked up 38 yards, and that was all for 1971. The leading rusher was Sayers' replacement, Don Shy, with 420 yards and an average carry of 3.6 yards. The season that had started so well ended in disillusionment, with the Bears again in third place and burdened with the same losing record, 6–8–0, they had the year before.

A few days after Christmas 1971, a Chicago newspaper carried a picture of George Halas, and on the other side of it one of Jim Dooley. The captions under each told the story succinctly: "The Firer" and "The Fired." Halas was asked why he had ousted his coach, and he was equally brief in his explanation. "The record speaks for itself," he said. Halas, of course, was referring to Dooley's overall four-year coaching record of 20 wins against 36 losses, and to his three consecutive losing seasons—something the Bears had never experienced before. Not everyone, however, blamed Dooley for all the Bears' problems of the late 1960s and early 1970s. There was even sympathy for him from some of the players. Gale Sayers said: "I hate to see him go, I thought he was a fine coach." And then added, "He never had a healthy team going for him."

The next question from the press was, naturally: Who would be the new coach? Halas smiled. "Well, I'll tell you, several months ago I got to see the movie *Patton* for the first time. I sat there and the adrenalin really started to flow. What a great Bear coach General Patton would have made, I thought. Then, for a flicker

Abe Gibron, for years one of the most fondly regarded members of the Bear organization by fans and the media alike, became the team's head coach in 1972. He had been an assistant coach for seven years and an active player for two (1958-59). Gibron probably will be better remembered in the Bear story for the famous barbecues and parties he used to throw for the team than for his three-year record as head coach. –Chicago Bears

of a minute, I thought I would come back as head coach. Then the flicker was over."

A month later, Halas named his new coach, the long-time Bear assistant that one newspaperman referred to as the "beloved behemoth," Abe Gibron. Behemoth he was in 1972, registering on the scales somewhere in the vicinity of 300 pounds. But Gibron had been a highly respected player in his day, a quick and tough offensive guard. He had played for the Bears back in 1958 and 1959, which was after a six-year stint with the Cleveland Browns and two with the Philadelphia Eagles. During those years, he went to four Pro Bowl games and in 1955 was named an All-Pro. He had been an assistant coach with the Bears since 1965. Gibron was also one of the most widely liked sports personalities in Chicago.

By 1972, any Chicagoan who was even remotely interested in football or who possessed some semblance of civic pride wanted to see the Bears restore themselves to the eminence they had once had in professional football. And every Bear fan hoped that the popular Abe Gibron would be the person to achieve that.

1971 SEASON	.428	
Won 6 Lost 8 Tied 0		
Jim Dooley — Coach	Bears	Opponents
Pittsburgh Steelers . . . .(H)	17	15
Minnesota Vikings. . . . .(A)	20	17
Los Angeles Rams . . . .(A)	3	17
New Orleans Saints . . . .(H)	35	14
San Francisco 49ers . . . .(A)	0	13
Detroit Lions . . . .(A)	28	23
Dallas Cowboys . . . .(H)	23	19
Green Bay Packers. . . . .(H)	14	17
Washington Redskins . . . .(H)	16	15
Detroit Lions . . . .(H)	3	28
Miami Dolphins . . . .(A)	3	34
Denver Broncos . . . .(A)	3	6
Green Bay Packers. . . . .(A)	10	31
Minnesota Vikings. . . . .(H)	10	27
Totals.	185	276

The Bears conducted a good draft for the 1972 season, acquiring a promising offensive lineman in Lionel Antoine, from Southern Illinois University; a defensive back, Craig Clemons, from Iowa; a defensive tackle, Jim Osborne, from Southern University; and a tight end and potential punter in Bob Parsons, from Penn State University. But sorely missed in the 1972 line-up would be Gale Sayers, whose war-torn knee forced him to retire before the season started.

But the Bears, new and old, did not seem to be in pursuit of what Chicagoans were clamoring for. Three losses and a tie in the first four games of the season were hardly what their fans had been looking forward to, but when the Bears came back to win three in a row—beating the Cleveland Browns, Minnesota Vikings, and St. Louis Cardinals—the mood changed to one of optimism again. Then, everything seemed to fall apart and the Bears lost six of the last seven games. They dropped from third place to the cellar of the NFC Central Division that year, with a record of 4–9–1. (Beginning in 1972, incidentally, tie games counted in the standings for the first time. A tie was rated as a half-game won and a half-game lost.)

Left-handed Bobby Douglass, drafted by the Bears in 1969, gets off a pass (top) against the Detroit Lions in 1972. Never rated highly as a passer, he was the Bears' principal quarterback during the 1971-73 era. What Douglass did best was carrying the ball, as he is doing here (bottom) against the Green Bay Packers in 1972. Even though he was a quarterback, he led the Bears in rushing that year, with 968 yards. His career average gain of 6.62 yards a carry is an all-time high for a Bear, and his season average gain of 6.87 yards (100-plus carries) is second in the NFL only to Beattie Feathers' 9.94, a record set in 1934. No. 78 on the Bears is guard Bob Newton. –Top, Chicago Bears; bottom, Pro Football Hall of Fame

Ron Smith (48) of the Bears moves out with a kickoff return behind the locomotive-like interference of Dick Butkus (51) in this game against the Los Angeles Rams in 1972. No. 70 on the Bears is tackle Andy Rice. That year, Smith returned kickoffs for a total of 924 yards, gaining 208 yards in a single game—both of these are all-time Bear records. –Chicago Bears

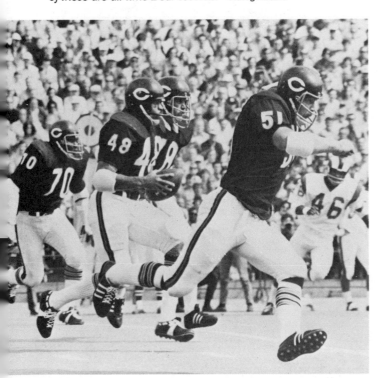

1972 SEASON　.307 Won 4　Lost 9　Tied 1 Abe Gibron — Coach	Bears	Opponents
Atlanta Falcons . . . .(H)	21	37
Los Angeles Rams . . . .(H)	13	13
Detroit Lions . . . .(H)	24	38
Green Bay Packers . . . .(A)	17	20
Cleveland Browns. . . . .(A)	17	0
Minnesota Vikings. . . . .(H)	13	10
St. Louis Cardinals . . . .(A)	27	10
Detroit Lions . . . .(A)	0	14
Green Bay Packers . . . .(H)	17	23
San Francisco 49ers . . . .(H)	21	34
Cincinnati Bengals . . . .(H)	3	13
Minnesota Vikings. . . . .(A)	10	23
Philadelphia Eagles. . . . .(A)	21	12
Oakland Raiders . . . .(A)	21	28
Totals.	225	275

A major problem was still throwing the football. The Bears ended the 1972 season with the worst passing statistics in the entire NFL. On the other hand, they led their conference in rushing, gaining a total of 2,360 yards, a healthy average of 169 per game. A total of 968 of those yards were contributed by Bobby Douglass, who that year set an all-time rushing record in the NFL for a quarterback. His passing completion percentage, however, was only 38%.

One sportswriter referred to the Bear offense at that time as "absolutely schizophrenic." Actually, the Bears had a split personality type of offense for a number of years before the 1972 season. The last time the Bears had displayed a balanced passing and running attack was back in 1965, rookie Gale Sayers' record-setting year.

Bobby Douglass led the NFL in average yards gained rushing that year, with 6.9 per carry, and Ron Smith topped the league in average kickoff returns, with 31 yards each attempt. Those were about the only highlights of the Bears' season. Abe Gibron's first year as coach was not exactly a happy one.

The plan for 1973 was one of developing the relatively young team they now had, with help from the college draft. The Bears signed defensive lineman Wally Chambers, from Eastern Kentucky University, as their first-round draft choice. He would become one of the great defensive tackles in Bear history. Another fine defender added that year was cornerback Allan Ellis, from UCLA. With the hope of bringing some help to the quarterbacking department, Gary Huff, from Florida State, was drafted on the second round. And running back Carl Garrett was acquired from the New England Patriots.

The start of the 1973 season was an obstacle course, with the first two games scheduled against the Dallas Cowboys and the Minnesota Vikings, two of the best teams in the league (both would win their respective divisions that year). The Bears played well against both, but not quite good enough, losing 20–17 to Dallas and 22–13 to the Vikings. The win the next week over the Denver Broncos, another respectable team that year, by the substantial score of 33–14, was heartening.

The Bears of 1973 were still in search of a quarterback. Bobby Douglass proved to be a wonderful runner, but the team lacked a passing attack. In an effort to create one, Coach Gibron replaced Douglass with rookie Gary Huff in the 10th game of the season. Huff made his debut against the Detroit Lions. He threw four interceptions, and the Bears were beaten 30–7. They also lost the remaining four games of the 1973 schedule and ended up again in last place in the NFC Central, with a worse record than the year before, 3–11–0.

It was now five years in a row that the Bears had posted losing seasons. It was something that George

Carl Garrett, acquired from the New England Patriots, tries to find a little running room in this 1973 game against the Los Angeles Rams. Leading interference for him is guard Glen Holloway (61). The Bears lost this game and 10 others—the second-worst season in the team's history. Garrett was the Bears' leading rusher of 1973, with 655 yards. –Chicago Bears

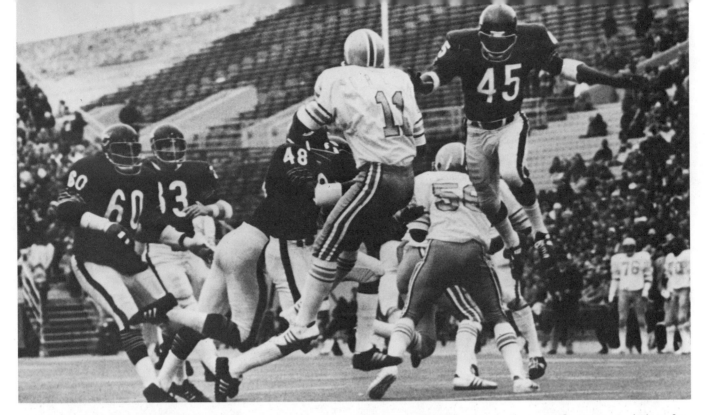

The Bears putting the rush on Houston Oiler punter Dave Green. Allan Ellis (48) almost blocks the punt. Soaring in to help is Joe Moore (45), while Wally Chambers (60) and Gary Kosins (33) look on. This was one of only three regular-season games the Bears won (35–14) in 1973. –Pro Football Hall of Fame

1973 SEASON .214
Won 3   Lost 11   Tied 0

Abe Gibron — Coach	Bears	Opponents
Dallas Cowboys . . . .(H)	17	20
Minnesota Vikings. . . . .(H)	13	22
Denver Broncos . . . .(A)	33	14
New Orleans Saints. . . . .(A)	16	21
Atlanta Falcons. . . . .(A)	6	46
New England Patriots . . . .(H)	10	13
Houston Oilers. . . . .(H)	35	14
Green Bay Packers. . . . .(A)	31	17
Kansas City Chiefs . . . .(A)	7	19
Detroit Lions . . . .(H)	7	30
Minnesota Vikings. . . . .(A)	13	31
Los Angeles Rams . . . .(H)	0	26
Detroit Lions . . . .(A)	7	40
Green Bay Packers. . . . .(H)	0	21
Totals.	195	334

and regular-season games. And still another pro football league would try to survive in competition with the NFL in the coming season. Although the World Football League signed up some of the NFL's best players, it didn't last long. Bad publicity, following disclosures of outlandishly padded attendance figures —among other things—would force it to fold in the middle of the 1975 season.

The radio voices familiar to Bear fans for so many years (1953-76) were those of Jack Brickhouse (right), who handled the play-by-play, and Irv Kupcinet, who provided the color. Brickhouse is, of course, the long-time voice of the Chicago Cubs. Kup, a syndicated newspaper columnist, was on the 1935 College All-Star team that played against the Bears and was the head linesman in the 1940 NFL championship game when the Bears demolished the Redskins 73–0. –WGN Radio

Halas was not at all accustomed to. In fact, only once before in their history had the Bears gone more than one year without winning over 50% of their regular-season games, and that was in 1952 and 1953, when they had records of 5–7–0 and 3–8–1. The five-year period beginning with the season of 1969 had been by far the darkest in the history of the Chicago Bears. Their losing streak was, unfortunately, not over yet.

Early in 1974, the NFL decided to extend the sudden-death overtime rule to include all pre-season

A NEW MAN AT THE TOP

IN THE SUMMER of 1974, Bear president George Halas, Jr., better known by his nickname, Mugs, was attending a meeting of the NFL Management Council. There were difficult times that year because the Council was running head-to-head in bargaining with the NFL Players Association and the threat of a strike loomed very large and very real. (It did indeed prove to be real, and the strike lasted from July through August, forcing the cancellation of the All-Star game.) Negotiations and meetings had been going on since the early spring, and by mid-summer it was feared that there might not even be a 1974 NFL season.

After one of the sessions, Mugs Halas was talking with long-time friend Jim Finks, who had resigned as vice-president and general manager of the Minnesota Vikings shortly after the team appeared in the Super Bowl earlier that year. Finks was now devoting all his time to the NFL Management Council, trying to help solve the problems that existed between the owners and players.

"What are you planning to do with yourself when this is all over?" Halas asked.

Jim Finks shrugged and then explained that he was considering various alternatives. He might even get out of football altogether, he said.

"What would you think about coming with us?"

Jim Finks, who had always had an abiding respect for the Bears and the Halas family, was surprised. "A possibility," he said, then nodded, "I'd be interested in talking about it."

The reputation Jim Finks had earned during his 10 years of management in the NFL was that of a "builder," one who could take the down-and-out team and mold it into a contender. That seemed an especially appropriate requirement for a top management position with the Chicago Bears in 1974.

After that brief conversation, a number of serious meetings ensued in Chicago between Mugs Halas and Finks. Then, on September 12, 1974, George Halas announced that Jim Finks had been hired as the new general manager, vice-president, and chief operating officer of the Bears. And the rebuilding program would begin in earnest. It was the first time in the history of the Chicago Bears that George Halas had turned over the control of the ball club's day-to-day operations to someone else. Even when Papa Bear was thousands of miles away and bogged down in a world war, no major decisions had been made without consulting him.

Jim Finks had played quarterback for the University of Tulsa. Drafted by the Pittsburgh Steelers in 1949, he was converted to a defensive back because the Steelers were still using the single-wing in those days. In 1952, when the Steelers adopted the T formation, he went back to quarterbacking. He was selected for the Pro Bowl in 1953, along with such other quarterbacks as

Jim Finks, executive vice-president, general manager, and chief operating officer of the Chicago Bears, came to the club in 1974 after having built the Minnesota Vikings into a team of Super Bowl caliber. –Chicago Bears

1974 SEASON	.286	
Won 4 Lost 10 Tied 0		
Abe Gibron — Coach	Bears	Opponents
Detroit Lions . . . .(H)	17	9
New York Jets . . . .(H)	21	23
Minnesota Vikings. . . . .(A)	7	11
New Orleans Saints . . . .(H)	24	10
Atlanta Falcons. . . . .(A)	10	13
Green Bay Packers. . . . .(H)	10	9
Buffalo Bills . . . .(A)	6	16
Minnesota Vikings. . . . .(H)	0	17
Green Bay Packers. . . . .(A)	3	20
San Francisco 49ers . . . .(H)	0	34
Detroit Lions . . . .(A)	17	34
New York Giants . . . .(H)	16	13
San Diego Chargers . . . .(A)	21	28
Washington Redskins . . . .(A)	0	42
Totals.	152	279

Otto Graham, Bobby Layne, and Norm Van Brocklin, and he led the NFL in completions and total passing yardage in 1955.

After his playing days ended, Finks assisted Terry Brennan by coaching the Notre Dame backfield, then went to the Canadian League to serve as general manager of the Calgary Stampeders. When he became general manager of the Minnesota Vikings in 1964, the team was entering its fourth NFL season, having posted a 10–30–2 record in its three-year history. The Vikings for the first time had a better than .500 season that year and ended in a tie for second place in the NFL Western Conference. During the 10 years Finks was with Minnesota, the Vikings became an NFL powerhouse, winning their division five times and playing in the Super Bowl twice.

Rebuilding the Bears would be an equal challenge for Finks. That became quite evident in 1974, the first year of his control, which turned out to be a 4–10–0 season and another last-place finish in the NFC Central Division. The lowest point of the season may have been when the Bears lost seven of their last eight games . . . or maybe it was the fact that they went 23 consecutive quarters in mid-season without scoring a single touchdown . . . or perhaps it was when the New York Giants traveled to Soldier Field and only 18,802 spectators came to the game and the Bears had the less than inspiring duty of claiming 36,951 "no-shows."

Then the changes came. Abe Gibron, who had compiled an 11–30–1 record in his three years as head coach, was relieved of his job, and Jack Pardee was hired to replace him. Pardee had played linebacker for the Los Angeles Rams for 13 seasons and the Washington Redskins for another two, then served as an assistant coach with the Redskins and as head coach of the World Football League's Florida Blazers.

The Bears then moved their pre-season training camp from Rensselaer, Indiana, where it had been conducted for the past 31 years, to the grounds of Lake Forest College in a suburb north of Chicago. But few players who had toiled in the Indiana cornfields the summer before would be making the trip to the new Bear training camp. All told, 76 players who were under contract in one form or another to the Bears were traded, waived, or released outright in 1975.

A new team was very definitely being built. And the cornerstone, it would turn out, was the Bears' first-round draft choice that year, running back Walter Payton, from Jackson State College.

The other new faces that joined the Bears in 1975 came by way of the draft or a trade, or as a result of the collapse of the World Football League. They included quarterback Bob Avellini (from Maryland University), running back Roland Harper (Louisiana Tech), cornerback Virgil Livers (Western Kentucky), wide receiver Steve Schubert (from the New England Patriots), defensive end Mike Hartenstine (Penn State), safety Doug Plank (Ohio State), offensive guard Noah Jackson (Tampa), tight end Greg Latta (Morgan State), running back Johnny Musso (Alabama), center Dan Neal (from the Baltimore Colts), center Dan Peiffer (Southeast Missouri State), offensive guard Revie

Sorey (Illinois), tackle Jeff Sevy (California), defensive tackle Ron Rydalch (Utah), and a new place-kicker, Bob Thomas (Notre Dame).

A returnee to the Bears, apparently forgiven for his vocal indiscretions back in 1969, was Virgil Carter, who was signed as a free agent. Carter had been released by the San Diego Chargers after their opening game, which he quarterbacked, and the Chargers lost 37–0, because the San Diego team signed up another quarterback, former Bear Bobby Douglass.

When the Bears came out for the regular season in 1975, there was only one relative old-timer left on the team, Doug Buffone. He had been outstanding as an outside linebacker in each of the nine years he had been with the Bears. He had also been unlucky enough

Bear linebacker Waymond Bryant (50) leaps to take a pass away from intended receiver Rich McGeorge of the Green Bay Packers in this 1974 game at Soldier Field, while defensive back Craig Clemons (45) moves in to help. The Bears won this Monday night game 10–9, but it was one of only four victories that season. –Pro Football Hall of Fame

Defensive back Doug Plank works out with a pair of dumbbells. Weight lifting is an integral part of the Bears' physical fitness training. The Bears' full-time physical, or strength, coordinator, Clyde Emrich, is a five-time U.S. champion and former Olympic weight lifter. –Bill Smith

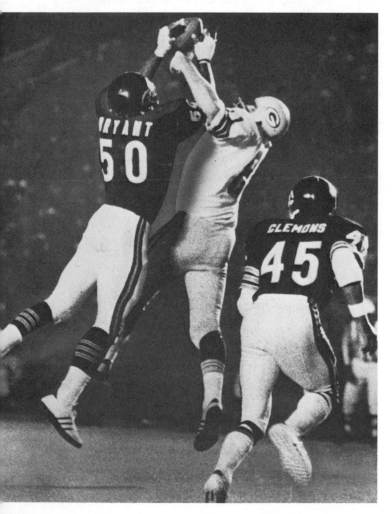

to have played many of those years in the shadow of Dick Butkus. But running backs, quarterbacks, and offensive linemen who opposed the Bears during those years knew he was one of the best players at his position in the NFL.

The "new" Chicago Bears took their learning lumps in 1975. It was, in fact, another dismal 4–10–0 season and another last-place finish. Gary Huff became the starting quarterback but late in the season, when it was clear the Bears were going nowhere, he was replaced by Bob Avellini. There appeared to be some hope for the future when the Bears managed to win two of their last three games that year.

Walter Payton also showed himself to be a potentially good running back, rushing for 679 yards. His average per carry was only 3.5, however. Payton's most impressive showing was in the last game of the season, when he gained a total net yardage of 300, including 134 yards rushing on 25 carries. It was the highest total yardage posted by a Bear since Gale Sayers toted up 339 against the Vikings back in 1966. Virgil Livers led the NFC in punt-return yardage (456) and Bo Rather became the Bears' leading receiver,

1975 SEASON .286

Won 4 Lost 10 Tied 0

Jack Pardee — Coach		Bears	Opponents
Baltimore Colts	(H)	7	35
Philadelphia Eagles	(H)	15	13
Minnesota Vikings	(A)	3	28
Detroit Lions	(A)	7	27
Pittsburgh Steelers	(A)	3	34
Minnesota Vikings	(H)	9	13
Miami Dolphins	(H)	13	46
Green Bay Packers	(H)	27	14
San Francisco 49ers	(A)	3	31
Los Angeles Rams	(A)	10	38
Green Bay Packers	(A)	7	28
Detroit Lions	(H)	25	21
St. Louis Cardinals	(H)	20	34
New Orleans Saints	(A)	42	17
Totals		191	379

with 39 catches for 685 yards. But the Bear defense gave up a total of 379 points, the most that any team in the NFC ceded that year.

At the end of the 1975 season, the Bears had the nucleus of their rebuilding efforts. To the core of their roster they would add: wide receiver James Scott (from Henderson Junior College), wide receiver Brian Baschnagel (Ohio State), tackle Dennis Lick (Wisconsin), and safety Gary Fencik (Yale) in 1976; quarterback Mike Phipps (from the Cleveland Browns), tackle Ted Albrecht (California), linebacker Gary Campbell (Colorado), fullback Robin Earl (Washington), halfback Art Best (Kent State), and quarterback Vince Evans (USC) in 1977; and defensive tackle Brad Shearer (Texas) plus three well-known veterans in tackle Alan Page (acquired from the Vikings), end and linebacker Tommy Hart (from the 49ers), and wide receiver Golden Richards (from the Cowboys) in 1978.

Bob Avellini was drafted by the Bears in 1975 and took over the team's quarterbacking chores in 1976. In 1977, he passed for more than 2,000 yards. –Chicago Bears

Soccer-style kicker Bob Thomas holds Bear records for career field-goals-made percentage (58.1) and single-season field-goals-made percentage (77.3), set in 1978. –Chicago Bears

Running a Team 1970s Style

How does the money come and go today with a professional football team like the Chicago Bears? A private auditing firm in 1976 compiled a pro forma combined statement of income for all teams for the NFL, based on the 1975 playing season. The following are the average income and outgo of cash for an NFL team in the mid-1970s.

Income of Average Club

Ticket sales (pre-season and regular season)	$4,202,000
Television and radio	2,442,000
Participating teams' shares of post-season games	244,000
Distributions from post-season games	276,000
Programs, concessions, films, and royalties	137,000
Miscellaneous	98,000
Total income	$7,399,000

Operating Expenses

Player costs

Pre-season	$ 248,000
Salaries, bonuses, and deferred compensation	2,503,000
Post-season	136,000
Player insurance trust	66,000
Medical expenses, workmen's compensation, and payroll taxes	184,000
General team expenses, including coaching, scouting, travel, training camp, uniforms, and equipment	1,290,000
Stadium costs	475,000
Box office and other services	326,000
League assessments, including officiating, security, publicity, legal and professional fees	245,000
General administrative expenses, including front office salaries, rent, utilities, insurance, charitable contributions, nonplaying employees' pension plans, professional fees, publicity and promotion	1,070,000
Total operating expenses	$6,543,000

Operating Profit	$ 856,000
Other expenses, including non-operating expenses and provision for income taxes	472,000
Net income	$ 384,000

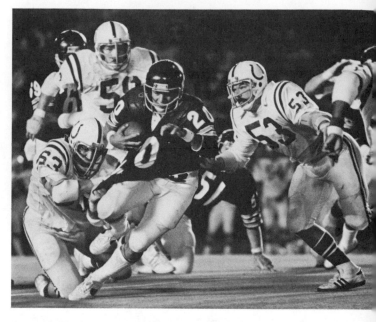

Bear halfback Walter Payton is noted for his gymnastic catapulting over defensive lines to deposit himself and the football in enemy end zones. Here, in a 1976 regular-season game against the Dallas Cowboys at Texas Stadium, he illustrates one of those classic leaps. –Bill Smith

Among the finest pass rushers ever to wear a Bear uniform, Wally Chambers (60) goes high in the air to bat at a pass thrown by Detroit Lion quarterback Joe Reed in this 1975 game. Double-teaming Chambers are Lynn Boden (62) and Jon Morris (63), who would play with the Bears in 1978. The Bears won the game 25–21, but their record was a repeat of 1974's dismal 4–10–0. –Pro Football Hall of Fame

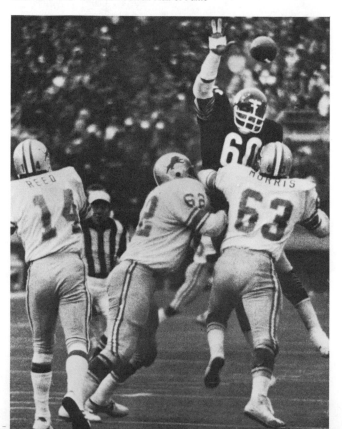

Jack Pardee talks with wide receiver Ron Shanklin on the sidelines during a game at Soldier Field in 1975, his first year as the Bears' head coach. During Pardee's three-year tenure as coach, the Bear teams would improve steadily, culminating in a trip to the NFL playoffs in 1977. –Pro Football Hall of Fame

With the new team things really did begin to change. In 1976 the Bears improved their record to 7–7–0, the first time they had achieved a .500 season in a long eight years, and it was good enough for a second-place finish in their division. Walter Payton emerged that year as one of the NFL's premier running backs, leading the NFC in rushing, with 1,390 yards (second only in the NFL to O. J. Simpson's 1,503 yards). He also tied with Chuck Foreman of the Vikings for the most touchdowns rushing (13) in the NFC.

The promise that the young Bears gave evidence of in 1976 was not so much in their won-loss record as it was in how they measured up to the teams they played. They had faced one of the most difficult schedules in the NFL that year and had made a respectable showing in six games against teams who would end up in the NFL playoffs. The Bears defeated the Washington Redskins and the Minnesota Vikings in two of these six games and lost two others by a single point each to the Oakland Raiders (28–27) and the Vikings (20–19). Both of these losses were due to the kicking game. Bob Avellini's completion percentage

1976 SEASON	.500	
Won 7　　Lost 7　　Tied 0		
Jack Pardee — Coach	Bears	Opponents
Detroit Lions . . . .(H)	10	3
San Francisco 49ers . . . .(A)	19	12
Atlanta Falcons. . . . .(H)	0	10
Washington Redskins . . . .(H)	33	7
Minnesota Vikings. . . . .(A)	19	20
Los Angeles Rams . . . .(A)	12	20
Dallas Cowboys . . . .(A)	21	31
Minnesota Vikings. . . . .(H)	14	13
Oakland Raiders. . . . .(H)	27	28
Green Bay Packers. . . . .(H)	24	13
Detroit Lions . . . .(A)	10	14
Green Bay Packers. . . . .(A)	16	10
Seattle Seahawks . . . .(A)	34	7
Denver Broncos . . . .(H)	14	28
Totals.	253	216

Bear halfback Walter Payton is noted for his gymnastic catapulting over defensive lines to deposit himself and the football in enemy end zones. Here, in a 1976 regular-season game against the Dallas Cowboys at Texas Stadium, he illustrates one of those classic leaps. –Bill Smith

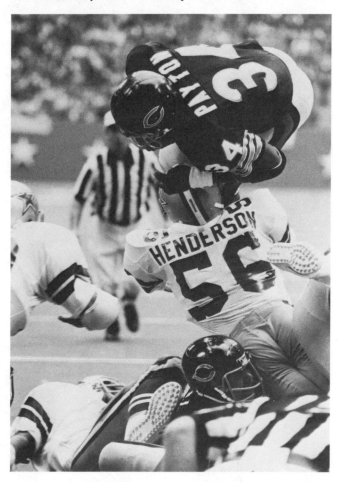

was only 44%, so there were still some problems with the quarterbacking situation. But all in all it was a heartening year, and when it was over both Walter Payton and Wally Chambers were named All-Pro. And as a result of the Bears' resurgence, Jack Pardee was named NFC Coach of the Year.

Then came 1977, one of the more tumultuous years in Bear history. The year began badly; in fact by mid-season the Bears had a disappointing 3–4 record. They then flew down to Houston to meet the Oilers at the Astrodome. Here the Bears had a good chance of turning their season around, because the Oilers had lost their last three games in a row. But the Oilers didn't

see it that way. Dan Pastorini threw for two touchdowns among his 11 completions that day. Wide receiver Billy ("White Shoes") Johnson ran 75 yards for one touchdown and 61 for another. Houston out-gained Chicago 489 yards to 125. The Bears registered a net loss of 12 yards passing that bleak Sunday afternoon. The final score was 47–0.

The Kansas City Chiefs, the AFC West's weakest team, with a 2–6 record, came to Soldier Field the week after the disaster in Houston.

At half-time the Bears trailed 17–0—and now they had been outscored 64–0 in their last six quarters of play. Then, when it appeared that the game would be a

This picture of a play execution, which looks as if it were specially choreographed for the photographer, won an award in the 1976 Pro Football Hall of Fame photo contest. The action was for real, however, and that is Walter Payton moving through a giant hole in the San Francisco 49er line after taking a handoff from Bob Avellini (7). Other Bears, in circular order, are Noah Jackson (65), Lionel Antoine (79), Bob Parsons (86), Dan Peiffer (53), Jeff Sevy, and Roland Harper. The photo was taken by M. Frederic Stein, then of the Chicago Daily News. *–Pro Football Hall of Fame*

The Bears' Walter Payton (right) and O. J. Simpson of the San Francisco 49ers exchange a few words before playing against each other at Candlestick Park in 1976. Payton took away Simpson's NFL record for most yards gained rushing in a single game, with 275 in 1977, but O.J. holds the record for most yards gained rushing in a season (2,003). –Bill Smith

shambles like the one the week before, the Bears suddenly came to life. In the third quarter, Brian Baschnagel returned a punt 49 yards to the Kansas City 28. A couple of plays later, Walter Payton followed with a brilliant, darting, 18-yard run to the 4-yard line, breaking five tackles on the way. After that, Payton dived over for the first Bear touchdown in what had been a long, long time.

With 7½ minutes left in the game, Payton again scored, this time from the 1-yard line, cutting Kansas City's lead to 17–14. The Chiefs, however, came up with a field goal, making it 20 to 14. Then, Bob Avellini threw to Payton, a 28-yard pass play that brought the football to the 18-yard line with just under three minutes left. Payton left the game after having the wind knocked out of him, but came back one play later. He got the ball on the 15, started wide to his left on a run,

then cut back sharply to the middle of the field against the flow of the pursuit as he crossed the line of scrimmage, and went into the end zone untouched with the tying touchdown. Bob Thomas converted, and the Bears led 21–20 with two minutes left. But the Chiefs came right back, all the way to the Bears' 14-yard line. Only about 30 seconds now remained in the game. The Bears were looking for a pass, but halfback Ed Podolak surprised everyone with an end run and went in for the touchdown. The successful kick for the extra point gave Kansas City a 27–21 lead.

At the kickoff there were only 24 seconds left, and the Bears' comeback from a 17-point deficit in the second half appeared to have been wasted. Those few fans who were not part of the mass exodus from Soldier Field after Podolak's touchdown then saw one of the most frantic but memorable comebacks in Bear

Walter Payton trying to gain yardage against Green Bay and Packer defenders Johnnie Gray (24) and Mike Butler (77) trying to stop him. Payton became the only Bear back in history to gain more than 1,000 yards in a season four times, and he did it consecutively (1976-79). He already owns a large number of other Bear records. –Chicago Bears

What had kept the Bears in the game that day was the running of Walter Payton. He gained 192 yards rushing against the Chiefs, which brought his total for the season beyond the 1,000-yard mark.

From that point on the Bears were a different team. The next week Payton set an NFL single-game rushing record when he ran for 275 yards, on 40 carries, against the Vikings. And the Bears continued on a six-game winning streak that would leave them in a tie with Minnesota for the division title but also secure for them a berth in the NFL playoffs, an experience they had not enjoyed in 14 years. But that did not come easily, and it did not become a reality until only a few seconds remained in an overtime period in the last game of the season.

Bear tackle Wally Chambers raises his arms in triumph after one of his many sacks of opposing quarterbacks. Chambers played in the defensive line of the Bears for five years and was named to the All-Pro team in 1976. –Chicago Bears

history. Brian Baschnagel returned the kickoff straight up the middle of the field to the Bears' 43 and immediately called a time-out. Avellini then dumped a short pass over the middle to rookie fullback Robin Earl, who headed diagonally across the field for the sideline, finally being run out-of-bounds at the Kansas City 37. Only 10 seconds remained. Avellini faded back to the 46. Tight end Greg Latta raced down the sidelines. Amazingly, he was open as the Chiefs concentrated on the Bears' wide receivers. Avellini lofted the ball high and long, and Latta caught it over the shoulder, running top speed into the end zone. The clock showed three seconds left. Thomas kicked the game-deciding extra point, and the Bears won 28–27.

The Chicago Bears of 1977. Front row (from left): equipment manager Ray Earley, equipment assistant Ken Earley, trainer Fred Caito, physical coordinator Clyde Emrich, assistant trainer Tom Wilkinson. Second row: assistant coach Sid Gillman, Bob Avellini, Vince Evans, Mike Phipps, Bob Thomas, Johnny Musso, Len Walterscheid, Virgil Livers, Art Best, Walter Payton, Roland Harper, Robin Earl, Craig Clemons, assistant coach Fred O'Connor. Third row: head coach Jack Pardee, Terry Schmidt, Gary Fencik, Doug Plank, Mike Spivey, Allan Ellis, Waymond Bryant, Mel Rogers, Dan Neal, Dan Peiffer, Tom Hicks, Doug Buffone, assistant coach Brad Ecklund. Fourth row: assistant coach Ross Fichtner, Don Rives, Jerry Muckensturm, Gary Campbell, Dan Jiggetts, Fred Dean, Ted Albrecht, Noah Jackson, Jim Osborne, Revie Sorey, Dennis Lick, Mike Hartenstine, Jerry Meyers, assistant coach Ray Callahan. Fifth row: special assistant Bob Bowser, Jeff Sevy, Ron Rydalch, Bo Rather, Chuck Bradley, Steve Rivera, Brian Baschnagel, Steve Schubert, Bob Parsons, Billy Newsome, Greg Latta, James Scott, assistant coach John Hilton. –Chicago Bears

That game was against the New York Giants, and it was like several important Bear-Giant contests of the past in that the condition of the field could affect the outcome. Remembering the "Sneakers Game" for the NFL championship in 1934 and the disaster that befell them in the title game of 1956, the Bears of 1977 came prepared for the elements they expected to confront them. But this time the field was covered with slush and snow. On snow-covered artificial turf, rubber-soled shoes would be a problem. And that is what the Bears had brought with them. A call from Ted Haracz, the Bears' public relations director, lined up a source for ordinary cleated football shoes. A ball boy with a police escort sped to the sporting goods store in New Jersey and purchased more than $1,000 worth of the shoes. He arrived back at the stadium before half-time. It would help.

A win was crucial for the Bears, because they were grasping desperately at the "wild-card berth" in the playoffs. The best they could possibly do in their division would be to tie the Vikings' record of 9–5–0. Minnesota, however, would win the division title because the particular tie-breaking procedure that ap-

plied to this situation came down to the point differential in the two Bear-Viking games, the title therefore going to the Vikings, who had won by six points, while the Bears had won by only three in the other game. The Bears, however, would have a chance for the wild-card spot, but only if they beat the Giants—if they lost or tied that last game, the Washington Redskins would get it.

The teams slipped, slid, and fumbled throughout the game. In the final period, the Giants led 6–3, but with six minutes remaining, fullback Robin Earl plunged over from the 5-yard line, giving the Bears a 9–6 lead. The extra point was blocked, which nearly proved to be disastrous. In the final minute, with the Giants less than 10 yards from the goal line, a New York receiver got open in the end zone on a pass play, only to drop the slippery ball. The Giants settled for a field goal by Joe Danelo, his third of the game, and the score was tied 9–9 at the end of regulation time.

In the overtime period, the Bears muffed two chances to win. The first was a 35-yard field goal missed by Bob Thomas. The second occurred when the Bears were at the Giants' 10-yard line. A bad

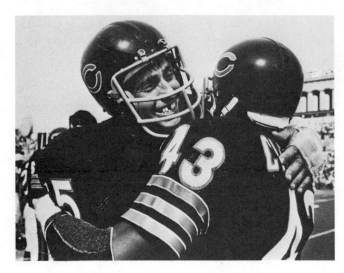

This picture of Bear linebacker Doug Buffone embracing defensive back Craig Clemons (43) won a 1977 Pro Football Hall of Fame photo contest award. The photograph was taken during an upbeat moment at Soldier Field by Perry C. Riddle, then of the Chicago Daily News. *–Pro Football Hall of Fame*

On a snowy December afternoon at Giants Stadium in East Rutherford, New Jersey, in 1977, Bob Thomas boots a 27-yard field goal with 12 seconds left in sudden-death overtime against New York. It gave the Bears a 12–9 victory and a place in the NFL playoffs for the first time since 1963. The holder is Bob Avellini. –UPI

snap from center nullified this opportunity, and the Giants took possession. Time was now running out. If no one scored, the game would end in a tie and the Bears would have to settle for watching the NFC playoffs on television.

With only two minutes left, the Giants appeared to have picked up a first down on a third-down run, but the gain was nullified by a penalty. The Bears held on the next play, forcing the Giants to punt, and they got the ball on the Giants' 45. Only 82 seconds remained in which to salvage the Bears' playoff dream.

As this lineman's hands illustrate, playing pro football today isn't any easier than it was back in 1920. –Vernon Biever

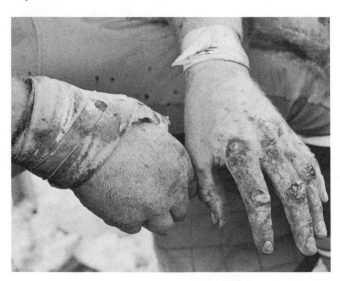

Bob Avellini hit Greg Latta with a pass out in the flat, but the play gained only two yards and the clock was running. Again Avellini looked for Latta; this time he connected with him down the middle for an 18-yard gain to the 25. With 42 seconds remaining, the Bears used their last time-out. When play resumed, Avellini faded back under a heavy pass rush. He was forced to dump the ball to Walter Payton, off to the side at about the line of scrimmage, who sloshed down the sidelines through the wet snow to the 10-yard line. He did not get out-of-bounds to stop the clock, however. With no time-outs left, the Bears' kicking team raced out onto the field. The clock was down to 12 seconds when the ball was centered. This time the snap and the hold were perfect, and Bob Thomas kicked the football directly through the center of the uprights—a 27-yard field goal that put the Bears in the playoffs. It was the first overtime victory for the Bears in their history.

The Bears only got to one game in the post-season. They lost the playoff to the Dallas Cowboys 37–7, a team that went on to win the Super Bowl that year. Still, they had exhibited a vast improvement: the project of rebuilding was moving along at a very impressive rate.

James Scott forged to the front of the Bear pass receivers in 1977, with 50 catches for 809 yards—the second-highest yardage in the conference and third highest in the NFL. Otherwise the year was all Walter Payton's. Besides the single-game rushing feat of 275 yards, Payton also shattered his own season-rushing record, which he had established the year before, by more than 450 yards. His total of 1,852 yards in 1977 was the most ever gained by a Chicago Bear runner. His 14 touchdowns and average of 5.5 yards per carry were also NFL highs for the year. Payton was an obvious All-Pro that year; he was also selected the NFL's Most Valuable Player of the Year by the Professional Football Writers Association and by various wire services and magazines, and the United Press named him Athlete of the Year. Chicago Bear fans were de-

lighted to again have an exciting running back in the mold of Gale Sayers, Red Grange, George McAfee, and Willie Galimore.

One loss after the season had ended, however, was an unexpected one. Coach Jack Pardee resigned to take the head coaching job with the Washington Redskins. His departure would be felt severely in the coming season. Pardee and the team had grown along with each other in the three seasons they had been together—from a last-place 4–10–0 to a playoff qualifier with a record of 9–5–0. Now a young Bear team faced the process of adapting to a new coach and a new staff.

Neill Armstrong, the defensive coach of the Minnesota Vikings for the previous eight years, was hired by Jim Finks to replace Jack Pardee. The transition that

Walter Payton gains a few yards on this rush against the Minnesota Vikings in 1977 at Soldier Field, during a game in which he set the NFL single-game rushing record, with 275 yards. He averaged 6.9 yards a carry as the Bears won 10–7. –UPI

Walter Payton's 1977 Records

Three NFL Records:

Most yards rushing, one game	275
Most rushing attempts, season	339
Most combined attempts,* season	373

Thirteen Chicago Bear Records (the three above plus):

Most yards rushing, season	1,852
Most touchdowns rushing, season†	14
Most seasons, 1,000 yards rushing†	2
Most consecutive seasons, 1,000 yards rushing	2
Most 200-yard rushing games, career	2
Most 200-yard rushing games, season	2
Most 100-yard rushing games, season	10
Most consecutive 100-yard rushing games	5
Most rushing attempts, game	40
Most combined attempts,* game	41

*Includes attempts on rushes, pass receptions, and returns of kickoffs, punts, interceptions, and fumbles.
†Tied with Gale Sayers.

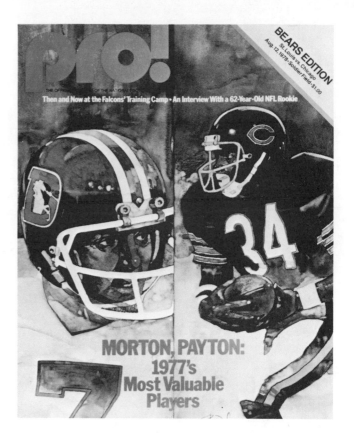

The Bears drew the Dallas Cowboys as their opponents in the 1977 divisional playoffs. Here, Bear linebacker Waymond Bryant (50) wrestles a scrambling Roger Staubach to the ground early in the game. But for most of the game, the Cowboys handled the Bears easily, removing them from further playoff contention by a score of 37–7. –UPI

The first year—1977—Bear running back Gale Sayers was eligible for induction into the Pro Football Hall of Fame was the year he was accorded that honor. He is shown at the hall in Canton, Ohio, just after the induction ceremony with the official presenter he requested, George Halas. –Pro Football Hall of Fame

Meeting the press, coach Jack Pardee talks while his boss Jim Finks ponders. The two men brought the Bears from a cellar-dwelling team in 1975 to the playoffs in 1977. –Bill Smith

1977 SEASON .643

Won 9   Lost 5   Tied 0

Jack Pardee — Coach	Bears	Opponents
Detroit Lions . . . .(H)	30	20
St. Louis Cardinals . . . .(A)	13	16
New Orleans Saints . . . .(H)	24	42
Los Angeles Rams . . . .(H)	24	23
Minnesota Vikings. . . . .(A)	16	22
Atlanta Falcons. . . . .(H)	10	16
Green Bay Packers . . . .(A)	26	0
Houston Oilers. . . . .(A)	0	47
Kansas City Chiefs . . . .(H)	28	27
Minnesota Vikings. . . . .(H)	10	7
Detroit Lions . . . .(A)	31	14
Tampa Bay Buccaneers. . . . .(A)	10	0
Green Bay Packers. . . . .(H)	21	10
New York Giants . . . .(A)	12	9
Totals.	255	253

Divisional Playoffs

	Bears	Opponents
Dallas Cowboys . . . .(A)	7	37

came with 1978 would need some time before it would become effective.

Beginning in 1978, the regular-season schedule was increased to 16 games and the pre-season games were cut back to four. For the Bears, the pre-season was nothing more than a series of trials and tribulations, as it turned out. They lost all four of their exhibition games, but in the sophisticated late 1970s everyone accepted the fact that the pre-season was a time of experimentation, out of which would come the proper men and methods to conduct a successful regular-season campaign.

And this seemed to be true for the Chicago Bears, who came on strong early, winning their first three games in a row. Bob Avellini was doing the quarter-backing, Walter Payton and Roland Harper the running. But then, everything collapsed, and the Bears lost their next eight consecutive games. They had done that only once before in their history, back in a period that spanned two seasons, from December 15, 1968, through November 2, 1969.

Neill Armstrong was named head coach of the Chicago Bears when Jack Pardee left after the 1977 season. Like Jim Finks, who hired him, Armstrong worked in the Canadian football league and then moved to the Minnesota Vikings before coming to the Bears. –Chicago Bears

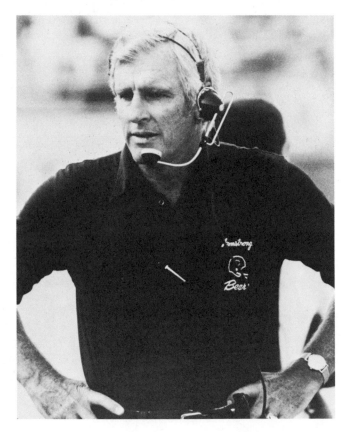

The obligatory spike. Bear end James Scott does it here in a game against the Lions at Detroit in 1978. It was the Bears' last victory before lapsing into an eight-game losing streak and then managing to win four of their last five games. –Bill Smith

The statistic was bad, there was no question about that. The only consolation was the fact that the Bears were within a play or two of winning every one of the games they lost in that eight-week period. In the words of Jim Finks, a losing streak of that kind was unfortunate, but it was the price the team had to pay as an entirely new coaching staff attempted to get its feet on solid football ground. "The coaching change inevitably retarded our progress," Finks said. "It did set us back, and we just have to ride out the situation."

Then the turn-around came again. The Bears wound up 1978 winning four of their last five games —one of them a shutout of the Packers—restoring hope that the rebuilding process was still moving ahead. They closed the season with a 7–9–0 record.

In 1978, Walter Payton became the first Chicago Bear to rush for more than 1,000 yards three times—and he did it in three consecutive years. His total of 1,395 yards was enough to lead the conference again, his third consecutive year for that honor. His running partner Roland Harper accounted for another 992 yards rushing. This was Harper's finest season so far in a Bear uniform.

Kicker Bob Thomas also had his best year, with a 77.3% field-goal percentage for the year, an all-time Bear record (Mac Percival's 69.4% had stood since 1968). Thomas also tied Percival's 1968 Bear record of 10 consecutive field goals.

And in that 1978 season, Doug Buffone set a different kind of record. He appeared in more games in a Chicago Bear uniform than any other player in the team's history—170 games since his first one as a rookie back in 1966.

The promise that the 1978 season ended on, with the Bears winning four of their last five games, carried exuberantly into the 1979 summer camp at Lake Forest. To add to that feeling, the draft had been a rich

1978 SEASON	.438	
Won 7 Lost 9 Tied 0		
Neill Armstrong — Coach	Bears	Opponents
St. Louis Cardinals . . . .(H)	17	10
San Francisco 49ers . . . .(A)	16	13
Detroit Lions . . . .(A)	19	0
Minnesota Vikings. . . . .(H)	20	24
Oakland Raiders. . . . .(H)	19	25
Green Bay Packers. . . . .(A)	14	24
Denver Broncos . . . .(A)	7	16
Tampa Bay Buccaneers. . . . .(A)	19	33
Detroit Lions . . . .(H)	17	21
Seattle Seahawks . . . .(H)	29	31
Minnesota Vikings. . . . .(A)	14	17
Atlanta Falcons. . . . .(H)	13	7
Tampa Bay Buccaneers. . . . .(H)	14	3
San Diego Chargers . . . .(A)	7	40
Green Bay Packers. . . . .(H)	14	0
Washington Redskins . . . .(A)	14	10
Totals.	253	274

Roland Harper explodes into the end zone against Seattle in 1978. The Bear fullback toted up 992 yards rushing for the season, averaging 4.1 yards per carry. –Bill Smith

Alan Page (82) illustrates his reputation as one of the quickest defensive linesmen in the game as he breaks through the Atlanta Falcon line in this 1978 game at Soldier Field. Page joined the Bears in 1978 and that year led the team in sacks (11½ in 10 games). –Bill Smith

Veteran linebacker Doug Buffone retired after the 1979 season, having appeared in more games for the Bears (186) than any other player in history. He also shares the Bear record for most seasons played (14). –Chicago Bears

Vince Evans took over as quarterback in the second game of the 1979 regular season and electrified Bear fans with a series of long bombs during the next few games, before a serious infection sidelined him. –Chicago Bears

harvest, the coaching staff and front office felt. The first round produced Dan Hampton, a quick, strong, 256-pound defensive tackle from the University of Arkansas, and Al Harris, a unanimous All-America defensive end from Arizona State. Rickey Watts, a wide receiver from Jim Finks's alma mater, the University of Tulsa, came in the second round, followed by running back Willie McClendon from Georgia in the third round; Lee Kunz, a linebacker from the University of Nebraska was a seventh-round pick. Leaving that year, however, would be some familiar Bear names, including Waymond Bryant, Johnny Musso, Jeff Sevy, and Art Best.

What would become a plague of injuries began early. Brad Shearer, the Bears' top draft pick the preceding year, would not put on a game uniform after the first pre-season game, and rookie Al Harris injured his knee even before that. The roster of injured would grow much longer before the end of the season.

The Bears of 1979 would offer Chicagoans a wild ride on an erratic course that ricocheted from confidence to hope to disappointment, that engendered excitement one week and brooding depression the next, elicited groans and shrieks of jubilation. It was to be a fretful, dramatic year, one in which the nail-biting would not reach its climax until the last Sunday of the regular season — two hours, in fact, after the Bears finished their last regular-season game.

The year began on a positive note. Even a good number of the nation's sportswriters were predicting that the Bears would win the NFC Central Division that year. Three straight victories in the pre-season, over the New York Jets, the New Orleans Saints, and the Cincinnati Bengals, made the fans think the prognostications might be right. It was certainly far more encouraging than the winless pre-season the Bears had suffered in 1978. The closing game of the pre-season gave them their first taste of defeat, when the St. Louis Cardinals beat them at Busch Memorial Stadium by a score of 10–7. Much more damaging than the loss, however, was the knee injury to Bear fullback Roland Harper, which would keep him out for the season and deny the Bears a back who contributed almost a thousand yards rushing the previous year as well as outstanding blocking for his running mate Walter Payton.

The Bears opened the regular season against the Green Bay Packers in Chicago at newly renovated Soldier Field. Fifty-five years old by 1979, and dubiously honored as the elder statesman of NFL arenas, Soldier Field had undergone a $3.5 million refashioning. New grandstands were added in the north end zone to raise the total seating capacity to 58,064 (an addition of a little more than 700 new seats), and a

Gary Fencik (45) takes part here in some of the mayhem that routinely goes on in the Bear secondary. Fencik came to the Bears in 1976 and led the team in tackles in 1977 and 1978 (133 and 130 respectively). In 1979 he was third, even though he missed two games during the season because of an injury. –Bill Smith

brand-new artificial turf covered the field. Nonetheless, the stadium still left a great deal to be desired.

Mike Phipps was taken from the Bears' quarterbacking turntable and given the starting assignment against the Packers. It was a scorcher in the mid-80s that afternoon and the game was as lethargic as the late summer doldrums, with the Bears winning by kicking two field goals to the Pack's one.

The defending division champs, the Minnesota Vikings, came to Soldier Field the following week, and the Bears revealed that they did have an offensive attack. Vince Evans came off the bench with about six minutes left in the half and shortly afterward launched a 56-yard bomb to James Scott. Walter Payton added two exciting touchdown runs, 43 and 26 yards respectively, and the Bears were impressive in a 26–7 win.

But then the decline started. The Dallas Cowboys, a 1978 contender in the Super Bowl, served the Bears their first loss of the season, 24–20. Still, the Bears played respectably and Dallas had to pull the game out in the last two minutes with one of Roger Staubach's patented last-moment touchdown marches. For Chicago, Vince Evans scored three touchdowns that day, running once and throwing bombs to James Scott and Golden Richards.

Then the Floridians struck. First, Miami hosted the Bears, and Larry Csonka mauled and bruised the Bear defense all afternoon. His three touchdowns contributed to an easy Dolphin victory. Next the Tampa Bay Buccaneers, undefeated and an amazing surprise in the NFC Central Division, came to Chicago and to the Bears' chagrin extended their winning streak. The Bears sank to a record of 2 wins and 3 losses. To add to their misery, Vince Evans during the following week came down with a staph infection in his back that would put him in the hospital for a month and out of action for the rest of the season. Bob Avellini was chosen to replace him as starting quarterback.

Mike Phipps nailed down the starting quarterback position midway through the 1979 season and offered Bear fans a surprising twist—a sustained passing attack. He posted an NFL quarterback rating of 69.7. –Chicago Bears

The Bears managed to sneak past the Buffalo Bills by a single touchdown on a dazzling fourth-down leap into the end zone by Walter Payton in the final quarter. It was but a brief respite, followed by the season's lowlight. The New England Patriots virtually took the Bears apart, 27–7.

There was discontent in the ranks. Only a few weeks earlier touted as probable division champs, the Bears were now languishing at the wrong end of the standings. The quarterbacks asked for a chance to present their case for a more wide-open offensive game plan. Their voices were heard apparently, because the Bears did change tactics, and for the fans it was as refreshing as a crisp autumn breeze sweeping in from Lake Michigan.

It began in the Minnesota Viking game the next Sunday. With the Bears trailing in the second half 17–14, Mike Phipps was brought from the bench to replace Avellini. Suddenly the Bears were a passing threat as Phipps threw for 200 yards and gave them a 27–17 lead in the fourth quarter. Unfortunately it was

frittered away as the Vikes came back with two touchdowns, the last with only 13 seconds remaining in the game. The Bears at the halfway mark in the season had a disappointing record of 3–5.

But the turnaround had begun. And when the Bears went out to Candlestick Park in San Francisco, they played a game remarkably reminiscent of the 1977 victory over the Kansas City Chiefs that put them on a track direct to the playoffs. The similarities were astonishing. The Bears were 3–5 going into both games; they won both games by the score of 28–27; each game was won with a desperation bomb in the fourth quarter; and both games signaled a surge that landed the team in the playoffs. The 1979 pass that did it was a fourth-down 49-yarder thrown by Phipps to James Scott.

With the adrenaline from that game pumping madly, the Bears crushed the Detroit Lions 35–7 in a game highlighted by Steve Schubert's 77-yard punt return for one touchdown and Terry Schmidt's interception runback for another. The victory was not without cost. Wide receiver James Scott broke his ankle and joined the ranks of Bears sidelined for the season.

The loss of Scott, however, offered rookie Rickey Watts his first real chance in the pros. He took advantage of it the following week against the Los

George "Mugs" Halas, Jr., Bear president, died in the early hours of December 16, 1979. Mugs Halas was a "behind-the-scenes" person, shunning the publicity that is so much a part of pro football, but he was widely admired throughout the NFL for his many contributions to the sport during a career that spanned 30 years. –Chicago Bears

Angeles Rams when he caught six passes for a total of 147 yards, the best pass-catching day (in number of yards gained) a Bear receiver had had since Dick Gordon back in 1970 grabbed five passes for 158 yards. It inspired the Bears to a comeback victory over the Rams (halftime score, Rams 16–Bears 7; final score, Bears 27–Rams 23).

The Bears handily defeated the New York Jets next, then went to Detroit on Thanksgiving Day. Just as fans started talking about playoff chances again, the Bears curled up and died on national television, losing 20–0 to the Lions. But wins in the next two weeks, over the Buccaneers and the Packers, brought the Bears right back into contention.

One game in the season remained. The Bears' chances of getting into the playoffs were rather complicated. Going into the final game, the Bears and Tampa Bay were tied for first place in their division with records of 9–6–0. For the Bears to be awarded the division crown, however, they had to win that Sunday and Tampa Bay had to lose or tie. If both teams won, the Buccaneers would earn the title because their record within the division was better than the Bears'.

On the other hand, the Bears also had a shot at a wild-card berth for the playoffs. To achieve that, the Bears would have to win and the Washington Redskins would have to lose. Not only that, the margins of the Bear victory and the Redskin loss would have to total at least 33 points. Then the Bears would be given the berth because the point differential between them and their opponents during the entire season would be better than that registered by Washington.

The St. Louis Cardinals came to Chicago that final Sunday. The day began with a searing Bear tragedy. Early that morning, December 16, the team's president, Mugs Halas, died unexpectedly, the victim of a

Rookie Rickey Watts races down the sideline against the St. Louis Cardinals, returning a kickoff 83 yards for a touchdown. The score helped the Bears ring up enough points to land them in the 1979 NFL playoffs. –Bill Smith

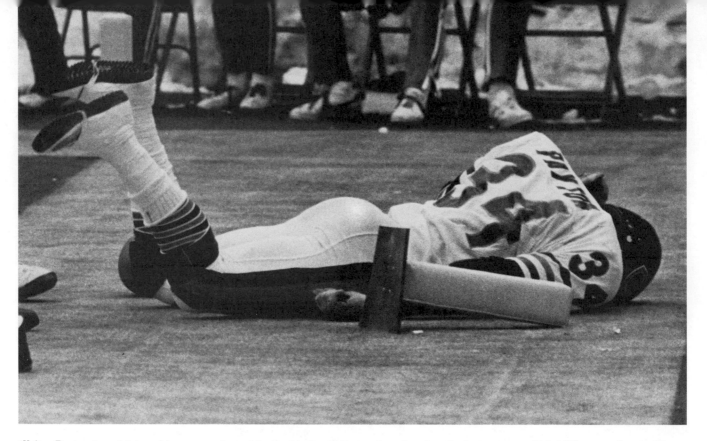

Walter Payton is not injured here, merely registering his frustration at learning that the longest run of his NFL career has just been nullified by a penalty back up the field. Payton had carried the ball 84 yards, all the way to the 1-foot line, in the 1979 playoff game against the Philadelphia Eagles, which the Bears eventually lost 27–17. –Bill Smith

heart attack. It was a deep and disturbing blow to everyone in the Bears' organization, in fact to everyone associated with the NFL. With a combination of things now to play their hearts out for, the Bears played inspired football that Sunday. They built a solid 21–0 lead by halftime. But during the intermission they learned that Tampa Bay had won. Their only chance now was to win big, then hope that Washington would lose by a wide enough margin to create a differential of 33 points. For the Bears, who had scored over 28 points only once all season, it was a large request.

It became even larger when St. Louis came out in the second half and scored a touchdown. With the missed extra point, the 21–6 score meant that the Bears had to chalk up another 18 points.

That's when Rickey Watts exploded. He took the Cardinal kickoff and after a few diversionary moves streaked down the sideline past the Cardinal bench, 83 yards and a touchdown. A short while later, he grabbed a short pass from Mike Phipps and turned it into a 38-yard gain, down to the Cardinal 5-yard line. Walter Payton carried the ball in for another Bear touchdown. Then with time winding down on the season, Phipps again looked for Watts, who raced a short pattern across the middle, took the pass at almost a complete standstill, faked one way, then whirled the other and raced toward the sideline and the goal line, stepping in with the Bears' sixth touchdown of the day.

The final score, 42–6; the Bears had come up with the needed 33 points and a few more to boot.

Only it all appeared to be for nothing. Washington, the Bears found out, had gone out in front of the Cowboys by a score of 17–0. Bear players showered and dressed as the Redskin-Cowboy game wore on. Many of them then gathered in the parking lot under Soldier Field to listen to the last minutes of the game on a car radio. It was dismal. With just four minutes remaining, the Redskins led 34–21 and they had possession of the ball. Suddenly there was a glimmer of hope: Washington fumbled and Dallas recovered on its own 35-yard line. It took Roger Staubach only three plays to put a touchdown on the scoreboard for Dallas. Washington then tried to run out the clock but was forced to punt with less than two minutes left. Again, Staubach marched the Cowboys down the field. With only 40 seconds left and the Bear players at Soldier Field still huddling around the car radio, now in dead silence, Staubach lofted a little lob pass right into the hands of Tony Hill as he streaked into the end zone. The crucial extra point was good, the final score Dallas 35, Washington 34. The Bears were in the playoffs.

More than 69,000 people filled the stadium in Philadelphia to watch the Bears take on the Eagles in the opening round of the NFL playoffs. The Bears came from behind to lead at the half 17–10, the result of two Walter Payton touchdowns and a Bob Thomas field goal. Unfortunately that ended the Bears' scoring for the day, even though that didn't appear to be the case when early in the third quarter Payton took the ball around end and dazzled the Eagle defenders with an 84-yard run to the Eagle 1-foot line. But it was

called back for an illegal-motion penalty. The Eagles benefited from several other calls during the second half and managed to add two touchdowns and a field goal, enough to dash any hopes the Bears might have had for advancing in the playoffs.

It had been a wonderfully exciting season, however. Walter Payton, with his fourth consecutive 1,000-yard season (1,610 in 1979), led the NFC in rushing, also for the fourth consecutive year. Doug Buffone ended his fine career, inscribing his name in Bear record books as the player to perform in the most Bear games ever (186). He also played for the most seasons and the most consecutive seasons (14), a record he shares with Bill George. And Mike Phipps proved that a Bear quarterback could indeed be a passing threat, tossing more touchdown passes than interceptions (only nine other NFL quarterbacks could claim that in 1979) and posting an impressive 69.7 NFL quarterback rating.

As a team, the Bears scored 306 points, an average of 19.1 points per game, the best they had posted since the 409-point season of 1965, when they averaged 29.2 points a game. The team ranked third in the NFL in defense, yielding only 249 points to their opponents, and led the NFC in pass interceptions with 29. The season was summed up best perhaps by defensive tackle Alan Page when he said, "I believe the importance of this season was not that we won 10 games or got into the playoffs. The most important thing about 1979 was that we learned to be winners."

1979 SEASON   .625
Won 10   Lost 6   Tied 0

Neill Armstrong — Coach		Bears	Opponents
Green Bay Packers	(H)	6	3
Minnesota Vikings	(H)	26	7
Dallas Cowboys	(A)	20	24
Miami Dolphins	(A)	16	31
Tampa Bay Buccaneers	(H)	13	17
Buffalo Bills	(A)	7	0
New England Patriots	(H)	7	27
Minnesota Vikings	(A)	27	30
San Francisco 49ers	(A)	28	27
Detroit Lions	(H)	35	7
Los Angeles Rams	(H)	27	23
New York Jets	(H)	23	13
Detroit Lions	(A)	0	20
Tampa Bay Buccaneers	(H)	14	0
Green Bay Packers	(A)	15	14
St. Louis Cardinals	(H)	42	6
Totals		306	249

Divisional Playoffs

Philadelphia Eagles	(A)	17	27

EXIT ARMSTRONG, ENTER DITKA

THERE WAS PERHAPS good reason for hope around Chicago as the Bears entered the decade of the 1980s, the seventh in their long history. The year before, they had posted the most wins (10) since that championship season of 1963. They had made the playoffs and were edged out by the Eagles in a game many felt the Bears would have won without several controversial calls by the officials. Now the Bears were almost unanimously picked to win their division, an honor that had eluded them for the past 15 years.

The team that would take the field for the 1980 season was basically the same as that of 1979. The defensive line was strong and respected throughout the NFL. Mike Phipps had comported himself well at quarterback in 1979 (his NFL rating of 69.7 was the best for a Bear quarterback since Jack Concannon registered an 81.3 back in 1969). There was also a lot of good feeling about his back-up, the still unproven Vince Evans, who was known to have an extraordinarily strong arm and possessed the added dimension of being a superb runner. And, of course, there was perennial All-Pro Walter Payton. The draft produced three players who, as it turned out, would see some playing time in the upcoming season—linebacker Otis Wilson (Louisville), running back Matt Suhey (Penn State), and tight end Bob Fisher (SMU).

In the pre-season, however, the Bears did not look like the team to dominate the NFC Central. After handling the New York Jets, they dropped three straight to the Cincinnati Bengals, Cleveland Browns, and St. Louis Cardinals, three less-than-awesome opponents (among the three they had a collective record in 1979 of 18–30).

Then, with the first game of the regular season, they stepped off on the proverbial wrong foot, a stumble that seemed to set the tone for all of 1980. The Bears traveled to Green Bay to take on the Packers on a sweltering early September afternoon. Both teams plodded through four quarters, at the end of which the score was tied 6–6. The Bears had fairly dominated the game, taking the ball inside Packer territory on seven of their nine possessions, but all they had to show for it was two field goals. Phipps completed 17 of 30 passes for 174 yards; on the other hand, he threw three interceptions that were instrumental in depriving the Bears of the points necessary to win the game in regulation time. And Payton was held to 65 yards on 31 rushing attempts, well below his usual average of more than four yards per carry.

But if the first four quarters were dissatisfying, the overtime period was a disaster. The Bears won the toss and elected to receive, but a holding penalty on the kickoff put them back on their own 10-yard line. With three more penalties the Bear offense moved the ball backward to their 3-yard line and then punted. The Packers, starting from good field position, got to the

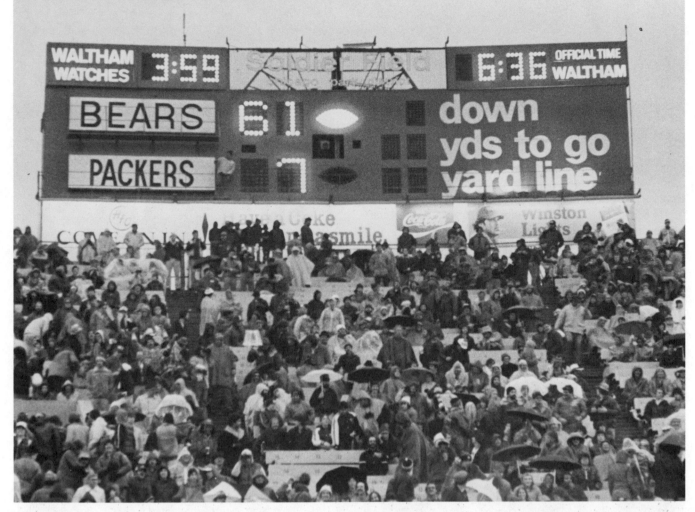

The scoreboard says it all. In this 1980 game the Bears tied the club record for most points scored in a regular-season game. Only in 1965, when they drubbed San Francisco 61–20, had they toted up as many points. (The Bear post-season record, of course, is 73 points, scored in the historic championship game of 1940 against the Washington Redskins.)–Bill Smith

Bears' 18-yard line with a 32-yard pass from Lynn Dickey to James Lofton. Moments later, Chester Marcol, who had earlier that day kicked field goals of 41 and 46 yards, came on to try to boot the Bears out of the game with a 34-yard attempt. Bear defender Alan Page broke through the Packers and solidly blocked the kick. Too solidly. The ball caromed right back into the arms of a surprised Chester Marcol, who hesitated a moment, then, realizing what had happened, took off on a Keystone Kop–like run that skirted around the mass of humanity piled at the line of scrimmage. No Bear laid a hand on him and he crossed the goal with the game-winning touchdown.

The pattern of Bear problems that would arise that year was all too evident in Green Bay—an unproductive offense, crucial penalties and turnovers, and a dose of downright misfortune. But the Bears rebounded the next week in their home opener and trounced the New Orleans Saints 22–3. Payton appeared to be in the best of form, picking up 183 yards rushing, the fourth best effort. of his career. One jaunt from scrimmage, a 69-yarder in the fourth quarter, was his longest touchdown run ever, and his average gain of 10.2 yards a carry was also a career high. Mike Phipps did not throw a single interception that day, although his passing stats were uninspiring, seven of 24 for 115 yards.

The Vikings came to town next, fallen giants who had won only seven of 16 games the year before. A mere shadow of their former selves, they were not considered a threat, at least at that point in the young season. But they annihilated Neill Armstrong's ill-fated Bears before the hometown fans. Vince Evans replaced Phipps in the first half with the Bears down 14–0, a clear message that the quarterbacking question was far from solved. The Bears trailed 28–0 in the fourth quarter before they finally got on the scoreboard. The only memory of the day worth preserving for Bear fans in the 34–14 debacle was an 89-yard bomb from Evans to Rickey Watts, the longest touchdown pass in Soldier Field since the Bears began playing there in 1971. Evans gained 204 yards in the air that day, although he was only 14 for 34 and had been sacked five times.

The next week it was the ever-awesome Pittsburgh Steelers, the reigning Super Bowl champs. A Bob Thomas field goal gave the Bears a 3–0 lead on their first possession, but then the Steelers blitzed them with 38 consecutive points, as Terry Bradshaw threw four touchdown passes among his 12 completions that day. Once again Vince Evans was called in to relieve Mike Phipps, but of the seven passes he threw he completed only two to Bear receivers while three were caught by Steeler pass defenders.

The Bears now had to face the Tampa Bay Buccaneers on a Monday night nationally televised game, a situation that had hardly proved conducive to Bear success in the past (they had won only three of their 10 previous Monday night encounters). But the Bears, as unpredictable as ever, rose to the occasion. They beat the Bucs 23–0, the second meeting in a row they had held Tampa Bay scoreless (14–0 in the latter half of 1979). Walter Payton produced his second 100-yard

Vince Evans (8), releasing a pass here, started 10 games for the Bears in 1980, winning the starting job from Mike Phipps and going on to have a fine year (a 53.2 completion percentage, 11 touchdown passes, and an NFL rating of 66.1). But he had a most disappointing season in 1981, ending up with the lowest quarterback rating (51.0) in the entire NFL.–Bill Smith

Tight end Bob Fisher (85) steps out after grabbing a Bear pass. Blocking for him is Dave Williams (22). Fisher was a rookie in 1980; his first pro catch was a 10-yard pass from Mike Phipps that he raced with for 46 more yards and a Bear touchdown. Williams, picked up as a free agent in 1979, became an all-purpose player for the team, filling in at fullback, returning kickoffs, even moving to wide receiver in 1981 when Bear injuries mandated it. –Chicago Bears/Bill Smith

rushing effort of the year (133 yards on 28 carries). When his statistics for the night were added to the Bear record book, Payton, just into his sixth pro season, became the club's all-time leader for combined net yards gained, surpassing the 9,435 yards Gale Sayers had amassed in his seven-year Bear career.

The Vikings then did it to the Bears again, this time a little less devastatingly, 13–7. The Bears beat the Lions a week later but fell to the Eagles 17–14. At the season's midway mark, they stood at a disenchanting 3–5–0, the fourth straight year they could claim such an unhappy record. And all those who had predicted a Bear coronation in the NFC Central in 1980 were swiftly revising their prognostications.

There was, of course, talk about Neill Armstrong's Bears being annual late-bloomers, flirting with remembrances of the seven wins in their last eight games the previous season. But that would not be the case in 1980.

The season's second half began with a loss to the Cleveland Browns; but Vince Evans, who had been the starting quarterback since the seventh game of the season, was impressive that Monday night. He completed 18 of 33 passes for 201 yards, including two for touchdowns, to Brian Baschnagel and Robin Earl.

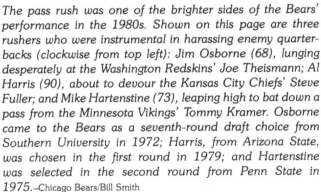

The pass rush was one of the brighter sides of the Bears' performance in the 1980s. Shown on this page are three rushers who were instrumental in harassing enemy quarterbacks (clockwise from top left): Jim Osborne (68), lunging desperately at the Washington Redskins' Joe Theismann; Al Harris (90), about to devour the Kansas City Chiefs' Steve Fuller; and Mike Hartenstine (73), leaping high to bat down a pass from the Minnesota Vikings' Tommy Kramer. Osborne came to the Bears as a seventh-round draft choice from Southern University in 1972; Harris, from Arizona State, was chosen in the first round in 1979; and Hartenstine was selected in the second round from Penn State in 1975. –Chicago Bears/Bill Smith

Evans also carried the ball seven yards for another touchdown. The following week he did even better, leading the Bears to a 35–21 swamping of the Washington Redskins. At Soldier Field, Evans picked up 210 yards passing (11 of 18), including three touchdown tosses: a 40-yarder to James Scott; one to Walter Payton that covered 54 yards; and another to Scott, a 12-yarder. Payton raced 50 yards for a touchdown and Roland Harper bulled in from the 2 to give the Bears a five-touchdown afternoon, their best offensive show thus far that year.

The glory was short-lived, however. The Bears fell to the Houston Oilers in a game in which Earl Campbell rushed for 206 yards and Payton was held to a mere

Under defensive coordinator Buddy Ryan, the Bears developed one of the more respected defenses in the NFL. Before coming to the Bears in 1978, Ryan had handled the defensive lines at Minnesota (1976-77) and the New York Jets (1968-75). Ryan was one of the few Bear mentors to earn praise from Papa Bear George Halas after the lackluster 1981 season. –Chicago Bears

60, and then lost to the Atlanta Falcons, who soared behind the passing of Steve Bartkowski (17 of 32 for 250 yards and three touchdowns). In the Atlanta game, 12 penalties were assessed against the Bears, and with more than 18 minutes remaining Payton was ejected after touching an official on the arm. The incident occurred at the Falcon ½-yard line after Payton was ruled to have fumbled, resulting in a turnover instead of a possible touchdown for the Bears. Payton protested the controversial call and spent the rest of the game on the bench as a consequence. With the season three-quarters over, the hapless Bears had a record of 4–8–0.

The Bears then bested the Lions for the second time that year in what was the shortest overtime game in NFL history. With the score tied at 17 at game's end, the Bears won the coin toss and chose to receive. Dave Williams took the kickoff at the 5 and raced 95 yards with it into the Lion end zone, thus triumphantly ending a 21-second overtime period.

The season's high point came against the Packers the following week at Soldier Field. The Bears were still smarting from that unorthodox loss up in Green Bay, which had launched their season down such a dismal trail. And the Bears got their revenge, matching their highest scoring total in regular-season play with 61 points (they had scored 61 against the 49ers in 1965). The total of 61 was also the most points scored by one team in any NFL game since 1973. And everyone had a good day. The defense allowed only one touchdown and total net yardage of 266. Vince Evans had his most productive day as a Bear, 18 completions in 22 attempts, a phenomenal mark of 81.8%. In doing so he picked up 316 yards, the most by a Bear passer since Jack Concannon threw for 338 against a different Green Bay team back in 1970. Evans was also credited with three touchdown passes that volatile afternoon— to Brian Baschnagel, Robin Earl, and Rickey Watts. Walter Payton gained 130 yards on 22 rushes. When he left the game, his replacement, Willie McClendon, added another 72 yards on only six carries. Lenny Walterscheid picked off a Packer pass and raced 36 yards for still another Bear score. The nine touchdowns the Bears posted that day tied the club record, which had been set in the previous 61-point splurge.

The Bears split the last two games of the year. They lost in overtime to the Cincinnati Bengals, their third overtime game of the season, an NFL record (it would be tied in 1981 by the New York Giants). Then, in the season's finale at Tampa, they slipped by the Buccaneers 14–13 to round out a 7–9–0 season.

The Bears, so highly touted before the season, dwelt in third place in their division, bettered by both the Minnesota Vikings and the Detroit Lions. It was a dismaying comedown from the 10–6–0 season of 1979.

Walter Payton gained more than 1,000 yards for the fifth consecutive year, extending his all-time Bear record. His 1,460 yards earned him the NFC rushing crown for the fifth consecutive season. He was also the only Bear to win a berth on the All-Pro team of 1980, the fifth time in his career he was so honored, and was the only Bear to go to the Pro Bowl. Quarterback Vince Evans had been erratic, but overall he had done a creditable job after taking over the starting slot. His completion ratio of 53.2% and NFL rating of 66.1 were respectable passing stats, especially for a man who had seen only limited action in prior years. James Scott had gained the most yards catching passes from Evans and Phipps, 696, but Payton led in receptions with 46.

On defense, Gary Fencik led the team in total tackles with 125, followed closely by Gary Campbell (121) and Jerry Muckensturm (120). Muckensturm had

Bob Parsons took over the Bear punting chores in 1974. Only Bobby Joe Green, who spent 12 years with the Bears (1962-73), has booted the ball more often for the team. Over the years Parsons has been extremely successful at killing the ball inside the 20-yard line and even inside the 10. He is also a constant threat as a passer or runner (he was a quarterback at Penn State) and can play tight end. Parsons's best year punting for the Bears was 1980, when he averaged 40.6 yards a kick.–Chicago Bears

Linebacker Jerry Muckensturm (58) led the Bears in solo tackles in 1980 with 101 and then was sidelined for the 1981 season with an injured shoulder. Before his injury, Muckensturm was one of only three Bears to hold down the left linebacking slot in 25 years, succeeding Bear stalwarts Doug Buffone (1967-78) and Joe Fortunato (1955-66). Muckensturm is shown here as he prepares to take on a block from Green Bay Packer running back Terdell Middleton.–Chicago Bears/Bill Smith

the most solo tackles (101). Alan Page blocked four kicks, by far the most that year, and his 9½ sacks were second to Dan Hampton's 11½. Lenny Walterscheid led the team in pass interceptions with four and also was the Bears' principal punt returner (averaging 7.2 yards on his 33 returns).

Dave Williams, whom the Bears had signed as a free agent the year before, proved to be the third best kickoff returner in the entire NFL, toting up 666 yards with an average return of 24.7 yards.

With the hope of injecting a little adrenaline into the Bears' offensive bloodstream, two new assistant coaches were hired for 1981. Ted Marchibroda was signed as offensive coordinator and given clear-cut orders to do something about the Bears' anemic passing attack. Marchibroda, who had guided George Allen's offenses with the Los Angeles Rams and the Washington Redskins, also had a fine record as head coach of the Baltimore Colts from 1975 through 1979 (in his first three seasons the Colts were 31–11–0, including three AFC East titles). He had been the instrumental tutor of both Roman Gabriel and Bert Jones. Taking over the

1980 Season	.438	
Won 7 Lost 9 Tied 0		
Neill Armstrong—Coach	Bears	Opponents
Green Bay Packers .... (A)	6	12
New Orleans Saints .... (H)	22	3
Minnesota Vikings .... (H)	14	34
Pittsburgh Steelers.......... (A)	3	38
Tampa Bay Buccaneers .... (H)	23	0
Minnesota Vikings .... (A)	7	13
Detroit Lions. .... (H)	24	7
Philadelphia Eagles .... (A)	14	17
Cleveland Browns.......... (A)	21	27
Washington Redskins........ (H)	35	21
Houston Oilers .... (H)	6	10
Atlanta Falcons .... (A)	17	28
Detroit Lions. .... (A)	23	17
Green Bay Packers .... (H)	61	7
Cincinnati Bengals.......... (H)	14	17
Tampa Bay Buccaneers .... (A)	14	13
Totals	304	264

offensive line was Dick Stanfel, who had served as line coach and offensive coordinator with the San Francisco 49ers and the New Orleans Saints, and as interim head coach for the Saints in 1980.

On the other hand, there would be a few departures. The most noticeable was that of wide receiver James Scott, who signed a more lucrative contract to play for the Montreal Alouettes in the Canadian Football League. From the defensive unit, Allan Ellis, a mainstay at cornerback since coming to the Bears in 1973, retired, his wounded knee unable to take another season. And linebacker Tom Hicks, a salary holdout, was simply let go.

But the Bears had a prosperous draft for 1981. Their first-round pick was Keith Van Horne, an All-American offensive tackle from Southern California. In the second round they snared middle linebacker Mike

Matt Suhey (26), a second-round draft choice out of Penn State in 1980, won the starting job at fullback in 1981, replacing Roland Harper. Above average as a blocker, Suhey gained 521 yards in 1981 on 150 carries (an average of 3.5 yards per carry) and bulled across the goalline three times for touchdowns. Here, he races past two Green Bay defenders, linebacker John Anderson (59) and tackle Terry Jones (63). –Chicago Bears/Bill Smith

Singletary (Baylor), another consensus All-American. The third round produced Ken Margerum (Stanford), a wide receiver with a reputation for having adhesive hands and who had a knack for making dazzling circus catches.

Three other draftees were also destined to see a good deal of action during the 1981 season: cornerback Reuben Henderson (San Diego State), punt returner and cornerback Jeff Fisher (Southern California), and safety Todd Bell (Ohio State). Signed as free agents were kicker John Roveto (Southwest Louisiana) and Marcus Anderson (Tulane) as well as three NFL veterans: linebacker Brian Cabral, guard Emanuel Zanders, and wide receiver Emery Moorehead.

Once again, the Bears appeared to be the odds-on favorite to rule the NFC Central. And once again, the Bears in the pre-season gave everyone who harbored such a notion some second thoughts, at least through the first two games. Losing to the New York Giants, they managed only one touchdown; then they came up scoreless in a loss to the Kansas City Chiefs the following week. The "new" offense seemed nowhere in sight. But it somehow proved productive enough to come away with victories against the Cincinnati Bengals (24–21) and the St. Louis Cardinals (31–27) before having to get down to the serious business of the regular season.

The Bears hosted the Green Bay Packers for the opener, the same ball club they had annihilated in the late weeks of the preceding season. The two teams had been going at it now since 1921, and over those 60 regular seasons, the Bears had won 66 games and the Packers 51, with six resulting in ties. The Bears had outscored the Pack 2,011 to 1,781.

Vince Evans had earned full right to the starting job at quarterback, and Roland Harper lined up in the backfield again with Walter Payton. Rickey Watts replaced James Scott at wide receiver, Brian Baschnagel was at flanker, and Bob Fisher got the nod to start at tight end. The offensive line was the same as the year before, with Ted Albrecht and Dennis Lick at tackles, Noah Jackson and Revie Sorey at guards, and Dan Neal at center.

Lee Kunz had replaced Tom Hicks as the starting middle linebacker, edging out rookie Mike Singletary for that job. Otis Wilson and Gary Campbell would flank him. Len Walterscheid had wrested the starting job at free safety from Doug Plank. Gary Fencik was at strong safety, and Terry Schmidt and rookie Reuben Henderson filled the cornerback slots. The front four were also the same as 1980—ends Dan Hampton and Mike Hartenstine and tackles Jim Osborne and Alan

Page (who had announced that this, his 15th pro season, would be the last).

It was sunny, 70-degree weather at Soldier Field as the kickoff that September 6 christened the 1981 season, but the Bear offense, it was soon evident, was as cold as a brutal Chicago winter. The same team that had run up 61 points against the Pack a year earlier was held scoreless the first half and picked up just 9 points in the second, while the Packers gathered 16 for the day. The Bears fumbled the ball six times, losing four of them, and drew 10 penalties (four more than the Packers). The most costly mistake was Matt Suhey's fumble at the ½-yard line with 30 seconds left in the game, depriving the Bears of a chance to score a game-tying touchdown. It exemplified the kind of frustrating turn of events that would haunt the Bears throughout the 1981 season.

The Bears expected to beat the 49ers when they traveled out to San Francisco the following week. They viewed San Francisco in terms of its lackluster 6–10–0 record for 1980, not as the team that would win 13 regular-season games in 1981, tops in the NFL, and go on to win the Super Bowl. But the Bears got a taste of the 49er magic when Joe Montana completed 20 of 32 passes for 287 yards, including three touchdown tosses. The Bears managed a 17–14 lead early in the third quarter, but the 49ers were indomitable and came back to win 28–17.

With the Bears 0–2 for two games they had expected to win, there was cause for concern. There was also a little line-up juggling. Robin Earl was now starting at tight end, and Matt Suhey had taken over the fullback slot from Roland Harper, who was still gimpy from injuries that had sidelined him in 1979 and part of 1980. Dennis Lick had only one more quarter to play before he would injure his knee and sit out the rest of the season, to be replaced by Dan Jiggetts at tackle. Among the most unexpected and certainly disconcerting injuries was to dependable kicker Bob Thomas, who hurt his leg in an accident off the field and would not return in 1981. An untried Hans Nielsen was assigned the kicking chores but after three games lost that job to John Roveto.

The Bears had beaten the Tampa Bay Buccaneers

Rookie Ken Margerum makes one of his more spectacular diving catches in this 1981 game against the Kansas City Chiefs. Margerum caught four passes for 48 yards to help the Bears to a 16–13 win. After four games, Margerum won a starting berth and went on to become the Bears' top receiver in terms of yardage (584 on 39 catches, the longest for 41 yards). –Bill Smith

Two familiar figures in the Bear defense of 1981 were linebacker Otis Wilson (55) and end Dan Hampton (99), putting the rush here on Joe Theismann of the Redskins. Wilson, the Bears' first-round draft choice in 1980, was second on the team in total tackles in 1981 with 81 (Gary Fencik was first with 135). Hampton, the top draft pick in 1979, led the Bears in sacks in 1980 with 11½ and tied Alan Page for those honors in 1981 with nine. –Chicago Bears

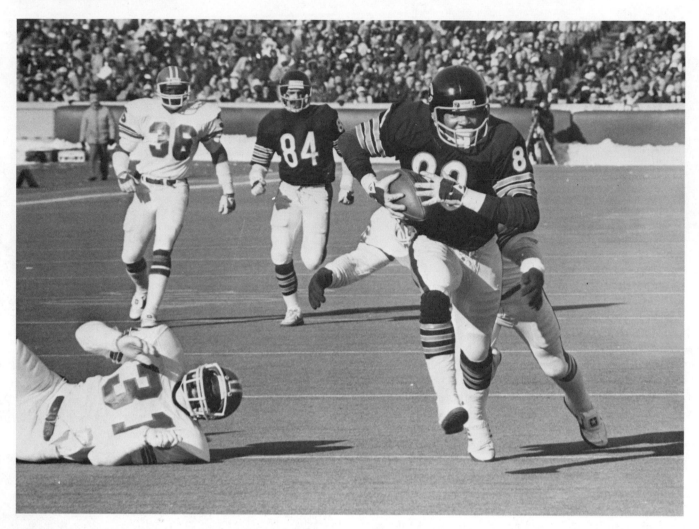

Rickey Watts (80) moves out with a Vince Evans pass in the closing game of 1981. The Bears upset the Denver Broncos 35–24 that afternoon, depriving them of a berth in the NFL playoffs. No. 84 is receiver Brian Baschnagel, who played with a broken arm through more than half the 1981 season and still had his best year, catching 34 passes for 554 yards. –Bill Smith

twice the year before and a total of six times in their eight previous encounters. The Buccaneers came to Chicago and beat the Bears on paper, racking up 450 total net yards to 247 and 22 first downs to 15. They outrushed the Bears 141 yards to 121 and outpassed them 309 yards to 126. On the other hand, the Bears were called for only three penalties, while the Buccaneers were assessed 101 yards on 14 infractions. And the Bears were the beneficiary of an 88-yard punt return for a touchdown by rookie Jeff Fisher, only one yard short of the all-time Bear record (Scooter McLean raced 89 yards back in 1942). As a result, the Bears beat the Bucs on the scoreboard 28–17.

The Los Angeles Rams, however, defeated the Bears at Soldier Field the following week 24–7. Walter Payton, still looking for his first 100-yard game of the year, rushed for only 45 yards on 17 carries. And Vince

Evans, whose stats for the day were one completion in eight attempts for three yards, was relieved by Bob Avellini, who in turn was replaced by Mike Phipps. The next week it was the Minnesota Vikings, this time a 24–21 loss, despite the fact that Evans posted what would prove to be his finest effort of the season (26 of 43 passes for 307 yards and two touchdowns). There had been some significant line-up changes for the Viking game. Ken Margerum got the first start of his pro career at flanker, and he led the team in receiving that day with 10 catches for 140 yards. Brian Baschnagel was moved to split end. In the offensive line, Emanuel Zanders replaced Revie Sorey, and first-round draft pick Keith Van Horne took the job at tackle from Dan Jiggetts. Doug Plank filled in at free safety for Len Walterscheid, who was undergoing knee surgery and would be lost for the season. The next week Al Harris moved into Mike Hartenstine's slot at defensive end.

The shake-up hardly helped. The Redskins and the Detroit Lions wrought double-barreled devastations: 24–7 and 48–17, and the Bears stood at a lowly record of 1–6–0, their worst start since 1975 (which had turned out to be a 4–10–0 year). Against the Redskins, Walter Payton, troubled with a shoulder injury, gained only five yards or five carries. And Vince Evans threw 37 passes but completed only eight and was tagged with four interceptions. Against the Lions, Marcus Anderson, filling in at split end for Brian Baschnagel, who had broken his arm in the previous game, electrified everyone in the Pontiac Silverdome when he took a Vince Evans pass 85 yards for a touchdown. (The Bear mark for the longest touchdown pass play is 98 yards, Bill Wade to John Farrington in 1961). But it was the only highlight of that bleak day. And the Lions had scored the most points against the Bears in the regular season since the Atlanta Falcons ran up 48 during the Bears' 1–13–0 season of 1969.

Around this time of disenchantment, owner George Halas surprised everyone by going over the heads (or around the ends) of general manager Jim Finks and head coach Neill Armstrong and hiring Jim Dooley to serve as "offense consultant" on the Bear coaching staff. Dooley, who had been the Bears' head coach from 1968 through 1971 (a record of 20–36–0), would be Papa Bear's "man in the huddle," as one scribe put it. It was a clear indication that Halas was moving back to a more active role in the team's management.

Walter Payton finally found his first 100-yard day in the season's eighth game (107 yards on 36 carries), against the San Diego Chargers, a team that *Pro Football Weekly* predicted would defeat the Bears by "around 24 points." Mike Singletary worked his way into the starting line-up for the game and would hold down the middle linebacking job for the remainder of the year. Brian Baschnagel was playing with a broken arm but still managed to catch five passes for 80 yards, and Ken Margerum grabbed four for 83 yards. And so the Bears beat the heavily favored Chargers 20–17. But at the season's midpoint, the Bears were in the cellar of the NFC Central, with a record of 2–6–0.

It was not destined to get a lot better, either. The Buccaneers broke the four-game win streak the Bears held over them down in Tampa, 20–10. The Bears then rebounded to knock off the Kansas City Chiefs 16–13, principally the result of John Roveto's three field goals, while Vince Evans completed only seven of 30 passes for 77 yards that day. The Packers rubbed it in, beating down the Bears 21–17 in Green Bay. Then the Lions did it again, this time 23–7, in a game in

Alan Page took off his helmet for the last time after the last game of the 1981 season, ending 15 years in the NFL. He played the final four years at defensive tackle for the Bears. Page retired with the dual distinctions of never having missed a regular-season game during his long career (218 in all) and being the only defensive player ever named the NFL's MVP (1971). He was named an All-Pro in nine of his first 11 seasons and played in eight Pro Bowls. As a Bear, Page chalked up three sacks in a single game four times, and he was notorious for blocking enemy kicks. –Chicago Bears

which Chicago gained only *24 net yards* all day, an all-time Bear low, and earned only four first downs. Vince Evans was four for 19 for 21 yards and two interceptions, and his reliever Bob Avellini was three of 10 for 20 yards and one interception.

On Thanksgiving Day, the Bears went to Dallas, where they lost 10–9 to the Cowboys, despite Payton's best effort of the year. He gained 179 yards on 38

Jim McMahon meets the Chicago press shortly after the 1982 NFL draft. The first quarterback the Bears had selected in the first round since 1951, McMahon, a consensus All-American from Brigham Young, set 56 NCAA Division 1 records for passing and total offense during his college career. At Brigham Young, he completed 653 of 1,060 passes (.616), including 84 for touchdowns. –Chicago Bears

Draft Trivia

The Chicago Bears have drafted only six quarterbacks in the first round since the NFL draft was instituted back in 1936. They are:

> *Sid Luckman (Columbia) 1939*
> *Frankie Albert (Stanford) 1942*
> *Johnny Lujack (Notre Dame) 1946*
> *Bobby Layne (Texas) 1948*
> *Bob Williams (Notre Dame) 1951*
> *Jim McMahon (Brigham Young) 1982*

carries, but the Bears and their record now sagged to 3–10–0.

The season was over for all practical purposes. The Bears were out of contention for a spot in the playoffs. The offense that was supposed to have opened up and changed the Bear fortunes so dramatically had never really gotten started. Still the defense was respectable, and it was largely through their efforts that the Bears emerged victorious in their last three games of the year. They sneaked by the Minnesota Vikings 10–9 on a fourth-quarter touchdown, a pass play from Avellini to Baschnagel that covered 72 yards. Then they astonished the Oakland Raiders 23–6, the defense accounting for six sacks that day. And finally they finished the season with a delightful 35–24 romp over the heavily favored Denver Broncos in Soldier Field. Tackle Alan Page ended his pro career that day in grand style, credited with 3½ sacks. Gary Fencik ran an interception back 69 yards for a touchdown, and big Al Harris took another one 44 yards for a score.

Thanks to the Bear defense, the club improved its record to 6–10–0, but it still was in last place in the NFC Central. Walter Payton rushed for more than 1,000 yards for the sixth straight year, but for the first time during that period he did not earn the NFC rushing title; his 1,222 yards left him behind George Rogers (New Orleans), Tony Dorsett (Dallas), Billy Sims (Detroit), Wilbert Montgomery (Philadelphia), Ottis Anderson (St. Louis), and William Andrews (Atlanta). And Payton's average carry of 3.6 yards was well below his career average of 4.5.

Gary Fencik was the only Bear to be honored as an All-Pro and to be invited to the Pro Bowl. But three Bears were named to the NFL All-Rookie team: Mike Singletary, Ken Margerum, and Keith Van Horne. Margerum led the club in yardage gained receiving (584 yards on 39 catches), although Walter Payton caught the most passes (41). Matt Suhey gained 521 yards rushing, an average of 3.5 per carry. Rookie Jeff Fisher was the NFC's second most productive punt returner with 509 yards, an all-time Bear record, and an average return of 11.8 yards.

From the defense, Gary Fencik toted up the most tackles (135) and most solo tackles (112), and led in interceptions (six). Alan Page had nine sacks, tied for the team high with Dan Hampton, and he also was the leader in blocking kicks (three).

When the depressing season was over, it was apparent there were going to be some major changes. The first hint came from owner George Halas, who had taken it upon himself to contact Tex Schramm, president of the Dallas Cowboys, and ask permission to talk to one of the Cowboy assistant coaches, Mike Ditka, about the possibility of working in Chicago. Papa Bear made it clear that the changes that would be made were going to be his alone. First he roundly praised the defensive coaching staff and announced that their jobs were secure. Then he fired Neill Armstrong as head coach and hired Mike Ditka to replace him. Ted Marchibroda resigned as offensive coordinator, and Ditka then hired Ed Hughes to replace him. Hughes had been with Ditka in Dallas from 1973 through 1976, handling the offensive backfield while Ditka guided the receivers and special teams, and had most recently been on the staff of the Philadelphia Eagles.

When it became apparent that fleet receiver James Scott would be returning from the Canadian Football League, George Halas and Jim Finks brought him back into the Bears' den with hopes that he would be a key to revitalizing the club's passing attack. As a further move in that direction, the Bears, with the fifth pick in the 1982 draft, selected All-American quarterback Jim McMahon of Brigham Young, the first time they had taken a quarterback in the first round since Bob Williams back in 1951.

There was little question that the Bears were in the process of rerouting their course through the 1980s. Things had not gone as well as the management and the fans had hoped. But then the Bears had traveled through some deserts before on their more than 60-year journey through the NFL. There were still plenty of crowns to go after down the road. And no one was thinking more about that than George Halas or Jim Finks or Mike Ditka.

Mike Ditka. –Chicago Bears

Mike Ditka was named head coach of the Bears for the 1982 season. At 42 years old, he came back to Chicago from the staff of the Dallas Cowboys, where he had been the assistant coach in charge of receivers and special teams since 1973. Ditka was well remembered in Chicago for his days as a tight end on the teams coached by George Halas from 1961 through 1966. He had been the NFL's Rookie of the Year in 1961 and was four times named an All-Pro (1961-64). In Bear history only Johnny Morris caught more passes than Ditka (356 to 316); only Morris caught more in a single season (93 to 75); and only Jim Keane in a single game (14 to 13). Ditka played two years with the Philadelphia Eagles and then four more with the Cowboys before retiring after the 1972 season. (In 1971, he had the distinction of catching the first Cowboy pass of the pre-season and the last of the post-season in Super Bowl VI.) When he finally left the game as a player, Ditka had caught 427 passes for 5,812 yards and had scored 43 touchdowns.

Ditka became only the 11th Bear head coach in 62 years, and vowed to bring to Chicago some of the Cowboys' fabled offense.

1981 Season	.375	
Won 6 Lost 10 Tied 0		
Neill Armstrong—Coach	Bears	Opponents
Green Bay Packers . . . . (H)	9	16
San Francisco 49ers. . . . . (A)	17	28
Tampa Bay Buccaneers . . . . (H)	28	17
Los Angeles Rams. . . . . (H)	7	24
Minnesota Vikings . . . . (A)	21	24
Washington Redskins. . . . . (H)	7	24
Detroit Lions. . . . . (A)	17	48
San Diego Chargers. . . . . (H)	20	17
Tampa Bay Buccaneers . . . . (A)	10	20
Kansas City Chiefs. . . . . (A)	16	13
Green Bay Packers . . . . (A)	17	21
Detroit Lions. . . . . (H)	7	23
Dallas Cowboys . . . . (A)	9	10
Minnesota Vikings . . . . (H)	10	9
Oakland Raiders . . . . (A)	23	6
Denver Broncos . . . . (H)	35	24
Totals	253	324

Halas Hall, the home of the Bears. The football complex on the campus of Lake Forest College was opened in 1979. The building, whose offices for coaches and management look out on the practice field, has three floors and covers 32,000 square feet. Inside, there are locker rooms, team meeting rooms, a player lounge, a racquetball court, weight-training rooms, a photo lab, a media workroom, private interview areas, offices, and a computer department. It is the site of the Bears' annual summer camp. –Chicago Bears

The Chicago Bears as well as professional football in general have changed considerably in the six decades they have both been in operation. The Chicago Bear organization of today no more resembles the one that existed back in 1920 than today's Saturn V moon rocket resembles the Model T Ford of that earlier era. The franchise fee of $50 that Curly Lambeau had to come up with to keep the Green Bay Packers in the league back in 1922 would now be valued in the millions of dollars.

Pro football franchises today are organizations of sophistication and modern technology. Computers and elaborate filming procedures supplement the human scouts and the human coaches. There are strength coordinators, public relations departments, and teams of technicians and office workers to make the whole thing run.

The teams of offensive-defensive 60-minute men with player/coaches of the 1920s have given way to two platoons of specialists, coached by specialists. Players have become year-round composites of athletes and businessmen. Professional football is a high-paying sport—million-dollar contracts exist where once a check for only $100 (and sometimes less than that) was written after a game. The competition for a position is brutal, and every player knows it.

The game has changed, so has the league, and so have the people who now watch it every Sunday or Saturday or Monday night. But pro football is the hard-hitting, bone-crunching contact sport it always was. And for those who play it, the one thing that hasn't changed is the feeling that comes before every game. The stomach-turning, mind-freezing, nerve-

The 1980s marked the Bears' seventh decade and seven decades of George Halas's affiliation with the team. As player, coach, promoter, and owner, he had been there from the start, through the tough times, and those of glory. Papa Bear's physical, but not spiritual, affiliation with the Bears ended with his death in 1983.—Chicago Bears

challenging, very physical and very mental reactions in those few moments before the opening kickoff are no different for the players of today than they were for George Halas, Dutch Sternaman, George Trafton, and the other Bears back in 1921 when they first showed up in Chicago with the dream of establishing a professional football team.

Mr. Bear, Walter Payton, steps out spiritedly in a game against the Dallas Cowboys. The Bears, who had previously lost seven of their ten encounters with Dallas, annihilated the Cowboys in 1985, 44–0, the worst defeat in Dallas history and the first time they were shutout in 218 games. No. 40 on the Cowboys is Bill Bates.—Chicago Bears

TURNING IT AROUND

THE TURNAROUND that George Halas had in mind when he hired Mike Ditka was not expected to be instantaneous. Coach Ditka knew that his mentor at Dallas, Tom Landry, one of the NFL's all-time winningest coaches, had not had a winning season in his first five years at the Cowboys' helm. For the last-place Bears that Ditka inherited, there were a lot of areas to flesh out and key positions that needed an infusion of new blood.

There was, of course, great hope that first-round draft choice Jim McMahon would, after a little pro experience, solve the quarterbacking problems Chicago had suffered since Bill Wade left in the mid-sixties. The Bears' second pick in the 1982 draft, tight end Tim Wrightman from UCLA, opted for the new USFL and would play in Chicago for the Blitz instead of the Bears. But several rookies did establish themselves on the Chicago roster, most notably: guard Kurt Becker of Michigan, running back Dennis Gentry from Baylor, and defensive tackle Henry Waechter of Nebraska.

The quarterbacking situation was far from solved on opening day at Detroit that year. Bob Avellini started and was relieved by Vince Evans, but neither did much in the 17–10 loss to the Lions. The following week, at Coach Ditka's regular season debut in Soldier Field, Avellini again got the start, completed only three of nine passes before retiring to the bench. Vince Evans came out for the second quarter, completed four passes, two to Bears receivers and two to New Orleans defenders, before he

joined Avellini on the sideline. Jim McMahon played the entire second half and completed 12 of 22 passes for 131 yards and, even though the Bears lost 10–0, it appeared a solution to the quarterbacking dilemma might be at hand. Ditka announced that McMahon would start the next game.

The next game, as it turned out, would not take place for more than two months because the players went on strike. But when it did, McMahon was on the field for the entire game and impressed the hometown fans, completing 16 of 27 passes for 233 yards and two touchdowns and leading the Bears to a 20–17 win over the Detroit Lions. The game-winning field goal by John Roveto was in fact set up by a long pass from McMahon to tight end Emery Moorehead. From that day forward the starting job was McMahon's, at least through the 1982 season.

Other problems remained, however. Among the most prominent was pass defense: Tommy Kramer of the Vikings passed for 342 yards and five touchdowns against the Bears in one game, Vince Ferragamo of the Rams for 509 yards and three TDs in another, and the Buccaneers' Doug Williams for 367 and two touchdowns in still another. At the end of the strike-shortened season, the Bears had a record of 3–6 and once again ended up in the cellar of the NFC Central division.

Many of the pieces that would fit so perfectly into place on the world champion Bears of 1985 were collected in the 1983 draft, certainly one of the Bears' most

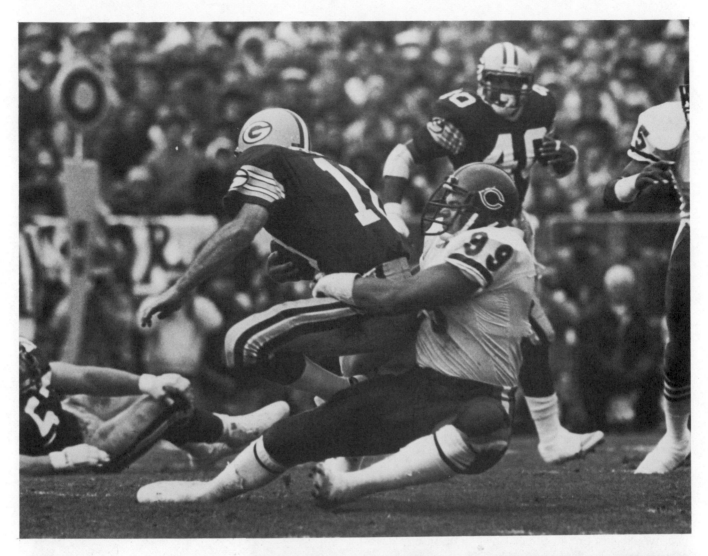

Defensive end Dan Hampton demonstrates dramatically the concept of having the quarterback in your grasp as he wrestles a scrambling Lynn Dickey of the Packers to the ground. Hampton was named All-Pro in both 1982 and 1984 and has gone to the Pro Bowl four times.—Chicago Bears

A trio of Bears converge on Oakland Raider quarterback David Humm in this 1981 game. The would-be sackers are Steve McMichael (76), Mike Hartenstine (73), and Jim Osborne (69). The Bears won the game 23–6.—Chicago Bears

On Second Thought . . .

Hiring Ditka Would Be Madness

The above headline appeared over then–Chicago Sun-Times *sportswriter John Schulian's column of January 5, 1982.*

Schulian observed in the column:" *'Ditka's a maniac,' a lapsed member of America's Team [the Dallas Cowboys, where Ditka was serving as an assistant coach] was saying Monday. But he is still odds-on to become the Bears' new head coach after George Halas's tawdry return to power and Neill Armstrong's inhumane firing. You can make of that scenario what you will, but some of the people who have known Ditka best in Dallas are wondering if there is a punchline to this joke. . . .*

"Again and again, you are confronted with visions of him [Ditka] throwing clipboards and cursing officials when he should be sending in the next play on offense or calling the next defense. He is, after all, a creature of brute force, the quintessential Midway monster, and such is not the stuff head coaches are made of. But if Ditka still wants to come back to Chicago, finding a position for him shouldn't be difficult. Even at his age, he would be a better tight end than any of the stiffs the Bears have there now."

lucrative in history. Seven of the collegians culled that year would start on the Super Bowl–bound Bears three seasons later. Jim Finks and Mike Ditka put their heads together and came up with these selections: in the first round, offensive tackle Jimbo Covert of Pittsburgh and wide receiver Willie Gault from Tennessee; in the second round defensive back Mike Richardson of Arizona State; from the third round, defensive back Dave Duerson out of Notre Dame; in the eighth round, defensive tackle Richard Dent from Tennessee State and guard Mark Bortz of Iowa; and finally free agent Dennis McKinnon, wide receiver from Florida State. By trade the Bears added tight end Jay Saldi from the Cowboys and offensive tackle Andy Frederick from the Browns.

After the last of the 1983 newcomers were signed, executive vice president and general manager Jim Finks resigned. George Halas named the club's treasurer, Jerry Vainisi, to serve as general manager in Finks's stead. Only a few weeks after the appointment, George Halas, Papa Bear, passed away at the age of 88, bringing to an end his 64-year association with the team as player, coach, president, and owner. On November 11, 1983, his grandson, Michael McCaskey, was appointed president and chief executive officer of the Bears.

1982 Season	.333		
Mike Ditka—Coach		Bears	Opponents
Detroit Lions. . . . . (A)		10	17
New Orleans Saints. . . . . (H)		0	10
Detroit Lions. . . . . (H)		20	17
Minnesota Vikings. . . . . (A)		7	35
New England Patriots . . . . (H)		26	13
Seattle Seahawks . . . . (A)		14	20
St. Louis Cardinals . . . . (H)		7	10
Los Angeles Rams . . . . (A)		34	26
Tampa Bay Buccaneers. . . . . . . (A)		23	26
Totals		141	174

The Bears showed some offensive spunk in winning three of their four preseason games in 1983, including one out in Los Angeles over the Raiders, champion of the AFC West the year before. But the fates, the good ones, that is, had not yet decided to accompany them onto the playing field. The Bears suffered a loss in the opener at home to the Atlanta Falcons and then beat the Buccaneers, 17–10, in a game highlighted by a 73-yard touchdown pass play from McMahon to Walter Payton and won with a fourth-quarter, 32-yard interception return for a touchdown by Terry Schmidt.

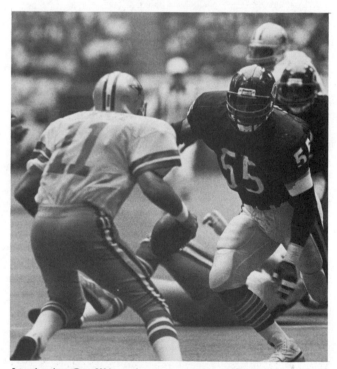

Linebacker Otis Wilson, here converging on Dallas quarterback Danny White, earned his first invitation to the Pro Bowl in 1985. He was credited with 11.5 sacks that year, second only to Richard Dent, and he picked off three passes, returning one for a touchdown.—Chicago Bears

Mike Richardson soars to snatch a Denver Bronco pass intended for Mike Harden. In 1985, Richardson ran one of his four interceptions that year back 90 yards in a game against the Redskins although he ended up one yard shy of the goal line. Chasing the action is Richardson's fellow cornerback Leslie Frazier.
—Chicago Bears

Eighteen teams in the NFL could testify firsthand to the veracity of this sign after the 1985 season closed with the Bears posting an overall record of 18–1.—Vernon Biever

Kenny Margerum makes one of his patented circus catches in this game against the Detroit Lions. Looking on futilely is safety James Hunter. Margerum had best year with Bears in his rookie season in 1981, when he led the team with 39 pass receptions, then sat out the 1984 season with a knee injury, and came back in '85 to catch 17 passes, two for touchdowns. —Chicago Bears

On the road, the fates were noticeably absent as the Bears dropped two overtime games in a row. The first was an exciting, surprise-filled contest down in New Orleans at the Superdome that was tied four times. The Bears struck first when McMahon hit rookie Willie Gault to mark the speedster's first NFL touchdown reception. And, in fact, they dominated the game statistically, their 493 net yards gained considerably more than the Saints' 332. Walter Payton produced one of the more memorable days of his career that afternoon, racing 49 yards for one touchdown and completing two out of two passes, both for touchdowns to Willie Gault. McMahon, playing erratically, was replaced by Vince Evans in the third quarter, but it was Payton's two TD tosses in the fourth quarter that kept Chicago in the game and, with a score of 31–31, sent it into overtime. But there, after about 11 minutes of play, New Orleans won it with a 41-yard field goal.

The following week the Bears were in Baltimore to face the Colts, the team that had posted the worst record in the league the year before (0–8–1). McMahon again had his troubles and was relieved in the second and third quarters by Evans, who produced two touchdowns in the fourth quarter, one on a 57-yard pass to Gault and the other on an eight-yard run with just over a minute remaining that tied the score at 19 apiece and brought about a sudden death extra period (Bob Thomas had kicked two field goals earlier but had also missed a crucial extra point). After nearly five minutes of overtime play, the Colts won it with a 33-yard field goal, and the Bears were a dismal 1–3.

Through the next six games the quarterbacking chores were shunted back and forth between McMahon and Evans, and the Bears managed to lose four of those contests. With a record of 3–7, the season was a starkly disappointing one. But before the tenth game, which turned out to be a 21–14 loss to the Rams out in Anaheim, Coach Ditka announced that he was going with McMahon for the rest of the season. The blond quarterback did not throw a touchdown pass in appreciation that day, but he did catch one on a razzle-dazzle play where he threw back to Walter Payton (constituting a lateral), then took off for the goal line himself and Payton hit him for a six-pointer.

After that the Bears' course was irrevocably reversed and they began the entertaining and gratifying journey

Richard Dent is spotlighted here trying to decapitate Packer running back Jesse Clark. In the six games the Bears and Packers have met since Mike Ditka took over as coach, Chicago has won four times, increasing their domination of the 65-year rivalry to 77 wins against 68 losses and nine ties. No. 21 is corner back Leslie Frazier, and on the ground is safety Dave Duerson.—Vernon Biever

that would end in the Superdome at Super Bowl XX. Behind McMahon's passing, the all-around play of Payton, the receptions of Gault and Dennis McKinnon, and a

1983 Season	.500	
Mike Ditka—Coach	**Bears**	**Opponents**
Atlanta Falcons . . . . (H)	17	20
Tampa Bay Buccaneers. . . . . . . (H)	17	10
New Orleans Saints. . . . . (A)	31	34
Baltimore Colts. . . . . (A)	19	22
Denver Broncos . . . . (H)	31	14
Minnesota Vikings. . . . . (A)	14	23
Detroit Lions. . . . . (A)	17	31
Philadelphia Eagles. . . . . (A)	7	6
Detroit Lions. . . . . (H)	17	38
Los Angeles Rams . . . . (A)	14	21
Philadelphia Eagles. . . . . (H)	17	14
Tampa Bay Buccaneers. . . . . . . (A)	27	0
San Francisco 49ers . . . . (H)	13	3
Green Bay Packers. . . . . (A)	28	31
Minnesota Vikings. . . . . (A)	19	13
Green Bay Packers . . . . (H)	23	21
Totals	311	301

defense that was coming into its own, the Bears won five of their last six games to end the season with a record of 8–8.

After the tenth game of the 1983 season, Mike Ditka's Bears coaching record stood at a grim six wins and 13 losses. From that point until journey's end in January 1986, Ditka would post a regular season record of 30–8, and 4–1 in postseason play.

During the 1983 season, Walter Payton rushed for 1,421 yards, the fourth best effort of his nine-year career and the fourth best that year in the NFL. He also caught the most passes (53). The 836 yards toted up by Willie Gault on pass receptions was the most by a Bear since Dick Gordon back in 1970 (1,026). Middle linebacker Mike Singletary, who made 120 solo tackles (28 more than the next Bear defender, Todd Bell) and recovered four fumbles, was named All-Pro. Defensive tackle Dan Hampton received an invitation to the Pro Bowl.

The Bears, so well bolstered by the draft of 1983, filled in a few more gaps in 1984. The most heralded was consensus All-American linebacker Wilber Marshall of Florida, chosen on the eleventh pick of the first round. In the second go-around the Bears picked another linebacker, Ron Rivera from California. Other selections who would qualify for Bear paychecks included offensive guard Stefan Humphries (Michigan), center Tom Andrews (Louisville), wide receiver Brad Anderson (Arizona), and defensive back Shaun Gayle (Ohio State). With Vince Evans gone to the USFL and Bob Avellini feeling his age on the football field, the Bears dealt for a pair of back-up quarterbacks and brought over Steve Fuller from the Rams for an eleventh-round draft choice in 1984 and sixth-round selection in 1985, and Rusty Lisch, claimed on waivers from the St. Louis Cardinals.

The Bears opened the 1984 season as impressively as they closed the previous year. A mauling of Tampa Bay at Soldier Field, 34–14, delighted the hometown crowd, on opening day, followed by a romp over the Denver Broncos, 27–0. The Bears scored all 27 points against Denver in the first half, and the defense held the Broncos to only 130 total yards the entire game. Jim McMahon got off a 61-yard bomb to Willie Gault for one of the touchdowns but suffered a broken bone in his throwing hand when he was hit after releasing the ball. Avellini filled in for him and the Bears went to their running game, a highlight of which was a 62-yard touchdown run by Walter Payton, his longest touchdown run from scrimmage ever (he had run for 76 yards against the Broncos in 1978, his longest run, but did not score on it). Payton rushed for 179 yards that day on 20 carries.

Three Bob Thomas field goals the following Sunday at Green Bay were enough to give the Bears another win, because the defense held the Packers to a single touchdown. The Bears had their first 3–0 start since 1978.

With McMahon on the bench and Buddy Ryan's defense out of kilter, the Bears were quickly brought back to reality at the Kingdome out in Seattle in the fourth game of the season. With four fumbles and three interceptions to their discredit, the Bears fell to the Seahawks 38–9. The next week, back at Soldier Field with McMahon quarterbacking but unable to pass effectively with his injured hand, they were mistreated by the Cowboys, 23–14.

Chicago got back on the winning track the following week, however, by drubbing the New Orleans Saints, 20–7; it was also the game in which Walter Payton broke Jim Brown's long-held NFL career rushing record of 12,312 yards. A loss to the Cardinals and impressive wins over the Vikings and Los Angeles Raiders gave the Bears a record of 7–3, an exact reversal of their won–lost column through ten games the year before. But there was a bleak side, too. In the game against the Raiders, McMahon took off running when he could not find a receiver and became the focal point of a brutal collision of Los Angeles tacklers. He left the game with what turned out to be a season-ending injury, a lacerated kidney. Steve Fuller was the heir apparent.

Fuller turned in a fine performance the next week, completing 21 of 27 passes for 240 yards against the Rams, and the Bears maintained a lead into the fourth quarter. But then they were devastated by a 63-yard bomb by Jeff Kemp to Henry Ellard and the powerful running of Eric Dickerson, whom they found they could not contain. The 17-point final period gave the Rams a 29–13 victory. But Fuller continued to play very well and led the Bears to wins over the Lions and Vikings, but unfortunately in the latter game he was forced to the sideline with a separated shoulder and would not return until the playoffs. On the brighter side of the Vikings' game, the victory clinched the division title for the Bears, the first time they had won the crown since 1963.

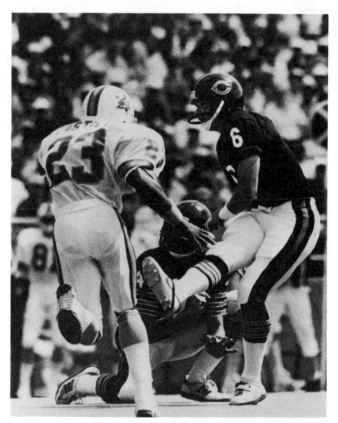

Rookie Kevin Butler boots one of his 31 field goals for 1985 against the Tampa Bay Buccaneers. Butler, a fourth-round draft choice from Georgia, beat out Bob Thomas, the Bears all-time leading scorer, and went on to break five team single-season kicking records: most field goals (31), most consecutive field goals (13), most points scored (144), best field goal percentage (81.6), and most field goal attempts (38).—Chicago Bears

Steve Fuller evades the rush of Doug English (78) and Ken Fantetti (57) of the Detroit Lions in this 1984 game. With Fuller filling in for injured Jim McMahon, the Bears defeated the Lions twice that year. Fuller, acquired from the Rams just before the '84 season, started four games and the two playoff games that year, and quarterbacked the team admirably when standing in, on occasion, for Jim McMahon in the championship season of 1985.—Chicago Bears

With Rusty Lisch at quarterback, however, the Bears lost to the San Diego Chargers and Green Bay Packers. An ancient but seasoned Greg Landry was signed as a free agent to quarterback the Bears through their last game of the regular season, which he did effectively in a 30–13 win over Detroit. The two losses in preceding games, however, cost the Bears the home field advantage in the playoffs and deprived the more ardent fans of seeing their team play in person in the postseason.

Only twice since 1963 (1977 and 1979) had a Bears team earned a place in the playoffs, and both those times they were quickly eliminated. Now they were slated to meet the Washington Redskins, winner of the NFL East and holder of a record of 11–5.

Washington had succeeded on the passing of Joe Theismann and the running of John Riggins, and they were a slight favorite that Sunday at RFK Stadium in Washington. The Skins scored first on a Mark Mosely field goal, but in the second quarter the Bears tied it when Bob Thomas booted a 34-yarder, then went ahead when Walter Payton shunned the run and lofted a 19-yard touchdown pass to tight end Pat Dunsmore. To open the second half, Steve Fuller hit Willie Gault with a short pass

and the world-class speedster broke a tackle and streaked all the way for a touchdown, turning what should have been a short gain into a 75-yard touchdown play. That and another TD pass from Fuller later in the period, this time to Dennis McKinnon, was enough to give Chicago its first postseason triumph since 1963.

The victory gained for the Bears the right to meet the San Francisco 49ers in the NFC championship game at Candlestick Park. Bill Walsh's 49ers were considered, quite rightly, the class of the league. Quarterbacked by All-Pro Joe Montana, with receivers like Freddie Solomon, Dwight Clark, and Russ Francis and runners like Wendall Tyler and Roger Craig, San Francisco had won 15 of their 16 regular season games and had trounced a fine New York Giants team the preceding week in the playoffs.

The Bears' defense kept them in the game during the first half, ceding only two field goals to the San Franciscans. But Steve Fuller could not get the Chicago offense moving. The 49ers did have the best defense in the NFL that year, having given up only 227 points, an average of about 14 a game, and the Bears bore witness to that January afternoon. They were unable to put a point on

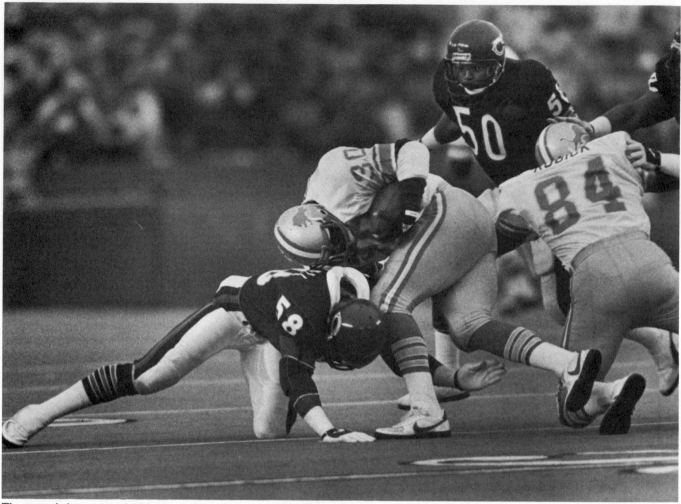

The crunch here is applied by linebacker Wilber Marshall (58) to Detroit running back James Jones, while Mike Singletary (50) observes from above. Marshall, a first-round draft pick from Florida in 1984, earned a starting assignment the following year and ended up ranking third in total tackles (78, with 60 solos, including six sacks).—Vernon Biever

the scoreboard all day, and the 49ers won it 23–0. 49er Ronnie Lott told a few Bear players as they walked off the field, "Next time bring your offense." It was a loss the Bears would remember well. And one they would gleefully and rapaciously avenge less than a year later.

The city of Chicago had not been treated to a major sports championship in more than two decades—not the Bears, Cubs, White Sox, Bulls, Blackhawks, DePaul. Not since 1963 when the Bears beat the New York Giants at Wrigley Field for the NFL crown and Loyola University surprised Cincinnati to take the NCAA basketball title had a crown come to the Windy City.

In 1986 the drought finally came to an end after what was surely one of the most exciting and colorful seasons in the Chicago Bears' 66-year history. With a rookie called Refrigerator; Walter Payton, the game's all-time most successful running back; a quarterback with a Mohawk-like haircut, reflector sunglasses, and inscribed headbands; a defense of epic intimidation; and with a

syncopated tuneful "Super Bowl Shuffle"; the Bears rewarded their loyal longtime fans and entertained an entire nation of sports buffs.

Even before the players began thinking about coming to summer camp, the team became the hub of sports speculation everywhere with a surprise first-round draft choice, a mountainous defensive tackle named William Perry, who weighed somewhere in the vicinity of 350 pounds when he played that position at Clemson. Nicknamed the "Refrigerator," Perry had been a consensus All-American in college, but questions were raised about his being able to play in the pros at his astonishing weight. Coach Ditka promised that Perry would trim down to 310 or so by the start of the regular season; defensive coordinator Buddy Ryan wondered aloud whether the team had wasted a precious first-round selection. Everyone around Chicago talked about the Refrigerator, but no one would have guessed that by season's end he would grace the cover of *Time* magazine and have attained the status of a near-national folk hero.

1984 Season	.625	
Mike Ditka—Coach	**Bears**	**Opponents**
Tampa Bay Buccaneers....... (H)	34	14
Denver Broncos .... (H)	27	0
Green Bay Packers.......... (A)	9	7
Seattle Seahawks .... (A)	9	38
Dallas Cowboys .... (H)	14	23
New Orleans Saints......... (H)	20	7
St. Louis Cardinals .... (A)	21	38
Tampa Bay Buccaneers....... (A)	44	9
Minnesota Vikings........... (H)	16	7
Los Angeles Raiders .... (H)	17	6
Los Angeles Rams .... (A)	13	29
Detroit Lions............... (H)	16	14
Minnesota Vikings........... (A)	34	3
San Diego Chargers .... (A)	7	20
Green Bay Packers.......... (H)	14	20
Detroit Lions............... (A)	30	13
Totals	325	248
Divisional Playoffs		
Washington Redskins .... (A)	23	19
NFC Championship		
San Francisco 49ers .... (A)	0	23

The draft also produced cornerback Reggie Phillips (Southern Methodist), wide receiver James Maness (Texas Christian), place kicker Kevin Butler (Georgia), who would wrest that job from the Bears' all-time leading point-scorer Bob Thomas, and running back Thomas Sanders (Texas A & M). Tight end Tim Wrightman, who had been the Bears' number-two choice in the 1982 draft, left the USFL and signed on as a free agent. Wide receiver and punt returner Keith Ortego (McNeese State) and quarterback Mike Tomczak also made the team as free agents.

Chicago faced a schedule that was far from easy. They were to play both of the previous season's Super Bowl participants, the 49ers and Dolphins, as well as such other highly regarded teams as the Dallas Cowboys, New York Jets, Washington Redskins, and New England Patriots.

It was a steamy opener at Soldier Field the first week in September, broilingly hot and much more suited to the visiting Buccaneers from Florida than the Chicagoans, who had become enured to playing in subfreezing temperatures and ice-riddled winds on their hometown turf. By halftime, the Bucs' James Wilder had rushed for 105 yards and the team had produced a 28–17 lead. But then Tampa Bay wilted. On their first possession of the second half, Steve DeBerg's pass was tipped by Richard Dent and picked off by Leslie Frazier, who returned it 29 yards for a touchdown. The Bears' defense virtually came to life that half and shut down the Bucs every time they had the ball. Behind the passing of Jim McMahon, his lacerated kidney fully healed, the Bears marched and capped it with a Jim McMahon-to-Matt Suhey touchdown pass later in the third quarter. A few moments after Shaun Gayle blocked a Tampa punt in the final period. McMahon carried the ball in for another Chicago touchdown. When it ended, the Bears had turned in a nice comeback win, 38–28, and it would prove to be the most points scored against the Bears all year.

The Bears' defense demonstrated just what a remarkable force it was the following week at Soldier Field. They did not allow the New England Patriots a point until the last period, when Craig James got free for a little pass from Tony Eason and the play carried 90 yards, which is the longest TD play ever in a Bears game at Soldier Field. It was not only their only score of the game, it was also only the second time in the entire game that the Patriots managed to get into Bear territory.

*The Honey Bears kicked up their heels for the last time for the Bears at the Super Bowl in New Orleans; they were disbanded after the 1985 season.—*Bill Smith.

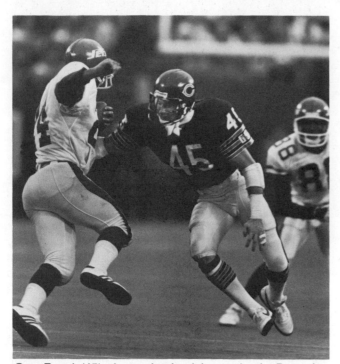

Gary Fencik (45), doing what he did more for the Bears than any other player in 1985, moves in to tackle New York Jets running back Freeman McNeil. The Monsters of the Midway beat the New Yorkers that day, 19—6 at Giants Stadium, to bring their record to 14—1 as they surged toward the Super Bowl. Fencik's 118 total tackles and 98 solos were both club highs for 1985, and his five interceptions were second only to Leslie Frazier's six. His 35 career interceptions are only two short of the club record, held by Richie Pettibon.—Vernon Biever

The next game was a Thursday night affair, and it was Jim McMahon's turn to dazzle in the spotlight. Benched throughout the first half with back and leg injuries, he came on in the third quarter with the Bears losing 17–9 and electrified the national television audience by throwing two consecutive touchdown passes. The first was a 70-yarder to Willie Gault; then, after an interception, he hit Dennis McKinnon for a 25-yard touchdown. When the Bears got the ball back, he completed a couple of short passes, found McKinnon again with a 43-yarder, and suddenly the eight-point deficit had been turned into a 30–17 lead. Minnesota was demoralized and the final score stood 33–24, Bears.

Against the Redskins, titleholder of the NFC East the year before, the Bears again got off to a shaky start, trailing 10–0 early in the second quarter. By the end of the game, however, the score was 45–10, Bears. After Washington's last score, Willie Gault caught the kickoff at his one yardline and streaked 99 yards through Redskin

defenders for a touchdown. It was the third longest in Bears history (Gale Sayers, 103 in 1967; Don Bingham, 100 in 1956; Willie Galimore, 99 in 1958), and it ignited a 31-point second quarter for the Bears. After this impressive win the Bears were 4–0 and alone at the top of the NFC Central. And now not just starry-eyed fans but even sportswriters were entertaining thoughts that this Chicago team might just be something special. Don Pierson of the *Chicago Tribune* observed, "Greatness is not measured in one-fourth of a season, but the Bears have won their games the way great teams win them. Somehow they find a way. They have come from behind in three of four games. They have won when they have controlled the ball and when they haven't. They have won despite injuries and holdouts. They have more than won; they have dominated."

But they did not dominate in the first half of all their games, and that was clearly displayed in Tampa Bay,

Walter Payton comes to the sideline after breaking the NFL all-time rushing record, which had been held since 1965 by Cleveland's Jim Brown. Payton surpassed the mark of 12,312 at Soldier Field in this game against New Orleans in 1984. Payton also holds a slew of other league records, including most combined yards gained, most games 100 + yards rushing, most rushing attempts, and most yards rushing in a game (275, against Minnesota in 1977). With him here is Bear media relations director Ken Valdiserri.—Chicago Bears

The first headband. Jim McMahon gave a whole new meaning to the wearing of headbands during the 1985 season, and an ulcer or two to league commissioner Pete Rozelle, who was not fond of players advertising products on NFL football fields.—Fred Roe

quarterback Joe Montana would remember well, sacked seven times that day. Coach Bill Walsh would also harbor some distressing memories; his team gained only 183 total yards and were held to a paltry 11 first downs, both the lowest any Walsh-coached San Francisco team had ever registered, and they gained only three yards rushing in the entire second half. For Chicago, Jim McMahon passed for 186 yards and Walter Payton rushed for 132 and, according to Coach Ditka, "We challenged them with our offensive and defensive lines. . . . The lines got the game balls." And the Refrigerator, William Perry, weighing in at about 320 pounds, made his debut as a running back. On each of two plunges at the end of the game he picked up two yards. Some said it was in retribution for Walsh's use of guard Guy McIntyre as a blocking back in their previous encounter in the NFC title game the year before; others that it was just a little Ditka

Jim McMahon, here chilling the proverbial spines of coach Mike Ditka and Bear fans everywhere who remember his near career-ending kidney injury when he ran with the ball the year before, races out of the reach of Jets All-Pro defensive end Mark Gastineau in this 1985 game. McMahon threw 15 touchdown passes in the '85 regular season, ran for three others, and caught a Walter Payton pass for still another. Then in the playoffs he threw two TD passes against the Giants, passed for one and ran for another against the Rams, and ran two in against the Patriots in the Super Bowl.—Fred Roe

where they found themselves on the short end of a 12–3 score at the intermission. True to form, however, the Bears bounced back with 17 unanswered points. The Bucs got back within one at 20–19 and had the Bears deep in their own territory, third and about four yards to go, with just over four minutes remaining in the game. McMahon hit Emory Moorehead for the first down and the Bears marched on for a game-clinching touchdown and won it 27–19. McMahon completed 14 of 17 passes in the second half, one a touchdown to Dennis McKinnon, and Walter Payton ran it in for two other TDs.

Now came the time for sweet revenge. And the setting was the same, Candlestick Park in San Francisco. The reigning national champion 49ers had lost two of their five games in 1985, but still were considered *the* team to beat in the league. And the Bears not only beat them, 26–10, they beat them up as well. It was a game

At Lambeau Field in Green Bay in 1985, William Perry, perhaps the only 300+-pound receiver in the history of the NFL, cradles the ball as if it were a baby while carrying it into the end zone. Perry had come out of the backfield to take a short pass from Jim McMahon. After having previously scored rushing, now on a pass reception, the Refrigerator was the subject of speculation as to just when he would start throwing passes for the Bears. Chicago won this game 16–10, the closest call they had all year, the loss to the Miami Dolphins notwithstanding. In the background is Bear tackle Andy Frederick (71).—Chicago Bears

whimsy emanating from the euphoria of leaving the city by the bay with a record of 6–0 and a triumph over last year's champs.

Now facing the Bears was a month of intra-divisional play, crucial to their hopes of a title-taking repeat. And Chicago did it, mauling Green Bay, Minnesota, the Packers again, and Detroit. In the first game, the Refrigerator scored his first touchdown by bursting through the Green Bay line to break a 7–7 tie. Earlier he had led the way into the end zone for Walter Payton by simply bowling over Packer linebacker George Cumby with one of the most devastating blocks ever seen in Soldier Field.

In the second of these games, the Bears intercepted five Vikings passes. In the third, up in Green Bay, Refrigerator Perry caught his first touchdown pass, coming out of the backfield from the four yardline, and Walter Payton rushed for 192 yards, his best day since he picked up an

identical amount against the Kansas City Chiefs back in 1977. After the game Ditka was asked when his defensive tackle/running back William Perry might be used as a passer and replied, "As soon as he jumps over the goal post." In the fourth game, it was the running of Payton (107 yards) and Matt Suhey (102 yards), the best defensive showing of the season (the Lions gaining only 106 total yards), and a not-to-be-ignored Refrigerator contributing two sacks over these four games.

After 10 games, the Bears were the only undefeated team in the NFL and could claim 16 wins in their last 17 games against NFC Central division teams and 15 wins in their last 17 games at Soldier Field.

Next on the agenda was Mike Ditka's former employer, the Dallas Cowboys in the unfriendly environs of Texas Stadium. Since 1960, the two teams had met 10 times and the Cowboys had won seven times, includ-

William "Refrigerator" Perry, the Bears first-round draft choice in 1985 as a defensive tackle out of Clemson, spikes the ball on the occasion of his first NFL touchdown. The reported 309-pound, reputed 325-pound Perry burst in from the one yardline to break a 7–7 tie with the Packers at Soldier Field, leading the way to a 23–7 victory. The "Fridge," as he was affectionately called, became a household word before the season was over—"the best thing to happen to fat since the invention of bacon," according to Chicago Sun-Times *columnist Ray Sons. Other Bears are Jim McMahon (9), guard Mark Bortz (62), and tackle Keith Van Horne (78).*—Chicago Bears

ing a 23–14 battering the year before in Soldier Field. In fact, the last time the Bears had beaten the Cowboys was back in 1971 when Dallas had a tight end named Mike Ditka on its roster.

On November 17, 1985, it was a day to remember . . . for the Bears. They devastated the NFC East-leading Cowboys 44–0, the worst defeat in Dallas's 26-year history. The Cowboys had not been shutout in 218 consecutive games until the Bears came down to Texas. For the Bears, it clinched the NFC Central title; for Walter Payton, it enabled him to post his ninth 1,000-yard rushing season; and for William Perry it got him more national news coverage when he picked up Payton, who was stopped short of the goalline, and tried to pitch him into the end zone.

Atlanta got a taste of the same in game 12, a 36–0 rout. With a record now of 12–0, Chicago fans could

enjoy the fact that only two teams in the history of the NFL had gone so far undefeated in a season (Bears of 1934 and Dolphins of 1972).

But, as Judy Holliday sang in *Bells Are Ringing,* all dreams must end. The dream of football perfection ended in Miami at the Orange Bowl. Super Bowl contender from the year before and leader of the AFC East, the Dolphins did it, bringing the Bears back to pro football reality with a 38–24 drubbing. The best defense in the NFL could not stop Dan Marino that Monday night, and the elusive quarterback threw three touchdown passes, converted several crucial third-down situations to Miami first downs, and guided the Dolphins to an insurmountable 31-point first half. The only thing of note to Chicago was that in the game Walter Payton broke still another NFL record by rushing for more than 100 yards in eight consecutive games (the mark of seven had been

Cornerback Leslie Frazier picks one off here against the Denver Broncos. Frazier has led the Bears in interceptions three years in a row, 1983–85 (tied with Gary Fencik in 1984), but suffered a serious knee injury at the end of the '85 season. No. 24 is cornerback Jeff Fisher.
—Chicago Bears

This is not a reprise of "Shall We Dance?" from The King and I. It is a 1985 meeting of sometime defensive tackle William Perry of the Bears and Dallas Cowboy Glenn Titensor. Although there appears to be no winner in this particular confrontation, the Bears embarrassed the Cowboys that day in Texas, thrashing them 44–0.
—Vernon Biever

shared by Payton, O. J. Simpson, and Earl Campbell).

The party was far from over for the Bears, however; it was just momentarily sidetracked. Sportswriters suggested it was good for them, that they would not go into the playoffs too cocky, that they would realize now they were indeed mortal.

As it turned out, the defeat was the only one of the season for the Bears. They leaped back on the win-wagon the following week by trimming the Indianapolis Colts. The New York Jets and Detroit Lions fell in subsequent weeks and the Bears ended the 1985 regular season with a handsome record of 15-1, by far the best in the NFL.

By dint of their record, the Bears had earned the home field advantage and faced the New York Giants in their first postseason encounter. The Giants had beaten the San Francisco 49ers in the wild-card playoff game and were coming off one of their finest seasons in some time. Phil Simms had stayed healthy and was one of the more impressive quarterbacks in the league, and Joe Morris had turned into one of the most productive running backs around. And, of course, there was the Giants' defense, second only to the Bears in 1985, which had such All-Pro caliber players as linebackers Lawrence Taylor and Harry Carson and end Leonard Marshall.

A quirky play got the Bears their first score of the game. Sean Landeta, the Giants' punter, only grazed the ball when he tried to boot one in the first quarter and Shaun Gayle scooped it up at the five and ran it in for a touchdown. Two touchdown passes from Jim McMahon to Dennis McKinnon in the third quarter served merely as frosting because the Bears' defense totally thwarted the Giants. The final score was 21–0, Bears.

In the other playoff game that weekend, the Los Angeles Rams also racked up a shutout, downing the Dallas Cowboys 20–0, which gave them the right to come to chilly Chicago for the NFC title game. A lot of eyebrows were raised when the oddsmakers made the Bears an 11-point favorite; after all, this was a conference championship game and the Rams had gone 11–5 during the regular season.

The Rams' biggest threat was perennial thousand-yard rusher Eric Dickerson, who had put together 55- and 40-yard touchdown runs and gained an NFL playoff record of 248 yards rushing against Dallas the week before. They also had a highly respected defense. But it was the Bears' defense that filled the spotlight the afternoon of January 12, 1986, in Soldier Field. For the second straight playoff game, they did not give up a single point. Dickerson managed only 46 yards on 17 carries and the entire Los Angeles offense was allowed a meager 130 total yards all day.

The Bears had a lot to high-five about in 1985. Here is a jubilant meeting between defense and offense: linebacker Otis Wilson (55) and wide receiver Dennis McKinnon (85).—Chicago Bears

Meanwhile Jim McMahon scrambled 16 yards for a touchdown and Kevin Butler booted a 32-yard field goal in the first quarter for the Bears. In the third quarter McMahon hit Willie Gault for a 22-yard touchdown, and in the final period, just in case someone had not noticed the defense's contributions, linebacker Wilber Marshall gobbled up a Los Angeles fumble and carried it 52 yards for another touchdown. Bears 24–Rams 0. And a ticket to the Super Bowl.

The Bears, to a man, wanted to take on the Miami Dolphins in the Super Bowl, the only team to have stained their otherwise perfect record. But the Dolphins were surprised by the New England Patriots in the AFC title tilt, 31–14, and they would not go to the Superdome in New Orleans.

The Bears were at the center of the traditional hype and hoopla the week before the Super Bowl—on Bourbon Street, at press conferences, everywhere, they were visible and viable. And they were a strong favorite after

Defensive end Richard Dent lunges upon the Giants' Phil Simms in the Bears first playoff game of 1985. Dent was credited with 3½ sacks that afternoon at Soldier Field. During the regular season he sacked other quarterbacks 17 times, the most in the NFC; after the season was over he could also claim All Pro honors, an invite to the Pro Bowl, and recognition as the Super Bowl MVP.—Fred Roe

1985 Season	.938	Bears	Opponents
Mike Ditka—Coach			
Tampa Bay Buccaneers . . . . (H)		38	28
New England Patriots . . . . (H)		20	7
Minnesota Vikings . . . . (A)		33	24
Washington Redskins . . . . (H)		45	10
Tampa Bay Buccaneers . . . . (A)		27	19
San Francisco 49ers . . . . (A)		26	10
Green Bay Packers . . . . (H)		23	7
Minnesota Vikings . . . . (H)		27	9
Green Bay Packers . . . . (A)		16	10
Detroit Lions . . . . (H)		24	3
Dallas Cowboys . . . . (A)		44	0
Atlanta Falcons . . . . (H)		36	0
Miami Dolphins . . . . (A)		24	38
Indianapolis Colts . . . . (H)		17	10
New York Jets . . . . (A)		19	6
Detroit Lions . . . . (A)		37	17
Totals		456	198
Divisional Playoffs			
New York Giants . . . . (H)		21	0
NFC Championship			
Los Angeles Rams . . . . (H)		24	0
Super Bowl XX			
New England Patriots (New Orleans)		46	10

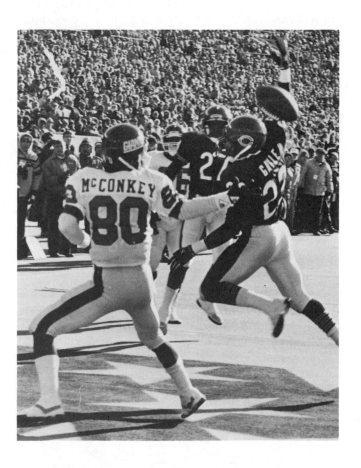

Cornerback Shaun Gayle breaks up a pass intended for New York Giants wide receiver Phil McConkey in the 1985 playoffs. The Bears' defense was spectacular that day, shutting the Giants out 21–0 and holding them to 32 yards rushing and 149 net yards passing (129 of which were on New York's final two possessions of the game when they were already down three touchdowns). In the background is cornerback Mike Richardson.—Fred Roe

Jim McMahon finds a wide-open Ken Margerum during the tilt with the Giants at Soldier Field, which, at day's end, enabled the Bears to move on to the NFC title game. The Giant pursuing the play is safety Kenny Hill (48).—Fred Roe

The story of the NFC championship game is pretty well summed up in this photo as Bear linebacker Ron Rivera (59) and tackle Henry Waechter (70) descend on fallen Ram ballcarrier Barry Redden (30). The Bear defense once again was faultless in a 24–0 romp that earned them the right to make the club's first Super Bowl appearance ever. No. 60 on Los Angeles is guard Dennis Harrah.—Vernon Biever

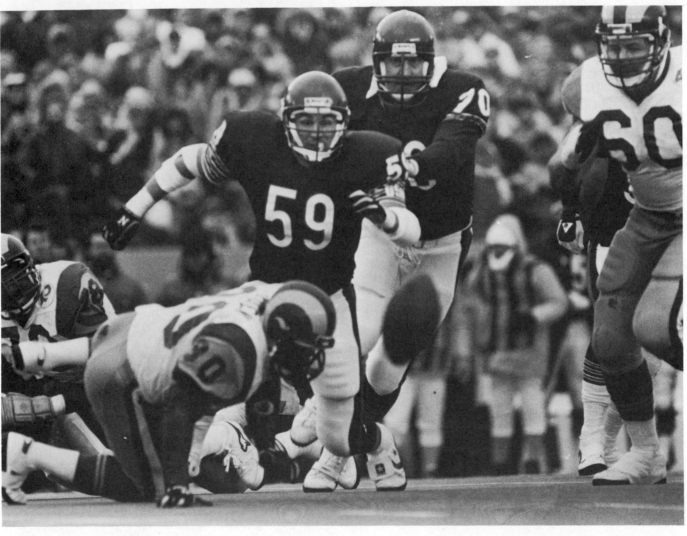

Notes and Quotes, 1985–86

Mike Ditka: "There are teams that are fair-haired and there are teams that aren't. There are teams named Smith and teams named Grabowski. The Rams are a Smith. We're a Grabowski."

Otis Wilson, describing his defensive teammates: "Mike Singletary is the quiet, Christian type; I'm the wild one; Fencik is the Ivy Leaguer; Dan Hampton is the politician; Steve McMichael is crazy. It makes for a wild bunch."

NFL Commissioner Pete Rozelle, on Jim McMahon's inscribed headbands: "I'm concerned that it will spread. I don't want our players running around like race-car drivers with patches all over them. Pretty soon, we'll have a center with a Big Mac on his fanny."

Mike McCaskey, Bears president, the week before Super Bowl XX: "Our secret weapon is the placebo effect. I don't know how the Patriots can counter that. That's when there's no evidence that the treatment works, but the patient thinks it works, so it does. The placebo effect and the man from Japan [Jim McMahon's acupuncturist who was treating him for a bruised buttock] are our secret weapons."

Dick Enberg, Super Bowl XX broadcaster, during the third quarter: "If it were a fight, they'd have to stop it."

Pete Brock, Patriots center assigned to block William Perry, after Super Bowl XX: "I'm not in a real talkative mood. So if you're hanging out for a quotable quote, it just ain't flowing."

He'd Be Upstairs Cheering

Virginia McCaskey, daughter of George Halas; wife of Ed, chairman of the board of the Bears; and mother of Mike, the club's president, talking after the Bears had just won the NFC conference championship at Soldier Field, January 12, 1986, and reported by columnist Bob Verdi in the Chicago Tribune: "Dad would relish this. Have you ever heard a crowd at a Bear game sing like they did? And it's not only this city and the nation. The night before, we met people from Tokyo, England, France; people who might not know anything about American football, but they love the Chicago Bears. . . .

"I've never had this much fun. I even laughed at a Bear game. I never thought I'd do that, because every yard used to be so serious. But at Green Bay, when William Perry scored the touchdown; and Dallas, when he tried to lift Walter Payton into the end zone . . . What would Dad have thought of the Refrigerator?

"Dad would have loved it all. The Bears were his life. Mugs, my brother [the Bears' former president until his death in 1979], it was his life too. He shares in this. And Jim Finks did the Bears a tremendous service during his years here.

"Dad would really enjoy this. He'd be upstairs cheering, taking notes. . . . He's with us. You don't see him, but he's still with us."

their systematic destruction of the Giants and Rams in the playoffs.

The Bears felt like champions as they roamed the streets of the French Quarter and prepared for the season's final confrontation. They did not look like world beaters on their first possession when Walter Payton fumbled and the New Englanders turned it into a three-point lead on a field goal.

But it was all over after that. In the same premier period, the Bears roared back with a McMahon to Gault 43-yard pass that set up the score-tying Kevin Butler field goal. Butler added another field goal, then Matt Suhey crashed in for a touchdown. The score was 13–3 at the end of the first quarter, and 23–3 at the half. A 21-point third quarter for the Bears and the game became a slaughterhouse. The final score was 46–10, and the Bears had the most lopsided Super Bowl victory in history.

It was a great day, it had been a great season. George Halas would have loved to be there. This was his kind of team, a winner peopled with the 1980s versions of Red Grange, Bronko Nagurski, Bulldog Turner, Sid Luckman, Gale Sayers, Dick Butkus. Papa Bear had to be happy.

Trivium

When Mike Ditka made his appearance at Super Bowl XX, he became only the third person in NFL history to have appeared in that classic as both a player and a head coach. The other two were Tom Flores (quarterback of Kansas City in Super Bowl IX and coach of the Raiders in Super Bowls XV and XVIII) and Forrest Gregg (tackle for Green Bay in Super Bowls I and II and coach of the Cincinnati Bengals in Super Bowl XVI). But Ditka holds the single honor of being the only head coach of a Super Bowl team to have scored a touchdown in the Super Bowl (a seven-yard pass from Roger Staubach in the Dallas Cowboys 24–3 win over the Dolphins in Super Bowl VI back in 1971).

Super Bowl Records

Set in SB XX

Bears

Most points, team	46
Largest victory margin	36
Most points, team, second half	23
Most points, team, third quarter	21
Most touchdowns, rushing	4

Patriots

Longest punt (Rich Camarillo)	62 yards
Most kickoff returns (Stephen Starring)	7
Fewest first downs, rushing	1
Fewest yards, rushing	7
Lowest rushing average	.6

Both Teams

Most points, third quarter	21
Most times sacked	10 (Patriots 7, Bears 3)

Tied in SB XX

Bears

Most points after touchdown (Kevin Butler)	5
Most safeties (Henry Waechter	1
Most touchdowns, rushing (Jim McMahon)	2
Most touchdowns, interception returns (Reggie Phillips)	1
Most fumbles recovered (Mike Singletary)	2
Most touchdowns, team	5
Most points after touchdown, team	5
Most safeties, team	1
Most touchdowns, interception returns, team	1

Patriots

Most times sacked, team	7
Most kickoff returns, team	7
Most fumbles lost, team	4

Both Teams

Most field goals	4 (Bears 3, Patriots 1)
Most touchdowns, rushing	4 (Bears 4)
Most kickoff returns	11 (Patriots 7, Bears 4)

An exultant Mike Ditka in 1984 after defeating the Washington Redskins 23–19 in the divisional playoff in the nation's capital. The coach would have much more to luxuriate in the following year when his Bears moved from conference title contender to the status of national champion.—Chicago Bears

The Refrigerator, William Perry, scores his fourth touchdown of 1985 in Super Bowl XX, plunging in from the one yardline to make the score 43–3 in the third quarter. The Bears were simply unstoppable that day, running up the widest winning margin in Super Bowl history. Chicago outrushed the Patriots 167 yards to 7, outpassed them 241 yards to 116, out-first-downed them 23-12, sacked their quarterback seven times, recovered four of their fumbles, and intercepted two of their passes.—Vernon Biever

The scoreboard says it all! —Vernon Biever

If the Dallas Cowboys in their heyday could be called America's Team, rookie Refrigerator Perry in 1985 could surely be dubbed "America's Mascot." With his 300-and-you-guess-what-pounds, a conspicuous gap in his upper plate, a plethora of commercials and advertisements, he was an unprecedented focus of attention for a rookie. The Bears going 18–1 and copping the Super Bowl Trophy did not hurt his popularity either. —Vernon Biever

The gesture and symbol of triumph. Bears president Mike McCaskey personifies it here with a triumphant fist and a hand on professional football's most prized possession, the Vince Lombardi Trophy, awarded to the Super Bowl victor. Behind him is an equally proud chairman of the Bears board, Ed McCaskey.—Chicago Bears

Super Bowl XX Trivia

—*"The more than 2,000 media credentials issued for Super Bowl XX is more than were issued for the Reagan–Gorbachev summit meeting." (Don Pierson, Chicago Tribune)*

—*The game was broadcast in 31 countries.*

—*The Superdome in New Orleans, site of the game, contains 52,000 square yards of carpeting, 400 miles of electrical cord, and 88 restrooms.*

—*Tickets cost $75 each regardless of location.*

—*Official attendance: 73,818*

—*Television audience: estimated at 115,000,000.*

—*Cost of a 30-second television commercial during the game: $550,000.*

SUPER BOWL XX

Matt Suhey dives in to score the Chicago Bears' first touchdown of the game. The defender is New England Patriots Fred Marion.—AP/
Wide World Photos

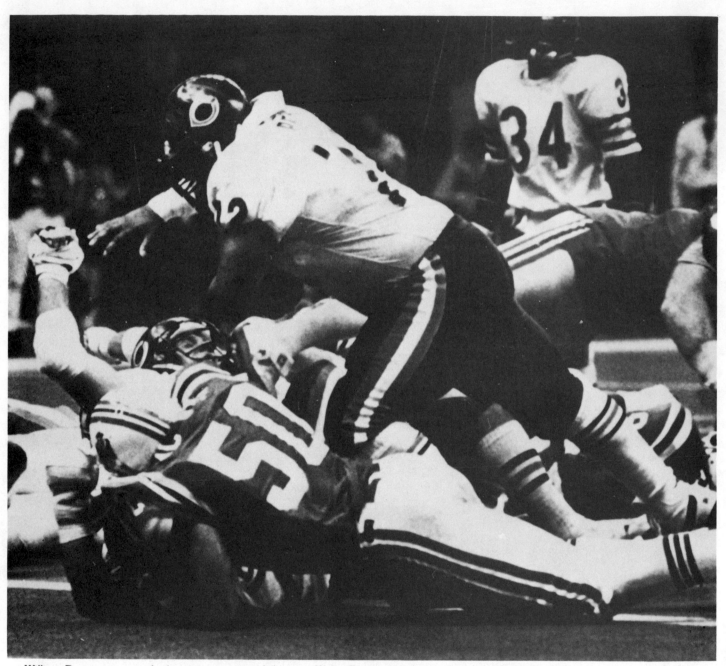

William Perry goes over the line to score a touchdown as Walter Payton watches in the background.—AP/Wide World Photos

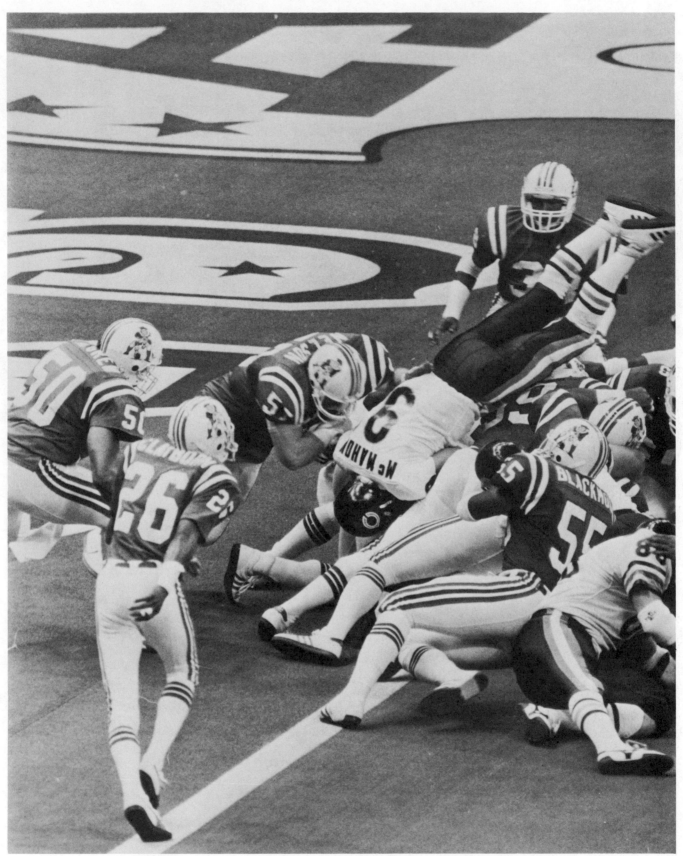

Jim McMahon dives into the end zone to score a touchdown. —AP/Wide World Photos

Receiver Willie Gault pulls in the ball as he beats New England Patriots Ronnie Lippett.—AP/Wide World Photos

Henry Waechter sacks New England Patriots Steve Grogan behind the goal line.—AP/Wide World Photos

Head coach Mike Ditka is carried on the shoulders of Steve McMichael, left, and William Perry and escorted by Willie Gault (83) and Maury Buford (8) after winning the Super Bowl XX.—AP/Wide World Photos

A crowd estimated at around 10,000 cheers and dances to the "Super Bowl Shuffle" in the Rush and Division Streets bar district Sunday night in Chicago. —AP/Wide World Photos

APPENDIX

INDIVIDUAL RECORDS

SERVICE

Seasons, Active Player

14   Bill George, 1952–65
      Doug Buffone, 1968–79
13   George Trafton, 1920–32
      Clyde ("Bulldog") Turner, 1940–52

Consecutive Seasons, Active Player

Same as above

Games, Lifetime

186   Doug Buffone, 1966–79
161   Bobby Joe Green, 1962–73
159   Bill George, 1952–65
155   Joe Fortunato, 1955–66

Consecutive Games, Lifetime

144   Bob Parsons, 1972–81
142   Doug Buffone, 1966–76
136   Richie Petitbon, 1959–68

Seasons, Head Coach

—See Coaching Records
30   George Halas, 1933–42, 1946–55,
      1958–67
10   George Halas/Dutch Sternaman,
      1920–29
4   Hunk Anderson/Luke Johnsos/
      Paddy Driscoll, 1942–45
      Jim Dooley, 1968–71
      Neill Armstrong, 1978–81

SCORING

Points, Lifetime

541   George Blanda, 1949–58
      (5-TD, 247-XP, 88-FG)
654   Walter Payton, 1975-81 (107-TD)
456   Mac Percival, 1967–73
      (159-XP, 99-FG)
430   Bob Thomas, 1975–81
      (169-XP, 87-FG)

Points, Season

144   Kevin Butler, 1985 (51-XP, 31-FG)
109   Johnny Lujack, 1950
      (11-TD, 34-XP, 3-FG)
100   Mac Percival, 1968 (25-XP, 25-FG)

Points, Rookie Season

132   Gale Sayers, 1965

Points, Game

36   Gale Sayers, 12/12/65

Consecutive Games, 1+ Points

83   George Blanda, 10/28/51–11/09/58
34   Johnny Lujack, 9/26/48–12/03/50

TOUCHDOWNS

Touchdowns, Lifetime

107   Walter Payton, 1975-84
      (98-rush, 9-rec)
59   Rick Casares, 1955–64
      (49-rush, 10-rec)
56   Gale Sayers, 1965–71
      (39-rush, 9-rec, 8-ret)

Touchdowns, Season

22   Gale Sayers, 1965
      (14-rush, 6-rec, 2-ret)
16   Walter Payton, 1977
      (14-rush, 2-rec)
      Walter Payton, 1979
      (14-rush, 2-rec)
14   Rick Casares, 1956
      (12-rush, 2-rec)

Touchdowns, Rookie Season

22   Gale Sayers, 1965*

Touchdowns, Game

6   Gale Sayers, 12/12/65†
      (4-rush, 1-rec, 1-ret)

Consecutive Games, 1+ Touchdowns

8   Rick Casares, 11/01/59–9/25/60
7   Ken Kavanaugh, 11/02/47–12/14/47
      Willie Galimore, 9/28/58–11/09/58
      Gale Sayers, 10/26/69–12/06/69
      Walter Payton, 10/03/76–11/14/76

EXTRA POINTS

Extra Points, Lifetime

247   George Blanda, 1949–58
169   Bob Thomas, 1975–81

Extra Points, Season

52   Roger Leclerc, 1965
45   George Blanda, 1956

Extra Points, Game

8   Bob Snyder, 11/14/43

Extra Points Attempted, Lifetime

250   George Blanda, 1949–58
187   Bob Thomas, 1975–81

Extra Points Attempted, Season

52   Ray ("Scooter") McLean, 1947
      Roger Leclerc, 1965
47   George Blanda, 1956
46   Johnny Lujack, 1948

Extra Points Attempted, Game

9   Bob Thomas, 12/07/80
8   Bob Snyder, 11/14/43
      George Blanda, 10/21/56
      Roger Leclerc, 11/25/62

* NFL record
† Tied for NFL record

Consecutive Extra Points, Lifetime

156   George Blanda, 10/28/51–10/21/56
143   Mac Percival, 11/19/67–11/04/73

Extra Points (no misses), Season

52   Roger Leclerc, 1965
37   George Blanda, 1955

Extra Points (no misses), Game

8   Bob Snyder, 11/14/43

FIELD GOALS

Field Goals, Lifetime

99   Mac Percival, 1967–73
88   George Blanda, 1949–58

Field Goals, Season

31   Kevin Butler, 1985
25   Mac Percival, 1968

Field Goals, Game

5   Roger Leclerc, 12/03/61
     Mac Percival, 10/20/68
4   Roger Leclerc, 11/17/63
     Mac Percival, 10/27/68
     Mac Percival, 11/15/70
     Bob Thomas, 10/03/76

Field Goals Attempted, Lifetime

201   George Blanda, 1949–58
182   Mac Percival, 1967–73

Field Goals Attempted, Season

38   Kevin Butler, 1985
36   Mac Percival, 1968

Field Goals Attempted, Game

7   Roger Leclerc, 11/17/63
6   George Blanda, 11/03/57

Consecutive Field Goals, Lifetime

13   Kevin Butler, 11/3/85–12/22/85
11   Bob Thomas, 11/11/84
10   Mac Percival, 10/20/68–11/03/68

Consecutive Games, 1+ Field Goals

12   George Blanda, 11/11/56–11/03/57
10   George Blanda, 11/14/54–11/20/55
     Mac Percival, 10/13/68–12/15/68

Longest Field Goal

55   Bob Thomas, 11/23/75
52   Lee Artoe, 10/27/40

Percentage, Lifetime (25+)

60.0   Bob Thomas, 1975–81
54.4   Mac Percival, 1967–73
51.4   Roger Leclerc, 1960–66

* NFL record

Percentage, Season (10+)

81.6   Kevin Butler, 1985
77.3   Bob Thomas, 1978
72.2   Bob Thomas, 1980

Field Goals (no misses), Game

5   Roger Leclerc, 12/03/61
     Mac Percival, 10/20/68
4   Mac Percival, 10/27/68
     Bob Thomas, 10/03/76

RUSHING
ATTEMPTS

Attempts, Lifetime

3,371   Walter Payton, 1975–85
1,386   Rick Casares, 1955–64
   991   Gale Sayers, 1965–71

Attempts, Season

369   Walter Payton. 1979*
339   Walter Payton, 1977, 1981
333   Walter Payton, 1978
317   Walter Payton, 1980
311   Walter Payton, 1976
236   Gale Sayers, 1969

Attempts, Game

40   Walter Payton, 11/20/77
39   Walter Payton, 10/07/79
38   Walter Payton, 11/26/81
36   Walter Payton, 11/07/76
     Walter Payton, 9/02/79
     Walter Payton, 10/25/81
33   Walter Payton, 11/13/77
     Walter Payton, 12/04/77
     Walter Payton, 12/16/79
     Walter Payton, 12/06/81

YARDAGE

Yards Gained, Lifetime

14,860   Walter Payton, 1975–85
 5,657   Rick Casares, 1955–64
 4,956   Gale Sayers, 1965–71

Seasons (1,000+)

6   Walter Payton, 1976–81
2   Gale Sayers, 1966, 1969
1   Beattie Feathers, 1934
     Rick Casares, 1956

Yards Gained, Season

1,852   Walter Payton, 1977
1,610   Walter Payton, 1979
1,460   Walter Payton, 1980
1,390   Walter Payton, 1976
1,231   Gale Sayers, 1966

Yards Gained, Game

275   Walter Payton, 1977*
205   Walter Payton, 1977
       Gale Sayers, 1968

Games, (100+) Lifetime

73   Walter Payton, 1975–85
20   Gale Sayers, 1965–71
13   Rick Casares, 1955–64

Consecutive Games (100+)

9   Walter Payton, 1984–85
5   Walter Payton, 11/13/77–12/11/77
3   Beattie Feathers, 9/30/34–10/10/34
     Rick Casares, 10/07/56–10/21/56
     Gale Sayers, 11/28/65–12/12/65
     Gale Sayers, 12/10/67–9/15/68
     Gale Sayers, 10/26/69–11/09/69
     Walter Payton, 10/03/76–10/17/76
     Walter Payton, 9/02/79–9/16/79
     Walter Payton, 10/21/79–11/4/79
     Walter Payton, 10/06/80–10/19/80

Games, (100+) Season

10   Walter Payton, 1977
 9   Walter Payton, 1979
 8   Walter Payton, 1980
 7   Rick Casares, 1956
      Walter Payton, 1976
 6   Walter Payton, 1978
 5   Beattie Feathers, 1934
      Gale Sayers, 1968

Longest Run from Scrimmage

86   Bill Osmanski, (TD) 10/15/39
85   Pete Stinchcomb, (TD) 11/20/21
82   Beattie Feathers, (TD) 10/10/34

Consecutive Seasons (1,000+)

6   Walter Payton, 1976–81

Games, (200+) Season

2   Walter Payton, 1977

Games, (200+) Career

2   Walter Payton, 1975–81

AVERAGE GAIN
Average Gain, Lifetime (250+)

6.62   Bobby Douglass, 1969–75
5.77   Beattie Feathers, 1934–37
5.00   Gale Sayers, 1965–71

Average Gain, Season (100+)

9.94   Beattie Feathers, 1934*
6.87   Bobby Douglass, 1972
6.20   Gale Sayers, 1968

Average Gain, Game (10+)

11.75   Joe Maniaci, 10/02/39
11.59   Gale Sayers, 12/18/66
11.18   Rick Casares, 12/16/56

TOUCHDOWNS
Touchdowns, Lifetime

71   Walter Payton, 1975–81
49   Rick Casares, 1955–64
39   Gale Sayers, 1965–71

Touchdowns, Season

14 Gale Sayers, 1965
      Walter Payton, 1977
      Walter Payton, 1979
13 Walter Payton, 1976
12 Rick Casares, 1956
11 Johnny Lujack, 1950
      Walter Payton, 1978

Touchdowns, Game

4 Rick Casares, 10/28/56
   Rick Casares, 12/06/59
   Gale Sayers, 12/12/65
   Bobby Douglass, 11/04/73

Consecutive Games, 1+ TDs

7 Gale Sayers, 10/26/69–12/06/69
   Walter Payton, 10/03/76–11/14/76
6 Beattie Feathers, 9/30/34–10/28/34
   Johnny Lujack, 10/01/50–11/12/50
   Rick Casares, 11/01/59–12/06/59
   Gale Sayers, 11/14/65–12/19/65

PASSING

Rating, Lifetime (400+ passes)

82.8 Jim McMahon, 1982–85
75.0 Sid Luckman, 1939–50
73.4 Bill Wade, 1961–66
72.8 Rudy Bukich, 1958–59, 1962–68

Rating, Season (100+)

107.8 Sid Luckman, 1943
 95.5 Sid Luckman, 1941
 93.7 Bill Wade, 1961

PASSES

Passes, Lifetime

1,744 Sid Luckman, 1939–50
1,407 Bill Wade, 1961–66
1,246 Ed Brown, 1954–61

Passes, Season

436 Vince Evans, 1981
412 Bill Wade, 1962
385 Jack Concannon, 1970

Passes, Game

57 Bill Wade, 10/25/64
52 Johnny Lujack, 10/23/49
50 Jack Concannon, 12/20/70

COMPLETIONS

Completions, Lifetime

904 Sid Luckman, 1939–50
767 Bill Wade, 1961–66
607 Ed Brown, 1954–61

Completions, Season

225 Bill Wade, 1962
195 Vince Evans, 1981
194 Jack Concannon, 1970

Completions, Game

33 Bill Wade, 10/25/64
31 Virgil Carter, 12/06/69
29 Johnny Lujack, 10/23/49

COMPLETION PERCENTAGE

Completion Percentage, Lifetime (250+ comp)

58.0 Jim McMahon, 1982–85
54.5 Bill Wade, 1961–66
54.0 Rudy Bukich, 1958–59, 1962–68

Completion Percentage, Season (60+)

61.9 Rudy Bukich, 1964
57.1 Sid Luckman, 1941
      Ed Brown, 1956

Completion Percentage, Game (10+)

86.7 Bob Williams, 10/12/52
83.3 Gene Ronzani, 10/22/44
      Ed Brown, 11/20/55
      Bill Wade, 11/08/64

YARDS PASSING

Yards Passing, Lifetime

14,686 Sid Luckman, 1939–50
 9,958 Bill Wade, 1961–66
 9,698 Ed Brown, 1954–61

Yards Passing, Season

3,172 Bill Wade, 1962
2,712 Sid Luckman, 1947
2,658 Johnny Lujack, 1949

Games, 300+ Yards, Lifetime

9 Bill Wade, 1961–66
4 George Blanda, 1949–58

Consecutive Games, 300+

2 Sid Luckman, 10/12/47–10/19/47
   George Blanda, 10/17/54–10/24/54
   Bill Wade, 10/14/62–10/21/62
   Bill Wade, 11/18/62–11/25/62

Games, 300+ Yards, Season

4 Bill Wade, 1962
3 Bill Wade, 1961

Yards Passing, Game

468 Johnny Lujack, 12/11/49
466 Bill Wade, 11/18/62
433 Sid Luckman, 11/14/43

Longest Pass Completion

98 Bill Wade (to John Farrington), (TD) 10/08/61
93 Jack Concannon (to Dick Gordon), (TD) 11/19/67
91 Ed Brown (to Willard Dewveall), (TD) 10/16/60

TOUCHDOWN PASSES

Touchdown Passes, Lifetime

137 Sid Luckman, 1939–50
 68 Bill Wade, 1961–66
 63 Ed Brown, 1954–61

Touchdown Passes, Season

28 Sid Luckman, 1943
24 Sid Luckman, 1947
23 Johnny Lujack, 1949

Touchdown Passes, Game

7 Sid Luckman, 11/14/43
6 Johnny Lujack, 12/11/49
5 Ray Buivid, 12/05/37

Consecutive Games, 1+ TD Pass

19 Sid Luckman, 11/22/42–11/26/44
14 Sid Luckman, 10/12/47–10/17/48

PASSES HAD INTERCEPTED

Passes Had Intercepted, Lifetime

132 Sid Luckman, 1939–50
 88 Ed Brown, 1954–61
 70 George Blanda, 1949–58

Passes Had Intercepted, Season

31 Sid Luckman, 1947
24 Bill Wade, 1962

Passes Had Intercepted, Game

7 Edmund ("Zeke") Bratkowski, 10/02/60

Passes (none intercepted), Game

46 Bill Wade, 10/11/64
38 Bill Wade, 10/04/64

PERCENTAGE INTERCEPTED

Lowest Percentage, Lifetime (400+ passes)

3.43 Jim McMahon, 1982–85
4.69 Bill Wade, 1961–66
5.13 Rudy Bukich, 1958–59, 1962–68

Lowest Percentage, Season (100+)

1.40 Jim McMahon, 1984
2.88 Rudy Bukich, 1965
3.10 Mike Phipps, 1979
3.37 Bill Wade, 1963

AVERAGE GAIN

Average Gain, Lifetime (400+ passes)

8.42 Sid Luckman, 1939–50
8.23 Bernie Masterson, 1934–40
7.79 Johnny Lujack, 1948–51

Average Gain, Season (100+)

10.860 Sid Luckman, 1943
 9.924 Sid Luckman, 1941
 9.923 Ed Brown, 1956

Average Gain, Game (10+)
17.09 Charlie O'Rourke, 11/22/42
16.88 Sid Luckman, 10/05/41
16.67 Gene Ronzani, 10/22/44

PASS RECEIVING

Pass Receptions, Lifetime
422 Walter Payton, 1975–85
356 Johnny Morris, 1958–67
316 Mike Ditka, 1961–66

Pass Receptions, Season
93 Johnny Morris, 1964
75 Mike Ditka, 1964

Pass Receptions, Game
14 Jim Keane, 10/23/49
13 Mike Ditka, 10/25/64

Consecutive Games, 1+
49 Mike Ditka, 12/03/61–10/10/65
30 Johnny Morris, 12/15/63–9/11/66

YARDS GAINED
Yards Gained, Lifetime
5,059 Johnny Morris, 1958–67
4,616 Harlon Hill, 1954–61

Seasons, 1,000+ Yards
2 Harlon Hill, 1954, 1956

Yards Gained, Season
1,200 Johnny Morris, 1964
1,128 Harlon Hill, 1956
1,124 Harlon Hill, 1954

Games 100+ Yards, Lifetime
19 Harlon Hill, 1954–61
15 Johnny Morris, 1958–67
14 Mike Ditka, 1961–66

Consecutive Games, 100+
3 Harlon Hill, 11/11/56–11/25/56

Games 100+ Yards, Season
7 Harlon Hill, 1954
6 Harlon Hill, 1956
Johnny Morris, 1964

Yards Gained, Game
214 Harlon Hill, 10/31/54
201 Johnny Morris, 11/18/62
198 Harlon Hill, 10/21/56

Longest Pass Reception
98 John Farrington (from Bill Wade),
(TD) 10/08/61
93 Dick Gordon (from Jack Concannon),
(TD) 11/19/67

91 Willard Dewveall (from Ed Brown),
(TD) 10/16/60

AVERAGE GAIN
Average Gain, Lifetime (75+ rec)
22.38 Ken Kavanaugh, 1940–41, 1945–50
21.67 Ray ("Scooter") McLean, 1940–47

Average Gain, Season (30+)
25.56 Ken Kavanaugh, 1947
24.98 Harlon Hill, 1954

Average Gain, Game (4+)
44.75 Dick Gordon, 11/19/67
37.50 Gene Schroeder, 12/16/51

TOUCHDOWNS
Touchdowns, Lifetime
50 Ken Kavanaugh, 1940–41, 1945–50
40 Harlon Hill, 1954–61

Touchdowns, Season
13 Ken Kavanaugh, 1947
Dick Gordon, 1970
12 Harlon Hill, 1954
Mike Ditka, 1961

Touchdowns, Game
4 Harlon Hill, 10/31/54
Mike Ditka, 10/13/63

Consecutive Games, 1+ TD
7 Ken Kavanaugh, 11/02/47–12/14/47
5 Mike Ditka, 10/22/61–11/19/61

INTERCEPTIONS BY

Interceptions By, Lifetime
37 Richie Petitbon, 1959–68
27 Bennie McRae, 1962–70
26 Dave Whitsell, 1961–66

Interceptions By, Season
9 Roosevelt Taylor, 1963
8 Clyde ("Bulldog") Turner, 1942
Johnny Lujack, 1948
Richie Petitbon, 1963

Interceptions By, Game
3 Bob Margarita, 11/11/45
Johnny Lujack, 9/26/48
Richie Petitbon, 9/24/67
Curtiss Gentry, 11/19/67
Ross Brupbacher, 12/12/76

Consecutive Games, 1+
4 Clyde ("Bulldog") Turner, 9/27/42–10/18/42
S. J. Whitman, 12/13/53–10/10/54
Ken Gorgal, 10/09/55–10/30/55

Erich Barnes, 10/12/58–11/02/58
Richie Petitbon, 12/10/61–9/23/62
Charlie Ford, 10/28/73–11/18/73

YARDS RETURNED
Yards Returned, Lifetime
643 Richie Petitbon, 1959–68
485 Bennie McRae, 1962–70
414 Roosevelt Taylor, 1961–69

Yards Returned, Season
212 Richie Petitbon, 1962
182 J. C. Caroline, 1956
172 Don Kindt, 1953
Roosevelt Taylor, 1963

Yards Returned, Game
101 Richie Petitbon, 12/09/62
96 Clyde ("Bulldog") Turner, 10/26/47
Roosevelt Taylor, 10/20/68
92 Todd Bell, 11/22/81

Longest Interception Return
101 Richie Petitbon, (TD) 12/09/62
96 Clyde ("Bulldog") Turner, (TD) 10/26/47
Roosevelt Taylor, (TD) 10/20/68
92 Todd Bell, 11/22/81

TOUCHDOWNS
Touchdowns, Lifetime
4 Bennie McRae, 1962–70
3 Richie Petitbon, 1959–68
Roosevelt Taylor, 1962–69

Touchdowns, Season
2 Gerry Weatherly, 1950
J. C. Caroline, 1956
Bennie McRae, 1967

Touchdowns, Game
1 By many players. Last:
Tom Hicks, 12/09/79

PUNTING
PUNTS
Punts, Lifetime
833 Bobby Joe Green, 1962–73
747 Bob Parsons, 1972–81
343 Ed Brown, 1954–61
243 Fred ("Curley") Morrison, 1950–53

Punts, Season
114 Bob Parsons, 1981
99 Bob Parsons, 1976
96 Bob Parsons, 1978
93 Bob Parsons, 1975

Punts, Game
14 Keith Molesworth, 12/10/33†

† Tied for NFL record

11 Ed Brown, 11/29/59
    Bobby Joe Green, 12/2/73
    Bob Parsons, 12/12/76

YARDS PUNTING

Yards Punting, Lifetime

35,057 Bobby Joe Green, 1962–73
28,870 Bob Parsons, 1972–81
13,912 Ed Brown, 1954–61
10,170 Fred ("Curley") Morrison,
        1950–53

Yards Punting, Season

4,531 Bob Parsons, 1981
3,726 Bob Parsons, 1976
3,625 Bob Parsons, 1975
3,549 Bob Parsons, 1978
3,486 Bob Parsons, 1979
3,408 Bob Parsons, 1974

Yards Punting, Game

517 Keith Molesworth, 12/10/33
476 Bob Parsons, 11/06/77
471 George Gulyanics, 11/14/48

Longest Punt

94 Joe Lintzenich, 11/16/31
79 George McAfee, 11/17/40
78 Sid Luckman, 10/31/43

AVERAGE

Average, Lifetime (75+ punts)

44.53 George Gulyanics, 1947–52
42.09 Bobby Joe Green, 1962–73
41.85 Fred ("Curley") Morrison, 1950–53

Average, Season (30+ punts)

46.47 Bobby Joe Green, 1963
44.52 Bobby Joe Green, 1964
44.22 George Gulyanics, 1948

Average, Game (4+ punts)

57.25 Fred ("Curley") Morrison, 11/16/52
53.40 Ed Brown, 10/30/60
52.43 Bobby Joe Green, 12/01/63

PUNT RETURNS

Punt Returns, Lifetime

112 George McAfee, 1940–41, 1945–50
104 Johnny Morris, 1958–67
103 Steve Schubert, 1975–79

Punt Returns, Season

43 Jeff Fisher, 1981
42 Virgil Livers, 1975

Punt Returns, Game

7 George McAfee, 10/15/50
   Ron Smith, 10/15/50
   Steve Schubert, 12/04/77

YARDS RETURNED

Yards Returned, Lifetime

1,431 George McAfee, 1940–41, 1945–50
  893 Johnny Morris, 1958–67
  866 Steve Schubert, 1975–79
  717 Virgil Livers, 1975–78
  635 J. R. Boone 1948–51

Yards Returned, Season

509 Jeff Fisher, 1981
456 Virgil Livers, 1975
417 George McAfee, 1948

Yards Returned, Game

134 Gale Sayers, 12/12/65
108 George McAfee, 10/10/48
102 Ray ("Scooter") McLean, 10/11/42

Longest Punt Return

89 Ray ("Scooter") McLean, (TD) 10/11/42
88 Jeff Fisher, (TD) 9/20/81
85 Gale Sayers, (TD) 12/12/65

AVERAGE RETURN

Average Return, Lifetime (25+)

14.81 Ray ("Scooter") McLean, 1940–47
14.48 Gale Sayers, 1965–71

Average Return, Season (1+ per game)

15.80 Harry Clark, 1943
14.88 Gale Sayers, 1965

Highest Average Return, Game (3+)

36.00 George McAfee, 10/10/48
34.00 Ray ("Scooter") McLean, 10/11/42
26.80 Gale Sayers, 12/12/65

TOUCHDOWNS

Touchdowns, Lifetime

3 Ray ("Scooter") McLean, 1940–47
   Steve Schubert, 1975–79
2 George McAfee, 1940–41, 1945–50
   Gale Sayers, 1965–71

KICKOFF RETURNS

Kickoff Returns, Lifetime

108 Cecil Turner, 1968–73
 91 Gale Sayers, 1965–71
 85 Ron Smith, 1965, 1970–72

Kickoff Returns, Season

31 Cecil Turner, 1971
30 Ron Smith, 1972

Kickoff Returns, Game

8 Brian Baschnagel, 11/06/77
6 Charlie Sumner, 11/27/55
   Ron Smith, 11/19/72
   Brian Baschnagel, 11/13/77

YARDS RETURNED

Yards Returned, Lifetime

2,781 Gale Sayers, 1965–71
2,616 Cecil Turner, 1968–73
2,263 Ron Smith, 1965, 1970–72

Yards Returned, Season

924 Ron Smith, 1972
754 Brian Baschnagel, 1976
752 Cecil Turner, 1970
718 Gale Sayers, 1966

Yards Returned, Game

208 Ron Smith, 11/19/72
185 Brian Baschnagel, 11/06/77
178 Ron Smith, 12/17/72
170 Gale Sayers, 10/17/65

Longest Kickoff Return

103 Gale Sayers, (TD) 9/17/67
100 Don Bingham, (TD) 11/18/56
 99 Willie Galimore, (TD) 10/04/58

AVERAGE RETURN

Average Return, Lifetime (25+)

30.56 Gale Sayers, 1965–71*
26.62 Ron Smith, 1965, 1970–72
25.58 Willie Galimore, 1957–63
24.70 Charlie Bivins, 1960–66

Average Return, Season (1+ per game)

37.69 Gale Sayers, 1967
32.70 Cecil Turner, 1970
31.71 Walter Payton, 1975

Average Return, Game (3+)

52.00 Cecil Turner, 9/19/70
48.67 Dick Gordon, 9/16/66
48.33 Gale Sayers, 12/03/67

TOUCHDOWNS

Touchdowns, Lifetime

6 Gale Sayers, 1965–71†
4 Cecil Turner, 1968–73

Touchdowns, Season

4 Cecil Turner, 1970†
3 Gale Sayers, 1967
2 Gale Sayers, 1966

FUMBLES

TOTAL FUMBLES RECOVERED

Fumbles Recovered, Lifetime

27 Dick Butkus, 1965–73 (2-Bear, 25-opp)
21 Joe Fortunato, 1955–66 (21-opp)
17 Bill George, 1952–65 (1-Bear, 16-opp)

* NFL record
† Tied for NFL record

Fumbles Recovered, Season

7   Dick Butkus, 1965 (1-Bear, 6-opp)
    Gary Huff, 1974 (7-Bear)
6   Don Kindt, 1947 (3-Bear, 3-opp)
    Jack Concannon, 1970 (6-Bear)

Fumbles Recovered, Game

3   Gary Huff, (3-Bear) 9/15/74
    Virgil Livers, (3-Bear) 10/05/75

BEAR FUMBLES RECOVERED

Bear Fumbles Recovered, Lifetime

13   Gale Sayers, 1965–71
10   Ed Brown, 1954–61
9   Johnny Morris, 1958–67
     Ron Bull, 1962–70

Bear Fumbles Recovered, Season

7   Gary Huff, 1974
6   Jack Concannon, 1970
5   Bobby Douglass, 1972

Bear Fumbles Recovered, Game

3   Gary Huff, 9/15/74
    Virgil Livers, 10/05/75

OPPONENTS' FUMBLES RECOVERED

Opponents' Fumbles Recovered, Lifetime

25   Dick Butkus, 1965–73
21   Joe Fortunato, 1955–66
16   Bill George, 1952–65

Opponents' Fumbles Recovered, Season

6   Dick Butkus, 1965
5   Ed O'Bradovich, 1962

Opponents' Fumbles Recovered, Game

2   By many players. Last: Dan
    Hampton, 9/16/79

YARDS RETURNED
(Total Fumbles)

Yards Returned, Lifetime

128   Charlie Sumner, 1955, 1958–60
      (128-opp)
111   Ed Sprinkle, 1944–55 (1-Bear,
      110-opp)
84   Larry Brink, 1954 (84-opp)

Yards Returned, Season

101   Charlie Sumner, 1958 (101-opp)
84   Larry Brink, 1954 (84-opp)
62   Bill Garrett, 1950 (62-opp)

Yards Returned, Game

86   Charlie Sumner, 12/07/58
84   Larry Brink, 11/28/54
62   Bill Garrett, 11/05/50

* NFL record
† Tied for NFL record

YARDS RETURNED
(Bear Fumbles)

Yards Returned, Lifetime

36   John Adams, 1959–62
24   Ike Hill, 1973–74
22   Ron Bull, 1962–70

Yards Returned, Season

36   John Adams, 1961
24   Ike Hill, 1973
21   Ron Bull, 1962

Yards Returned, Game

36   John Adams, 11/19/61
24   Ike Hill, 11/12/73
21   Ron Bull, 11/04/62

Longest Return, Bear Fumble

36   John Adams, 11/19/61
24   Ike Hill, 11/12/73
21   Ron Bull, 11/04/62

YARDS RETURNED
(Opponents' Fumbles)

Yards Returned, Lifetime

128   Charlie Sumner, 1955, 1958–60
110   Ed Sprinkle, 1944–55
84   Larry Brink, 1954

Yards Returned, Season

101   Charlie Sumner, 1958
84   Larry Brink, 1954
62   Bill Garrett, 1950

Yards Returned, Game

86   Charlie Sumner, 12/07/58
84   Larry Brink, 11/28/54
62   Bill Garrett, 11/05/50

Longest Return (Opponents' Fumble)

98   George Halas, (TD) 11/04/23
86   Charlie Sumner, (TD) 12/07/58
84   Larry Brink, (TD) 11/28/54

TOUCHDOWNS
(Total Fumbles)

Touchdowns, Lifetime

2   Fred Evans, 1948 (2-opp)
    Ken Kavanaugh, 1940–41, 1945–50
    (2-Bear)
    Ed Sprinkle, 1944–55 (2-opp)
    Mike Ditka, 1961–66 (2–Bear)

Touchdowns, Season

2   Fred Evans, 1948 (2-opp)

Touchdowns, Game

2   Fred Evans, 11/28/48 (2-opp)

TOUCHDOWNS
(Bear Fumbles)

Touchdowns, Lifetime

2   Ken Kavanaugh, 1940–41, 1945–50†
    Mike Ditka, 1961–66†

Touchdowns, Game

1   By many players. Last: Johnny
    Musso, 11/31/76

TOUCHDOWNS
(Opponents' Fumbles)

Touchdowns, Lifetime

2   Fred Evans, 1948
    Ed Sprinkle, 1944–55

Touchdowns, Season

2   Fred Evans, 1948†

Touchdowns, Game

2   Fred Evans, 11/28/48*

TAKE-AWAYS
(Interceptions and Opponents' Fumbles Recovered)

Take-Aways, Lifetime

47   Dick Butkus, 1965–73
     (22-int, 25-opp fum rec)
44   Richie Petitbon, 1959–68
     (37-int, 7-opp fum rec)
37   Joe Fortunato, 1955–66
     (16-int, 21-opp fum rec)

Take-Aways, Season

12   Roosevelt Taylor, 1963
     (9-int, 3-opp fum rec)
11   Dick Butkus, 1965
     (5-int, 6-opp fum rec)
10   Richie Petitbon, 1963
     (8-int, 2-opp fum rec)
     Ross Brupbacher, 1977
     (7-int, 3-opp fum rec)

Take-Aways, Game

4   Bill George, (2-int, 2-opp fum rec)
    12/03/61

COMBINED NET YARDS GAINED

(Includes Attempts and Yards Gained on
Rushes, Pass Receptions, and All Returns)

ATTEMPTS

Attempts, Lifetime

3,810   Walter Payton, 1975–85
1,579   Rick Casares, 1955–64
1,234   Gale Sayers, 1965–71

Attempts, Season

426   Walter Payton, 1984
400   Walter Payton, 1979
383   Walter Payton, 1978

(Combined Net Yards Gained—*continued*)

380	Walter Payton, 1981		32	Jon Arnett, 11/15/64		
373	Walter Payton, 1977†			Jim Harrison, 10/23/72		
363	Walter Payton, 1981		31	Rick Casares, 11/18/56		
327	Walter Payton, 1976			Walter Payton, 9/19/76		
			30	Rick Casares, 10/09/60		

Attempts, Game

41	Walter Payton, 11/20/77
	Walter Payton, 10/07/79
37	Walter Payton, 11/07/76
34	Walter Payton, 11/13/77
	Walter Payton, 12/11/77
33	Walter Payton, 12/04/77

YARDS GAINED

Yards Gained, Lifetime

22,153	Walter Payton, 1975–85
9,435	Gale Sayers, 1965–71
8,276	Johnny Morris, 1958–67
7,308	Rick Casares, 1955–64

Yards Gained, Season

2,440	Gale Sayers, 1966
2,272	Gale Sayers, 1965
2,216	Walter Payton, 1977
1,923	Walter Payton, 1979
1,875	Walter Payton, 1978
1,689	Gale Sayers, 1967

Yards Gained, Game

339	Gale Sayers, 12/18/66
336	Gale Sayers, 12/12/65
300	Walter Payton, 12/21/75

CAREER LEADING SCORERS
100+ Points

Player (Pos.)	Seasons	Years	Rush	Rec.	Ret.	XP	FG	Pts.
Bob Thomas (k)	1975-84	10	0	0	0	245/268	128/205	629
Walter Payton (hb)	1975-85	11	98	11	0	0/0	0/0	654
George Blanda (k-qb)	1949-58	10	0	0	0	247/250	88/201	541
Mac Percival (k)	1967-73	7	0	0	0	159/162	99/182	456
Roger Leclerc (k)	1960-66	7	0	0	0	152/158	75/146	377
Jack Manders (fb-lb-hb-db-k)	1933-40	8	11	6	2	133/x	40/0	367
Rick Casares (fb)	1955-64	10	49	10	0	0/0	0/0	354
Gale Sayers (rb)	1965-71	7	39	9	8	0/0	0/0	336
Ken Kavanaugh (e)	1940-41, 45-50	8	0	50	2	1/1	0/0	313
Johnny Lujack (qb-k)	1948-51	4	21	0	0	130/136	4/9	268
Harlon Hill (e)	1954-61	8	0	40	0	0/0	0/0	240
George McAfee (hb-db)	1940-41, 45-50	8	22	11	6	0/0	0/0	234
Ray ("Scooter") McLean (hb-db)	1940-47	8	6	21	3	45/54	0/1	225
Willie Galimore (rb)	1957-63	7	26	10	1	0/0	0/0	222
Johnny Morris (rb-wr)	1958-67	10	5	31	1	0/0	0/0	222
Mike Ditka (te)	1961-66	6	0	34	2	0/0	0/0	216
Hugh Gallarneau (hb)	1941-42, 45-47	5	26	7	2	0/0	0/0	210
Dick Gordon (wr)	1965-71	7	0	35	0	0/0	0/0	210
Bill McColl (e)	1952-59	8	0	25	1	0/0	0/0	156
Jim Keane (e)	1946-51	6	0	23	0	0/0	0/0	138
Gary Famiglietti (fb-hb)	1938-45	8	20	1	0	1/2	0/0	127
Bill Osmanski (fb)	1939-43, 46-47	7	20	1	0	0/0	0/0	126
George Gulyanics (hb)	1947-52	6	19	2	0	0/0	0/0	126
Bobby Douglass (qb)	1969-75	7	20	0	0	1/1	0/0	121
Bill Karr (e)	1933-38	6	1	18	1	0/0	0/0	120
James Scott (wr)	1976-80, 82	6	0	20	0	0/0	0/0	120
Joe Maniaci (fb-hb)	1938-41	4	12	0	2	24/25	3/6	117
Harry Clark (hb-db)	1940-43	4	8	9	2	1/1	0/0	115
Julie Rykovich (hb)	1949-51	3	17	2	0	0/0	0/0	114
Bronko Nagurski (fb)	1930-37, 43	9	18	0	0	4/x	0/0	112
George Wilson (e)	1937-46	7	0	15	3	0/0	0/0	108
Billy Stone (hb)	1951-54	4	8	10	0	0/0	0/0	108
Roland Harper	1975-78, 80-82	7	15	3	0	0/0	0/0	108
John Hoffman (fb-e-lb)	1949-56	8	7	9	1	0/0	0/0	*104
John Aveni (k-e)	1959-60	2	0	0	0	51/57	17/35	102
Matt Suhey (fb)	1980-85	6	15	4	0	0/0	0/0	114

CAREER LEADING RUSHERS
(1,000+ Yards)

Player (Pos)	Yrs.	Seasons	Att.	Yards	Avg.	TD
Walter Payton (hb)	11	1975-85	3,351	14,860	4.43	98
Rick Casares (fb)	10	1955-64	1,386	5,657	4.08	49
Gale Sayers (hb)	7	1965-71	991	4,956	5.00	39
Roland Harper	7	1975-81	754	3,037	4.03	15
Willie Galimore (hb)	7	1957-63	670	2,985	4.46	26
Ron Bull (hb-fb)	9	1962-70	787	2,871	3.65	9
Bronko Nagurski (fb)	9	1930-37, 1943	633	2,778	4.39	18
Bobby Douglas (qb)	7	1969-75	373	2,470	6.62	20
Ray Nolting (hb)	8	1936-43	508	2,285	4.50	10
George Gulyanics (hb)	6	1947-52	509	2,081	4.09	19
Gary Famiglietti (fb-hb)	8	1938-45	505	1,927	3.82	20
Matt Suhey (fb)	6	1980-85	630	2,348	3.73	15
Beattie Feathers (hb)	4	1934-37	320	1,846	5.77	14
Bill Osmanski (fb)	7	1939-43, 1946-47	368	1,753	4.76	20
George McAfee (hb)	8	1940-41, 1945-50	341	1,685	4.94	22
Jack Manders (fb-hb)	8	1933-40	451	1,586	3.52	11
Hugh Gallarneau (hb)	5	1941-42, 1945-47	343	1,421	4.14	26
John Hoffman (fb-hb)	8	1949-56	317	1,366	4.31	7
Joe Maniaci (fb-hb)	4	1938-41	260	1,295	4.98	12
Harry Clark (hb)	4	1940-43	262	1,209	4.61	8
Gene Ronzani (qb-hb-fb)	8	1933-38, 1944-45	260	1,153	4.43	1
Julie Rykovich (hb)	3	1949-51	293	1,133	3.87	17
John ("Kayo") Dottley (fb)	3	1951-53	250	1,122	4.49	7
Keith Molesworth (hb-qb)	7	1931-37	348	1,105	3.18	7
Jim Harrison (fb)	4	1971-74	308	1,099	3.57	4
Bobby Watkins (hb)	3	1955-57	235	1,041	4.43	11
Johnny Morris (hb-wr)	10	1958-67	224	1,040	4.64	5
Fred ("Curley") Morrison (fb-hb)	4	1950-53	285	1,022	3.59	6
Joe Marconi (fb)	5	1962-66	275	1,002	3.64	9
Carl Garrett (hb)	2	1973-74	271	1,001	3.69	6

CAREER LEADING PASSERS (400 + Passes)

Player	Seasons	No.	Comp.	Pct. Comp.	Yards	Avg. Gain	TD	Pct. TD	Int.	Pct. Int.	Rating*
Jim McMahon	1982–85	961	558	58.0	5,223	9.36	44	4.6	33	3.4	82.0
Sid Luckman	1939–50	1,744	904	51.8	14,686	8.42	137	7.9	132	7.6	75.0
Bill Wade	1961–66	1,407	767	54.5	9,958	7.08	68	4.8	66	4.7	73.4
Rudy Bukich	1958–59, 1962–68	878	474	54.0	6,254	7.12	46	5.2	45	5.1	72.8
Johnny Lujack	1948–51	808	404	50.0	6,295	7.79	41	5.1	54	6.7	65.3
Ed Brown	1954–61	1,246	607	48.7	9.698	7.78	63	5.1	88	7.1	62.5
Mike Phipps	1977–81	482	253	52.5	2,806	5.82	15	3.1	27	5.6	57.1
Bernie Masterson	1934–40	409	156	38.1	3,366	8.23	34	8.3	38	9.3	57.1
Jack Concannon	1967–71	951	486	51.1	5,222	5.49	31	3.3	52	5.5	55.6
Bob Avellini	1975–81	1,037	522	50.3	6,739	6.50	33	3.2	66	6.4	55.1
Vince Evans	1977–81	780	376	48.2	4,939	6.33	26	3.3	42	5.4	57.1
George Blanda	1949–58	988	445	45.0	5,936	6.01	48	4.9	70	7.1	51.4
Gary Huff	1973–76	614	310	50.5	3,271	5.33	12	2.0	34	5.5	50.1
Bobby Douglass	1969–75	895	376	42.0	4,932	5.51	30	3.4	51	5.7	47.6
Edmund ("Zeke") Bratkowski	1954, 1957–60, 1972	537	263	49.0	3,639	6.78	24	4.5	58	10.8	46.6

*Based on official NFL rating system.

CAREER LEADING RECEIVERS (CATCHES)
(100 + Pass Receptions)

Players (Pos.)	Seasons	Year	No.	Yards	Avg.	TD
Walter Payton (rb)	1975–85	11	422	3,939	9.3	11
Johnny Morris (rb-wr)	1958–67	10	356	5,059	14.2	31
Mike Ditka (te)	1961–66	6	316	4,503	14.3	34
Dick Gordon (wr)	1965–71	7	238	3,550	14.9	7
Harlon Hill (e)	1954–61	8	226	4,616	20.4	40
Jim Dooley (wr)	1952–54, 56–57, 59–62	9	211	3,172	15.0	16
Jim Keanes (e)	1946–51	6	206	3,031	14.7	23
Bill McColl (e)	1952–59	8	201	2,815	14.0	25
Rick Casares (fb)	1955–64	10	182	1,538	8.5	10
James Scott (wr)	196–80, 82	6	177	3,202	18.1	20
Ron Bull (hb-fb)	1962–70	9	163	1,404	8.6	4
Ken Kavanaugh (e)	1940–41, 45–50	8	162	3,626	22.4	50
John Hoffman (e)	1949–56	8	136	1,870	13.8	9
Brian Baschnagel (wr)	1976–84	9	134	2,024	15.1	9
Roland Harper (rb)	1975–78, 80–82	7	128	1,013	7.9	3
George Farmer (wr)	1970–75	6	113	1,909	16.9	10
Gale Sayers (hb)	1965–71	7	112	1,307	11.7	9
George Wilson (e)	1937–46	10	111	1,342	12.1	15
Bob Wallace (wr)	1968–72	5	109	1,403	12.9	9
Gene Schroeder (e)	1951–52, 54–57	6	104	1,870	18.0	13
Ray ("Scooter") McLean (rb)	1940–47	8	103	2,232	21.7	21

CAREER LEADING INTERCEPTORS
(15 + Interceptions)

Player (Pos.)	Seasons	Years	No.	Yards	Avg.	TD
Richie Petitbon (s)	1959–68	10	37	643	17.4	3
Gary Fencik (s)	1976–85	10	35	446	12.9	1
Bennie McRae (cb)	1962–70	9	27	485	18.0	4
Dave Whitsell (cb)	1961–66	6	26	397	15.3	2
George McAfee (db)	1940–41, 1945–50	8	25	350	14.0	1
J. C. Caroline (db)	1956–65	10	24	405	16.9	2
Doug Buffone (lb)	1966–79	14	24	211	8.8	0
Roosevelt Taylor (s)	1961–69	9	23	414	18.0	3
Allan Ellis (cb)	1973–77, 1979-80	7	22	185	8.4	1
Dick Butkus (lb)	1965–73	9	22	166	7.5	0
Don Kindt (db-lb)	1947–55	9	21	348	16.6	1
Terry Schmidt (cb)	1976–84	2	21	141	6.7	2
Ray ("Scooter") McLean (db)	1940–47	8	18	258	14.3	0
Bill George (lb)	1952–65	14	18	144	8.0	0
Sid Luckman (db)	1939–50	12	17	310	18.2	2
Clyde ("Bulldog") Turner (lb)	1940–52	13	17	298	17.5	2
Noah Mullins (db)	1946–48	3	16	308	19.3	1
Charlie Sumner (db)	1955, 1958–60	4	16	251	15.7	0
Joe Fortunato (lb)	1955–66	12	16	156	9.8	1
Joe Taylor (cb)	1967–74	8	15	178	11.9	0

CAREER LEADING PUNTERS (70+ Punts)

Player	Seasons	No.	Yards	Avg.
George Gulyanics	1947–52	113	5,032	44.5
Bobby Joe Green	1962–73	833	35,057	42.1
Fred ("Curley") Morrison	1950–53	243	10,170	41.9
Ed Brown	1954–61	343	13,912	40.6
Edmund ("Zeke") Bratkowski	1954, 1957–60	76	3,023	39.8

CAREER LEADING PUNT RETURNERS
(20+ Punt Returns)

Player	Seasons	No.	Yards	Avg.	TD
Ray ("Scooter") McLean	1940–47	42	622	14.8	3
Gale Sayers	1965–71	27	391	14.5	2
George McAfee	1940–41, 1945–50	112	1,431	12.8	2
Noah Mullins	1946–48	20	236	11.8	0
J. R. Boone	1948–51	56	635	11.3	0
Hugh Gallarneau	1941–42, 1945–47	24	243	10.1	0
Dennis McKinnon	1983–85	43	387	9.0	1
Jeff Fisher	1981–84	123	1,137	9.2	1
Virgil Livers	1975–78	86	738	8.6	0
Johnny Morris	1958–67	104	893	8.6	1
Steve Schubert	1975–79	103	866	8.4	3
Lenny Walterscheid	1977–81	57	424	7.4	0
Wilford White	1951–52	37	248	6.7	0
Jon Arnett	1964–66	45	298	6.6	0
Eddie Macon	1952–53	24	142	5.9	0

CAREER LEADING KICKOFF RETURNERS
(20+ Kickoff Returns)

Player	Seasons	No.	Yards	Avg.	TD
Gale Sayers	1965–71	91	2,781	30.6	6
Eddie Macon	1952–53	22	672	30.6	0
Harry Clark	1940–43	23	643	28.0	0
Frank Minini	1947–48	23	631	27.4	0
Ron Smith	1965, 1970–72	85	2,263	26.6	1
Leon Campbell	1952–54	24	638	26.6	1
Ken Grandberry	1974	22	568	25.8	0
Willie Galimore	1957–63	43	1,100	25.6	1
Charlie Bivins	1960–66	62	1,531	24.7	0
Lenny Walterscheid	1977–81	34	833	24.5	0
Cecil Turner	1968–73	108	2,616	24.2	4
Brian Baschnagel	1976–81	86	2,060	24.0	1
Roosevelt Taylor	1961–69	25	598	23.9	0
Ron Drzewiecki	1955, 57	38	906	23.8	0
Jon Arnett	1964–66	22	520	23.6	0
Ike Hill	1973–74	27	637	23.6	1
Dick Gordon	1965–71	58	1,362	23.5	0
Johnny Morris	1958–67	54	1,267	23.5	0
Chuck Hunsinger	1950–52	31	717	23.1	0
Fred ("Curley") Morrison	1950–53	31	698	22.5	0
Ray ("Scooter") McLean	1940–47	22	492	22.4	0

ANNUAL SCORING LEADERS

Year	Player	TD	PAT	FG	Pts.
1985	Butler, Kevin	0	51	31	144
1984	Thomas, Bob	0	35	22	101
1983	Thomas, Bob	0	35	14	77
1982	Moorehead, Emery	5	0	0	30
1981	Roveto, John	0	19	10	49
1980	Thomas, Bob	0	35	13	74
1979	Payton, Walter	16	0	0	96
1978	Thomas, Bob	0	26	17	77
1977	Payton, Walter	16	0	0	96
1976	Payton, Walter	13	0	0	78
1975	Thomas, Bob	0	18	13	57
1974	Roder, Mirro	0	18	13	57
1973	Roder, Mirro	0	11	8	35
1972	Percival, Mac	0	26	12	62
1971	Percival, Mac	0	18	15	63
1970	Percival, Mac	0	28	20	88
1969	Percival, Mac	0	26	8	50
1968	Percival, Mac	0	25	25	100
1967	Sayers, Gale	12	0	0	72
1966	Leclerc, Roger	0	24	18	78
1965	Sayers, Gale	22	0	0	132
1964	Morris, Johnny	10	0	0	60
1963	Ditka, Mike	8	0	0	48
1962	Leclerc, Roger	0	36	13	75
1961	Ditka, Mike	12	0	0	72
1960	Aveni, John	0	23	7	44
1959	Casares, Rick	12	0	0	72
1958	Galimore, Willie	12	0	0	72
1957	Blanda, George	1	23	14	71
1956	Casares, Rick	14	0	0	84
1955	Blanda, George	2	37	11	82
1954	Hill, Harlon	12	0	0	72
1953	Blanda, George	0	27	7	48
1952	Blanda, George	1	30	6	54
1951	Lujack, Johnny	7	10	0	52
1950	Lujack, Johnny	11	34	3	109
1949	Lujack, Johnny	2	42	1	57
1948	Lujack, Johnny	1	44	0	50
1947	Kavanaugh, Ken	13	0	0	78
1946	Gallarneau, Hugh	8	0	0	48

ANNUAL RUSHING LEADERS

Year	Player	Yards	Att.	TD
1985	Payton, Walter	1,551	324	9
1984	Payton, Walter	1,684	381	11
1983	Payton, Walter	1,421	314	6
1982	Payton, Walter	596	148	1
1981	Payton, Walter	1,222	339	6
1980	Payton, Walter	1,460	317	6
1979	Payton, Walter	1,610	369	14
1978	Payton, Walter	1,395	333	11
1977	Payton, Walter	1,852	339	14
1976	Payton, Walter	1,390	311	13
1975	Payton, Walter	679	196	7
1974	Grandberry, Ken	475	144	2
1973	Garrett, Carl	655	175	5
1972	Douglass, Bobby	968	141	8
1971	Shy, Don	420	116	2
1970	Montgomery, Ross	229	62	0
1969	Sayers, Gale	1,032	236	8
1968	Sayers, Gale	856	138	2
1967	Sayers, Gale	880	186	7
1966	Sayers, Gale	1,231	229	8
1965	Sayers, Gale	867	166	14
1964	Arnett, Jon	400	119	1
1963	Marconi, Joe	446	118	2
1962	Marconi, Joe	406	89	5
1961	Galimore, Willie	707	153	4
1960	Casares, Rick	566	160	5
1959	Casares, Rick	699	177	10
1958	Casares, Rick	651	176	2
1957	Casares, Rick	700	204	6
1956	Casares, Rick	1,126	234	12
1955	Casares, Rick	672	125	4
1954	Jagade, Chick	498	157	3
1953	Morrison, Fred	307	95	2
1952	Morrison, Fred	367	95	3
1951	Dottley, John	670	127	3
1950	Gulyanics, George	571	146	2
1949	Gulyanics, George	452	102	5
1948	Gulyanics, George	439	119	4

(Annual Rushing Leaders—*continued*)

Year	Player			
1947	Osmanski, Joe	328	64	1
1946	Gallarneau, Hugh	476	112	7
1945	Margarita, Bob	497	112	3
1944	Margarita, Bob	463	88	4
1943	Clark, Harry	556	120	3
1942	Famiglietti, Gary	503	118	8
1941	McAfee, George	474	65	9
1940	Nolting, Ray	373	78	2
1939	Osmanski, Bill	699	121	8
1938	Nolting, Ray	297	63	2
	Francis, Sam	297	85	3
1937	Nolting, Ray	424	106	2
1936	Nagurski, Bronko	529	122	3
1935	Ronzani, Gene	356	79	2
1934	Feathers, Beattie	1,004	101	1
1933	Nagurski, Bronko	553	128	1

ANNUAL PASSING LEADERS

Year	Player	Att.	Comp.	Yards	TD	Int.	Rating
1985	McMahon, Jim	313	178	2,392	15	11	82.8
1984	McMahon, Jim	143	85	1,146	8	2	97.8
1983	McMahon, Jim	295	175	2,184	12	13	77.7
1982	McMahon, Jim	210	120	1,501	9	7	80.1
1981	Evans, Vince	436	195	2,354	11	20	51.0
1980	Evans, Vince	278	148	2,039	11	16	66.1
1979	Phipps, Mike	255	134	1,535	9	8	69.7
1978	Avellini, Bob	264	141	1,718	5	16	54.6
1977	Avellini, Bob	293	194	2,004	11	18	61.7
1976	Avellini, Bob	271	118	1,580	8	15	49.7
1975	Avellini, Bob	126	67	942	6	11	57.4
	Huff, Gary	205	114	1,083	3	9	57.1
1974	Huff, Gary	283	142	1,663	6	17	50.4
1973	Douglass, Bobby	174	81	1,057	5	7	59.2
1972	Douglass, Bobby	198	75	1,246	9	12	49.5
1971	Douglass, Bobby	225	91	1,164	7	15	38.7
1970	Concannon, Jack	385	194	2,130	16	18	61.6
1969	Concannon, Jack	160	87	1,783	4	8	81.3
	Douglass, Bobby	148	68	773	5	8	50.9
1968	Concannon, Jack	143	71	715	5	9	49.8
1967	Concannon, Jack	186	92	1,260	6	14	51.0
1966	Bukich, Rudy	309	147	1,858	10	21	49.1
1965	Bukich, Rudy	312	176	2,641	20	9	93.6
1964	Bukich, Rudy	160	99	1,099	12	7	89.0
1963	Wade, Bill	356	192	2,301	15	12	73.8
1962	Wade, Bill	412	225	3,172	18	24	70.2
1961	Wade, Bill	250	139	2,258	22	13	93.7
1960	Brown, Ed	149	59	1,079	7	11	50.1
1959	Brown, Ed	247	125	1,881	13	10	77.0
1958	Brown, Ed	218	101	1,418	10	17	51.0
1957	Brown, Ed	185	84	1,321	6	16	44.5
1956	Brown, Ed	168	96	1,667	11	12	83.1
1955	Brown, Ed	164	85	1,307	9	10	71.4
1954	Bratkowski, Zeke	130	67	1,087	8	17	60.9
1953	Blanda, George	362	169	2,164	14	24	51.4
1952	Romanik, Steve	126	49	772	4	11	34.5
1951	Lujack, Johnny	176	85	1,295	3	8	59.9
1950	Lujack, Johnny	254	121	1,731	4	21	40.9
1949	Lujack, Johnny	312	162	2,658	23	22	75.9
1948	Luckman, Sid	163	89	1,047	13	14	65.2
1947	Luckman, Sid	323	176	2,712	24	31	67.6
1946	Luckman, Sid	229	110	1,826	17	16	70.8
1945	Luckman, Sid	217	117	1,725	14	10	82.6
1944	Luckman, Sid	143	71	1,018	11	11	66.8
1943	Luckman, Sid	202	110	2,194	28	12	107.8
1942	Luckman, Sid	105	57	1,023	10	13	80.0
1941	Luckman, Sid	119	68	1,181	9	6	95.5
1940	Luckman, Sid	105	48	941	6	9	60.7
1939	Masterson, Bernie	113	44	914	5	9	49.6
1938	Masterson, Bernie	112	46	848	7	9	55.6
1937	Masterson, Bernie	72	26	615	6	7	55.8

ANNUAL RECEIVING LEADERS CATCHES

Year	Player	No.	Yards	TD
1985	Payton, Walter	49	483	2
1984	Payton, Walter	45	368	0
1983	Payton, Walter	53	607	2
1982	Suhey, Matt	36	333	0
1981	Payton, Walter	41	379	.2
1980	Payton, Walter	46	367	1
1979	Williams, Dave	42	354	5
1978	Payton, Walter	50	480	0
1977	Scott, James	50	809	3
1976	Harper, Roland	29	291	1
1975	Rather, Bo	39	685	2
1974	Wade, Charlie	39	683	1
1973	Garrett, Carl	23	292	0
1972	Thomas, Earl	20	365	3
1971	Farmer, George	46	737	5
1970	Gordon, Dick	71	1,026	13
1969	Wallace, Bob	47	553	5
1968	Gordon, Dick	29	477	4
1967	Gordon, Dick	31	524	5
1966	Sayers, Gale	34	447	2
1965	Morris, Johnny	53	846	4
1964	Morris, Johnny	93	1,200	10
1963	Ditka, Mike	59	794	8
1962	Ditka, Mike	58	904	5
	Morris, Johnny	58	889	5
1961	Ditka, Mike	56	1,076	12
1960	Dewveall, Willard	43	804	3
1959	Dooley, Jim	41	580	3
1958	McColl, Bill	35	517	8
1957	Dooley, Jim	37	530	1
1956	Hill, Harlon	47	1,128	11
1955	Hill, Harlon	42	789	9
1954	Hill, Harlon	45	1,124	12
1953	Dooley, Jim	53	841	4
1952	Schroeder, Gene	39	660	6
1951	Hoffman, John	28	394	2
1950	Keane, Jim	36	433	0
1949	Keane, Jim	47	696	6
1948	Keane, Jim	30	414	3
1947	Keane, Jim	64	910	10
1946	Kavanaugh, Ken	18	337	5
1945	Wilson, George	28	259	3
1944	Wilson, George	24	265	4
1943	Clark, Harry	23	535	7
1942	McLean, Ray	19	571	8
1941	Plasman, Dick	14	283	0
1940	Kavanaugh, Ken	12	276	3
1939	Plasman, Dick	19	403	3
1938	Karr, William	14	253	4
1937	McDonald, Lester	11	179	4
1936	Hewitt, Bill	15	358	0
1935	Johnsos, Luke	19	298	4
1934	Hewitt, Bill	10	151	5
1933	Hewitt, Bill	16	273	2
1932	Johnsos, Luke	24	321	2

ANNUAL INTERCEPTION LEADERS

Year	Player	No.	Yards
1985	Frazier, Leslie	6	119
1984	Fencik, Gary	5	102
	Frazier, Leslie	5	89
1983	Frazier, Leslie	7	135
1982	Schmidt, Terry	4	39
1981	Fencik, Gary	6	121
1980	Walterscheid, Lenny	4	84
1979	Schmidt, Terry	6	44
	Fencik, Gary	6	31
1978	Fencik, Gary	4	77
1977	Ellis, Allan	6	23
1976	Brupbacher, Ross	7	49
1975	Clemons, Craig	2	109
	Plank, Doug	2	50
	Livers, Virgil	2	40
	Ellis, Allan	2	4
1974	Clemons, Craig	4	84
1973	Lyle, Garry	5	62
1972	Ford, Charlie	7	104
1971	Ford, Charlie	5	46
1970	Buffone, Doug	4	33
1969	Taylor, Joe	3	37
	Daniels, Dick	3	37
	Youngblood, George	3	22
1968	McRae, Bennie	4	41
1967	McRae, Bennie	5	94
	Petitbon, Richie	5	93
	Taylor, Roosevelt	5	19
1966	Petitbon, Richie	4	34
1965	Butkus, Dick	5	84
1964	Caroline, J. C.	2	84
	Whitsell, Dave	2	57
	Taylor, Roosevelt	2	45
	McRae, Bennie	2	44
	George, Bill	2	28
1963	Taylor, Roosevelt	9	172
1962	Petitbon, Richie	6	212
1961	Whitsell, Dave	6	123
1960	Caroline, J. C.	3	31
1959	Barnes, Erich	5	67
1958	Sumner, Charles	6	67
1957	Johnson, Jack	4	36
1956	Caroline, J. C.	6	182
1955	Sumner, Charles	7	162
1954	Whitman, S. J.	5	117
1953	Kindt, Don	6	172
1952	Dooley, Jim	5	30
1951	Schroeder, Gene	5	62
1950	Davis, Harper	5	59
1949	McAfee, George	6	76
1948	Lujack, Johnny	8	131
1947	Mullins, Noah	6	113
1946	Farris, Tom	4	43
1945	Margarita, Bob	6	79
1944	Grygo, Al	4	79
1943	Clark, Harry	5	32
1942	Turner, Clyde	8	96
1941	McAfee, George	6	78
1940	Clark, Harry	4	62
	Famiglietti, Gary	4	18
	McAfee, George	4	50

ANNUAL PUNTING LEADERS

Year	Player	No.	Avg.
1985	Buford, Maury	68	42.2
1984	Finzer, Dave	83	40.1
1983	Parsons, Bob	79	36.9
1982	Parsons, Bob	58	41.3
1981	Parsons, Bob	114	39.7
1980	Parsons, Bob	79	40.6
1979	Parsons, Bob	92	37.9
1978	Parsons, Bob	96	37.0
1977	Parsons, Bob	80	40.4
1976	Parsons, Bob	99	37.6
1975	Parsons, Bob	93	39.0
1974	Parsons, Bob	90	37.8
1973	Green, Bobby Joe	82	40.5
1972	Green, Bobby Joe	67	41.2
1971	Green, Bobby Joe	77	40.1
1970	Green, Bobby Joe	83	40.9
1969	Green, Bobby Joe	76	39.0
1968	Green, Bobby Joe	27	42.3
1967	Green, Bobby Joe	79	42.9
1966	Green, Bobby Joe	80	41.9
1965	Green, Bobby Joe	58	42.7
1964	Green, Bobby Joe	71	44.5
1963	Green, Bobby Joe	64	46.5
1962	Green, Bobby Joe	69	43.7
1961	Brown, Ed	58	42.2
1960	Brown, Ed	56	39.8
1959	Brown, Ed	64	41.2
1958	Brown, Ed	27	42.2
1957	Brown, Ed	34	40.1
1956	Brown, Ed	42	39.1
1955	Brown, Ed	44	40.1
1954	Bratkowski, Zeke	39	41.0
1953	Morrison, Fred	65	42.6
1952	Morrison, Fred	64	42.3
1951	Morrison, Fred	57	39.0
1950	Morrison, Fred	57	43.3
1949	Gulyanics, George	29	47.2
1948	Gulyanics, George	55	44.2
1947	Gulyanics, George	23	44.8
1946	Luckman, Sid	33	37.4
1945	Luckman, Sid	36	36.0
1944	McEnulty, Doug	25	39.8
1943	Luckman, Sid	34	35.9
1942	Luckman, Sid	24	40.6
1941	Luckman, Sid	13	41.1
1940	Luckman, Sid	27	42.5
1939	Luckman, Sid	27	43.3

ANNUAL PUNT RETURN LEADERS

Year	Player	No.	Yards	Avg.
1985	Taylor, Ken	25	198	7.9
1984	Fischer, Jeff	58	492	8.5
1983	McKinnon, Dennis	34	316	9.3
1982	Fischer, Jeff	9	65	7.2
1981	Fisher, Jeff	43	509	11.8
1980	Walterscheid, Lenny	33	239	7.2
1979	Schubert, Steve	25	238	9.5
1978	Schubert, Steve	27	229	8.5
1977	Schubert, Steve	31	291	9.4
1976	Livers, Virgil	28	205	7.3
1975	Livers, Virgil	42	456	10.9
1974	Hill, Ike	33	183	5.5
1973	Hill, Ike	36	204	5.7

(Annual Punt Return Leaders—continued)

Year	Player	No.	Yards	Avg.
1972	Smith, Ron	26	163	6.3
1971	Smith, Ron	26	194	7.5
1970	Cole, Linzy	14	83	5.9
1969	Lyle, Garry	12	78	6.5
1968	Turner, Cecil	9	19	2.1
1967	Gordon, Dick	12	82	6.8
1966	Arnett, Jon	15	58	3.9
1965	Sayers, Gale	16	238	14.9
1964	Arnett, Jon	19	188	9.9
1963	Morris, Johnny	16	164	10.3
1962	Morris, Johnny	20	208	10.4
1961	Morris, Johnny	23	155	6.7
1960	Morris, Johnny	13	75	5.8
1959	Morris, Johnny	14	171	12.2
1958	Morris, Johnny	14	96	6.9
1957	Drzewiecki, Ron	22	64	2.9
1956	Jeter, Perry	6	66	11.0
	Smith, Ray	6	66	11.0
1955	Drzewiecki, Ron	20	100	5.0
1954	Stone, Billy	14	40	2.9
1953	Macon, Ed	17	68	4.0
1952	White, Roy	23	117	5.1
1951	White, Roy	14	131	9.4
1950	McAfee, George	33	284	8.6
1949	McAfee, George	24	279	11.6
1948	McAfee, George	30	417	13.9
1947	McAfee, George	18	261	14.5
1946	Gallarneau, Hugh	10	99	9.9
1945	Margarita, Bob	7	66	9.4
1944	Grygo, Al	11	100	9.1
1943	Clark, Harry	10	158	15.8
1942	Gallarneau, Hugh	9	101	11.2
1941	Swisher, Bob	7	101	14.4
	McAfee, George	5	158	31.6

ANNUAL KICKOFF RETURN LEADERS

Year	Player	No.	Yards	Avg.
1985	Gault, Willie	22	577	26.2
1984	Cameron, Jack	26	485	18.7
1983	Gault, Willie	13	276	21.2
1982	Watts, Rickey	14	330	23.6
1981	Williams, Dave	23	486	21.1
1980	Williams, Dave	27	666	24.7
1979	Walterscheid, Lenny	19	427	22.5
1978	Baschnagel, Brian	20	455	22.8
1977	Baschnagel, Brian	23	557	24.2
1976	Baschnagel, Brian	29	754	26.0
1975	Payton, Walter	14	444	31.7
1974	Grandberry, Ken	22	568	25.8
1973	Hill, Ike	27	637	23.6
1972	Smith, Ron	30	924	30.8
1971	Smith, Ron	26	671	25.8
1970	Turner, Cecil	23	752	32.7
1969	Sayers, Gale	14	339	24.2
1968	Turner, Cecil	20	363	18.2
1967	Sayers, Gale	16	603	37.7
1966	Sayers, Gale	23	718	31.2
1965	Sayers, Gale	21	660	31.4
1964	Martin, Billy	24	534	22.3
1963	Bull, Ronnie	7	105	15.0
1962	Martin, Billy	25	515	20.6
1961	Bivins, Charles	25	668	26.7
1960	Galimore, Willie	12	292	24.3
1959	Morris, Johnny	17	438	25.8
1958	Morris, Johnny	16	399	24.9
1957	Drzewiecki, Ron	13	315	24.2
1956	Bingham, Don	17	444	26.1
1955	Drzewiecki, Ron	25	591	23.6
1954	Jagade, Chick	11	195	17.7
1953	Macon, Ed	13	373	28.7
1952	Macon, Ed	9	299	33.2
1951	Morrison, Fred	13	353	27.2
1950	Hunsinger, Chuck	23	343	14.9
1949	Dreyer, Wally	13	338	26.0
1948	Minini, Frank	12	370	30.8
1947	Minini, Frank	11	261	23.7
1946	Osmanski, Bill	8	203	25.4
1945	Margarita, Bob	10	155	15.5
1944	Margarita, Bob	12	279	23.3
1943	Clark, Harry	13	326	25.1
1942	Gallarneau, Hugh	6	151	25.2
1941	McAfee, George	7	223	31.9

COACHING RECORDS

Years	Coach		Won	Lost	Tied	Pct.
1982–85	Mike Ditka					
		Regular Season	35	20	0	.636
		Playoffs	4	1	0	.800
1978–81	Neill Armstrong					
		Regular Season	30	34	0	.469
		Playoffs	0	1	0	.000
1975–77	Jack Pardee					
		Regular Season	20	22	0	.476
		Playoffs	0	1	0	.00
1972–74	Abe Gibron					
		Regular Season	11	30	1	.262
1968–71	Jim Dooley					
		Regular Season	20	36	0	.357
1958–67	George Halas					
		Regular Season	75	53	6	.560
		Playoffs	1	0	0	1.000
1956–57	Paddy Driscoll					
		Regular Season	14	9	1	.583
		Playoffs	0	1	0	.000
1946–55	George Halas					
		Regular Season	75	42	2	.630
		Playoffs	1	1	0	.500
1942–45*	Hunk Anderson, Luke Johnsos, Paddy Driscoll					
		Regular Season	23	11	2	.639
		Playoffs	1	1	0	.500
1933–42*	George Halas					
		Regular Season	84	22	4	.764
		Playoffs	4	2	0	.667
1930–32	Ralph Jones					
		Regular Season	24	10	7	.585
		Playoffs	1	0	0	1.000
1920–29	George Halas & Dutch Sternaman					
		Regular Season	85	31	19	.630

*Halas was head coach for the first five games of the 1942 season, then he went on active duty with the U.S. Navy. The remaining six league games and the NFL championship game that year were coached by Anderson, Johnsos, and Driscoll.

CHICAGO BEARS ALL-PRO HONOR ROLL

Eight times:	Bill George
	George Connor (counting elections to offensive and defensive teams three times)
Seven times:	Sid Luckman
Six times:	Bulldog Turner
	Dick Butkus
Five times:	Danny Fortmann
	Gale Sayers
	Walter Payton

CHICAGO BEARS RETIRED JERSEY NUMBERS

3	Bronko Nagurski	56	Bill Hewitt
5	George McAfee	61	Bill George
28	Willie Galimore	66	Bulldog Turner
41	Brian Piccolo	77	Red Grange
42	Sid Luckman		

THE BEST DAYS

200-Yard Rushing Games

				Attempts
275	Walter Payton	11/20/77	vs. Vikings	40
205	Walter Payton	10/30/77	vs. Packers	23
	Gale Sayers	11/03/68	vs. Packers	24

400-Yard Passing Games

				Attempts	Completions
468	Johnny Lujack	12/11/49	vs. Cardinals	39	24
466	Bill Wade	11/18/62	vs. Cowboys	46	28
433	Sid Luckman	11/14/43	vs. Giants	32	21

200-Yard Pass Receiving Games

				Receptions
214	Harlon Hill	10/31/54	vs. 49ers	7
201	Johnny Morris	11/18/62	vs. Cowboys	10

CHICAGO BEARS IN THE PRO FOOTBALL HALL OF FAME

	Position	With Bears	Inducted
Doug Atkins	E	1955–66	1982
George Blanda	QB, K	1949–58	1981
Dick Butkus	LB	1965–73	1979
George Connor	T, LB	1948–55	1975
	Asst. Coach	1956–57	
Paddy Driscoll	HB	1926–31	1965
	Coach	1956–57	
	Asst. Coach	1941–55, 1958–62	
Danny Fortmann	G	1936–43	1965
Bill George	LB	1952–66	1974
	Asst. Coach	1972	
Red Grange*	HB	1925, 1929–34	1963
	Asst. Coach	1933–40	
George Halas*	E	1920–29	1963
	Coach	1920–29, 1933–42, 1946–55, 1958–67	

	Position	With Bears	Inducted
Ed Healey	T	1922–27	1964
Bill Hewitt	E	1932–36	1971
Sid Luckman	QB	1939–50	1965
	Asst. Coach	1954, 1956–70	
Link Lyman	T	1926–28, 1930–31, 1933–34	1964
George McAfee	HB	1940–41, 1945–50	1966
George Musso	G, T	1933–44 1945–50	1982
Bronko Nagurski*	FB, T	1930–37, 1943	1963
Gale Sayers	HB	1965–71	1977
Joe Stydahar	T	1936–42, 1945–46	1967
	Asst. Coach	1963–64	
George Trafton	C	1920–32	1964
Bulldog Turner	C, LB	1940–52	1966
	Asst. Coach	1952–56	

*Denotes charter member

DOUG ATKINS

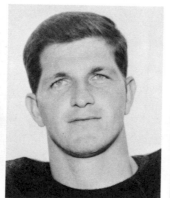

GEORGE BLANDA

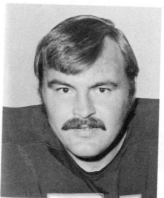

DICK BUTKUS

GEORGE CONNOR

PADDY DRISCOLL

DANNY FORTMANN

BILL GEORGE

RED GRANGE

GEORGE HALAS   ED HEALEY   BILL HEWITT   SID LUCKMAN

LINK LYMAN   GEORGE McAFEE   GEORGE MUSSO   BRONKO NAGURSKI

GALE SAYERS   JOE STYDAHAR   GEORGE TRAFTON   BULLDOG TURNER

Photo Credits: *picture of Halas—Sternaman Collection; of Atkins, Grange, Lyman, Musso, and Trafton—Pro Football Hall of Fame; of Blanda, Butkus, Connor, Driscoll, Fortmann, George, Healey, Hewitt, Luckman, McAfee, Nagurski, Sayers, Stydahar, and Turner—The Chicago Bears*

INDEX